A PUBLIC FAITH

A PUBLIC FAITH

From Constantine to the Medieval World,
A.D. 312–600

IVOR J. DAVIDSON

The Baker History of the Church, Vol. 2

John D. Woodbridge and David F. Wright,
Consulting Editors

Tim Dowley, Series Editor

BakerBooks
Grand Rapids, Michigan

Published by Baker Books
a division of Baker Publishing Group
P.O. Box 6287, Grand Rapids, MI 49516-6287
www.bakerbooks.com

U.S. translation first published April 2005. This edition published by arrangement with Monarch Books, Mayfield House, 256 Banbury Road, Oxford, OX2 7DH.

Printed in the United States of America

Library of Congress Cataloging-in-Publication Data
Davidson, Ivor J.
    The birth of the church : from Jesus to Constantine, AD 30/312 / Ivor J. Davidson.
        p.   cm.—(The Baker history of the church ; v. 1)
    Includes bibliographical references and index.
    ISBN 0-8010-1270-8 (cloth)
    1. Church history—Primitive and early church, ca. 30–600. I. Title. II. Series.
BR165.D368 2005
270.1—dc22   2004011988

ISBN 0-8010-1270-8 (cloth : v. 1)
ISBN 0-8010-1275-9 (cloth : v. 2)

CONTENTS

MAPS AND ILLUSTRATIONS

6

PREFACE

This book takes up the story begun in the first volume in this series, *The Birth of the Church*, which deals with the history of Christianity from its beginnings to the early fourth century. In that book I endeavored to sketch something of the social, political, and cultural context within which early Christianity developed, to describe the major ways in which the first Christian communities came to be organized, and to assess what Christian conversion, consolidation, challenge, and expansion entailed in the first centuries of the faith. Much of this background is clearly vital for an understanding of issues, movements, and developments discussed in the present book, and readers are referred back to *The Birth of the Church* at numerous points in order to avoid repetition of material here. While certainly not essential, it may well be desirable to peruse the first volume in conjunction with this one.

The aims of this book—a combination of readability, balanced assessment, and broad comprehensiveness in treatment—are as they were for volume 1. So too are the author's caveats about the feasibility of realizing them. As before, I remain all too conscious of what has not been said, of the areas where the temptation to expand on both detail and analysis has had to be resisted, and of the perils of oversimplifying complex situations in the quest for brevity. I am especially aware of the insidious dangers of Westernizing or Europeanizing the early history of Christianity in writing as a Western person for English-speaking readers. It is all too easy to forget that the Greco-Roman world never represented the sum total of the relevant territory of the Christian faith in this period and that believers whose homes lay elsewhere, deep in the heart of Asia and in non-Roman as well as Roman Africa, had vital and distinctive roles to play in missionary endeavors, ascetic zeal, scholarship, spirituality, and theology. As we stand at the beginning of the twenty-first century, when Christianity is patently becoming less and less a Western-dominated affair and more and more a movement whose statistical strength is concentrated in Asia and Africa (plus, of course, Latin America), we need to be reminded of the degree to which some of these developments represent a return to very ancient roots. If a good deal of the focus of this book necessarily remains trained upon happenings in the Mediterranean world, that is not the whole story. Readers are encouraged to be alert to the crucial significance of developments elsewhere and to recollect that churches were flourishing in large swaths of the East centuries before the evangelism of Northern Europe had seriously begun.

"Macrohistory," not least the attempt to describe entire centuries of developments in the space of a few pages, is in many quarters an unfashionable business these days. All too often, such efforts run the risk of suggesting that all the various subhistories of a period can be reduced to a single story, or of producing a "top-down" narrative that speaks primarily of large-scale political and cultural happenings—the world of the powerful and the educated, the recognized and the privileged—rather than of the experiences and perspectives of ordinary people living their lives in social circumstances that were far more mundane. I have tried to avoid some of the cruder evidences of such tendencies and instead draw attention to the reality that the assumptions, arguments, and achievements of the famous few must never be treated as the only history that matters. In every age, it is through the faith and witness of the vast, innumerable ranks of ordinary Christians that the gospel has been lived and encountered. I have tried to ensure that those who are too often forgotten—women, ascetics, lay believers, poets, devotional writers, and those who challenged established patterns—have also been given some kind of place, and that it is not only the obvious bishops, preachers, politicians, and thinkers of whom we hear, vital though the latter inevitably remain. Symbolism, ritual, art, and music are also discussed, however briefly, and some effort has been made to give consideration to Christian morality and practice. In an ideal world, much more would be said about each of these aspects, but within the constraints of word limits I have tried to say something at least and to point to resources that will take things further. At every stage, I have endeavored to present human subjects "warts and all" and to resist hagiography or the kind of onward-and-upward approach to history that ignores the messiness, failings, setbacks, and sufferings of Christian people in every age.

In various sections of the book, perhaps most obviously in chapters 2–3 and 7–8, the discussion necessarily involves a fair degree of theological detail. This preoccupation doubtless reflects something of my own interests, but I submit that it is also of vital importance for an understanding of the intellectual and spiritual development of Christianity in this period. Many of the figures encountered in this book would have been deeply puzzled by later tendencies to compartmentalize faith—to differentiate, say, between doctrine and spirituality, between theology and biblical exegesis, or between church activities and private belief—and for that reason, among others, I have been concerned to overcome such false polarities by allowing the complex interweaving of faith and practice, doctrine and politics, ethics and worship to come across in its own terms. I hope that readers will persevere with the challenges that such an approach sometimes presents and that the theological debates can be seen for what they were in their own context. Once again, the reading list offers a selection of further literature for those who wish to pursue these and other matters in more depth. As in *The Birth of the Church*, the list is deliberately restricted to English-language material and to books rather than journal literature or Internet resources; I continue to believe that books are the right place to start, and many of the best examples are suggested here. A number of the theological guides listed in the general section and under the specific chapter headings in the bibliography will provide much further stimulus to those who seek it.

Caveats duly entered, I hope that the work may prove of some value not only to beginners in church history but also to those whose interest in these crucial centuries of the Christian story is of longer standing. I am extremely grateful, once again, to Dr. Tim Dowley for his encouragement, care, and commitment to the series and for all his work on this book as on its predecessor. I appreciate also the comments of an anonymous reader of the manuscript. I am very grateful once more to Baker Books for their sponsorship of the series and to Tony Collins and the staff of Monarch Books in London for their excellent work throughout. Special thanks to my editor at Baker, Paul Brinkerhoff, who has overseen the project with efficiency throughout, and to Chad Allen for his further kindness; thanks also, once again, to Lois Stück for Americanizing my text and to Kathleen Strattan for indexing the book. It is a pleasure to work with Baker's team of dedicated and gifted people. Professor David Wright has offered encouragement and wise counsel, as ever. My thanks to Associate Professor Robert Hannah for his picture of the Arch of Constantine and to all others in New Zealand, the U.K., and the U.S. who assisted with artwork in essential ways. For research assistance, I again thank Jacqui Davis; for maps, Bill Mooney; and for funds, the University of Otago. For enduring the frustrations of the authorial process at close quarters, it is, as always, Julie whom I must thank most.

Ivor J. Davidson
Dunedin, New Zealand
September 2004

THE DAWN OF A NEW AGE

Christianity in the Early Fourth Century

As the fourth century began, Christianity had come a very long way from its beginnings in Palestine. It had spread far beyond its origins in Judaism and had won Gentile converts all over the Roman world and well beyond. It had weathered many storms, including official persecution both small- and large-scale, widespread popular indifference or opposition to its ideas, and a great deal of failure, dispute, and division among its followers. It had developed sophisticated intellectual traditions in the articulation and defense of its essential teachings and had evolved structures of discipline, spirituality, and ministry that spoke of its social organization and the energy of its inner life.

It had touched individuals at all levels of society and had made disciples among people of widely differing ethnic, religious, and cultural backgrounds. Its communities of worshipers varied enormously in size, but they were to be found from Syria and Persia to the extremes of Western Europe, from Egypt and North Africa to Britain, the Balkans, Armenia, and Georgia. Christianity was by no means confined to imperial Roman territory; many of its most flourishing churches and spiritual traditions were concentrated deep in the heart of Asia and in significant parts of Africa. In a world in which new religious movements were plentiful and pluralism was a fact of life, this one faith—which declared that its message was for all but demanded exclusive commitment to the one God and to his Christ—had become a remarkably powerful force. Within the Roman Empire as a whole, 10 percent or more of the population called themselves Christians, and there were very significant numbers in regions that lay far beyond the Romans' control.

The majority of believers were still located in urban areas, and in many regions people who lived in the countryside remained untouched by Christian evangelism. Nevertheless, in the last quarter of the third century Christianity had also spread quite significantly in rural areas, and there had been a measurable decline in popular enthusiasm for some of the cults of regional deities. Christians still often met in private houses, but in many places their meeting rooms were officially recognized as church property, their clergy were publicly accepted as leaders, and their rituals, teachings, and patterns of organization were witnessed routinely by society at large. The majority of people in the Roman world remained unconcerned by the Christians' behavior; rumors of their odd ways were rife, and it was always possible to laugh at the Christians or blame them when times were difficult, but it was not easy to avoid their presence or escape the effects of their zeal in the densely packed, face-to-face environments of ancient urban society. Indeed, at an individual level, many ordinary folk probably got on perfectly well with their Christian neighbors, and some admired their commitment to their lifestyle. Christians were increasingly to be found in quite affluent circumstances and in responsible positions, in administration, in economic activity, in the professions, and in the imperial household itself. All in all, there were simply too many of them to ignore.

And this, indeed, was the problem. Not for the first time, it had become apparent to the authorities that the Christians were a political liability. There was significant sympathy in the Roman world for the idea that there was in the end a single divine being behind or beyond all the gods and goddesses of classical religion. The Christians, however—like their Jewish progenitors and fellow eccentrics—seemed to take the obligations of their monotheism far too seriously. For generations, the followers of Christ had been notoriously awkward in their attitude to the imperial cult, refusing to compromise their devotion to their Lord by acknowledging the emperor as divine or offering sacrifice to Rome's traditional gods. While the third century had seen large numbers of Christians brought to heel, either as traitors to their cause or as martyrs for it, there were enduring uncertainties as to their loyalty. The empire was crucially dependent upon a strong and reliable military force; some Christians refused to serve in the army altogether, and others risked offending Rome's guardian divinities by making the sign of the cross when they went into battle.

In a world where things could easily go wrong, the Christians were too big a risk to Rome's security. It was time to deal with them once and for all.

"The Great Persecution"

Moves were made first to purge believers from the Roman army. Much more extensive action followed. "The Great Persecution," which began in 303–304, was an attempt to crush the Christians en bloc.[1] At first there was some effort to avoid bloodshed; the strategy was to curtail the Christians' rights, remove believers from significant positions, confiscate their property, arrest their leaders, and burn their Scriptures. But things soon became more menacing still when all citizens of the empire were compelled on penalty of death to offer sacrifices to Rome's gods.

The oppressions that ensued varied considerably in range, intensity, and duration, and their ultimate effects were much more severe in the Eastern parts of the empire than they were in the West. In the East, the emperors Galerius and Maximin Daia sought to crush Christianity with brutal resolve, imprisoning, deporting, and torturing those who refused to comply with their orders. As in earlier trials, there were many believers who capitulated under pressure, but many also held out to the end, suffering death for their steadfastness or surviving to bear terrible scars for the rest of their days.

However dreadful the costs, Christians endured. Galerius died in May 311, issuing an amnesty to Christians on his deathbed and appealing for their prayers on his behalf and for the Roman state. Little changed. Maximin renewed the persecutions with passion, wreaking terrible havoc on the Egyptian churches in particular; but his days too were numbered. Events were determined by a power struggle between the four remaining imperial rulers: Maximin in Asia Minor, Syria, and Egypt; Licinius, a former confidant of Galerius (who had become senior emperor in the East) in the Balkans; Maxentius in Italy and North Africa; and Constantine, the son of Constantius, the former Augustus of the West, who by this time had control of Britain, Gaul, and Spain. Constantine made an alliance with Licinius, Maxentius with Maximin. On 28 October 312, Constantine defeated Maxentius at the Milvian Bridge just outside Rome and secured full control of the West. His victory was said to have taken place under the sign of the cross of Christ and with the favor of the Christian God.

Arch of Constantine in Rome, commemorating his victory at the Milvian Bridge in A.D. 312. Illustration from Robert Hannah. Used by permission.

Constantine had already over several years adopted a policy of toleration toward Christians, and Maxentius had also exercised a broadly tolerant approach in the West. The vicious treatment adopted by Maximin in the East was now opposed by both Constantine and Licinius. Constantine ordered the cessation of persecution in all areas of the empire, aiming particularly at reining in Maximin in the East. Maximin issued an edict of toleration for the Eastern provinces, granting the right of Christians to practice their beliefs, though making no offer to restore their property. In February 313 Constantine and Licinius met in Milan and cemented an alliance by the marriage of Licinius to Constantine's half sister Constantia. They agreed on a policy of religious liberty in their joint territories. Two months later, Licinius succeeded in defeating Maximin in battle at Adrianople, after allegedly praying to "the supreme God" for assistance. Licinius was master of the East, Constantine of the West.

The End of Persecution

In June 313 Licinius issued a circular to his provincial governors, in his own name and Constantine's, ordering that all persecution of Christians was to cease and that lands and properties belonging to individual Christians and to the churches as corporate entities were to be restored. There was to be freedom for all to worship according to their conscience. This so-called "Edict of Milan" did not derive, as its conventional name misleadingly suggests, from the meeting of Constantine and Licinius in Milan a few months earlier, but it did reflect a strategy on which the two had clearly already agreed. It was the formal declaration that the oppressions were at an end. Maximin took his own life, and the last vestiges of his persecution in the East died away.

The partnership of Constantine and Licinius was nevertheless fragile. Constantine had plainly nursed ambitions to become sole emperor from the start, and it was not long before he and Licinius fell out. Licinius's attachment to tolerance had been thinner than Constantine's, and as he began to lose ground to Constantine, he resorted once again to persecuting Christians as alleged partisans of his opponent. His anti-Christian measures grew in intensity over the following years, and he canceled the legal privileges of the churches and sought to suppress Christian activities. In the end, however, Licinius was no match for Constantine, who took his erstwhile ally's mounting hostility to the Christians as a justification for a final showdown. By the end of 324 Constantine had defeated and deposed Licinius, and the harassment of Christians was no more. Constantine had already bestowed considerable favors upon the churches and their leaders over the preceding years. An emperor who openly treated Christianity as none of his predecessors had ever done was now in sole charge of the Roman world.

How Christian Was Constantine?

But how Christian was Constantine? As far as his Christian eulogists were concerned, his victory at the Milvian Bridge was directly attributable to his commitment to the Christian God, of whose reality he had already become convinced, and his turn to Christ was the dawning of a new age of divine grace for the Roman Empire. Everything that had happened over the succeeding years was part of the inevitable ascendancy of God's chosen ruler, and the assured triumph over the forces of evil by a divinely anointed leader, called to establish a model order based upon Christian principles.

Constantine's open sponsorship of the Christian cause seems clear-cut from around or before the time of his defeat of Maxentius, and there is no doubt that his actions over the subsequent years went far beyond a policy of mere toleration. As we shall see in more detail in the pages that follow, under his regime Christians became direct beneficiaries of considerable financial, legal, and cultural largesse, suggestive of a conviction that their cause was not only acceptable in political terms but morally and spiritually true. In a fashion altogether without precedent in the history of the Roman Empire, the churches became the recipients of explicit social favor, and the overall pattern of belief held by the followers of Jesus was blessed with the emperor's personal patronage.

Yet there were many ambiguities about Constantine's actual religious convictions. The military sign that he had reportedly ordered his troops to paint on their shields at the Milvian Bridge—a cross in the form of a *Chi-Rho* monogram, symbolizing the name of Christ[2]—was perhaps an adaptation of an existing Roman cavalry standard, whose associations were clearly not Christian at all. Constantine's emblem came to be known, at any rate, as the *Labarum*, which may imply that its shape could also be associated with the *labrys*, or double-axe, which was a traditional symbol of the cult of Zeus.

The story that Constantine experienced a vision of the cross in the sky prior to battle[3] is in other versions presented as a vision of the pagan Sun-god. This deity was certainly of enduring importance to him. The coins he issued in his early years as emperor included images of *Sol Invictus*, "the Unconquered Sun," as well as symbols of various other pagan gods, and the still-extant triumphal arch later erected in Rome to celebrate his victory over Maxentius also depicts *Sol Invictus* as Constantine's protector and refers simply to "the divinity," unspecified. When in 321 Constantine declared the first day of the week as a public holiday (or at least a day when nonessential labor was discouraged and public institutions such as the law-courts could be open only for the charitable purpose of freeing slaves), his stated reason was not to facilitate Christian worship or practice as such but to respect "the venerable day of the Sun."

If there is any truth in the account of Constantine's vision of the cross, it is conceivable that he somehow associated a personal guardian deity, the Sun-god, with the God of the Christians. It was not difficult to align such conventional images with the scriptural idea of Christ as "the sun of righteousness" (cf. Mal. 4:2). Christian preachers had often connected the notion of Christ as the light of salvation with the nature of the sun as the source of human light, and there had long been popular rumors that Christians were involved in a version of sun-worship because they met together on Sundays. A mosaic from a late-third- or early-fourth-century tomb found under St. Peter's in Rome expressly depicts Christ as Apollo the Sun-god in his chariot, and Constantine utilized an image of

Apollo in a public statue of himself in his new city of Constantinople on the Bosphorus. For Constantine, the amalgamation of the conventional symbolism of his preferred deity with the doctrine of the Christian God may have been quite easy.

In view of these and other equivocal associations, the story of Constantine's conversion is one of the most complex and controverted chapters in Christian history. Did Constantine genuinely become Christian or not? Some interpreters believe he never became a true disciple of Christ but simply chose to exploit the significance of Christianity within the Roman world for his own ends. The consequences of his actions, it is said, were disastrous for the spiritual integrity of the church and rendered its doctrine and practice liable to political pressures and cultural fads in ways that have never been entirely undone, even in the twenty-first century. To others, conversely, Constantine was a real champion of the faith, and his conversion was a marvelous moving of divine providence that opened up opportunities for the expansion and recognition of Christianity far beyond anything that the first followers of Jesus could have imagined.

Given the existence of such widely different views, how is Constantine to be assessed? It is with this question, and the diversity of evidence that affects the attempt to answer it, that our story in this book begins. While it is possible to overstate the significance of Constantine's conversion for the narrative of the Christian churches in history—Constantine was not the first ruler to adopt Christianity, and in Asia and Africa countless believers never did belong within the bounds of his empire—almost everything we shall be considering in the chapters that follow was affected at one level or another by the political watershed of the early fourth century. Whatever we say about Constantine himself, from his time onwards the air that Christians breathed would never be quite the same again. For good or ill—and perhaps, in different ways, for both—a new era had indeed dawned for the Christian faith.

1

CONSTANTINE
AND THE CHURCHES

▼

Constantine and Pagan Religion

If Constantine became a Christian in 311 or 312, he did not allow it
entirely to revolutionize his behavior with regard to traditional religion.
His coinage over a number of years continued to depict pagan deities;
he retained the pagan high priest's title of *Pontifex Maximus*, held by
all emperors since Augustus; and he did little if anything to curtail
the imperial cult. It appears that he came to deplore animal sacrifices
and to favor the appointment of Christian officials who would not perform such rites, but there is no evidence that he discontinued them. As
his legislation about Sunday indicated, even his pro-Christian actions
could appeal to non-Christian ideas. At the very least, we must say that
Constantine took pains to demonstrate his sensitivity to the cultural
importance of conventional religious symbols.

Favoring the Christians

Nevertheless, Constantine's public patronage of Christianity was evident very soon after his defeat of Maxentius. If the God of the Christians

had granted him his victory at the Milvian Bridge, Constantine would not be slow to acknowledge the debt. Having opted for a policy of toleration all along, from as early as 313 he began to show open favor to the followers of Jesus. It was not only a matter of persecution officially coming to an end—Constantine engaged in the positive promotion of Christian interests. He passed legislation that legitimized the church as a public body with official status: no longer was Christianity to be a fringe or clandestine movement, but an entity with legal rights and considerable social privileges.

Over a period of years, a raft of legal measures advanced the church's interests. The clergy were exempted from civic duties and from taxation. Bishops were allowed to adjudicate in various civil cases, and it became possible legally to free slaves before the church in the presence of a bishop. For the first time, Christian pastors were appointed as military chaplains. The church was allowed to receive legacies from rich individuals. Sometimes the benefits to Christians came at simultaneous cost to others. Jews, traditionally excluded from serving on town councils, were deemed no longer to deserve this exemption; the Jews lost as the Christians gained. Laws were enacted to debar upper-class citizens from applying to become clerics simply in order to secure relief from municipal obligations. Christians were preferred for administrative posts of many kinds, to the detriment of others with possibly better practical qualifications.

One example of a Christian professional who benefited was Lactantius (ca. 250–325), a teacher of rhetoric who had formerly served at Diocletian's court in Nicomedia until the outbreak of persecution in 303. Now in his old age, Lactantius was appointed tutor to Constantine's young son, Crispus. Over the past few years, Lactantius had been engaged in writing an elegant Latin exposition of the Christian faith, with conventional polemic on the errors of pagan religion, called *Divine Institutes*. Aiming to persuade intellectual critics of the truth of the Christian way, Lactantius argued that Christ was the fulfillment of prophecies and expectations found in pagan as well as biblical sources (Constantine himself pointed to the story of a virgin-born hero in Virgil's fourth *Eclogue* as "messianic") and commended the humanity that characterized Christian ethics. Lactantius's venomous pamphlet, *On the Deaths of the Persecutors*, produced in the period 313–315, was written by a man who believed that Constantine was a Christian champion. It depicts the painful deaths suffered by those who harassed the churches, especially Galerius and Maximin, as divine judgments upon them for their wickedness; the martyrs had been avenged by God. A valuable source on the persecutions, the work's strong note of Christian triumphalism hints at the spirit of political assurance that affected many in the churches.[1]

Constantine devoted large sums of money to the rebuilding of churches after the ravages of the persecutions, and he financed the copying of the Scriptures in the aftermath of the widespread destruction of sacred texts. A matter of days after his victory at the Milvian Bridge, he donated to the church in Rome the site of a former imperial residence and began the construction of the great edifice that would eventually become the basilica of St. John Lateran. New churches were erected at the shrines marking the presumed graves of Peter and Paul and at the burial place of St. Lawrence, the most celebrated of the Roman deacons martyred under Valerian in 258.[2] The palace where Constantine's mother, Helena, resided was said to house a relic of the true cross upon which Christ had been crucified, and this site would also become a great church. In addition, Constantine endowed the Christian community with vast resources to provide for the maintenance of all these properties and for the extension of charity to the needy.

Nor was the expenditure confined to Rome. The East, too, was given splendid buildings in Nicomedia, Antioch, and elsewhere. Palestine became a particular center of attention, a sacred region to be reclaimed for Christian veneration. In Jerusalem, Helena had discovered what was said to be the true cross, and the alleged site of Jesus's burial was identified under a pagan shrine erected by Hadrian. A new Church of the Resurrection was financed to mark the spot (parts of the building still survive beneath the later Church of the Holy Sepulchre). In Bethlehem, Constantine's wealth funded the grand basilica of the Holy Nativity. The *terra sancta*, the "Holy Land," became a vital place of Christian pilgrimage, and believers began to flock to see the places where their Lord had walked, talked, suffered, and died.

Visits to holy sites had been a common phenomenon for centuries in the Greco-Roman world, and there is some evidence of Christians making their way to Palestine as pilgrims in the third century. In the wake of Constantine's and Helena's influence, such journeys multiplied. By the later fourth century they were a major draw for those eager for the spiritual experience of witnessing the landscape in which so many of the Bible's stories were set and of being where Jesus had been. The places in question were not regarded as special in themselves, but they were believed to have been invested with a particular sanctity by virtue of the holy people who had walked within them—above all, Jesus himself. The growth of pilgrimages would have major, long-term consequences for

Christian spirituality and for the spread of ideas, liturgical practices, and the cults of the saints and their relics among the churches at large.[3]

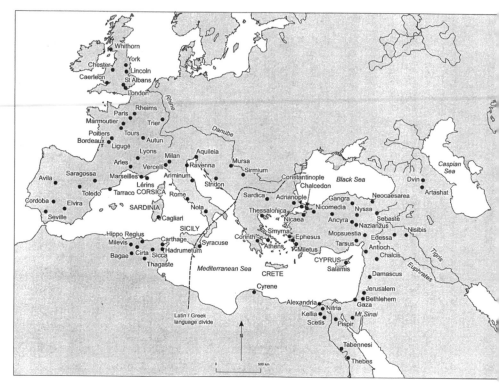

Christianity in the fourth and fifth centuries, showing some of the major sites mentioned in the text.

Constantine Becomes Sole Emperor

Constantine's largesse was bestowed over the teens and twenties of the fourth century. During these years, he was also steadily at work to consolidate his political position and secure absolute power. It was clear that he had aimed at sole rule all along. Despite his agreement with Licinius in 313, from early on his relationship with his colleague was not easy. By 316 they had fallen out, and Licinius lost a good deal of the East to Constantine's control. This induced Licinius to revive a policy of hostility toward Christians in his remaining territories, first by reversing their legal privileges and then, in later years, by actively seeking to persecute believers in Armenia. While he had shown tolerance to

Christians before and after 313 and had taken a Christian wife, Licinius did not share Constantine's enthusiasm for wholehearted favoritism towards the churches, and once the two had parted company Licinius came to regard Christian leaders as partisans of his enemy. He was not mistaken, for Constantine actively sought to enlist Eastern bishops in support of his political cause.

Licinius's anti-Christian measures slowly became more intense, and in the end they provided Constantine with a pretext for a showdown. In September 324 he defeated his former ally in battle at Chrysopolis, near the entrance to the Bosphorus, and thus became sole ruler of the Roman world. Licinius was imprisoned and then executed. Constantine had achieved his self-professed mission as one called by God to reunite the empire. All the imperial subjects were called upon to worship the one true God. A majority, naturally, refused to do any such thing, and religious coercion was forbidden as a way of securing their compliance, but there were probably widespread conversions to Christianity of at least a nominal kind.

Constantinople: "New Rome"

Following his defeat of Licinius, Constantine conceived the idea of building a new city, a "new Rome" in the East on the historic site of Byzantium, at the gateway to the Black Sea. The plan, said to have originated in divine revelation, was for a Christian city, undefiled by pagan cults and associations, to be known as "Constantinople," which would serve as the center of a new, "Christian" empire. The construction of the city took until 330, and during those years Constantine lived mostly at Nicomedia, contenting himself with occasional visits to inspect the progress on his vast project. The new city would contain no temples but was to have a number of churches, the most splendid of which would be the Church of the Holy Wisdom (Sancta Sophia), adjacent to the imperial palace, symbolizing the essential relationship between the emperor and the church.

Although the city was dedicated with great pomp in 330, only one of the basilicas was completed during Constantine's lifetime—the Church of the Holy Apostles, which was intended to serve as the emperor's tomb; there he would be interred as the thirteenth and final "apostle" of the gospel of Christ. The Church of the Holy Wisdom was not finished until 360, under Constantine's son Constantius II. All the same, Constantine's city was a magnificent place in his own time, endowed with great public buildings and much plundered artwork (especially statues removed from pagan shrines) and populated with a new senatorial elite, enticed to the East by various promises of status and wealth. His courtiers were summoned to worship the "God of Victory" each Sunday and were required to listen to their sovereign's counsel on religious and moral matters.

Rome had already started to wane in political significance, as the real capital of the empire had come to be wherever the emperor himself was based, and in the West cities such as Trier had begun to take on new importance as places of imperial residence. Constantine did not visit Rome after 326, and after the establishment of Constantinople, Rome's political decline was accelerated.[4] The senatorial class of Constantinople may technically have been inferior to that of Rome, but it was based in the city that the emperor had designed to embody his image, and it was there that he chose to be. The emperor's last trip to Rome had been filled with unpleasantness, and quarrels within his household had led to the execution of both his son Crispus and his second wife, Fausta. Fausta's palace on the Lateran was handed over to Silvester, the bishop, to serve as his official residence.[5] Henceforth, the most important man in Rome, it seemed, was the city's bishop.

Episcopal Admiration: Eusebius of Caesarea

Not surprisingly, Constantine had plenty of grateful admirers and willing counselors among the church's leaders. Ossius of Cordoba (ca. 256–357) served as a kind of special adviser to the emperor, and there were many other bishops who looked on Constantine as a political saint. The most famous among them was Eusebius (ca. 260–340), who became bishop of Caesarea around 314. A former student of the learned Origenist scholar and martyr Pamphilus, Eusebius was already well into middle age when the persecution in the East had struck, and he had been obliged to flee from Caesarea to Tyre and then Egypt, where he had spent some time in prison. Rehabilitated under Constantine, he was to play a prominent, if controversial, role in the doctrinal disputes of the 320s. His accounts of the persecutions emphasize the barbarity of those who sought to crush Christianity and the futility of their schemes.

Eusebius's vast and ambitious defense of the faith against its critics and persecutors found expression in a wide range of literary projects, but it was focused especially in the pair of treatises, *Preparation for the Gospel* and *Demonstration* [or "Proof"] *of the Gospel*. The latter does not survive intact. Both works see the Christian gospel as the obvious fulfillment of pagan

Eusebius of Caesarea. Illustration from André Thevet, *Les Vrais Portraits et Vies des Hommes Illustres* (Paris, 1584), Special Collections Library, University of Michigan. Used by permission.

and Jewish expectations, and over everything looms the shadow of Constantine, under whose providential beneficence the church had reached its apogee in history. The same exultance pervades the text for which Eusebius is best known, his famous *Ecclesiastical History*, the first attempt to give an overall account of the story of Christianity. Eusebius's qualities as a historian are complex to assess, and at many points his work needs to be set alongside other historical evidence, not least from archaeology, but his depiction of the church's progress remains a classic resource, no matter how tendentious its style.

Written over a period of many years, the *Ecclesiastical History* reflects various revisions as political circumstances changed, from the end of persecution in 311 to the defeat of Licinius in 324. It climaxes with the conversion and reign of Constantine as virtually the fulfillment of the kingdom of God on earth. According to God's good purpose, the coming together of church and empire represents for Eusebius the definitive convergence of faith and politics in the interests of Christ's cause. In an elaborative, four-book eulogy known as the *Life of Constantine*, completed after its subject's death, Eusebius carves out forever his hero's place as the representative of God on earth.[6]

The Donatists

Constantine's generosity brought its own problems, however. In North Africa the emperor found rival Christian claims for his favors. There, two distinct groups both claimed to represent the catholic church. The division between them lay in the area of discipline and the purity of the church. This was hardly a surprising source of strife, given the serious disputes that had arisen in North Africa about such matters over several generations, not least in the 250s.[7] In Constantine's world, however, differences of this kind were affected by a potent new factor—the prospect of imperial patronage for those who could persuade the civil authorities that theirs was the true position. For centuries Christians had appealed to emperors, but never before had the prospects of success involved the political rewards that were now at stake.

Around 311 or 312 a new bishop, Caecilian, had been appointed in Carthage. He had been rejected by a large number of the region's Christians, for it was rumored (unfairly, as it turned out) that one of the clerics who had consecrated him, Felix of Aptungi, had been a *traditor*—a person who had handed over his copy of the Scriptures to be burned during the persecutions. The dissenters had appointed a candidate of their own, one Majorinus, as a rival bishop, and in 313 he in turn had been succeeded by an individual named Donatus. Caecilian's challengers came primarily from Numidia, or the rural areas of modern-day eastern Algeria, but they quickly gathered support more widely and had probably come to constitute a substantial minority if not a majority of North Africa's Christians. For them, the spirit of Tertullian and Cyprian was strong,[8] and those who had been involved in the disgrace of *traditio*, or handing over the Scriptures, were guilty of terrible apostasy. Betrayal of Christ was not confined to the offering of pagan sacrifice (as it tended to be seen in the East); it was also present in the surrender of consecrated property, especially of the sacred texts of the faith.

Like the Novatianists before them,[9] the "Donatists," or partisans of Donatus, insisted that the true church was to be found among those who had maintained a steadfast testimony in the face of oppression. They also had a series of petty grievances alongside their doctrinal arguments. The last bishop of Carthage, Mensurius, had himself cooperated with the authorities, desisting from holding regular worship services and handing over some of his own books for destruction (though he had claimed the volumes in question were works of heretical theology). Caecilian had been his chief deacon, and he had allegedly tried to interfere even with the work of providing for the physical needs of the believers who had been imprisoned for their defiance of the magistrates.[10] He had also rebuked a wealthy Christian woman named Lucilla for her zealous devotion to a relic of a martyr. (She apparently made a habit of producing in church a bone from a martyr of disputed status and kissing it exuberantly.) Finally, on Mensurius's death, Caecilian had got himself elected very precipitately, and he had not extended the usual courtesy of giving the Numidians' local bishop a leading role in the consecration ceremony.

It is clear that the dispute had its immediate causes in a mixture of personal resentments as much as in theological differences. Clerical ambitions had been frustrated, a prominent Christian woman had been offended, and there were feelings that the new bishop was unworthy of his office, both on personal grounds and in view of his associations with those who had compromised their faith. In reality, some of the Numidian clergy themselves were probably guilty of *traditio* and other lapses, and their charges against Felix were unfounded. The fact that Majorinus, the first choice as rival bishop, was a member of Lucilla's household further hints at the degree of intrigue at work. Caecilian, for his part, found support in the church at Rome. He was evidently prepared to accept the Roman position on baptism, which was that any baptism was valid if carried out in faith and into the divine name, regardless of the minister officiating. This agreement with Rome provoked further fury from the Donatists, who held, with Cyprian, that only baptism carried out within the catholic communion was a true sacrament—and this meant, in their eyes, baptism within *their* fellowship, not Caecilian's.

The Donatists, resenting the prospect that Caecilian's church should be the recipient of generous imperial funds and civil privileges, appealed to Constantine. To the emperor, the affair seemed like a distant, parochial quarrel over personalities—which is essentially what it was at first. It is easy to see, however, why the stakes were so high within North Africa itself: the rival parties were contending for significant practical advantages as well as for spiritual status. In some areas it seems Donatist clergy had been favored by sympathetic local authorities, while in others those loyal to Caecilian were receiving the right to funds and to fiscal exemptions. Constantine's generosity to the church had brought about a situation in which he had to adjudicate in a dispute between Christians without any real awareness of the doctrinal emphases presented by the two sides.

Constantine opted to take Caecilian's side from the start, evidently under the influence of Miltiades, the bishop of Rome. An imperial commission decided against Donatus, but his supporters presented a series of petitions in protest. At a gathering of bishops at Arles in 314, the Donatists' fate was sealed: Caecilian was exonerated, and the Roman practice of baptism was officially endorsed as relevant for the North African situation. In 316 Constantine heard a further appeal by the Donatists. Finding once more in favor of Caecilian, he then attempted to coerce the Donatists by a variety of measures between 317 and 321, and a number of them lost their lives. In the end, however, the emperor had no stomach for such persecution, and he decided to desist from this course. The difficulties suffered by the Donatists only intensified their resolve, as they gloried all the more in their status as the real people of God, prepared to pay the price for their faith as their spiritual forebears had done. Donatus was a charismatic leader, and there was some real plausibility in the claims of his partisans that his community represented the authentic traditions of North African zeal. Their enthusiasm for their position was only fueled by the hardening of political attitudes against them.

As is clear from their willingness to appeal to the emperor for justice, the Donatists had at first been as eager as their opponents to exact what they could from the state. However, the decisive refusal of their claims had stirred up more belligerent feelings about Rome in some quarters. Donatism cannot be characterized as simply a political protest movement, nor can it be seen as an indigenous, rural force at odds with the Romanized catholic Christianity of Carthage. Nevertheless, in the course of the fourth century there would be associations between some elements of the Donatist movement and certain strains of nationalist militancy for whom the prospect of martyrdom only heightened the glory of the cause of opposition to Roman authority. Such links were undoubtedly an embarrassment to many Donatists, for to them zeal for Christ was not to be tainted by confusion with other ideals. Yet it is not difficult to imagine how ecclesiastical separatism might appeal to those who had experienced economic poverty and social disaffection.

The Donatist schism would completely dominate North African church life for well over a century, and the issues it raised would elicit significant theological reflection in the West in the later fourth and early fifth centuries, as we shall see in chapter 6 (see pp. 171–79). Constantine was not the last emperor to try to squash the Donatists; he was only the first to fail.

Dispute in the East: Arius

Constantine found that it was not only Western Christians who could not agree among themselves. When he took control of the East in 324, he soon discovered that the Greek churches, too, were acutely divided. This time, the quarrel was not about ecclesiastical discipline as such nor about the nature of the church. It was about something even more momentous—how to conceive of the person of Christ himself.

The background to the conflict lay in the church of Alexandria. Around 318 a presbyter of the church in that city, Arius, had got himself embroiled in a dispute with his bishop, Alexander. Arius (256–336), a Libyan by birth, was the leader of one of the regional congregations of Alexandria called Baucalis. He was a popular preacher with a high reputation for his personal character and his devotion to asceticism, and he had a solid band of local followers. We cannot be sure whether Arius had been rebuked by Alexander for his ideas or whether Arius had in fact made bold to criticize his bishop for his teaching, which he suspected of veering towards modalism[11] in his doctrine of God—the latter may be more likely.

The details of Arius's own position, both at this stage and later on, are very difficult to uncover, for much of our evidence comes from those who were his opponents then or (in most cases) subsequently, who naturally had their own reasons for presenting his ideas in a negative way from the beginning. Even the writings we do possess by Arius himself—a couple of letters and some fragments of a poem called *Thalia* ("Banquet"), which illustrate the ability Arius is said to have had to set theological ideas to verse or to the style of popular songs—survive because they were deliberately selected by his critics to show up his views in the worst possible light. Often Arius is alleged to have held opinions and said things that he probably did not. There is no doubt that his beliefs need to be distinguished from those espoused by many of the people who later came to be called "Arians"; some of the diverse forms of Arianism that unfolded in the course of the fourth century were far removed from the teachings of Arius himself.

Arius's enemies depicted him as a devious philosopher, led astray by his fondness for subtle, logical analysis. In reality, it is clear that Arius saw himself as a conservative, holding to the doctrinal traditions he had inherited, and seeking to anchor them in biblical texts rather than speculative metaphysics. This is not to say that Arius was not a thinker of some ability, with a knowledge of both Stoic and Platonist ideas; but it is to say that he was uninterested in the pursuit of ideas in detachment from the proclamation of a practical version of the Christian story. Arius needs to be seen as belonging in some sense within an existing Alexandrian tradition, and some scholars believe that his teaching began as simply an exaggeration of Origen's emphasis on the transcendence of the one God.[12]

There is certainly good reason to believe that Arius was driven by a desire to safeguard the uniqueness and perfection of God against the contingencies of change and suffering, and one of his main concerns was to find a way of interpreting the story of Jesus that did not jeopardize the essential *otherness* of God. Christ's participation in human vulnerability was, for Arius, the evidence that he should not be thought of as God in exactly the same sense as the God he called "Father." Christ was indeed known as the "Son" of God, but this, Arius argued, was a title given to him by divine grace and favor. The Son was to be thought of as a unique being produced by God to be the instrument by which the rest of creation was affected. As the only begotten one (John 1:18) his origins lay before time, but he was not coeternal with the Father. He was "the firstborn over all creation" (Col. 1:15), and the Wisdom brought forth as the first of the Lord's works (Prov. 8:22–36), and thus exalted over all other creatures. He might even be said to be "divine," but he remained a creature. He was not God as God is God.

In Arius's view, Christ was able to live a perfect human life by the will of God, but solely because of this. The Son was not by nature sinless and immutable in the way that God the Father is, and he could not fully know God himself, though he was enabled to reveal the Father to the world. By virtue of the moral life that he lived, triumphing over real temptations and evil, Jesus set an example for the rest of humanity to pursue. By following in his footsteps, Arius insisted, his Sonship can become ours by grace. The practical business of human salvation seems to have lain close to the heart of Arius's teaching.

Dealing with Arius

Whatever the motives behind Arius's actions, his views created a storm that far outlasted Constantine's era. In many ways that storm has never entirely abated in the subsequent story of the Christian church, and its consequences will certainly occupy us a great deal more in the period with which we are concerned in this book. Not only in the East but also in the West, the disputes over Arianism were of enormous importance both for the churches and for the Roman Empire itself.

In the first instance, events unfolded as follows. Arius wrote to Alexander, setting out his view of God. He presented himself as following the traditions in which he had been taught and seeking to be obedient to his bishop. He claimed to believe in one God, the Father, who is "alone unbegotten, alone everlasting, alone unbegun. . . ." The Son is God's offspring, begotten of the Unbegotten, and thus a creature; he is not *homoousios*, "of one substance," with the Father. On the basis of this teaching, Alexander initiated action against Arius, and he and his immediate supporters were censured.

Arius contacted Eusebius, bishop of Nicomedia (not to be confused with Eusebius of Caesarea), complaining that he had not been treated fairly by Alexander. Close to the imperial court, Eusebius of Nicomedia was in an important position to sponsor Arius's cause, and he succeeded in broadening the base of those who were sympathetic to his ideas. Arius also appealed to other clergy, protesting his orthodoxy and hinting at associations with the views of Lucian of Antioch, an influential teacher who had been martyred in 312. Despite what was once assumed, it is unlikely that he had actually been a pupil of Lucian, but he endeavored to identify himself with Lucian's authority for his own ends.

Alexander, for his part, issued an encyclical letter, informing the churches at large that Arius had been condemned by the bishops of Egypt and Libya. Alexander insisted that Arius's teaching was seriously in error: Arius held that God was not always a Father, that his Word was not from eternity but was made out of nothing, and that there was a time when the Son "was not." Formally excommunicated, Arius and a group of his supporters, including six presbyters, six deacons, and two bishops from Libya, were obliged to leave their churches. However, like his bishop, Arius continued to be in correspondence with a wide range of other churchmen, and his backers grew increasingly numerous, not only in Nicomedia but also in Palestine and Syria. His most powerful ecclesiastical advocate proved to be the bishop of Caesarea, Eusebius, who got himself into serious trouble for his efforts to champion Arius's position.

By late 324 the churches of the East were sharply divided between those that sided with Arius and those that endorsed the line taken by Alexander. Constantine's first instinct was to attempt to broker a settlement between the primary parties. He wrote to Alexander and Arius, urging them to put behind them the apparently trivial events that had led to their original dispute, but stating that the synodical excommunication of Arius and his fellow clergy remained valid; restoration for them could take place only as laymen and only on his, the emperor's, say-so. The letter was dispatched to Alexandria through Ossius of Cordoba, who pressed the view that while tolerance and forgiveness were necessary, Arius was in the end obliged to respect the authority of his bishop and submit to his discipline.

Constantine had made a commendable attempt to settle things, but he did not succeed. Early in 325 a synod at Antioch elected a staunch opponent of Arius, Eustathius, as the new bishop of Antioch and vigorously asserted its belief that the begottenness of God the Son did not mean that the Son was a creature; the Son was mysteriously begotten as the image of the Father and must not be thought of as ever having been nonexistent. Three bishops dissented from this position, one of whom was Eusebius of Caesarea. They were provisionally excommunicated, pending ratification of the judgment at a council to be held at Ancyra in Galatia (modern Ankara in Turkey) a few weeks later.

It is not clear whether the council was originally Constantine's plan or whether it was first suggested by the bishop of Ancyra, Marcellus, whose fierce opposition to Arius's teaching led him to hold that the Son so shares the Father's characteristics that there are not distinct *hypostaseis* or persons within God at all—a view that would subsequently generate considerable controversy of its own. At any rate, Constantine was eager to see a settlement to the doctrinal wrangling, for the dispute that had started in Alexandria was not only undermining ecclesiastical relations throughout the East but was quite capable of spreading toward the West and making a mockery of his dream of presenting an empire unified politically as well as theologically. As far as he was concerned, the whole affair was about something trifling, and the sooner it was over, the better.

The Council of Nicaea

A council at Ancyra, presided over by Marcellus, was highly likely to favor Arius's opponents. It was also inconvenient for the emperor himself. Constantine thus changed the venue to Nicaea, near Nicomedia (the modern Isnik), so that he could attend in person. His alleged reasons were that the air was better there and that Nicaea, just across the Bosphorus, would be more accessible for Western churchmen. It is quite likely that the maneuvering of Eusebius of Nicomedia also influenced the decision.

The Council of Nicaea was duly convened on 20 May 325. It assembled not on church property but in an imperial building, and Constantine himself chaired the opening session. It was the largest gathering of churchmen called up to that time. The total number of bishops present was probably around 220, all of them transported, housed, and fed at public expense in accordance with Constantine's policy of beneficence toward the clergy. Technically they represented all parts of the empire, though in reality the great majority were from the East. The handful of Westerners included Ossius of Cordoba and two presbyters sent by Bishop Sylvester of Rome. The open supporters of Arius perhaps numbered about twenty in all. After Constantine had solemnly exhorted the delegates to reach an agreement, he handed over the formal presidency of the Council to Ossius. The emperor did not directly stage-manage the proceedings, but he stamped his authority upon the occasion from the start, and none of the participants was unaware of his determination that a solution be found to the crisis that Arius had started.

The deliberations at Nicaea went on for two months. No precise record of their details, official or otherwise, has come down to us, and our knowledge of what happened must be pieced together from various kinds of later evidence. It appears to have been decided quite early on that the theology of Arius and his followers was unacceptable. Among Arius's opponents, however, there was no clear view as to what should be presented as an alternative statement of faith. Some, like Marcellus, believed that the whole scheme that had been inherited from Origen's language of "three *hypostaseis*" was deficient: the fundamental feature of God, they held, is his unity, and the distinction between the Father and the Son is essentially a temporal one relative to creation. Occupying the middle ground, and almost certainly the largest group among the delegates, were those who wanted to remain faithful to the traditional *Logos* models of the Greek church[13] without endorsing Arius's formulation that the Son is lesser in being than the Father. The challenge lay in trying to come up with a statement that would express the relationship of the Father and the Son in a way that neither reduced the divinity of the Son nor rendered the distinction between the Father and the Son merely a matter of different temporal manifestations.

In the search for answers, the role of Eusebius of Caesarea proved significant. Constantine, perhaps swayed by Eusebius's willingness to emphasize in his *Ecclesiastical History* the triumph of the emperor over Licinius, evidently made it clear that he disapproved of the censure of Eusebius at Antioch. Eusebius presented a creed of his own to the council for approval, claiming that it represented his traditional position—it was, he said, the creed he had professed at baptism and had always taught as a churchman. Part of Eusebius's creed affirmed belief in the Son as the Only-begotten of the Father, to be spoken of as "God from God, Light from Light, Life from Life, Only-begotten Son, firstborn of all creation, before all ages begotten from the Father. . . ." Eusebius himself tells us that Constantine expressed his approval of this language and proposed that it be adopted, with the addition of the word *homoousios* ("of one substance") to describe the relationship of the Son to the Father's divinity.[14]

Eusebius's evidence is naturally concerned to justify its author's stance and to magnify the part played by Constantine, who wisely recognized truth when he heard it. In the wake of his condemnation at Antioch, Eusebius can hardly have been in any position to engineer a settlement to the debate; he was in a situation in which he had to clear his own name. The creed he proposed in defense of his orthodoxy was not his creation but was rooted in an existing Palestinian or Syrian tradition.

There were, in fact, subtle but important differences between the wording of Eusebius's creed and the statement that was finally adopted at Nicaea, and Eusebius was only able to agree to the final Nicene formula after considerable evasion. Much negotiation undoubtedly went on after Eusebius's statement of self-defense had been sanctioned by the emperor. Nevertheless, some of the phraseology that had emerged in his effort to justify his orthodoxy helped to shape the ultimate result of the council's labors.

The Creed of Nicaea

In the end, the following definition was proposed:

> We believe in one God, the Father Almighty, Maker of all things visible and invisible.
> And in one Lord Jesus Christ, the Son of God, begotten of the Father, Only-begotten, that is, from the substance [ousia] of the Father; God from God, Light from Light, true God from true God, begotten not made, of one substance [homoousios] with the Father, by whom all things were made; who for us human beings and for our salvation came down and was incarnate, was made human, suffered, and rose again the third day, ascended into heaven, and is coming to judge the living and the dead.
> And in the Holy Spirit.

After these clauses, the following statements were added:

> And those who say, "There was when he was not," and "Before his generation he was not," and "He came to be from nothing," or those who pretend that the Son of God is of other reality [hypostasis] or substance [ousia], the catholic and apostolic church anathematizes.

Together, these affirmations make up the original Creed of Nicaea. The wording of the creed that is generally known as the "Nicene Creed" today does not in fact derive from this council but from a formula endorsed by another gathering later on, the Council of Constantinople in 381 (see pp. 95–98). Scholars often designate the 325 creed "N" and the 381 creed "C" in order to clarify the distinction. Strictly speaking, the statement usually designated the Nicene Creed ought to be known as the Niceno-Constantinopolitan Creed—though this represents something of a mouthful for liturgical practice.

The most immediately striking aspect of the Creed of Nicaea is that the word that Eusebius claims Constantine had suggested, *homoousios* ("of one substance"), found its way into the heart of the statement in the long second clause on the relationship of the Son to the Father. It is not entirely clear why this term in particular was championed. Constantine can hardly be credited with introducing it on his own initiative, and it has often been assumed that Ossius may have been behind it. It fits quite well with traditional Western ways of speaking of the "one substance" (*una substantia*) of the Father, the Son, and the Holy Spirit, and in some such sense it also resonates with the emphasis of Eustathius and Marcellus on the essential oneness of God's being.

Homoousios was, however, a word with a difficult history. For a start, it was not biblical, which meant that the council was proposing to talk about the nature of the Godhead in terms that were philosophical or conceptual rather than in language drawn directly from the Scriptures. For Arius and those sympathetic to him, this was a serious problem, for they believed sound theology ought to be biblical in its idiom. The term may conceivably have been used by Origen to speak of the Son as the true offspring of the Father, but its more immediate associations were much more negative. First introduced into theological discourse by Gnostic teachers to describe the way in which heavenly powers participated in the fullness of God, *homoousios* had been employed in the 260s by Libyan bishops whom Dionysius of Alexandria had condemned as modalists and, in a somewhat different sense, by Paul of Samosata, who was condemned by the Council of Antioch in 268 for so stressing the oneness of God that he denied the preexistence of the Son.[15] More significantly still, Arius himself had, as we have seen, already repudiated the word; to him, it was "Manichaean,"[16] for it suggested that the Godhead could somehow be divided into two parts in a quasi-materialistic way, as if a part of the Father could be split off from his being and known as "the Son."

On the face of things, therefore, the omens were poor. Yet the outcome of the council was virtually unanimous. All but two of the bishops agreed to sign the creed. The dissenters, Theonas of Marmarica and Secundus of Ptolemais, were both from Libya, where Arius had particularly loyal support. They suffered exile, as did Arius himself. The rest, it seemed, were at one, and Constantine had got his way; the church was united in its opposition to the teaching of Arius.

The reality, however, was far more complex. The apparently all-important *homoousios* could in fact be understood in a variety of ways. Literally, it meant "same in being." But what was "sameness" here? To be "the same as" can mean to be "identical to" in a specific sense or "exactly like" in a generic sense. The "being" in question is also vague: a human

and an animal may both be described as "beings," but one has one form
of "being" (or "nature" or "substance") and the other another. For staunch
enemies of Arius, such as Eustathius and Marcellus, *homoousios* meant
"one and the same being." For Eusebius of Caesarea, on the other hand,
it meant "exactly like in being"—potentially a very significant difference.
Is the Son *the same as* God in his being, or is he *exactly like* God in his
being? To Eusebius and many other Greek bishops it seemed much
better to say that he is like God. In their eyes, the claim that he is *the
same as* God would imply that there is no distinction between the Son
and the Father. Such an impression would compromise the role of the
Father as the source of the Godhead and suggest that *Father* and *Son*
are not distinct persons within the Godhead but only different modes
in which the one God appears at different times.[17]

The anathemas contained in the last section of the Creed of Nicaea
were certainly designed to condemn explicitly the language of Arius
with regard to the Son as a *created* being with a beginning at some point
in the will of God, but the positive definition of the Son's status was
capable of being endorsed by plenty of churchmen whose sympathies
lay more with Arius than with Alexander. Constantine may or may not
have had the inherent ambiguity of *homoousios* explained to him, but
its semantic slipperiness seemed to provide exactly what he needed: a
formula on which the majority of the bishops could agree.

The Canons of Nicaea

In addition to the creed, Nicaea bequeathed some other important legacies to the churches. Twenty "canons" or rules were issued, dealing with
a number of practical and organizational matters. They set out prescriptions for clergy and laity, aimed at standardizing discipline throughout
the many branches of the church on issues such as the necessity of a
period of probation after baptism prior to ordination, the functions of
deacons, and the process for valid episcopal consecrations. Bishops were
barred from transferring from one see to another, and it was decided
that generally they ought to be installed by the entire episcopate of an
area or by a minimum of three other bishops.

Most crucially, the canons of Nicaea enshrined the principle that
certain churches had a right to exercise authority over certain others. Alexandria, Antioch, and Rome were recognized as having rights
respectively over the entire provincial territories of Egypt and Libya,
Syria, and southern Italy. Their bishops were deemed to have specific

duties as "metropolitans," or leaders of an entire province rather than just a local diocese. They were to hold jurisdiction over other bishops within their provinces and have the right of veto over episcopal candidates in these regions. Special honor was said to be due to the see of Aelia, or Jerusalem, though not to the detriment of the metropolitan rights of Caesarea. Within a few years, the new see of Constantinople would aspire to belong to the same elite grouping, but it took another century or so for the church in Constantine's city to achieve a position of significance, and even then its bishops never became as powerful as their colleagues in Rome.[18]

Other topics dealt with at Nicaea included the question of the date of Easter, which had been a matter of significant controversy since the second century.[19] It was decreed that Easter was now to be observed in accordance with the practice of Rome and Alexandria, and thus independently of any Jewish reckoning of 14 Nisan (Passover time). More important, in structural terms, were the canons' judgments concerning the reconciliation of schismatics. Novatianists were to be readmitted to communion with the catholic church on the basis of simple compliance with penitential discipline. Followers of Paul of Samosata in Antioch were, however, to be (re)baptized, though their clergy were to be then deemed eligible for office within the catholic church.[20]

Among the other dissidents mentioned, the most recent were the Melitians in Egypt. They were followers of a prominent Coptic bishop, Melitius of Lycopolis, who at the height of the Great Persecution had taken it upon himself to organize the church of Alexandria after its bishop, Peter, had gone into hiding, in a bid to ensure that its activities continued in defiance of the authorities. Melitius had ordained a number of individuals who could provide pastoral care and lead worship in the midst of the crisis, both outside and within Alexandria.[21] Peter had soon returned, and Melitius had been arrested for his activities but had attracted solid support for his actions. There were accusations that Peter had been prepared to compromise his faith and that he was willing to readmit the lapsed on lenient grounds. Such charges continued even after Peter had been incarcerated himself. In the end, Melitius and his followers had separated themselves from Peter and his supporters, the Melitians establishing a "church of the martyrs," and members of the two parties had kept aloof from each other even when they were called to suffer together for their faith.

Peter had at length been martyred in 311, but Melitius lived on. The Council of Nicaea determined that he be stripped of his office, but those ordained by him were to be reconciled and could serve as clerics if they consented to be part of the mainstream communion in Alexandria. These terms proved sufficient to win over some of the Melitians over the next few years, but not all, and some of the former Melitian clergy proved a thorn in the flesh of the Alexandrian episcopate for a long time to come. The schism Melitius had produced never spread beyond Africa, but it long outlasted its founder. Despite appearances, its underlying causes were less to do with a clash of rigorism and moderatism and more about the competitiveness of episcopal authority among the churches of Egypt and Libya. Alexandria could brook no challenge from what it regarded as the culturally inferior representatives of Christianity elsewhere, and there were some long-standing tensions surrounding the respective rights of churchmen inside and outside the metropolis.

The Aftermath of the Council

The Council of Nicaea concluded in late July 325 with a banquet to celebrate the twentieth year of Constantine's reign. The bishops dispersed, having shared in their patron's bounty and, so it seemed, satisfied his ends. The decision to condemn Arius and those who stood by him was relayed to the churches of Egypt and Libya, and the dispute that had begun between Alexander and his priest was supposedly settled. Nicaea symbolized the extent to which churchmen could be pressed into subscribing to an ideal of oneness, even when that oneness was sustained on very flimsy foundations.

So long as the serious doctrinal issues that continued to divide Christians could be ignored, all might be well. Inevitably, however, it did not take long for the cracks to appear in the unity that Constantine prided himself on having secured. A matter of weeks later, Eusebius of Nicomedia, having signed the creed, proceeded to extend communion to Arians who had been condemned by the council. Similar behavior was adopted by another signatory, Theognis, bishop of Nicaea—the very place where the council had met. Constantine was outraged: their actions were, in his mind, political treason as well as doctrinal perfidy. The two senior bishops were removed from their posts by imperial command and sent into exile. They appealed, protesting that they had, after all, assented to the Creed of Nicaea, and at a meeting of an ecclesiastical court at Nicaea around 327 or 328 the decision was reversed, with the emperor's approval.

Meanwhile, Arius had sent a statement of his faith to Constantine in which he professed his beliefs to be both scriptural and traditional. He pointedly omitted all reference to the Creed of Nicaea. Although the creed would in time come to be regarded as a product of the first of the great "ecumenical" councils of the church (i.e., the findings of representatives from churches all over the *oikoumene* or the "whole inhabited world"),[22] and its statement on the person of Christ would be seen as a benchmark of catholic orthodoxy, it is quite clear that this was by no means its status at this point. At the same meeting that reinstated Eusebius of Nicomedia and Theognis of Nicaea, Arius's plea was accepted, and he was recalled from exile.

Despite this judgment, Arius's personal influence remained limited. The most prominent of his advocates, once again, was Eusebius of Nicomedia, and it was in no small measure thanks to his efforts that Arius's cause gained fresh momentum from around 328. In Egypt, Alexander ignored the order to readmit Arius to communion, and when Alexander died in April 328 the request remained unanswered. His successor, a young man by the name of Athanasius, was equally determined not to comply. Arius had been condemned for heresy, and as far as Athanasius was concerned his ideas remained erroneous, no matter what subtle maneuvers he or his allies might be prepared to make in order to secure his rehabilitation.

Athanasius

Athanasius is one of the most significant figures in Christian history. Controversial in his own day, he has always elicited diverse assessments: many consider him a spiritual giant and a champion of orthodoxy; others believe he was a cunning political strategist who was not averse to using extreme measures, including physical violence, to achieve his ends. His shortcomings are difficult to deny, but he was without question a man of outstanding gifts, and his influence as a theologian was enormous, as we shall see further in the next chapter.

Born around 299, probably in Alexandria, Athanasius was brought up in a Christian environment, and he became a servant of the church at an early age. As a young deacon, he acted as secretary to Alexander and accompanied him to Nicaea in 325. Designated by Alexander as his successor, he was consecrated bishop of Alexandria on 8 June 328. Almost immediately he ran into a storm of challenges to his authority. Rumors spread that his election was invalid for a variety of reasons, including his youthfulness (he was just short of thirty—the usual recognized age for a bishop), his status as a deacon rather than a priest at

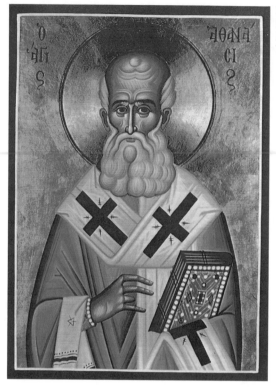

Icon of Athanasius. Illustration from Holy Transfiguration Monastery, Boston, MA. Used by permission.

the time, and the fact that he had been consecrated by only a minority of Egyptian bishops.

The opposition was orchestrated from the start by former Melitian clerics in particular, who refused to accept Athanasius and elected their own candidate as bishop in his stead. They then accused Athanasius of treating them in an oppressive and unjust manner and of using violence and intimidation to force them into submission. It is entirely probable that Athanasius indeed did not hesitate to use rough treatment, including beatings and imprisonment, to bring dissidents into line or to curtail their power to get in his way. Such tactics were certainly deployed by later bishops of Alexandria, and there is good evidence to suggest that they took their cue from Athanasius's example.

In the early 330s, some of Athanasius's Melitian enemies within Egypt began to form a loose alliance with pro-Arian believers elsewhere. The Melitians were not Arian in their own doctrinal sympathies—indeed, they would later invent the claim that Melitius condemned Arius before Alexander did. They were, however, quite willing to listen to and supplement stories put about by those who had other reasons to resent what Athanasius stood for and who were outraged at his refusal to accept Arius back into his church. There were allegations that Alexandria's bishop was to blame for all kinds of crimes including financial impropriety, sexual depravity, sacrilege, involvement in magic, and even murder. There is little likelihood that Athanasius was guilty of the more outlandish activities of which he was accused, but the charges of coercion and intimidation did have some substance, and the combined influence of

Eusebius of Nicomedia and an assortment of other foes meant that he was subject to investigation.

By 335 Constantine was in a mood to reconcile Arian sympathizers. Encouraged by the Eusebians, his calculation was that the peace of his empire would be best promoted by the restoration of all those supporters of Arius whose conduct looked likely to pose no risk to stability. The ceremonial expression of reunification would be the dedication of the great new Church of the Resurrection in Jerusalem. Constantine invited churchmen from all over the empire, including those designated as Arians. Reconciliation, however, presupposed the settlement of political as well as doctrinal matters. At a meeting of bishops in Tyre in 335, presided over by an imperial official, the Eusebian party secured condemnation of Athanasius for conduct unbecoming a bishop; he was deposed from his see and excommunicated. His crimes had nothing to do formally with his doctrinal position; they lay squarely in his moral behavior.

Athanasius, knowing he was heavily outnumbered by his adversaries, had expected to be condemned, and he appealed in person to Constantine, who had meanwhile gone ahead with his dedication ceremony in Jerusalem. At first the emperor was inclined to take his side, but (allegedly after Athanasius had threatened to call a dock strike in Alexandria to disrupt the vital grain supply from Egypt to Constantinople if he did not get his way) he was induced to believe that the Alexandrian church would be better off without him, and he decided to banish the turbulent bishop to Trier in Gaul. Shortly afterwards the fiercely anti-Arian Marcellus of Ancyra was also removed from his bishopric and sent into exile by a council in Constantinople, partly as a result of the machinations of Eusebius and his party. It was alleged that Marcellus had insulted Helena, the emperor's mother, when she was on a recent visit to Palestine and Syria. In reality, it was his theology that was objectionable. He spoke of God as essentially single and as threefold only in the processes of creation and redemption. To many, this seemed like a fresh outbreak of the heresy for which Sabellius had been condemned over a century earlier.[23]

Athanasius had been removed on moral and political grounds, Marcellus on doctrinal ones, but the result, in practical terms, was the same. The Eusebian cause triumphed, and Constantine's quest for unity was pursued at the cost of a benign indifference to the events of 325. As far as imperial policy was concerned, Nicaea was just a stage in a political process—important in its own time in patching up a kind of settlement between warring churchmen, and significant in terms of what it said about the emperor's relationship to the church, but not a strict test by which to determine the acceptability of episcopal behavior. Constantine's perception was that those who had preferred a broad interpretation of the issues appeared to be numerically on the winning side—and they often seemed to behave better than their opponents. A pragmatic approach held the best prospects for peace.

In this climate there was little reason why Arius himself should not be officially rehabilitated, even if his personal significance as a political player was well and truly over. By now an aging and physically frail figure, he had ceased to be of any real importance to ecclesiastical affairs; he may originally have sparked the controversies that would forever be associated with his name, but long before his death the issues were being fought out by churchmen much more prominent than he. Legend has it that he was mysteriously struck down in the streets of Constantinople in 336 on the night before he was due to be restored—perhaps the victim of a deadly disease, perhaps poisoned—and that he met his end as a forlorn figure in a public latrine. The truth will probably never be known, and we cannot say whether Arius was forgiven or not. The reality was that for everyone other than Arius himself, it had probably ceased to matter.

The Death and Legacy of Constantine

In the spring of the following year, Constantine fell ill. Knowing that his time was short, he at last received Christian baptism, clad as a catechumen, at the hands of Eusebius of Nicomedia. His life as a baptized believer was very brief. He died at Pentecost, on 22 May 337, while making plans for a military expedition against the Persians, the chief rivals to his dominion in the East, whose invasions of the kingdom of Armenia had been occupying his attentions militarily and politically for some time.

The Armenians had become the first nation to embrace Christianity officially a quarter of a century earlier when their king, Tiridates, was converted under the influence of Gregory "the Illuminator" (ca. 240–332), an Armenian noble who had become a Christian in Cappadocia and returned to evangelize his native land. It is clear that Constantine saw his planned assault on the Persians as a kind of holy war of Christianized forces against an infidel power threatening Christian territories. For Constantine himself, the encounter was not to be, and the outcome of Rome's engagement with Persia would not in fact be settled until 350. Constantine was buried in the sepulchre he had planned for himself in

Constantinople, in the splendid Church of the Holy Apostles—supposedly the thirteenth in the line of Christ's specially chosen emissaries. His senate, nonetheless, afforded him deification in traditional Roman style.

The death of Constantine brought to a close a strategic period. Whatever Constantine's personal motivations, his political regime had witnessed a substantial revolution in the status of the Christian faith in the Roman world. The churches had gone from being at best a tolerated and often a harassed flock, obliged to live a precarious existence in the world and trust in God rather than the arm of flesh, to being an officially recognized institution, in possession of considerable social, economic, and cultural privileges. As the early history of both Donatism and Arianism showed, the decisions of church leaders on matters of the faith were now bound up as never before with the whims and stratagems of secular authority, and the process of framing statements of Christian belief was capable of being powerfully influenced by political interests, often regardless of biblical or spiritual considerations. The shape of imperial preferences, with the significant material benefits that they brought, might all too readily determine the courses adopted by churchmen, and when Christians disagreed about issues of belief and practice, their appeals to the state could mean serious trouble for those who lost out in the competition for the emperor's favor. The dangers of intolerance and the incentive to impose uniformity rather than negotiate differences were given impetus such as had not existed in earlier ages.

Some historians believe these changes were disastrous for the integrity of Christianity and for the purity of the churches. "Constantinianism," they say, fatally compromised vital elements of the Christian witness and rendered the faith susceptible to the dangers of cultural entrenchment and complacency. The prophetic and countercultural aspects of the gospel were diluted. The problems may not have been apparent all at once, but in the longer term the conversion of Constantine led inevitably to the emergence of "Christendom" and the equation of Christian faith with politics, ethnicity, and privilege rather than with personal discipleship of Jesus and the inhabiting of a living tradition whose obligations included the need to confront the corruptions of worldly power. "Caesaropapism," the control of the church by secular political interests, had been instituted, and from its baneful influences Christianity, especially in Europe, would never recover.

Others consider Constantine's legacy a much more positive thing. Even if it did lead to particular challenges for the defining of the relationship between Christianity and society as a whole, it proved overall a very valuable force for the expansion of the faith. The endorsement of Christ at the highest levels of Roman power afforded unprecedented opportunities for the mission of the church. According to this perspective, the world had been specially prepared by God for the coming of Jesus in the establishment of Greco-Roman civilization; now this same political and cultural sphere had been remarkably reconfigured so that the truth of what God had done in Jesus was recognized by powers and authorities and made available to vastly larger constituencies.

As far as Constantine's own spiritual position is concerned, we must acknowledge that we simply have no access to his private beliefs. Whether his Christian convictions were genuine or purely expedient is something we are not able to determine. There is certainly much to suggest that his grasp of the subtleties of Christian doctrine was always poor and that he never did appreciate why it might ultimately matter greatly to Christians that the person of Christ should be defined in certain precise terms and not others, or that the visible purity of the church as a communion should be an issue of major concern to many believers. On the other hand, weakness of theological acumen or deficiency of spiritual insight does not necessarily imply lack of faith, and there is no evidence that Constantine ever deviated from his public commitment to Christianity, even if his expression of that commitment only became more comprehensive over time. In the end, the truth about Constantine's inner spirit must remain mysterious.

For many of the Christians of his own time, Constantine's reign brought a welcome end to repression and provided opportunities for social expansion and political influence that previous generations of believers would have found unimaginable. His generosity to the churches created many new structures, human as well as physical: Christianity was the official faith of the imperial household; the emperor was God's vicegerent; bishops were the leaders among a new and growing elite, gifted with money, status, and prestige. Constantine also accomplished much in political and social terms: his military campaigns on the frontiers of his empire restored a fair measure of security, especially in the West, and his economic policies secured a prosperity that for much of the third century had been a forgotten experience for a majority in the Roman world.

Yet, however remarkable the changes, Constantine's actions did not turn the Roman Empire into a Christian realm, nor could they render the real spiritual challenges of the Christian gospel any more palatable than they had ever been. The profession of Christianity did not become a compulsory thing, nor did Constantine repress traditional religions, even if he plundered the treasuries of pagan temples to assist with the funding of his Christian imperial architecture. The Roman world certainly did not become a theocracy, and the majority of its inhabitants remained indifferent or hostile to Christ. Christians were still a minority who regularly suffered ridicule and scorn at both private and public levels. Over the course of the fourth century, people would begin to join the churches in much larger numbers than ever before, but this in turn would create significant challenges for those who needed to instruct them in the moral responsibilities of living a Christian life (see pp. 248–54). To Eusebius, Constantine may have been the new Moses, who had led the church out of bondage into the promised land of recognition, power, and wealth. To others—the losers among the emperor's diverse ecclesiastical petitioners, such as the Donatists or, ultimately, Athanasius—Constantine's declaration of personal faith brought no special favoritism. The emperor may have professed to be Christian, but that did not mean the state was always on your side.

Arguably the most important effects of the so-called "Constantinian revolution" lay not so much at the level of external conditions, or in the benefits accruing to the churches in material terms, as in developments brought about internally, in the *minds* of those within the Roman Empire who called themselves believers. To be Christian was now, in theory, a matter of fashion rather than fear: to be a follower of Christ was not to be a devotee of a socially repugnant cause but to share the faith of the emperor himself. What Constantine set in motion was the beginnings of a gradual process of "Christianization"—a wide-ranging and overt assimilation of Christian symbolism and culture into the identity of the Roman Empire. It is crucial to remember that vast numbers of Christians lived in regions to the east that were not part of Constantine's domain, and for many of them this association of Christianity with the imperial ethos would have seemed a strange development. Faith had never been a "Roman" affair in anything like this way before. Thoroughgoing Christian transformation of the Roman world certainly did not happen with Constantine—or indeed with any other emperor after him—but the policies he pursued, whatever their inspiration, did prove to be the roots from which other developments followed, and in time these would alter the character of the Christian church forever.

The nature of Constantine's conversion and his role as political patron of Christianity will always remain controversial, and interpreters are likely to go on arguing about whether the social privileging of the Christian faith that took place under his authority was good or bad for the church in spiritual terms. One thing is clear, and that is that whether we think Constantine's identification with the Christian cause was a triumph or a disaster, the controversies that surfaced in the churches during his regime only endured and intensified in the generations after his death. Beneath the facade of unity that Constantine's *Realpolitik* constructed, there were still plenty of intellectual, social, and practical differences lurking and many serious issues yet to be confronted.

Nowhere was this more powerfully true than in the case of Arianism. In a host of ways, the questions that Arius and his supporters had opened up would dominate the church's horizons for years to come. In the world after Constantine, the manner in which these questions were dealt with could no longer take the forms that might have been assumed in previous ages. A new age of high-profile theological politics had begun.

2

THE POLITICS
OF ARIANISM

▼

Constantine's Heirs

Constantine intended his empire to be divided between his dynastic heirs.
As well as his three sons—Constantine II, Constantius, and Constans—
there were also two nephews, but after his death these nephews and
all other potential bidders for power were swiftly removed in a bloody
military purge, leaving control entirely with the sons. After a period
of negotiation, they agreed to share their responsibilities as follows:
Constantine II would govern the provinces of the West (Gaul, Spain,
and Britain); Constantius would be in charge of Asia Minor, Egypt, and
Syria (the biggest challenge, given the presence of the militant Persian
Empire on the borders); while the youngest, the teenager Constans,
would hold authority over Italy, North Africa, and the Balkans.

Relations between the brothers were difficult on several levels. Brought
up as Christians, they inherited their father's belief that the faith of
Christ was to be the unitary religion of the Roman Empire, but each
of them had also absorbed the idea that one emperor was ample for
the task of implementing this policy. The rivalry between them and the

varying doctrinal sympathies that emerged as a result of their power struggle were to prove of significance for the churches. In a world in which Christianity was officially favored, theological differences were no longer a matter only for clergy or committed believers but also for their imperial masters. The disputes that had arisen over the views of Arius and his followers were destined to be fought out in close connection with political processes. Christians may still have been in a minority, but the fortunes of their doctrinal affairs were bound up with developments in high places.

The effects of these links were felt all over the Roman world, and it is not possible to plot a simple course that looks at the story of the church in the fourth century in just one location at a time. The political outworking of the Arian controversies took place in a variety of related contexts at once, and the complexity of the process can only be appreciated by treating the churches of the Roman Empire as a whole. Through it all, we must remember that the ordinary life of Christian worship and witness in all kinds of places went on in its own multicolored fashion, and the churches continued to develop and grow in ways that are not directly reflected in the details of the intellectual disputes in which clergy and other leaders engaged. The grand-scale events of theological debate are only one side of the story; people continued to be converted, to witness, to shine, to struggle, and to fail wherever the gospel was heard, and the practical effects of Christian spirituality were felt in a million ways that are not recorded by the narratives of such affairs.[1]

Nevertheless, in the post-Constantinian environment, the overall situation of the communities to which believers belonged was unavoidably linked to larger political happenings. It is worth exploring the course of these developments in a little detail, for the complexity of the theological debates of the fourth century reveals the extent to which matters that affected the future life of the churches were conditioned by the larger social and cultural context within which Christians existed. Issues of great theological and spiritual significance for the shape of the Christian life as a whole were thought through and fought out amid the messiness and the contingencies of a volatile political world. The overall number of people professing Christianity at one level or another may have grown by well over twenty million during the first half of the fourth century, and this was the church scene into which they came. Rates of conversion and fidelity to the faith were affected by the twists and turns of imperial policy as well as by the messages proclaimed by bishops. Indeed, the freedom of churchmen to articulate their convictions was in no small measure connected with the decisions of those in charge of their wider political habitat.

Ongoing Doctrinal Tensions

In June 337 an amnesty was extended to exiled bishops such as Athanasius and Marcellus of Ancyra, allowing them to return to their sees. Things did not go smoothly, however. On Athanasius's return to Alexandria in November, he found significant local hostility. As one who had been condemned by an official council in 335, he was deemed to have forfeited the right to his see, and a rival bishop, Gregory, was shortly installed in his stead. After a brief period in hiding, Athanasius was forced to flee. Constantius was disinclined to listen to his pleas, for his doctrinal alignment was already clear, and it was not in Athanasius's favor; he was in the process of backing the transference of Eusebius of Nicomedia to become his new bishop in Constantinople. Constantius's sympathies plainly lay with those who felt that Arius's teaching was not entirely wrong.

Meantime, Marcellus too had met with opposition. Both he and Athanasius withdrew to Rome, where they were warmly welcomed by the recently installed bishop, Julius. Though he had only been in office for a few months, Julius had already begun to make his mark as a confident and outspoken leader. Under his guidance, the see of Rome—which, for all the privileges it had received from Constantine, had played only a modest part in the major doctrinal debates of recent years—began to assert its authority more strongly in the East. By welcoming the dissident bishops as refugees from inappropriate displays of Eastern justice, Julius demonstrated his commitment to the non-Eusebian reading of the Creed of Nicaea. He also challenged the judgment of the synods in the East that had excommunicated Athanasius and Marcellus. At a council of bishops in Rome in 340, the exiled bishops were cleared of all blame and declared to be the rightful leaders of their respective churches. Julius then flatly informed his Eastern colleagues of this judgment, claiming that Rome possessed an official right, going back to the apostle Peter himself, to function as a court of appeals in matters of Eastern as well as Western justice.

There was, in reality, no basis for such a claim, and not surprisingly the Eastern churchmen were not amused. Not for the first time, they felt, Rome had overreached its authority. Their attitude was sharpened by recent political developments. The young Constans had not taken kindly to the assumption of his brother Constantine II that Constans should take directions from him, and the two had fought, resulting in the death of Constantine II. Constans now controlled two-thirds of the empire, while Constantius was increasingly preoccupied with the problem of Persia. As part of his determination to make his political weight count, Constans sponsored the claims of Rome against the position adopted by the bishops in his brother's territory. It suited him very well that there were growing tensions between the churchmen of the West and the East. If Eusebius of Nicomedia's influence dominated the bishops in the East, Constans could use *his* support for Rome and a stricter understanding of Nicene theology to increase the pressure on Constantius. Political and doctrinal divisions converged.

In 341 a group of Eastern bishops assembled at Antioch to celebrate the completion of a great new church, the "golden" basilica, which had been begun by Constantine and was now, at last, ready to be dedicated under Constantius. While there, they met to consider their own response to the tensions that the Roman situation had generated. Eusebius of Nicomedia was clearly an influential party. While the bishops strongly disavowed that they had Arian sympathies themselves, they nevertheless refused to accept the Roman church's acquittal of Marcellus, whose views they once again declared to be heretical. They rejected the right of the Roman church to contest the decisions of duly constituted Eastern synods, arguing that such claims were novel and unfounded. They declared their fidelity to the theology of "one only-begotten Son of God" who "before all ages subsisted and coexisted with the Father who begot him." In its full form, the creed issued at Antioch spoke of the Son as "begotten from the Father before all ages, God from God, . . . exact Image of the Godhead, substance, will, power, and glory of the Father." The Holy Spirit was declared to be a third *hypostasis*, genuinely distinct from the Father and the Son.

By design, the position agreed upon at Antioch was meant to refute both a thoroughgoing Arian view and what was seen as the equally dangerous error of Marcellus's teaching. Some of the language used by the council consciously harked back to Nicaea and to ways of affirming the full deity of Christ that were well established in the East. The bishops acknowledged that there never was a time when the Son did not exist and insisted that Christ must be thought of as "from" God. At the same time, in strongly emphasizing the reality of the distinctions within the Godhead, they repudiated any suggestion that the three divine persons could be thought of as simply different modes of being, relevant only to specific phases in the history of creation and redemption. The Son was begotten of the Father "before all ages" and would "sit on the Father's right hand not only in this age but also in that to come"; his "kingdom," they declared, "shall have no end."[2]

To many Christian leaders in the West, however, the stance adopted at Antioch was highly suspicious. How could a council dominated by the influence of Eusebius fail to have Arian tendencies? The Eastern bishops may have claimed to be anti-Arian, but they made no mention of Nicaea's most difficult word, *homoousios*, and their reference to the Son as "the exact Image of the . . . substance . . . of the Father" was susceptible to a variety of interpretations, despite the language that accompanied it denouncing Arian notions of the Son as a creature. Talk of "three *hypostaseis*," translated into Latin, sounded like a belief in three gods, for it came out, literally, as "three *substantiae*." Were the Eastern leaders not perilously close to a form of tritheism (belief in three gods rather than one) in so pressing the distinctions within the Godhead?

Together, the actions of Julius and the decisions of Antioch potentially added up to a very serious situation, especially in view of the political machinations in the background. The dispute that had supposedly been settled at Nicaea in 325 was not only alive and well but was threatening to split the churches of the East and the West. Many Eastern Christians resented the arrogant presumption of Rome in daring to countermand the judgments of their bishops, and they regarded the Latin-speaking church as ignorant of the subtleties of theological language. In the West, by the same token, there was fear of the cleverness of the Greeks and strong suspicion of their agendas.

Politically, the Western situation was the stronger, in the light of Constans's status and his large territorial advantage. Athanasius continued to engage in a vigorous campaign to drum up wider Western support for his cause, and he succeeded in winning over a growing number of allies. During the winter of 341–342, Eusebius of Nicomedia died in Constantinople, and his see was fought over by rival claimants. There were also widespread disturbances in other Eastern churches in which local Christians refused to accept the presence of bishops with whose teaching they disagreed. There seemed to be growing disunity at the political heart of the Eastern cause.

The Council of Sardica

Under pressure from his brother, and realizing the gravity of the situation—no ruler could tolerate public riots over matters of Christian doctrine such as were either occurring or threatening to occur in a number of places—Constantius accepted that urgent action was needed to diffuse the tensions. Julius of Rome had suggested that a council of both Eastern and Western bishops should be convened to seek a settlement, and the two emperors agreed. The council was to meet at Sardica, modern Sofia in Bulgaria. The site was in Constans's territory but very close to the border with the East. There is some doubt as to the precise date when the gathering took place, but it was probably in 343.

The mood was bitter. The Westerners—unusually—were in a majority, and affairs were to be conducted under the primary guidance of Ossius of Cordoba, who had played such a prominent role at Nicaea. The Eastern contingent refused to sit down with them on the grounds that the deposed bishops, Athanasius and Marcellus, were present (now along with other dissidents, including Paul, the fiercely anti-Eusebian bishop from Constantinople). The Eastern churchmen withdrew across the frontier to Philippopolis in Thrace and began to hold a synod of their own.

The two camps then proceeded to hurl abuse at one another. The Eastern bishops issued a fresh excommunication of Athanasius and Marcellus and declared that all who supported them were unworthy to continue in their sees. Both Julius and Ossius were among those anathematized. The Western leaders responded in kind, excommunicating the present incumbents of the sees of Alexandria and Ancyra and declaring that the teaching of Marcellus was indeed orthodox. In addition, the Western churchmen rather unwisely issued a statement of their belief that, in defending Marcellus, contained a distinctly modalist interpretation of God's nature as one "substance." They also condemned two bishops from the Danube region who had gone over to the Greek side. Among a number of canons on the subject of episcopal discipline, the West included an explicit claim that the church of Rome possessed the right of final say in the case of appeals by Greek churchmen.

The Council of Sardica was a fiasco that showed up the worst excesses of petty politics, intolerance, and un-Christian behavior among the churches' leaders. It had done nothing to heal the divisions it had been called to deal with; the very separation that had been threatened seemed effectively to have taken place. Even if the Western representatives had allowed themselves to be used as pawns in Constans's strategy to take over his brother's territory and be sole ruler, and even if the Eastern bishops had made principled mountains out of procedural molehills, there was certainly a serious lack of willingness on both sides to understand and engage with differing opinions. Christian spokesmen from the two spheres of the Roman world had divided into mutually distrustful parties, wedded to different conceptions of how to specify a shared commitment to the deity of Christ, and adducing competing claims to ecclesiastical authority.

All the same, schism of a technical kind had not quite happened, and diplomatic relations were not broken off. There was very strong political pressure for a settlement, and ground needed to be yielded on both sides. The Eastern leaders drew up a further doctrinal statement, known as the "creed of the long lines" (it ran to some 1,400 words). They spoke of Christ as "like the Father in all things" and set out in some detail why a large number of churchmen were so opposed to the teaching of Marcellus. Their document made no mention, however, of Athanasius, who was frankly embarrassed by the crudity of the West's defense of Marcellan ideas at Sardica. This creed was presented at Rome in 345, and while it did not produce immediate success, a period of difficult negotiation seems to have ensued.

The Return of Athanasius

The consequence of these overtures was that the Western bishops increasingly edged away from their support for the Marcellan theology, while their Eastern colleagues, nervous at threats from Constans of civil war, decided that they were prepared to countenance Athanasius once again, especially as he began to distance himself from Marcellus. The death of Gregory, Athanasius's replacement in Alexandria, provided further timely help. In the spring of 346 Athanasius and Constantius were reconciled, and in October of that year Athanasius was able to reenter Alexandria. He is said to have been received back with great public enthusiasm and was able to spend almost the next ten years there—the longest single stretch he ever managed in proper charge of his see.

The late 340s brought a period of relative peace, but the stability was fragile. Although some historians have spoken of a "golden decade" of Athanasius's influence after his return to Alexandria, in reality he continued to face much opposition, and, as far as many in the East were concerned, he was tolerated rather than approved. In 349 a council at Antioch condemned him once again and recommended the appointment of George, a bishop from Cappadocia, in his place. The nomination, however, needed to be ratified by Constantius, and he had other things on his mind. Not only had he been involved for years in the bitter campaign against Persia: he now faced serious trouble elsewhere as well.

In February 350 Constans was murdered in Gaul in a military coup led by an officer named Magnus Magnentius, and Constantius was determined to crush the usurper. Interestingly, both Magnentius and Constantius sought Athanasius's support for their causes—an indication of the symbolic significance that Athanasius had come to assume in international politics, whatever his antagonists in the church were saying. Constantius was prepared to squash the deposition order against him in order to win him around. Athanasius offered no backing to Magnentius's envoys, though the bishop's enemies would afterwards accuse him of colluding in secret with the challenger.

Constantius's Drive for Unity

Meantime, however, Constantius's position became increasingly complicated. In September 351 he won a major battle against Magnentius at Mursa in Pannonia (modern-day Osijek in Croatia). The encounter took place in the territory of a bishop called Valens, who was a fierce critic of Athanasius (the Balkan region generally had been influenced by Arian sympathizers for many years). In return for supporting Constantius spiritually in his hour of crisis, Valens became a valued imperial adviser, and when Magnentius finally fell in 353 and Constantius became sole emperor, Valens was in a strong position to divert him from his openness towards Athanasius. Constantius's main object in ecclesiastical affairs was to achieve unity, and he was willing to adopt whatever means were necessary to unite the clergy of both East and West around a shared confessional position.

As had been clear at Sardica, Athanasius's periods of exile in Gaul (335–337) and Rome (339–346) and his vigorous literary campaigns had ensured that he enjoyed widespread support in the West. Amid all the doctrinal tensions, the churches had continued to grow considerably in Gaul and elsewhere in the West, and the number of bishoprics had expanded accordingly. Many of these churchmen were sympathetic to Athanasius. It was also clear, however, that a fair number of them had only a very thin grasp of the doctrinal details at stake in his disputes with his Eastern colleagues. Closely encouraged by Valens and others, Constantius endeavored to persuade the Latin bishops that their loyalties were misplaced and that wisdom dictated they should subscribe to a more flexible understanding of Christ's status. If necessary, the emperor was prepared to bribe bishops to induce them to fall into line or to remove them and send them into exile if they refused to comply.

At councils convened in Arles in 353 and Milan in 355, he secured a reversal of existing Western endorsements of Athanasius.

A number of bishops resisted Constantius's demands, and opposition came to a head at Milan when the dissidents were summoned before the emperor and confronted with an ultimatum to condemn Athanasius or face removal. Among those who suffered exile at this stage or not long afterwards were Liberius, Julius's successor in Rome,[3] Hilary of Poitiers, Dionysius of Milan, Eusebius of Vercelli, and the fiery zealot, Lucifer of Cagliari in Sardinia. Several of them would later go on to join Athanasius in lambasting Constantius as a tyrant and even as the Antichrist himself for his opposition to the true faith.

Hilary of Poitiers

The most capable theologian among these exiled leaders was Hilary, who had become bishop of Poitiers around 350. We know almost nothing about Hilary's early life, but he was probably born around 315 and had received a good classical education prior to embarking on his ecclesiastical career. As a bishop, he had early on revealed his allegiance to Nicaea and had severed relations with other Gaulish bishops who had succumbed to political pressure and acquiesced in the condemnation of Athanasius. In 356 he was implicated in a political revolt led by a Frankish soldier and was condemned and sent into exile in Phrygia, where he spent the next four years. The experience proved formative. In Asia he came into contact with Eastern doctrinal debates firsthand and became more aware of the varying strategies adopted in the Greek-speaking churches by those who were hostile to the legacy of Arius. When at length he returned to the West in 360, Hilary became a firm opponent of Arian theology, both in Gaul and farther afield, to the extent that his activities earned him the title of "the Athanasius of the West."

In some ways this designation is misleading, for Hilary did not wholeheartedly champion the word *homoousios* as Athanasius came to do, preferring to say (as a large number of Eastern churchmen did) that Christ was "like" God the Father in essence rather than equal to him as such—a formula that Athanasius was not willing to accept. Nevertheless, Hilary certainly was a passionate antagonist of Arian doctrine, and in helping to spearhead resistance to its logic he made a substantial contribution to the development of a serious intellectual theology in the Latin West.

One of a number of works Hilary wrote in exile[4] was a twelve-book treatise, *On the Trinity*, which presents an elaborate defense of the divine nature of God the Son. So strong is Hilary's affirmation of the preexistence of Christ, in fact, that he ends up painting a rather Docetic picture of the incarnation: Jesus's humanity is eclipsed by his divinity. Of the Holy Spirit, Hilary has less to say, and in that sense he does not offer any full-orbed doctrine of the Trinity as such, but he does see the Spirit as engaged in activities that are divine in character. Hilary was very much a biblical theologian, and he wrote spiritually focused commentaries on Matthew's Gospel and on the Psalms, which draw on Eastern sources such as Origen. He was also the first definite writer of hymns in Latin. Though only small fragments of a few of these hymns survive, they point to Hilary's attempt to use spiritual songs as a popular way of impressing sound doctrine upon ordinary believers. It was a technique that would be much used in Christian practice, not least in the later fourth-century West.

The Expansion of Constantius's Cause in Missionary Settings

For all the efforts of Hilary and others, the more flexible theology favored by Constantius continued to spread, not only within the Roman Empire but beyond as Christianity was taken to other constituencies. The Goths, the amalgam of Germanic tribes concentrated between the Rhine and the Danube, had been subject to Christian influences since at least the 250s, when they had invaded Cappadocia and taken among their prisoners a number of believers, including church leaders. A descendant of one of these captured Christian families was a young man whom the Goths called Wulfila(s) or Ulfila(s), "Little Wolf."

Ulfila (ca. 311–383) was brought up among the Goths but was in Constantinople in the late 330s or very early 340s. There he was consecrated by Eusebius, the former bishop of Nicomedia who was by then head of the church in Constantinople, to go as bishop to the Goths. The intention presumably was that he would consolidate a Christian constituency that already existed among the Goths north of the Danube. However, Ulfila also conducted a vigorous missionary campaign among other Gothic tribes, first in Dacia (modern Romania) and then, after encountering some persecution from those who equated the spread of Christianity with the encroachment of Roman power, in Moesia (Bulgaria), south of the Danube.

The "apostle to the Goths" met with considerable success, and he attracted many converts. One of his greatest achievements was the translation of the Greek Scriptures into the Gothic language for the first time. This was a considerable work of scholarship, for in order to do the job Ulfila had to invent an alphabet, made up of a combination of Greek letters and runes. It was said that he deliberately left out the books of Kings (which included what we call 1 and 2 Samuel) because the Goths were warlike enough already and were not to be encouraged to read further militaristic stories, but his delay in translating these texts probably did not mean he intended to exclude them from the biblical canon. His translation was very literal. It was incomplete when he died, and only parts of it survive, almost all of them New Testament passages.

Probably on account of his associations with Eusebius, Ulfila was not at all enthusiastic about claims that the Son is exactly equal to the Father and preferred to say that he is "like" him. Gothic Christianity thus inherited a doctrinal position that was far removed from Athanasius's. As we shall see in chapters 11 and 12, the impact of such teaching would have significant consequences in the longer term for the relationship between the imperial churches and the faith of the peoples the Romans called "barbarians," but in Ulfila's time it looked as if a non-Athanasian perspective was spreading very successfully in the West, both within and outside Rome's borders.

Constantius also endeavored to dilute support for Athanasius in other missionary contexts. His effort to bring converted peoples from outside the empire under the umbrella of his own doctrinal preferences was driven partly by a desire to extend his own authority and partly by a wish to minimize the political risks of allowing distinctive theological attachments to take root among those who remained beyond imperial control.

For instance, in northern Ethiopia the gospel had been spread in the second quarter of the fourth century under the influence of two young men from Tyre, Frumentius and Edesius, who had been captured and held prisoner by the ruler of the ancient kingdom of Aksum, which was at that time the major political power in the Red Sea region. The two had shared their faith with some success, and members of the royal household had been converted, including the king, Ezana. Frumentius had subsequently returned to Alexandria and had been consecrated bishop of Aksum by Athanasius, of whom he was a loyal supporter. When Constantius heard of his activities around 356–357, he wrote a strong letter to the princes of Aksum, insisting that Frumentius be dispatched to Alexandria at once to be reconsecrated by Bishop George, who by then had supplanted Athanasius and was a firm partisan of a very different view of the status of God the Son.

"Nicene" and "Arian" Parties

In the midst of the events of the 350s, renewed attention was being paid to the Creed of Nicaea. Some time early in the decade Athanasius wrote a work called *On the Council of Nicaea*, in which for the first time he proposed that the creed of 325, and the term *homoousios* in particular, should be treated as the watchword of doctrinal orthodoxy. Nothing less would do than an unqualified confession that Christ was literally "of one substance" with God. At the Council of Milan in 355, Eusebius of Vercelli suggested that the Nicene statement as a whole ought to be signed by those present, even if Athanasius was condemned (though he did not draw attention to the import of the word *homoousios* itself). In retrospect, his failure to achieve such a goal is perhaps less significant than the fact that here for the first time the Creed of Nicaea was suggested as a standard around which a gathering of disputing bishops might unite. In the ensuing years, more and more reference would be made to this benchmark by Athanasius and those loyal to him, and an explicit polarization emerged between the "Nicenes" and the "Arians."

By early 356 Athanasius had been obliged to flee Alexandria once more, this time under threat from military force. He spent the next six years in hiding, living principally among monks in the deserts of Egypt and Libya, though occasionally venturing back under cover into Alexandria. He continued to enjoy extensive loyalty in his metropolitan heartland, and his imposed successor, George, had considerable difficulties in asserting his presence. George himself was forced to take flight late in 358 after almost being beaten to death by a hostile mob, and although he managed to return briefly three years later, he was imprisoned and lynched not long afterwards, when word of Constantius's death reached the city.

More Radical Forms of Arianism

George's theology was close to versions of Arianism being promoted elsewhere. In 357 Eudoxius, an Arian who had previously been bishop of Germanicia in Syria, gained control of the church in Antioch. He was much influenced by a man named Aetius, a former deacon who had then worked as a lay-teacher for some years before being reappointed as a deacon by George of Alexandria. Aetius was an able thinker with a considerable ability in logic, and he applied his mind to the question of the causal relationship between God the Father and God the Son. Quite unlike Arius, Aetius was apparently not much interested in the Bible, nor did he offer any real exposition of the incarnation; his concern lay with the *philosophical* problem of what terms such as "Father" and "Son" might mean when applied to the being of God.

If the Son is begotten or generated, Aetius reasoned, surely the Son is "caused" by God. It is of the essence of God, however, to be "unbegotten" or ingenerate. Therefore, the Son cannot be said to be "of the same substance" with the Father. This idea gave rise to the belief that the Son's essence is "unlike" (*anomoios*) the Father's. Aetius did not use this term himself, but it later came to be associated with those who followed his reasoning.[5] One of his chief disciples was Eunomius, who was briefly bishop of Cyzicus in Pontus in 360 and who was ordained in Antioch by Eudoxius. Eunomius was much more inclined than Aetius to discuss scriptural texts, but he taught that the Son is *heteroousios*, "of a different substance" from God. The Son may conceivably be said to be "like" the Father in his activities and will, Eunomius argued, but not like God in his essence. Eunomius even went so far as to say that God cannot know more about his essence than his human creatures can, for the essence of God is his unbegottenness, and that unbegottenness can be known by us.

This kind of teaching was obviously a great deal more radical than anything that Arius had ever said, and for that reason it has often been labeled by modern scholars "neo-Arian," though many of its opponents in the fourth century tended to blur the distinctions between the ideas of Aetius and Eunomius and other Arian positions. All were part of a close family of errors. Even so, Aetius's and Eunomius's views ran directly contrary not only to the convictions of Athanasius and his Western supporters but also to the traditional beliefs of most Christians in the East, where it had been conventional to say that the Son's divinity consists in his "likeness" to the Father in his being, will, and power.

Anomoians and *Homoiousians*

The position of the mainstream within the Eastern churches was argued strongly at a gathering in Ancyra in 358. Under the leadership of Basil, the local bishop who was the successor of Marcellus and a staunch opponent of the theology that Eudoxius and George were encouraging,[6] a majority of Greek churchmen decided to seek Constantius's approval of the formula that the Son is *homoios kat'ousian*, "like in being" to the Father. As a result, they came to be known as *homoiousians*: instead of saying that the Son is *homoousios* with the Father, as Nicaea had done, they said that he is *homoiousios*. By the addition of a single Greek letter, an iota, they pinpointed exactly what their reading of Nicaea had been all along: the "sameness" spoken of in *homoousios* was understood to mean "similarity," not "identity," for they believed identity collapsed the distinctions within the Godhead. The Son is not *identical* in being to the Father but *like* the Father in being—the perfect image of the Father's will.

The *homoiousians* were firmly against the ideas of people like Aetius and Eunomius, but they were also resistant to understandings of the relationship between the Father and the Son that they felt misrepresented the way in which the two are one. For Basil and his followers, the *homoiousian* formula offered a middle way between what they saw as the equal and opposite extremes of the so-called *anomoians* on the one hand and the strict *homoousians* on the other—a path that avoided both an unworthy separation of the Son from the Father in essential terms and, at the same time, the danger of modalism, in which the distinctions within the Godhead were destroyed altogether.[7]

The "Blasphemy" of Sirmium

Basil of Ancyra was an astute political operator, and at first he succeeded in persuading Constantius that the *homoiousios* formula made most sense as a mechanism for unifying the churches. Constantius took a certain whimsical pleasure in theological debate, but, much like his father in 325, he was primarily interested in finding a political solution that would command widespread support. He recognized that the *anomoian* line was certainly not going to achieve that purpose; the *homoiousian* suggestion, on the other hand, seemed to him to offer real possibilities.

Basil's success with Constantius represented a direct challenge to the influence of Valens of Mursa. Assisted by his close associates Ursacius of Singidunum and Germanicus of Sirmium, Valens had accomplished much. At a small gathering of bishops in Sirmium in 357, he had even managed to induce the very elderly Ossius of Cordoba (who was by now well into his nineties if not around one hundred) to agree that reference to divine essence was best avoided altogether. Expressing themselves in Latin, the bishops argued that the language of *substantia* or what the Greeks called *ousia*, "essence," conjured up crudely corporeal images of God.

In a bid to promote unity, the bishops issued a statement drawing attention to the biblical references that implied that the Father is greater than the Son (especially John 14:28). The Son, it was said, is divine only in a secondary manner and must therefore be thought of as subordinate to the Father. Such views had been conventional in the East for a very long time, and the manifesto attracted some support in the West as well. However, far too much water had passed under the bridge for such a formula not to sound decidedly Arian to many ears. In North Africa and in Gaul it met with much disfavor. Hilary of Poitiers referred to it as "the Blasphemy of Sirmium,"[8] and the reputation of the frail Ossius, after all that he had achieved, never recovered from his lapse so late in life.

Valens and Basil were opposed to Athanasius's insistence that there had to be absolute equality of being between the Father and the Son, but they differed strongly on how to phrase an alternative. Constantius's quest for a unifying creed was complicated by the advice of two churchmen who were urging him to go in rather different directions. Valens advocated a return to biblical language and an avoidance of all reference to divine essence; Basil held that the formula "of similar essence" offered the best way forward. After inclining to Basil's position for a time in 358, Constantius turned once again to Valens and his allies. Another creed of Sirmium was worked out, which rejected *homoousios* and *homoiousios* equally. All such language was to be shunned as unscriptural and divisive. It was proposed that the Son ought to be confessed as simply "like" (*homoios*) the Father, without any mention of essence. This was a deliberate fudge, for it left unspecified what the "likeness" in question consisted of. As far as Basil was concerned, the legacy of Sirmium was dangerous in its vagueness; unless the church spelled out the sense in which the Son is "like" the Father, how could thoroughgoing Arianism be avoided?

In principle, at least four major positions had now emerged. At what we might loosely call the extreme "left" in doctrinal terms were the so-called *anomoians* or *heteroousians*; at the extreme "right" were the strict *homoousians*; and in the middle were the competing alternatives of the *homoiousians* and the *homoians*. Constantius was convinced that both of the extremes were untenable in political terms, but it was also increasingly plain to him that there was no consensus in the middle.

The Twin Councils of Unity

In the summer of 359 Constantius agreed to convene a great gathering of churchmen from both the East and the West. Because there were now so many bishops represented in the two parts of the empire, it was arranged that two separate meetings would be held: the Easterners would assemble at Seleucia, close to the southern coast of Asia Minor and the Westerners at Ariminum (Rimini) in Italy.[9] At least this was the justification for the twofold gathering; in reality, the division helped the emperor to extort what he had decided he really wanted: support for Valens's *homoian* position.

Closely supervised by imperial commissioners, the bishops were not intended to engage in genuinely free debate but to achieve a consensus in support of a *homoian* compromise. The larger Western council yielded first. The opponents of *homoianism* were outwitted by the machinations of Valens and his allies, who successfully appealed to the emperor in Constantinople against the dissenters. On 10 October, at the small town of Nike in Thrace, the pro-Nicene emissaries gave in and signed a revised version of the creed of Sirmium. The smaller Eastern council followed suit, though not without a genuine struggle on the part of the large majority who wanted to stick to the *homoiousian* tradition and who fought hard against the schemes of the leading *homoians*, Acacius of Caesarea, Eudoxius of Antioch, and George of Alexandria.

Both parties sent delegations to Constantius, but by the end of the year the *homoiousians* were obliged to concede defeat. The revised creed of Sirmium, agreed to by the Westerners at Nike and ratified by them at Ariminum, was endorsed. The *homoiousians* felt betrayed by their Western colleagues and had little option but to yield. In Constantinople, early in 360 at a council of seventy-two mostly Eastern bishops dominated by Acacius, it was settled that terms such as "essence" and *hypostasis* were henceforth to be dropped as unscriptural, and the Son was to be confessed to be simply "like the Father, as the Scriptures declare and teach." No detail was given as to what exactly this meant.

The events of 359–360 marked the ostensible triumph not only of Valens's theology but also of Constantius's pragmatism. By getting a majority of churchmen from both East and West to support the *homoian* doctrine, the emperor imagined he had secured a formula that would end the bitter wrangling that had gone on since 325. In his mind, Seleucia and Ariminum were his Nicaea—the counterpart of the great conciliar settlement that his father Constantine had masterminded. They were, for a new age, a means of uniting the Christians in the interests of uniting the empire. The difference this time, Constantius hoped, was that the ambiguity over which the churches had fought ever since Nicaea had now been taken to a new level; by deliberately avoiding precision, it ought to be possible to accommodate the sensibilities of as many Christians as possible on all sides and thus prevent the divisions that had at various points threatened the political stability of the Roman world over the past generation.

The problem with all this in practice, inevitably, was that there were plenty of strong dissenters. The theology of Seleucia and Ariminum was not meant to lend support to the theological line to which Arius was distantly related. Aetius, who refused to concede that the Son is "like" the Father, was removed from his lowly office of deacon in Antioch and sent into exile. But to those who held, as both the *homoiousians* and the strict Nicenes did in their quite different ways, that mere unspecified "likeness" was not enough, the new, simpler creed represented an act of treachery and the betrayal of all the effort that had been made for so long to safeguard the divinity of the Son. Twenty years later Jerome would write, of the decision at Ariminum, that "the whole world groaned and marveled to find itself Arian."[10] Constantius had brought East and West together, but he had done so by promoting a position that offered little or no defense against explicit Arianism.

A number of *homoiousians*, including Basil of Ancyra, were removed from their sees and sent into exile. In some cases, the extent to which their successors were Arian in tendency was all too clear. In Constantinople the ousted *homoiousian* Bishop Macedonius was replaced by the proudly *homoian* Eudoxius—an erstwhile disciple of Aetius himself. In Cyzicus in Pontus, the *homoiousian* Eleusius was followed by the clearly Arian Eunomius. Constantius's solution to the divisions was plainly no solution at all. A *homoian* creed may have been declared the official doctrine of the empire, but it was offensive not only to Athanasius and his allies but also to large numbers of moderate Eastern churchmen who (whatever the possible weaknesses of their own arguments) considered themselves no less opposed to Arianism than the strict Nicenes were.

Reflecting on the Status of Christ: Athanasius and the Logic of Faith

Viewed in the longer term, the debates of the late 350s served to crystallize as never before the issues that surrounded Arianism in all its forms. If it was unacceptable to say that the Son is less than fully

God, why was this so? What did it mean to confess that Christ is the perfect image of the Father? Should it be said that the Only-begotten is similar to the Unbegotten, and if so, similar in what sense? And is "similar" good enough? Surely the Son is *equal to* God when it comes to his divine nature; but how could this be argued without confusing the Father and the Son? These kinds of questions had occupied able Christian minds, especially in the East, for a good while, and no one offered more powerful answers to them than Athanasius.

In a fairly early work, *On the Incarnation*,[11] Athanasius had adumbrated the logic that remained central to his understanding of the Christian gospel. The incarnation was the entry of the uncreated God into the world of created, and now fallen, reality in order to rescue human beings, made in God's image, from the corruption and death to which sin had reduced them. Only the assumption of humanity by one who is himself fully divine could effect a change in this creaturely state; by becoming human and living a human life, the divine Word, who is in himself the true image of God, restored the image of God that is marred in us. Athanasius spoke of the work of salvation as a divinizing of human nature; Christ "was made human so that we might be made divine."[12]

In his *Orations against the Arians*, written a few years later, Athanasius elaborates on this reasoning. If Christ is less than God, he argues, then salvation becomes impossible. If it takes the Word to enter the human condition to deal with the effects of fallenness and sin, then it is vital that the Son who is Savior is absolutely equal to God. Anything less than a full assertion of equality of substance between the Father and the Son renders the story of human salvation utterly illogical. Athanasius adopted other language in addition to the *homoousios* formula to express this point—speaking, for example, of the Son as necessarily uncreated in order to be free in himself from the taint that affects the whole of created reality. His basic thrust, however, is always the same: it is not sufficient to say simply that the Father and the Son are alike in terms of purpose or will; they must be deemed to be one in *ontological* terms—that is, to be one in their *being*.

Athanasius considered the *homoian* doctrine to be hopeless, for it deliberately evaded the task of pinning down what "likeness" meant. In practice, it was no better than its polar opposite, the view of the *anomoians*, for it could not account any better for the process of salvation or explain why Christ should be honored and prayed to if he is not absolutely God in himself. And what about the *homoiousians*? They at least recognized that reference to divine essence was necessary. Nevertheless, Athanasius could not concede that anything less than a forceful assertion of equality of substance was adequate as a way of expressing the reality of the relations within the Godhead. A Christ who is merely "of similar substance" is not the Savior whom sinners need or the Lord whom Christians worship.

Evaluating the Issues

To modern readers, the complex and strange-sounding slogans bandied about in the fourth century can seem like an absurd game of words, in which theologians split hairs about the inscrutable mysteries of God's inner being. The great eighteenth-century historian of the later Roman Empire, Edward Gibbon, famously characterized the differences between the *homoousians* and the *homoiousians* as the division of Christendom over an iota.[13] How could it possibly matter that much whether the Son of God was confessed to be "identical" to God the Father or simply "like" God in his essence?

Gibbon thought debates of this kind merely illustrated the absurdities and intolerance of early Christian reasoning. But even those who have no wish to dismiss the importance of orthodox tradition may find the technicalities over which the bishops argued to be bizarre. Do not the subtleties of the distinctions and the fury of the political fighting between believers of both East and West suggest that the real Jesus they all claimed to have experienced—the one who deserved to be worshiped and followed in the realities of daily Christian living—had been forgotten?

There is little doubt that some of the protagonists in the disputes over Arianism did lose sight of the degree to which they shared a common inheritance of faith, and they often ignored the extent to which their deliberations were conditioned by cultural differences and political interests, both ecclesiastical and civil. Behavior such as that at Sardica was outrageous among Christians by any reckoning, and even where the consequences of dogmatism and the exclusion of dissent were less striking, there were generally distasteful political machinations of one kind or another. It was often easier to engage in name-calling and scare-mongering about one's opponents than to listen to their arguments.

The divisions between the churches of the East and the West were deepened not only by political factors but by a mutual lack of understanding of theological nuances. The problem was especially bad on the Western side, where Latin simply could not convey some of the finer distinctions that the more flexible structures of Greek were able to make. In both parts of the empire, many who were dubbed "Arians" held widely divergent views, and some were a very long way from the ideas of the man with whose name they were being associated. It is also worth remembering that a great deal of the theological debate on all sides went on over the heads of the majority of believers, who did not (and often could not) read the technical discussions of their leaders or listen to the debates of bishops in their synods and councils.

Nevertheless, when the controversies of the generation after Nicaea are viewed as a whole, however turgid the rhetoric and however tortuous the politics, the real issues at stake were manifestly of considerable importance to the integrity of the Christian gospel and to the practical outworking of Christian piety. If Christ was not fully and unambiguously equal to God, how could he be what Christians claimed he was—their true Savior and worthy Lord? Whatever we may say about some of Athanasius's tactics, he had put his finger on the heart of the matter, and his ways of articulating his arguments mark him as one of the greatest of theologians. As another profound Christian intellectual, Irenaeus, had discerned before him,[14] Athanasius understood that God must be thought of as both the creator of the universe and its only means of remedy from the plight into which the disruptive effects of evil have brought it. The incarnation of the divine Word in Jesus Christ represents the supreme action of divinity within creation, a union of God and humanity that transforms the whole of reality.

As Athanasius appreciated, only a fully divine Christ could effect the change that a fallen realm requires, out of its bondage to decay and into glorious union with its maker. Only a fully divine Christ could revolutionize the human plight and bring human beings to the destiny for which God intended them—the ultimate status of being partakers of the divine nature (cf. 2 Pet. 1:4). If the expression of these truths required a strict insistence on the *homoousios* formula over against every other construal of the relationship of the Son to the Father, so be it. Anything less—however well-intentioned or skillfully argued—was, sooner or later, a capitulation to the fatal misconception to which Arius's reasoning had given rise years earlier: the idea that Christ was not God as God is God.

In 360–361 the political prospects for Athanasius's theology did not look promising. He himself was in exile once again, and many of his sympathizers were similarly estranged from their sees. But things were soon to change in quite remarkable ways. These years also witnessed the demise of Constantius and the return of a much more sinister phenomenon in imperial politics: an emperor who had no time for Christianity at all, whatever its doctrinal flavor. Yet contrary to all that might have been expected, the official revival of paganism would bring with it some positive prospects for ecclesiastical progress. The individual who championed the anti-Christian agenda did not hold power for long, and despite his attempts to exacerbate the friction that existed among the churches, there would within a very short time be a resurgence of Christianity in general, and of the Nicene faith in particular, against its challengers.

3

The Churches in the Greek East, 361–381

▼

Julian: The Rise of a Post-Christian Emperor

Flavius Claudius Julianus, known to us as Julian, was born in Constantinople around 331. A cousin of Constantius, his grandfather had been a member of Diocletian's tetrarchy, and his father and several of his other male relatives were among those who had perished in the political purge following Constantine's death in 337. Julian had a secluded but intellectually rich upbringing. Along with his half-brother Gallus, he spent the formative years of his youth on an isolated imperial estate in Cappadocia but received a very good education in Greek literature, rhetoric, and philosophy. He was taught by some of the most respected teachers of his day, first in Asia Minor and later in Athens. He was also given a grounding in the Christian faith. He was baptized as a believer and is said to have been a sincere worshiper in his boyhood, serving as a reader in the church at Nicomedia.

In his late teens, however, Julian's studies in philosophy and the charisma of a number of his mentors, especially a Neoplatonist mystic called

Maximus of Ephesus, had begun to convince him that Christianity had some significant deficiencies. Around the age of twenty Julian secretly abandoned the Christian faith and was initiated into the Chaldean theurgical rites, a mystical Eastern system that believed that the divine was to be approached by a process of magical acts rather than by rational, cognitive apprehension.[1] His resentment of Christianity was probably intensified by Constantius's actions in 354, when Gallus was executed for treason and Julian himself narrowly escaped a similar fate. At this stage, however, he did not publicize his renunciation of the faith, judging it expedient to keep his views to himself and a small circle of intellectual confidants. Officially he continued to observe Christian worship.

Designated "Caesar" in 355, Julian spent the following years in Gaul pacifying the Germanic tribes, who had again been causing major problems for the Roman authorities with their incursions across the Rhine frontier. He proved very successful in his military tactics and won widespread admiration from his troops. When orders were given in early 360 for a large part of his army to transfer to the East to assist in Constantius's campaign against Persia, his forces mutinied and proclaimed him emperor instead. Apparently reluctant at first to accept this challenge, by the following year he decided to go ahead. Now openly championing the pagan gods, he began to march East to confront his cousin. It promised to be a decisive clash between the Christian emperor and the daring advocate of paganism. The encounter, however, never took place. In October of 361 Constantius fell ill in Cilicia, and by 3 November he was dead. Civil war had been averted, and Julian entered Constantinople the next month as sole emperor. An unabashed promoter of pagan religion and thought was once again in charge of the Roman world. Julian "the Apostate" (as he came to be known by his Christian enemies) was on the throne.

The Promotion of Paganism

Constantius had pursued an actively anti-pagan policy in a number of ways. Already in the 340s both he and Constans had taken measures to close shrines and halt some pagan rituals. Around 347 a converted astrologer from Sicily, Julius Firmicus Maternus, wrote a tract to both emperors urging them to engage in a vigorous campaign to stamp out pagan idolatry by force, and it is quite likely that his work, entitled *On the Error of Profane Religions*, reflected a mood to which its addressees were sympathetic. As sole emperor, Constantius had forbidden pagan sacrifices, closed temples, and ordered that the Altar of Victory, a major symbol of Rome's non-Christian past, be removed from the Senate-house in Rome when he addressed the senators in 357. His extension of fiscal and civic privileges to Christian clergy had been accompanied in some instances by a corresponding preparedness to ridicule pagan priests and secular thinkers. By contrast, Christians flourished in a number of prominent public roles.

There was, to be sure, plenty of resentment of Christianity and Christians among traditionally minded aristocrats, and many conventional religious observances and pagan festivals and holidays were still widely kept. With the exception of areas such as North Africa and parts of the Nile Valley, paganism was still very firmly entrenched in much of the countryside, especially in Italy and Gaul, and even in regions where rural Christianity had grown its forms of piety were often subject to lingering influences from traditional cults. In the cities, too, where the churches had always been strongest, polytheism still had plenty of socially advantaged and intellectually sophisticated advocates who were able to make their voices heard in sometimes menacing ways. For all the privileges the Christians had acquired, even now they made up at best just over half of the imperial population, and such an estimate is on the widest possible construal of the description "Christian." Nevertheless, on any reckoning the religious scene in the Roman world in 361 was hardly what it had been fifty years earlier. It was this that Julian was determined to change.

One of Julian's earliest moves as emperor was to promulgate an edict of religious toleration. Designed to allow for the revival of pagan cults, the measure inevitably brought a corresponding reversal of the privileges extended to Christianity. Throughout the East, Julian repaired pagan temples and altars that had fallen into disarray and built new ones. Pagan priesthoods were reorganized, and high moral standards were pressed upon their incumbents. To deepen their social impact, the priesthoods were deliberately structured to imitate the church's patterns; high priests were appointed with quasi-episcopal jurisdiction over regional territories and responsibilities for providing charity to the needy in their areas. Julian himself, as *Pontifex Maximus*,[2] observed daily animal sacrifices and avidly consulted soothsayers and pagan oracles. He showed a fascination for augury, divination, and astrology. The syncretistic Neoplatonism by which he had been influenced encouraged him to blend the concepts and categories of philosophical ethics with a conventional Greco-Roman interest in the interpretation of mysterious signs.

Julian promoted a renaissance of Greek culture in all its forms, advocating Hellenism as an all-embracing system of not only religion and philosophy but art, literature, drama, music, and science. The supremacy of such a tradition, with its rich influences on the history of Roman civilization, had been eroded by the spread of Christianity. The "Galileans"—Julian's preferred name for the followers of Jesus—were to blame for a decline in the civic and political prestige of Rome; the way to restore the empire to its true greatness was by recovering Greek *paideia*, or high culture. Julian preached this message all over the East with a passion that often demeaned his status. He restructured his court and parts of the civil service in ways that subtly discriminated against Christians. Though he did not actively persecute Christian officials, his appointment procedures showed a marked preference for pagans and for those who were willing to renounce Christian allegiances.

Perhaps the most notorious aspect of Julian's legislation related to education. In 362 Christians were forbidden to teach classical literature in schools, a move that even pagan writers who admired Julian, such as the historian Ammianus Marcellinus, considered harsh.[3] A subsequent ruling directed provincial magistrates to bar Christians from employment in the teaching profession altogether. These judgments suggest that there were by this time quite significant numbers of Christians occupying these roles, otherwise Julian would presumably not have perceived the need for such a measure. Julian's policies were astute attempts to choke off Christians' access to education, for in the absence of any special church system of schooling Christians remained entirely dependent on pagan schools and their traditional curricula. If the competence to teach in these schools was dependent upon allegiance to pagan religion, and if there was to be an active promotion of paganism in teaching, this would potentially cause major problems for Christians. In time, they might even stand to lose one of their most important missionary weapons: the ability to speak and write in correct Greek and Latin. Julian sought deliberately to dismantle the bridge between the gospel and Greek culture that educated Christian apologists had labored to construct.[4]

Julian's method of diminishing Christianity was to expose it to ridicule, and he endeavored to do this by various means and with increasing intensity. He mocked Christian bishops, refused to receive delegations from Christian officials, and deprived clergy of many of the immunities and honors with which they had been favored under Constantine. In his expansive writings and correspondence, Julian belittled the claims of Christian theology and sneered at the narratives of the Scriptures as fabricated tales, greatly inferior to the sophisticated truths of the Greek myths as told by Homer and Hesiod. During the winter of 362–363, while pressed by a number of serious practical problems (he had moved to Antioch in preparation for a fresh assault on Persia the following spring, but he faced considerable unpopularity for his personal style and his inability to deal with food shortages, famine, and economic collapse in the city), he wrote a work called *Against the Galileans* in which he attacked the followers of Jesus, both past and present, as misguided, foolish, and corrupt.

Against the Galileans

Only parts of the first section of Julian's treatise survive, preserved in a refutation written by Cyril, bishop of Alexandria, in the late 430s. Julian was a figure with personal experience of the Christian faith and an awareness of its texts and doctrinal history, and he was in a position to attack Christian beliefs and morals as a former insider. The extant fragments of the work seem crude and hastily written, but it is significant that long after Julian's death, and in very different political circumstances, a Christian leader such as Cyril should have considered his text still deserved rebuttal.[5] Julian's principal contention was that the Christians could not ground their religion in ancestral customs comparable to those of Greco-Roman antiquity. From the perspective of a world that greatly prized antiquity in ideas, Christian claims about the nature of God, creation, Jesus, and the Scriptures were very recent in origin, and their system was vastly inferior to that of Hellenistic Roman wisdom. Julian was almost certainly influenced by the famous attacks on Christianity in the previous century by Porphyry, whose writings continued to be regarded as among the most significant of reasoned challenges to Christian beliefs.[6]

In addition to his fairly conventional points about Christian doctrine and ethics, however, Julian offered a distinctive criticism of his own. To his mind, the Christian faith amounted to an apostasy from Judaism, and Christian understandings of the Hebrew Scriptures were a travesty of Jewish prophecy. Julian consciously turned the tables on the Christian strategy of citing the Hebrew Bible in support of Christian claims about Jesus. It was not that Julian favored the Jews on principle: he strongly despised their religion as well. Nevertheless, he chose to show some favor toward them in order to assist in the diminishing of Christianity. In the second half of 362 he went so far as to order the reconstruction of the temple in Jerusalem, perhaps in a bid to fulfill a pagan oracle or to try to invalidate the prophecy of Jesus about the temple's destruction. What more potent symbol of the failure of the Christian faith might there be than the restoration of the Jewish sacrificial cultus in the very place that Jesus had said would no longer be the locus of God's presence to Israel?

The rebuilding project in Jerusalem, however, was abandoned after a very short time in the wake of an earthquake and a fire. But although Julian's scheme had failed, his efforts to use the Jews against the Christians would not easily be forgotten. Wealthy Jews had collaborated with the apostate emperor to finance the reconstruction enterprise, and there were fears in some Christians' minds that Julian had planned not only to restore the temple but to allow the Jews to reclaim the city from which they had long been banned. For generations to come such prospects alarmed many Christians, and there were bitter attacks by Christian leaders on the possibility of countenancing such an apparent vindication of Judaism.

Enthusiasm, Apathy, Oppression

Julian's opposition to Christianity naturally struck a chord with many pagan intellectuals and aesthetes, and he enjoyed sympathy, support, and stimulus from a number of prominent thinkers, teachers, and literary figures. The best known of these was the great Antiochene scholar Libanius, whose lectures in rhetoric he had attended (against advice) in his youth and with whom he enjoyed a close relationship ever after. Another was Maximus of Ephesus, who had been instrumental in his departure from Christianity in the first place and who continued to serve as a religious adviser and interpreter of prophecies. With such men Julian corresponded, and from them he received predictable praise.

There were also plenty of nominal Christians who were happy to relinquish their associations with the church if it would assist their career prospects or raise their social standing. The aristocrat appointed to the urban prefecture of Constantinople, Domitius Modestus, was one such former Christian who had held high office under Constantius (he returned to the church after Julian's death). In addition to these networks of ideological encouragers and political retainers, Julian could also count on support of a cruder sort. In some places, the local populace could be stirred into a frenzy of anti-Christian sentiment, such as happened in Emesa in Syria, where the believers were subjected to public indignities and their bishop was cruelly tortured.

In many cities of the East, however, local officials could not share the emperor's enthusiasm for a restoration of defunct religious symbols, and the populace as a whole was often apathetic about the rituals of the old gods. In rural areas, celebration of the ceremonial aspects of pagan religion, such as harvest festivals, was still widespread, and there were plenty of traditions that had remained unscathed from pre-Christian times. Nevertheless, Julian's fervent advocacy of pagan ritual and his attempt to render paganism structurally similar to Christianity did not command pervasive respect where it was most needed, in the cities and towns where cultural life was most vibrant. Christianity provided interesting ceremonies of its own, and its cultic practices (if not its ethical demands) sometimes seemed less arduous than the elaborate protocols required by other religions. In some places, Julian was either resented or laughed at, and in parts of Syria and Asia Minor his new temples were ignored and even desecrated.

As well as eliciting the sympathy of his cultured supporters, outrages such as the destruction of temples not surprisingly encouraged Julian into more punitive attempts to impose his will. Although he had determined at first not to turn the Christians into martyrs, he came to permit outbreaks of physical persecution in various areas of the East. The numbers of those affected were not high, but a few Christians were tortured and put to death. When the temple of Apollo at Daphne near Antioch was destroyed by fire in October 362, Julian blamed the local Christians and punished them by closing their church. In January of the following year, a number of executions took place of Christians in the army, where there was some powerful resentment of the demand to participate in pagan rites.

Julian's End

Just over a month later, Julian set out on his campaign against Persia. He had, as ever, consulted a range of augurs and soothsayers, but this time, it is said, he elected to press ahead despite many signs that the expedition was ill-omened. Convinced that he was fighting a war that would confirm the providential favor of the traditional gods, he embarked on a poorly thought-out advance on Ctesiphon, the Persian capital, while a force under the command of his cousin pursued a simultaneous movement southwards from Armenia. The attempt on Ctesiphon failed, and Julian was fatally wounded while engaged in a counteroffensive against the pursuing Persian forces; he died the same evening in his tent, on 26 June 363.

Julian had sustained a thrust from a lance, and there was some doubt as to who was responsible. The probable culprit was an Arab auxiliary soldier on the Persian side, but various wild rumors began to circulate that the emperor had been killed by one of his own men—some said by accident, others by design—or even that he had committed suicide. Libanius subsequently hinted that the emperor had probably been slain by a Christian, but this was almost certainly a response to the Christian rejoicing at his death rather than a serious claim. Various legends also grew up as to Julian's final gesture and words. It was alleged that he spattered in the air some of the blood from his wound and, speaking to the Sun-god, said, "Be satisfied."[7] In the fifth century, it was said that he had in fact addressed himself to the Jesus he had despised and confessed, "You have conquered, Galilean."[8] It is impossible to ascertain the truth of any of these stories.

Julian died at age thirty-two, after a reign of barely eighteen months. His attempt to return the Roman world to a pre-Christian state had failed completely, but viewed from the perspective of his supporters it had been a remarkably bold effort. His inability to succeed testified to the strength of the hold that Christianity had acquired upon the Roman world. Though paganism did gain new momentum in some areas, not least in Gaul and in Britain, overall the Christian faith had become far too deeply rooted in fourth-century society to be removed by nostalgic commendations of an idealized past, symbolic celebrations of the splendors of Greek culture, or doctrinaire appeals to rekindle traditional cultic practices.

Julian's orations, letters, and treatises continued to circulate after his death, to be cited by his fans and refuted by his foes. Eulogists such as Libanius naturally extolled his virtues as one who had earned divine status. Julian had been deified in the old style, and his burial place in Tarsus became in time invested with special sanctity for some. For Christians, though, his death was inevitably a cause for celebration. His successor, Jovian, a military officer who managed to get the remainder of the Roman forces out of Persia and negotiate a costly peace with the enemy, was a Christian, and there was no chance of a return to the pro-pagan policies. On 16 September 363 Christianity was once again declared to be the favored religion of the Roman Empire.

The Churches in the 360s

One of Julian's ways of trying to discredit Christianity had been to allow exiled bishops to return to their sees. On the surface this was an act of toleration: churchmen were to be able to hold to their various beliefs without fear of political reprisal. At a deeper level, however, Julian's motive, as many people realized, was to spread further dissension among Christians by facilitating their theological disagreements. Calculating that the bishops would soon be quarreling among themselves, his aim was to play off pro-Nicenes and Arians against each other. He would make them all look equally foolish on account of their inability even to agree about how to define the relationship between their Savior and God, and thus undermine their ability to stand together against the emperor's policies and weaken the credibility of their message for potential converts.

In this area as in others, however, the results of Julian's policies were not as he expected. Though there were some notable exceptions, many Christians saw the political and social changes around them as a reason to revisit their differences and to think hard about which path they really wished to take in such a climate. Some had seized the chance to press their own local causes or make their feelings known about unwanted leaders. Donatist clergy exulted in a newfound political freedom in North Africa, and their cause experienced a powerful resurgence that endured for more than a generation, to the great detriment of the catholic churches of Numidia and Mauretania. In Alexandria, even before Julian had made any moves, the news of Constantius's death had proved sufficient to stir a local mob to seize the unpopular bishop George and lynch him. They may have been only mildly reproved by the new emperor, but such expressions of civil unrest can hardly have been what he wanted to encourage.

Tensions were still rife in many quarters under Julian, but it was clear that some leaders were prepared to think more pragmatically than before about the way forward. In a world of such political uncertainty, what was the most prudent course to take toward overcoming the disunity of the churches, and which direction would ensure that the truths that really mattered were safeguarded? Athanasius was able to return to Alexandria in February 362. Amid the changed political environment, even he had begun to realize that in some respects the *homoousians* and the *homoiousians* were in the end fighting for a broadly similar commitment—the assertion of the divinity of Christ over against principled forms of genuine Arianism. In the summer of 362 he convened a small council of bishops in Alexandria and managed to assemble devotees of diverse positions. The purpose of the gathering was to deal with a crisis that had arisen in the church at Antioch, where the local Christians had divided into competing factions on doctrinal grounds.

The roots of the problem went right back to the period after Nicaea. One group at Antioch, led by a presbyter named Paulinus, professed loyalty to the memory of the former Bishop Eustathius, who had been removed in the late 320s. The other party was led by Meletius. Meletius (not to be confused with Melitius, who had led the schism in Egypt fifty years before; see pp. 37–38) had been appointed bishop in 360 when Eudoxius, the patron of Aetius, had been transferred to Constantinople, but he had been speedily deposed when it was discovered that he had clear anti-Arian tendencies; his replacement was an old-fashioned supporter of Arius named Euzoius. On the demise of Constantius, Meletius had been able to return, but although he had a good deal of support elsewhere, his legitimacy at a local level was challenged by the group led by Paulinus, who regarded him as "soft" on the question of the vital *homoousios* formula.

The church of Antioch was thus divided into what might be deemed hard-line and moderate factions. Both communities endorsed the creed of Nicaea and resisted Arianism; where they disagreed was on the old question of the divine distinctions. For those under Paulinus, the traditional Eustathian and Marcellan logic of one *hypostasis* held sway; for the Meletians, it was vital to affirm that there are three *hypostaseis* in God. Athanasius's natural sympathies lay with Paulinus, as did those of the Westerners present at the council, not least the bishop of Rome. This, however, was unacceptable to most of the Eastern bishops, who strongly suspected Paulinus of Sabellian tendencies.[9] The council decided that if Arianism were repudiated, Nicaea confessed, and the divinity of the Holy Spirit acknowledged, the Meletians could be accepted as true believers. In a document addressed to the church at Antioch, it was suggested that if all sides were agreed on the non-negotiable standard of the Creed of Nicaea, it was acceptable to speak of three *hypostaseis*—so long as there was a corresponding affirmation of the three as being "of one substance."

Athanasius could concede that much, but the practical split in Antioch remained unresolved, for in the aftermath of the council Alexandria and Rome insisted on recognizing Paulinus. At a synod in Antioch in October 362 Athanasius formally endorsed Paulinus, and the schism deepened. Both Alexandria and Rome continued to resist overtures from offended Easterners to moderate their stance in the years ahead, and the mess in Antioch continued until 388. The belligerent sponsorship of Paulinus by Athanasius in particular may well have actually hindered the strict Nicene cause in the East in the late 360s and early 370s.

Although it did not succeed in reunifying the church in Antioch, the council of Alexandria helped to refine the verbal currency of theological discourse. The Council of Nicaea had treated *hypostasis* and *ousia* as interchangeable terms, and this had caused some considerable confusion, especially in the West, since it was not clear when people were speaking of three *persons* and when they were speaking of three *Godheads*. The council of Alexandria marked the beginnings of an attempt to distinguish the two. It was deemed acceptable to say, as most in the East had traditionally wanted to do, that there are three *hypostaseis*. But, at the same time, in insisting on the word *homoousios*, it was implied that there must be a single *ousia*, or divine essence, equally present in each of the three.

For some in the Latin-speaking churches, talk of three *hypostaseis* would continue to be problematic, for it still sounded like three *substantiae*, or a doctrine of three gods. In the East, however, the church was beginning to refine a distinction that would be crucial to subsequent trinitarian theology: there are three subsistences in God but only one divine essence.

Further Political Changes and Athanasius's Later Years

Athanasius's importance as the church's leading international politician began to fade somewhat in the 360s. After being forced into exile once more toward the end of 362 when he incurred the ire of Julian for baptizing some aristocratic pagan women in Alexandria, he was able to return after Julian's death. Under Jovian he became once again a dutiful and influential supporter of the emperor, losing no opportunity to press upon him the essential importance of the *homoousios* formula. Jovian's reign was short, however, and his sympathy for the Nicene cause did not have time to express itself in concrete policies. After only eight months in power, Jovian died in February 364, and he was succeeded by another Christian and military man, Valentinian I.

Valentinian moved to reinstate a system of two rulers—one for each part of the empire. A Westerner himself, he took the Western provinces under his own charge; the East he allotted to his younger brother, Valens. Valentinian would rule until 375, Valens until 378. The division of power had important implications for the churches. Valentinian was sympathetic to the Nicene position, but he attempted to pursue a policy of toleration for most forms of religion and to keep his personal piety free from strong doctrinal affiliations. First and foremost a soldier-emperor, his main concern was with the security of the empire's frontiers, not the promotion of a particular religious agenda. There was no active repression of pagan cults; the historian Ammianus attests that Valentinian "tolerated all the various cults, and never troubled anyone."[10]

In keeping with the same attitude of flexibility, Valentinian was also prepared to allow *homoian* clergy to dominate in various churches. Valens, on the other hand, openly promoted the *homoian* cause as agreed at Ariminum and Seleucia. In a great many Eastern sees there were rival claimants for office, and Valens's clear preference was for *homoian* candidates. The consequence was exile for both *homoiousians* and *homoousians*; those who had been removed by Constantius and allowed back under Julian were once again dismissed. Athanasius experienced a fifth and final spell of exile in 365–366. After his return, he spent his remaining years mainly engrossed in local affairs in Egypt. He died in Alexandria on 2/3 May 373.

Aside from his contributions to doctrinal debate and the theological treatises he penned, Athanasius's most important achievement was his powerful consolidation of his church. For a leader who was obliged to spend so much time away from his see, he succeeded in building up a remarkably strong Christian community both in Alexandria and farther afield in Egypt. He constructed impressive numbers of churches and presided over a considerable system of material charity to the poor, the sick, and the needy. He did a great deal to forge links with the large communities of ascetics in the Coptic churches (see pp. 138–43). He actively promoted monasticism and female virginity and offered extensive advice and teaching to ascetics, simultaneously exhorting them to maintain their devotion to self-denial and to embrace wholeheartedly the doctrine of Nicaea.

In his *Festal Letters*, written annually (according to an existing Alexandrian custom) to announce the date of Easter, Athanasius offered spiritual guidance on a wide range of practical matters. The most famous of these letters, the thirty-ninth, for 367, addressed the question of Scripture in the church and set out the first extant list of the twenty-seven books that make up our New Testament. The context of the letter is highly practical: Athanasius warned against false teachers who presented their own wisdom as opposed to the truths of Scripture, in particular those he calls "Melitians," who sponsored spurious works purporting to convey revelations supplementary to Christ's teachings. By delineating the parameters of biblical authority, Athanasius helped to strengthen the authority of the catholic bishops who deployed these canonical books in their churches all over Egypt and Libya.[11]

New Doctrinal Controversies

In addition to the enduring wrangles over Nicaea, and in direct connection with them, the 360s had seen the rise of other issues that would
dominate theological debate for the next generation. These issues were
already in some evidence at the Council of Alexandria in 362, and their
significance grew considerably in the years that followed, precipitating
further divisions among Christians across large parts of the Roman world,
especially in the East. Two themes in particular were of importance.
One was a further debate concerning the person of Christ. Although
connected with the controversies surrounding Arianism, it had a different emphasis from the main disputes we have considered thus far. The
other issue related to the status of the Holy Spirit. It is worth looking
at each of these in turn.

The Human Soul of Christ

From Origen onward, some attention had been paid to the relationship between the divine Word and what we might perhaps call the
"human psychology" of Jesus—though psychological theorizing in any
modern sense clearly cannot be read back into the early Christian
period. For the Arians, the general assumption was that in the incarnate
Christ the functions of the soul were performed directly by the divine
Word. Significantly, most of their critics implied much the same, even
if they disagreed radically about what it meant to say that the Word
was divine.

Athanasius himself had little to say on the matter. Scholars differ as to
whether this was because he denied—or came to deny—that Christ possessed a created soul or because a full-blown defense of the idea simply
seemed unnecessary for most of the period within which Athanasius
operated.[12] Either way, Athanasius believed the Word is always to be
seen as the subject of the experiences of the incarnate Christ, since from
first to last the incarnation is about a divine act of salvation. Athanasius
could even say that Jesus had merely imitated human weaknesses such as
ignorance, fatigue, or physical need—a claim that was perilously Docetic
in tone. In the context of Athanasius's theology as a whole, allegations
of Docetism are in reality quite inappropriate, since Athanasius made a
very great deal of the fact that the incarnation involved the assumption
by God of material, creaturely reality. Nevertheless, it is possible to see

how the question could have arisen as to whether this involved the assumption of an actual human mind or soul as well as a body.

The subject came up at Alexandria in 362, for Eustathius of Antioch had taught that the incarnation had to be seen as a union of the Word with an individual human being, so that the emotional experiences of Jesus were to be attributed not to the Word but to the faculties of the human being with whom he was united. This teaching was controversial because to some it sounded suspiciously akin to adoptionism: had the Word adopted an independently existing human being, or did the humanity of Christ derive every aspect of its reality from the activity of the Word? The Council of Alexandria agreed that the incarnation was not to be thought of as a case of a mere man being *indwelt* by the Word, after the fashion of a prophet uniquely inspired by divine energy, but as "the Word himself became man for us from Mary after the flesh."[13] The accompanying exposition of what this entailed, however, fudged the issue, probably deliberately, and failed to make it clear whether the Word *constituted* the soul of Jesus or *possessed* his soul.

Apollinaris

One of Athanasius's closest friends and most loyal allies was Apollinaris (ca. 310–390), bishop of the Syrian seaport of Laodicea. Apollinaris had paid a high price for his support of Athanasius and had known what it was to be excommunicated and ridiculed for his staunch dedication to Nicaea. During the reign of Julian, he had bravely spoken up for the interests of Christian teachers and had demonstrated the versatility of his own intellect by composing a verse rendering of the Pentateuch and a version of the Gospels and Epistles cast in the form of Platonic dialogues. Although only fragments of his many writings survive, we can see from these that he was an astute thinker and an able writer, whose main concern was to explore the implications of the theology that Athanasius had been advancing.

Apollinaris was deeply worried by the language adopted with reference to Christ by the believers in Antioch. In 375 (two years after the death of Athanasius) he brazenly interfered in the affairs of the Antiochene church to establish a teacher who would in his eyes provide the local Christians with the right teaching about the humanity of Jesus. Apparently ignoring Paulinus (and his existing rivals, Meletius and Euzoius), he installed one of his own associates, Vitalis, as bishop. This move was in keeping with the position that Apollinaris had already adopted throughout the 360s. As far as he was concerned, it was, of course, absolutely right to assert the divinity of the incarnate Word, but this could not mean that the Word had united himself to an individual man—that was the old adoptionist heresy of Paul of Samosata a century earlier.[14]

In order to safeguard the fundamental integrity of the divine Word, Apollinaris reasoned, it was necessary to say that the humanity of Christ was different from that of other people. If Christ had possessed an independent human mind, his sinlessness would have been compromised, for the mind is the source of sin and rebellion against God. In addition, the incarnate Lord would have had two different personalities—one divine and one human. Instead, in him the normal, fallible human mind was replaced by the divine mind of the Word; the Word directed all that Jesus did and said. Jesus was a perfect human being, but his perfection was guaranteed and effected by the Word's agency. Sometimes Apollinaris spoke of the constitution of Christ in twofold terms as simply the union of Word and flesh; at other times he saw the Word as united to a body and a created animal soul (*psyche*)—but in either case the Word was always the driving force.

Logically, Apollinaris was simply trying to follow some of the standard assumptions of Alexandrian theology as it had developed under the influence of Athanasius in particular. Human beings, this tradition held, are fallen because their minds, left to themselves, have naturally drifted off into sin. They are in a state from which they cannot deliver themselves. The incarnation is the coming of one who conquers all temptation to sin and who is thus able, by virtue of his divine power, to remedy the fallen human condition. Like Athanasius, Apollinaris was adamant that the incarnation was not just the inspiration of an ordinary human being with divine wisdom; it was the inbreaking of divine presence substantially into the fallen human realm. But at the point where Athanasius had been vague—the question of whether or not the incarnate Christ possessed a rational soul—Apollinaris was definite and negative. Divine inbreaking meant the existence of one whose mind was not like the mind of others. To all intents and purposes, Christ was God the Son with a human body.

The Cappadocian Fathers

As his career as a committed churchman and champion of Nicaea made clear, Apollinaris had no desire whatsoever to be radical. His views, disseminated through his preaching and his extensive writings, found sympathy among a number of Eastern Christians who regarded his teaching on Christ as uncontroversial. However, his ideas also stirred up

Basil of Caesarea. Illustration from André Thevet, *Les Vrais Portraits et Vies des Hommes Illustres* (Paris, 1584), Special Collections Library, University of Michigan. Used by permission.

considerable debate in the mid-370s. By this time Athanasius had passed from the scene, and his place as the leading Greek theologian of the day came to be filled by others. The group of churchmen who effectively took over Athanasius's role at the forefront of theological discussion in the East were among the most remarkable in the history of early Christianity. The "Cappadocian Fathers," as we have come to call them collectively, were primarily Basil ("Basil the Great"), bishop of Caesarea in Pontus (ca. 329–379), his close friend Gregory of Nazianzus ("Gregory the Theologian," ca. 329–389), and Basil's younger brother, also called Gregory, who became bishop of Nyssa (ca. 330–395).

Basil and Gregory of Nyssa came from a family of both aristocratic wealth and notable piety. Their older sister, Macrina (ca. 327–380), was a convert to asceticism, and in the late 350s she had persuaded her mother, Emmelia, to establish an ascetic regime on their estate near Caesarea, where another brother, Naucratius, also lived as a partial hermit. The lifestyle adopted by the family attracted other ascetics, and the estate became an important monastic center, in which women were the most prominent members. Macrina left us no writings, but her spiritual dedication was posthumously celebrated in a biography written by Gregory of Nyssa, which reveals the extent to which she did pioneering work. Macrina clearly exercised a formative spiritual influence upon her brothers, and it is regrettable that her importance has often been overlooked. Another significant but neglected figure was Gregory of Nazianzus's cousin, Amphilochius (ca. 340–395), who became bishop of Iconium in 373. He also wrote on a variety of theological subjects and played an influential role in doctrinal debate, though his works for the most part survive only in fragmentary form. Arguably there were five great Cappadocian theologians, not three, even if the main literary legacy of the group is limited to the three whose names are most famous.

Gregory of Nazianzus. Illustration from André Thevet, *Les Vrais Portraits et Vies des Hommes Illustres* (Paris, 1584), Special Collections Library, University of Michigan. Used by permission.

Gregory of Nazianzus became forever associated with the name of the town in Cappadocia where he was born, though it was his father, not he, who was bishop there. He himself nominally held for a time a small see in a backward Cappadocian village called Sasima, near the border with Armenia, but he never resided in the place. He spent most of his adult life in Nazianzus, Seleucia, and Constantinople, in the last of which he was briefly bishop in 381. Although he enjoyed imperial favor, his presence was opposed at a local level, formally on the grounds that he could not be moved from one see to another, but in reality because his doctrinal opinions were unpopular with several of his fellow churchmen. He passed his last years in monastic seclusion on his family estate.

The Cappadocian Fathers combined learning and culture with a zealous attachment to Christian asceticism. Basil had received a first-class education in Constantinople and Athens; Gregory of Nazianzus had studied in Palestine, Alexandria, and Athens (where he and Basil became friends, and where he was also a contemporary of Julian); and Gregory of Nyssa had been instructed in rhetoric by his cultivated older brother and worked as a teacher himself before becoming a bishop. All of them were literary figures, accomplished orators, and elegant writers. Gregory of Nazianzus in particular was a composer of verse as well as prose, who left a significant number of poems in addition to a large body of letters and a collection of theological orations that evince both intellectual acuity and rhetorical skill. Gregory of Nyssa was the most prolific writer of the three, whose works covered theology, exegesis, spirituality, mysticism, and asceticism; though his style is often difficult for modern readers to appreciate, he was an outstanding thinker and speculative theologian.

The Cappadocians' mediation of Greek values and ideas into Christian culture was a considerable element in the evolution of a Hellenistic-

Christian synthesis in the late fourth century, particularly in the formation of a distinctive theology nurtured by both classical and biblical influences. Basil's teaching on the monastic life and his organizational skills in implementing his ideas were of lasting significance in Eastern asceticism, and we shall return to their importance in chapter 5 (see pp. 145–47). The profound and sophisticated teaching of Gregory of Nyssa on the spiritual journey of the life of faith was of great value in the development of a Christian mystical tradition.[15]

It is for their contributions to doctrinal discussion, however, that the Cappadocians are most famous. Apollinaris's teaching was tackled by the two Gregories, most acutely by Gregory of Nazianzus, whose abilities in this and other areas of contemporary debate earned him his classical designation as "Gregory the Theologian." Basil found himself in a rather awkward position, for it was evidently thanks to Apollinaris that he had first become persuaded of the importance of the Nicene *homoousios* formula, and the two had enjoyed a positive relationship. Obliged to condemn Apollinaris's interference in Antioch and express his support of Meletius, Basil did come out firmly against his former mentor's ideas, but his grasp of the details was somewhat weak.

Gregory of Nazianzus: "The Unassumed Is the Unhealed"

By the late 370s, Apollinaris's ideas were being widely condemned both in the East and in Rome, and he and his supporters were in schism from the catholic church. But what was to be done with his theology? Some of the criticisms issued against him were not altogether fair. He was accused, for example, of impugning the virginal conception of Jesus and of teaching a quasi-Gnostic doctrine that the flesh of Christ was not derived from regular human material. These kinds of charges were clearly wide of the mark. Nevertheless, there were serious issues at stake in his claims. It was Gregory of Nazianzus who put his finger on the real difficulty. If one aspect of human nature, the possession of a normal human mind, was missing in Christ, how genuinely human was his life?

So far from being marginal, Gregory of Nazianzus argued, it is the mind that by nature stands most in need of salvation, for it was by an exercise of the mind (the will) that human beings fell into sin in the first place in their proud attempt to elevate themselves in defiance of God's commands. In what would become the most famous sentence he ever wrote, Gregory diagnosed the fatal weakness in Apollinarianism: "The unassumed is the unhealed; but that which is united to the Godhead is saved."[16] For Gregory, the gospel of the incarnation was the good news that *all* of what it means to be human, *including* the mind, is taken by God, and all of the human is healed, transformed, and indeed divinized as a consequence of that process.

Gregory had no quarrel with the principle that the Word is the active subject in incarnation, but he insisted that the "flesh" assumed by the Word was not just a human body but the entirety of human nature. If Apollinaris was right, human salvation would be inconceivable. As it was, the saving action of God in Christ embraced every part of the human condition, in all its need and inability to deal with its own plight.

The Status of the Holy Spirit

The other great debate that arose in the East in the second half of the fourth century concerned the status of the Holy Spirit. Athanasius had turned his attention to the theology of the Spirit in the late 350s in letters written to his close friend Serapion, bishop of Thmuis in the Nile delta. Up to that time the place of the Holy Spirit had been decidedly neglected in most theological discussion. The Creed of Nicaea had presented a major affirmation of the equal divinity of God the Son, but when it came to the Spirit it had stated simply: "And [we believe] in the Holy Spirit." There was no further specification of what such confession might mean in detail. Serapion had asked Athanasius for advice on how to deal with a group of believers who were quite willing to acknowledge the deity of the Son but insisted that the Holy Spirit should be thought of as a creature, the supreme being among the "ministering spirits" mentioned in Hebrews 1:14.

Athanasius referred to such people as *Tropikoi,* on the grounds that they interpreted the Scriptures tropologically or allegorically (Greek *tropikos,* "figuratively") where they proved awkward for their case. They focused on only a few texts and read them this way in order to avoid the plain testimony of the wider scriptural witness that the Spirit is fully divine. The Spirit is not simply an exalted angel, Athanasius argued; he is the divine life-giver, the Spirit of Christ within. He is thus of necessity coequal with the Son, just as the Son is coequal with the Father. As in Athanasius's case concerning the status of the Son, the argument turned on the nature of salvation: if human beings are genuinely sanctified and divinized, this process takes place by the agency of Christ's Spirit, and if the Spirit is only a creature, he is incapable of effecting it. If the Holy Spirit is the one who brings the life of God to humanity, he cannot be a created being any more than the Son is; he too must be fully divine, and *homoousios* with God the Father. At the Council of Alexandria in 362 an anathema was pronounced upon "those who say that the Holy Spirit is a creature and separate from the essence of Christ."[17]

In the 360s other deniers of the Spirit's divinity emerged in the East. Though unconnected to the *Tropikoi*, they made some quite similar claims. Their opponents called them the *Pneumatomachoi*, or "Spirit-fighters"—those who contested the biblical teaching about the Holy Spirit. They were later also called "Macedonians," after Macedonius, the *homoiousian* bishop in Constantinople, who was exiled in 360 and died around 362. It was alleged that Macedonius had similarly held that the Spirit is only a creature. There is, however, no evidence to confirm the allegation, and the association is probably spurious. Those who earned the label of "Spirit-fighters" were numerous in Asia Minor in the 370s. Perhaps their most prominent representative was Eustathius, bishop of Sebaste in Pontus.[18] Eustathius had earlier influenced Basil in his enthusiasm for monasticism (see p. 146), but the two came to disagree significantly about the status of the Spirit.

Basil on the Spirit

Basil's treatise *On the Holy Spirit*, written around 374–375, is among his most important works, although its approach to the controversy about the Spirit is a good deal less direct than that taken by Athanasius twenty years earlier. Basil does not explicitly say that the Spirit is God, on the grounds that this is nowhere stated in precisely such terms in Scripture, and he pointedly avoids using the term *homoousios* of the Spirit. His diffidence caused considerable discomfort among others committed to the Nicene cause, who feared that he was failing to take a strong enough stand in defense of the Spirit's divinity. Some modern scholars have argued that Basil's own background in the *homoiousian* theology typical of the East was not quite abandoned in the early 370s and that his wariness indicated a lack of conviction about the *homoousian* position.

Arguably, however, his approach was strategic. The "Spirit-fighters" refused to move beyond the letter of Scripture, and they insisted on keeping to the minimalism of Nicaea. If Basil had argued too closely on the basis of biblical texts, his opponents could have offered alternative ways of reading them, and if he had argued on the basis of the Nicene tradition, they could have pointed to the indubitable fact that Nicaea spoke only of believing in the Holy Spirit without any further specification as to the

Spirit's relationship to God. Basil's tactic, therefore, was to say that there is a difference between what had been spelled out in public and what was confessed in private in the spiritual experience of believers.

The divinity of the Spirit, Basil suggests, is something that needs to be personally experienced in the life of faith and especially in the liturgy of the church. If Christians are baptized into the name of the Father, the Son, and the Holy Spirit, and if the Holy Spirit is mentioned alongside the Father and the Son in prayers of blessing, then the Spirit is implicitly on the same level as the Father and the Son. The usual doxology took the form, "Glory be to the Father, through the Son, in the Holy Spirit," and Basil had incurred criticism for also using an alternative wording, "Glory be to the Father, *and/with* the Son, *and/with* the Holy Spirit." He argued that both versions were valid and that the latter in fact brought out even better the equality in status of the three persons. Basil may have been cautious about going beyond the letter of Scripture in talking of the Spirit, but his basic convictions were not in doubt: the Spirit is of the same order of being as the Father and the Son.

The Messalians

Basil may also have had other reasons for his wariness about stating this directly. In the last quarter of the fourth century and the first generation of the fifth, there was a good deal of controversy in Asia Minor over the activities of a group of ascetics known as the "Messalians," whose influence had spread across from Syria. Their name derives from the Syriac for "the praying ones," and sometimes the Messalians were known by the equivalent Greek designation, the "Euchites" (from the Greek *euchomai*, "I pray"). They believed that they were called to live in a state of constant prayer and complete dependence upon God. They were accused by their critics of holding the view that the devil continues to be present in the baptized and that only by intense prayer and ascetic meditation is it possible to triumph over evil influences. They lived a life of detachment not only from society but also from the routine liturgy of the church, roughing it and existing on whatever charitable donations of food came their way.

The Messalians placed great importance upon prayer to the Holy Spirit; it was by the Spirit's enabling that freedom from the concerns of the world and the flesh could be attained. Their enthusiasm represented something of a challenge to mainstream churchmen who also advocated asceticism. On the one hand, they pursued certain commendable ideals of self-denial and contemplation; on the other, they regarded the Holy

Spirit as operating independently of the sacramental life of the church and its regular channels of episcopal authority. Basil undoubtedly had sympathies with some of what the early Asian Messalians stood for—indeed, a part of his treatise *On the Holy Spirit* later came to be circulated in the company of works clearly influenced by Messalianism.[19] The Messalians would be condemned at a number of church assemblies, especially the Council of Ephesus in 431 (see pp. 204–5), but there was widespread admiration in orthodox circles for elements of their teaching. Basil may well have been torn between an instinctive approval of their stress on the Spirit's power and, at the same time, a strong concern to insist upon the importance of regular church structures.

Clarifying Theological Language

The exploration of the status of the Holy Spirit was part of a much larger theological contribution on the part of the Cappadocian Fathers. Prior to his treatise on the Holy Spirit, Basil had produced a major work, *Against Eunomius*, which sought to refute, among other aspects of Eunomius's teaching, his view that God cannot know more about his own essence than humans can. Against this claim, Basil insisted that God is by definition unknowable and ineffable in his essence. The same argument was elaborated further, in response to replies by Eunomius, by the two Gregories, who contended that God's incomprehensibility is grounded in his nature as uncreated. God is revealed through his activities or energies, but his essence in itself is unapproachable. It is precisely through the energies of God that creatures are given to appreciate how unknowable God's inner nature is, and thus they are led to worship him.

In the process of thinking through such claims, the Cappadocians gradually contributed to a very important theological synthesis. Around 375 Basil suggested—or at any rate influenced the acceptance of—a distinction between two words that had caused immense controversy for a very long time: *ousia* and *hypostasis*. It had been accepted at Alexandria in 362 that different ways of using these words did not necessarily mean different doctrinal positions, but only in clarifying the relationship between the terms could this concession be given any theological precision. Basil pointed out that *ousia* and *hypostasis* could not be regarded as referring to the same entities. The *ousia* of God is God's unknowable essence, his transcendent divine being. The word *hypostasis*, however, can only refer to the concrete manifestations of God, and of these there are three, all equally divine yet distinct: the Father, the Son, and the Holy Spirit. In God there is one *ousia* but three *hypostaseis*.

The distinction between *ousia* and *hypostaseis* was adopted by Gregory of Nyssa and Gregory of Nazianzus. Recent scholarship has drawn attention to the fact that the actual language of "one *ousia*, three *hypostaseis*" does not appear often in the Cappadocians' writings, and so it is better to avoid descriptions such as "the Cappadocian settlement"[20] in referring to their theological arguments. Gregory of Nyssa and Gregory of Nazianzus also used a variety of other terms in differentiating the oneness and the threeness in God. Nevertheless, a distinction between what the three divine persons are as particular agents of divine action and what they are equally together as God was fundamental to the Cappadocians' thinking. Gregory of Nyssa argued that if there is an association between the Father, the Son, and the Holy Spirit in their outward activities it is because there is a unity in their nature: *ousia* is the inscrutable divine being shared equally by the three *hypostaseis*.

Gregory of Nazianzus went on to reason that the three *hypostaseis* are distinguished by their different "idioms" or characteristics: the Father is unbegotten, the Son is begotten, and (on the basis of John 15:26) the Spirit "proceeds" or "goes forth from" the Father. These distinctions are thus grounded in the intrinsically necessary relations that constitute the being of God. For Gregory of Nazianzus, it was essential that all three are said to be "of one substance" and that the Spirit is acknowledged to be fully God.

A Triune God, or Three Gods?

The most obvious danger with all of this was tritheism: surely, if the distinctions between the *hypostaseis* were pressed, the doctrine ended up speaking not of *one* God but of *three*? The risk of such an impression was not alleviated by the fact that Gregory of Nyssa tentatively drew an analogy between the three *hypostaseis*, all of whom are equally divine, and three human individuals, such as the apostles Peter, James, and John, all of whom were equally human. Did this not imply that the Father, the Son, and the Holy Spirit are three independent or autonomous selves?

Gregory of Nyssa did not in fact make very much of such parallels,[21] for he was well aware that they were inexact and potentially misleading, and he adduced plenty of other arguments as well in seeking to describe how the three divine persons are also vitally one. In his little work entitled *To Ablabius: On Why There Are Not Three Gods*, he contends that the term *God* can only be used in the singular and that God is inherently incomposite. The distinctions between the three relate only to their different modes of origin or to the ways in which the divine *ousia* is shared by them. Each of the three possesses real, substantive identity within the being of the one God but also shares in the life of the other two. At the heart of all that the three do lies a unity of will, purpose, and power.[22]

In later theology, a more developed form of something akin to this model would be given the name *perichoresis*, from a Greek word meaning "to go around"; the three divine *hypostaseis* effectively "go around" one another—that is, they make room for or yield space to one another.[23] Such a principle would also later come to be known as "coinherence": the three dynamically interpenetrate or permeate one another so that everything that belongs to one belongs to the others. The way in which God is God is as three, yet the three cannot be thought of except as one. God is, in his inner being, inherently relational.

Such concepts were, and are, impossible for finite minds to grasp, but they carry important implications for a Christian understanding of the nature of God and his relationship to the world. Modern theologians have explored these implications in some intriguing ways, arguing that the Cappadocian Fathers laid the groundwork for a whole understanding of what it might mean to speak of "personhood" at a human as well as a divine level. If human beings are created in the image of a God whose being is constituted this way, then a proper conception of personal existence in creaturely terms needs to be inferred from the nature of the creator's own tripersonal relatedness. Consideration of the character of God as a "being-in-communion" may be of great importance for Christian reflection on political and social issues, not least for an understanding of the nature of the church as the community of God's people in history.

Some modern thinking in this area exaggerates the degree to which the seeds of such ideas are present in the Cappadocians. More seriously still, some of the cruder forms of the "social trinitarianism" supposedly extrapolated from fourth-century principles come perilously close to suggesting that the nature of God can be used as a cipher for merely human agendas about social equality. In so doing they risk idolatry by invoking God's name to sanction human ideals. No matter how worthy certain notions of personhood as relational may be in themselves, in terms of the Christian logic of salvation the fellowship of God as Trinity is experienced by grace, not emulated by creaturely ingenuity. No human social configuration can ever presume to replicate the holy and mysterious relations that exist within God.

Nevertheless, the doctrine of the Trinity undoubtedly does contain many profound principles for the practical outworking of life in the presence of the God who gives himself to be known in Jesus Christ and by his Holy Spirit. The Cappadocian Fathers would not have approved of some of what has been advocated in their name, but in their sophisticated expositions of trinitarian theology they provided much food for further thought in these areas.

Political Developments

While the debates went on about the person of Christ and the status of the Holy Spirit, momentous developments were taking place on the political scene, and these significantly affected the course of the controversies over matters of doctrine. On 9 August 378 the Eastern emperor Valens was killed in combat with the Goths at the Battle of Adrianople in modern-day Bulgaria. The battle was a cataclysmic defeat for the Roman forces; two-thirds of the emperor's army and most of his senior officers died with him. In the West, Valens's nephew Gratian had been in charge since 375, following the death of his father Valentinian. Gratian himself was still a teenager when he took office, and he was required to share his command nominally with his four-year-old half-brother, Valentinian II. Gratian was surrounded by a cohort of Christian aristocrats, some of whom took as much pride in their privileged background and influential position as they did in their faith. (The most eminent among them, Gratian's tutor Ausonius, a cultivated poet and rhetorician from Gaul, professed belief in Christ but was always a scholar first and a Christian second.)[24]

When news came of the disaster at Adrianople, Gratian was still only twenty-one, and he had more than enough to do to keep control of his own territory from his court in distant Trier in the Mosel valley. Yet the military situation demanded a swift response. At this critical moment, Gratian made the wise decision to appoint a talented young Spanish commander, Theodosius, to save the Eastern provinces.

Theodosius: A Nicene Emperor

On 19 January 379 Theodosius was proclaimed emperor in the East. He proved highly efficient in discharging his duties, and within a matter of months he had succeeded in repelling the Goths and stabilizing a very dangerous political situation. His tactics involved diplomacy as well as

Roman coin showing the emperor Theodosius I.
Illustration from Otago Museum, Dunedin,
New Zealand. Used by permission.

bloodshed; over the following years he extended a policy that had been tried to a lesser degree in earlier years of bringing numbers of Goths into alliance with Rome as confederates and military recruits, calculating that it was better to have them fighting for the empire than against it (see pp. 296–98).

In terms of Christian doctrine, Theodosius had strong pro-Nicene inclinations from the start. In February 380 he issued from his base in Thessalonica an edict to "all peoples" to follow the catholic faith, and that faith was defined with reference to the teachings held by Damasus, bishop of Rome, and Peter, bishop of Alexandria. Scholars debate whether this edict was a binding legal injunction, implicitly threatening imperial retribution for those who refused to comply, or simply a manifesto statement, indicating the new emperor's personal preferences. The latter is more likely, and it seems plain that in terms of society at large the policy can only have been aimed originally at people attached to the churches. Nevertheless, the edict indicated Theodosius's determination to have his say in theological affairs, and his doctrinal affinities were unambiguous. After recovering from an illness in the summer of 380, he was baptized by a pro-Nicene bishop, Acholius, at Thessalonica.

Theodosius's preferences may have been clear, but he soon discovered on moving to Constantinople that it was not at all easy to impose them on others. Whatever his edict to "all peoples" was about, it was bound to bring him trouble. In very large swaths of the East, Arianism of one kind or another prevailed in the churches, and among its opponents there were widespread divisions. Pro-Nicene believers still disagreed about the teachings of Apollinaris, and there remained significant disputes, especially in Antioch, over the issue of whether it was appropriate to speak of one *hypostasis* in God, as the Marcellan, Eustathian, and Paulinian traditions contended, or three *hypostaseis*, as the Cappadocians argued. Basil had by now passed from the scene; the two Gregories had much support, but by no means was there a consensus about their teaching or about their support for Meletius of Antioch. The prospects for a political sponsorship of Nicene theology did not look very promising. In Constantinople, Bishop Demophilus refused to comply with Theodosius's decree, preferring to remain faithful to his *homoian* past. He was removed from his see but proceeded to take his congregation into effective exile with him outside the city walls. Gregory of Nazianzus, who had been consolidating the Nicene position in one of the capital's suburban churches, looked like the obvious person to succeed him, but he was forestalled by the sudden consecration of a most unlikely candidate, a former Cynic philosopher named Maximus, who enjoyed the support of the church in Alexandria, and who Gregory had imagined was loyal to him. The tussle had a great deal to do with internecine rivalries and the desire of Peter of Alexandria to assert his authority as superior to that of Constantinople.

The Council of Constantinople

On 10 January 381 Theodosius promulgated a further decree. This time he did not refer to the faith as followed in Rome or Alexandria, but he expressly outlawed a group of heresies including Arianism and Eunomianism. Those who adhered to these systems were to be deprived of the right of assembly, and those who persisted in rebelling were to be expelled from their communities. In May the emperor called a general ecclesiastical council to meet in Constantinople.

Although from the fifth century on the occasion would come to be regarded as the second "ecumenical" council (Nicaea being the first, of course), its 150 delegates were all from the East and mostly from Asia Minor and Syria. There was no representative from Rome, and the newly appointed bishop of Alexandria, Timothy, came with no great enthusiasm. The city of Constantinople itself was full of Christian gossip: "If you ask for change," wrote Gregory of Nyssa, "the man launches into a theological discussion about 'begotten' and 'unbegotten'; if you enquire about the price of bread, the answer is given that the Father is greater and the Son subordinate; if you remark that the bath is nice, the man pronounces that the Son is from non-existence."[25]

The presidency of the council was given to Meletius of Antioch, despite the strong ill-will that had prevailed against him in Rome and Alexandria. The delegates at first decided that Gregory of Nazianzus ought to be appointed bishop of Constantinople after all, but things soon became complicated. Meletius died while the assembly was in session, and Gregory was appointed to take his place. Bitter disputes promptly ensued about the imminent situations in both Antioch and Constantinople. Gregory's elevation was opposed on the grounds that it was technically invalid according to the Nicene canons for him to be moved from his existing see of Sasima. In reality, a large number of the bishops resented his proposal that Meletius ought to be replaced by Paulinus after all, in order to appease the West.

Gregory resigned his presidency and left the council highly offended, to spend the remainder of his days in Cappadocia engaged in writing. (Among the various works he produced in this period was a verse autobiography in which he lamented the harsh treatment he had received at the hands of his colleagues.) To take charge in Antioch the council elected Flavian, a member of Meletius's clergy. Constantinople was given a neutral candidate, a distinguished layman, the senator Nectarius, who was untainted by partisan associations; he was duly baptized and installed. Such rapid elevations of laymen were not unusual, though they were officially discouraged, and Nectarius's was by no means the last in Constantinople.

As Nicaea had done, the Council of Constantinople issued a number (though a much smaller number) of canons. Among these was one that decreed that the bishop of Constantinople should have "primacy of honor" next to the bishop of Rome, "because Constantinople is New Rome." This judgment was resented both in Alexandria, where it was felt that Constantinople had been unduly privileged in the face of Alexandria's distinguished tradition, and—not surprisingly—in Rome itself, where it was objected that primacy rested upon more than just the secular status of the city. There would long be hostility from the West toward the claim, and toward the council's refusal to recognize Paulinus of Antioch even after Meletius's death. The canon was not finally accepted by Rome until the Fourth Lateran Council in 1215.

The main significance of the Council of Constantinople does not lie, though, in the arrangements it decided upon for a certain group of sees, however important the churches in question and however controversial the decisions proved to be. The council's greatest claim to fame lies in the doctrinal position with which it came to be associated. In accordance with Theodosius's wishes, the bishops reaffirmed the faith of Nicaea and condemned a number of heresies, including the views of "the Eunomians, . . . the Arians, . . . the Pneumatomachians, the Sabellians, the Marcellans, . . . and the Apollinarians." There was, additionally, condemnation of the opinions of "the Photinians," people connected with the beliefs of Photinus, bishop of Sirmium around 344, who had allegedly taught an adoptionist view of Christ; they too had already been proscribed by Theodosius.

The Niceno-Constantinopolitan Creed

No formal doctrinal statement issued by the council survives. At the Council of Chalcedon in 451 (see pp. 212–15) a longer version of the Creed of Nicaea was espoused that was said to derive from Constantinople. It was claimed that the Creed of Nicaea had been modified in 381 in the light of the controversies that had ensued since 325. There are certainly strong core resemblances between the Creed of Constantinople (*C*) and that of Nicaea (*N*), but the likelihood is that *C* was a separate creed affirmed at Constantinople in addition to *N*. *C* was probably not drawn up for the first time in 381; it may well have derived from an existing formulation used in the church in Constantinople. Whatever the origins of *C*, though, it is *this* creed, deriving from Constantinople rather than from Nicaea, that constitutes the basis of what we have come to call "the Nicene Creed." Formally it ought to be known as "the Niceno-Constantinopolitan Creed." While it echoes many of the emphases of the original Creed of Nicaea, its detail goes further in various respects. The full text reads as follows:

We believe in one God, the Father Almighty, maker of heaven and earth, and of all things visible and invisible;

And in one Lord Jesus Christ, the only-begotten Son of God, begotten of the Father before all ages, light from light, true God from true God, begotten not made, of one substance [*homoousios*] with the Father, through whom all things were made; who for us human beings and for our salvation came down from heaven and was incarnate of the Holy Spirit and the Virgin Mary and became human, and was crucified for us under Pontius Pilate, and suffered and was buried, and rose again on the third day according to the Scriptures, and ascended into heaven, and sits on the right hand of the Father, and will come again with glory to judge the living and the dead, of whose kingdom there shall be no end;

And in the Holy Spirit, the Lord and the life-giver, who proceeds from the Father, who with the Father and the Son is together worshiped and together glorified, who spoke through the prophets;

In one holy, catholic, and apostolic church.

We confess one baptism for the confession of sins; we look forward to the resurrection of the dead and the life of the world to come. Amen.

The wording differs from that of the Creed of Nicaea at a number of points, and there is an absence of the anathemas attached to the end of the creed of 325. The Son's kingdom is said to be without end, over against the ideas of teachers such as Marcellus of Ancyra who held that the kingdom of Christ was an earthly affair that would one day be yielded up to God the Father. There is confession of belief in the church as "one, holy, catholic, and apostolic," a description that would in time become fundamental to theological analysis of the nature of the church as the body of Christ in the world.[26] There are additional clauses on baptism and on the Christian hope in the resurrection of the dead and the life of the world to come.

The most distinctive feature of the Niceno-Constantinopolitan Creed, however, is its clause on the Holy Spirit. Whereas Nicaea simply confessed belief in the Spirit, here the Spirit is acknowledged in biblical terms as "the Lord" (2 Cor. 3:17) and "the life-giver" (2 Cor. 3:6) and as jointly worshiped with the Father and the Son. There is no direct claim that the Spirit is either *homoousios* with the Father or to be called "God" as such. The preference for biblical language and the avoidance of the term *homoousios* for the Spirit may hint at an effort to conciliate those who had difficulties in affirming the divinity of the Spirit in express terms.

Nevertheless, there are clear evidences of the influence of the kind of theology of which the Cappadocians were the leading champions in the East in the 370s and 380s. The Son is said to be "the only-begotten Son of God, begotten of the Father before all ages," and thus, while derived from the Father, a distinct person from him. The Spirit "proceeds from the Father," and is also distinct. The Spirit performs divine functions and is worthy of equal worship with the Father and the Son. The plain thrust of the confession is that there are three eternal *hypostaseis*, all on the same level of divine being, distinct yet indivisible.

While some of the most mature exposition of this theology by figures such as Gregory of Nyssa postdated the council,[27] the creed from Constantinople reflected the nature of the discussions that had gone on over the past generation about Christ and the Spirit, and its language was expressive of the essential approach that Gregory favored. Not only were the Son and the Spirit coequal with the Father; all three were together declared to be one God. The outcome of the proceedings of 381 was the effective enshrinement of the whole pro-Nicene tradition as it had evolved over the past two generations and the official rejection of any theology that played down the status of the Son or the Spirit in relation to God the Father.

East and West

All the same, the Council of Constantinople could hardly be called an "ecumenical" gathering in any real sense of the word, and in the West little attention was paid to its declarations for some years. Its practical decisions about church authority were also surrounded with contention. If its doctrinal affirmations did not generate decades of further strife comparable to the disputes that had followed Nicaea, this was in part because the world of Theodosius was a place in which the Nicene faith was destined to prevail in structural terms.

In the aftermath of the council, Theodosius enacted legislation forbidding Arians and other heretics, including the Apollinarians, to construct buildings for worship, and shortly afterward he ordered the removal of bishops and other clergy who espoused unorthodox teaching. This time he was careful to define orthodoxy with reference to the views pertaining in the major Eastern sees, without mention of Rome. As far as he was concerned, the Eastern bishops' agreement at Constantinople had marked out the boundaries of the true faith, and those who refused to abide within them were to be removed from positions of influence in the churches more widely.

But Theodosius was still emperor only in the East. What about the churches in the West? Arianism of one kind or another had continued to enjoy widespread support in the West throughout the third quarter of the fourth century. For all the efforts of figures such as Hilary and the price paid by some of Athanasius's loyal supporters for their opposition to the wishes of Constantius, a good many Western Christian leaders had not been very clear about the real issues at stake. On the whole, Latin theology had lagged far behind its Greek counterpart in sophistication. As events had shown, a majority of Western bishops were quite capable of being pushed into repudiating Athanasius and supporting a policy of consensus that plainly leaned in an Arian direction. *Homoian* clergy had been dominant in various significant sees, and they had remained undisturbed under the tolerant regime of Valentinian I. Valentinian's successor, Gratian, was a devout youth, but in his earliest period as emperor he lacked both the theological knowledge and the maturity of character to take a firm stand, and he was subject for some time to conflicting doctrinal pressures.

In the end, Arianism would fail in the major Western churches as well, but the success of the Nicene faith in the West no less than in the East was a hard-won affair, and in the second half of the fourth century there was opposition still to be faced. In the next chapter, we turn our attention to the consolidation of Christianity in the West over the course of the later fourth and early fifth centuries. This period saw the political demise of Arianism and a furthering of the social and cultural development of the churches in the Western Roman Empire. It produced some remarkable Christian figures, whose preoccupations extended well beyond opposition to false doctrine and whose intellectual, organizational, and spiritual legacies to the future of Western Christianity would be considerable.

4

CONSOLIDATION
IN THE WEST

▼

Ambrose of Milan

The church leader who contributed more than any other to the ultimate erosion of Arianism in the West was Ambrose (ca. 339–397), bishop of Milan from 374. Ambrose ranks as one of the most impressive of all bishops in the early church. The son of the praetorian prefect of the Gauls, one of the chief officials of the empire, his father died when he was still a child. Ambrose and his sister, Marcellina, and brother, Satyrus, were brought up in Rome in a home with strong Christian influences. His sister took vows of chastity and devoted herself to a spiritual life in her teens; Ambrose and his brother were given a typical classical education and pursued careers in the imperial civil service. Thanks to some assiduous networking and the patronage of an influential senator, Sextus Petronius Probus, Ambrose attained at a relatively early age the important position of governor of the province of Aemilia-Liguria in northern Italy. His headquarters were in the city of Milan.

The see of Milan had been occupied since 355 by a prominent *homoian*, Auxentius. Despite sustained opposition from Hilary of Poitiers and

Ambrose of Milan. Illustration from André Thevet, *Les Vrais Portraits et Vies des Hommes Illustres* (Paris, 1584), Special Collections Library, University of Michigan. Used by permission.

others, and a fair degree of dissent at a local level, Auxentius had proved an effective bishop, and he had a secure following. When he died in 374, a majority of Milan's clergy were committed to perpetuating his *homoian* legacy. The city's Nicenes, however, had other ideas. Turmoil erupted over the election of his successor, and in his capacity as governor Ambrose intervened in order to keep the peace. In the midst of his effort to forestall public disorder, he found himself unexpectedly called upon to assume the episcopal role in person. The story goes that a child's voice was heard to cry, "Ambrose, bishop!" and at this the warring parties united in support of the governor's candidacy. In reality, things can hardly have been so neat, but Ambrose was evidently regarded by a majority as an acceptable choice to take over the leadership of the Milanese church at a critical time.

Ambrose himself was reluctant. He already had pro-Nicene sympathies, but, like many believers of the time, despite his Christian upbringing he remained unbaptized. He was also seriously ill-equipped in terms of theological preparation to take on the task of guiding a large church torn apart by doctrinal differences. However, after securing the sanction of the emperor Valentinian I, he gave in and accepted the challenge. He was baptized by a Nicene clergyman and passed rapidly through the various grades of church office in the space of a single week, prior to being consecrated bishop on 7 December 374. From these unlikely beginnings, his episcopate would last for twenty-two years and witness the transformation of the social fortunes of the catholic faith in the West, not just in northern Italy but much farther afield.

Ambrose's activities during his early years as bishop were restricted by the strength of the opposition he faced and his own unpreparedness as a spiritual instructor. Nevertheless, a combination of natural gift, the grooming he had received for his former career as an administrator, and sheer hard work brought a good deal of progress in a relatively short time. He devoted himself to study, reading in Greek authorities including Philo, Origen, and Basil of Caesarea. His fluency in the Greek language enabled him quickly to assimilate the techniques of Alexandrian exegesis and, in a general sense at least, the strategies of pro-Nicene apologetics. Ambrose was a very capable orator, and his sermons, based especially upon the Old Testament, soon displayed a range of reading and an intensity of pastoral concern. His ability to interpret the Scriptures spiritually impressed his hearers.[1] He was also familiar with important elements of Greek philosophy, particularly Neoplatonism; he could evoke phrases of Plotinus and others in his preaching, and his applications of scriptural narratives were affected by Platonist conceptions of the relationship between matter and spirit.

Ambrose's Themes

Ambrose was not much of an original thinker, but he was capable of producing highly effective syntheses of other people's ideas. His main achievement in intellectual terms lay in his transmission of Greek Nicene thinking into Latin, through his sermons and by writing. He left a significant corpus of written works, many of which derive in part from his homilies. He wrote exegetical treatments of the six days of creation in Genesis 1 (the *Hexaemeron*, or "Six Days," borrowing heavily from a work of the same name by Basil), of Hebrew saints such as Job and David, and of various Psalms and parts of Luke's Gospel.

Ambrose also proved a gifted hymn-writer, and he introduced to Milan the Greek practice of congregational singing, recognizing the value of hymns as a medium of doctrinal instruction. By getting his people to sing simple yet moving hymns celebrating a fully consubstantial Christ and a truly divine Spirit, he impressed upon them the essential truths of Nicene orthodoxy. Though only a few of his compositions survive, the character of the Ambrosian hymn exercised a major influence on the subsequent direction of Western liturgy.

One of Ambrose's most famous hymns was written to celebrate the birth of Jesus. It rejoices in the miracle of the virginal conception and the conjunction of divinity and humanity in Christ, whose incarnation is pictured as a journey from heaven to earth, indeed even into the depths of hell, and back again to the throne of God for the sake of human salvation. In its allusions to the Psalms, its doctrinal emphases, its delight in the mystery of the Messiah's person and work, and its imagery of Christ as the light of the world, it is typical of Ambrose's style:

> Hearken, you who rule Israel,
> you who sit above the Cherubim,
> appear before Ephraim, rouse
> your power and come! [Ps. 80:1–2]
>
> Come, redeemer of the nations,
> show forth the birth from the virgin,
> let all the world marvel:
> such a birth befits God.
>
> Not from the seed of a man,
> but by a mystical inbreathing
> the Word of God was made flesh
> and the fruit of the womb flourished.
>
> The womb of the virgin swells,
> the door of chastity remains closed,
> the banners of virtue are radiant:
> God dwells in his temple.
>
> Let him come forth from his bridal chamber,
> the royal hall of chastity,
> a giant of twofold substance,
> eager to run his course. [cf. Ps. 19:5][2]
>
> His going out is from the Father,
> his coming back is to the Father;
> his journey is as far as hell,
> his return is to the throne of God.
>
> Equal to the eternal Father,
> he girds on the trophy of flesh,
> fortifying the weakness of our body
> with his enduring strength.
>
> May your crib now shine forth
> and the night breathe a new light
> that no night may disturb,
> and may it beam with constant faith.

As well as his sermons, expository texts, and hymns, Ambrose produced a number of doctrinal works, a large body of correspondence with churchmen and political leaders, and an important range of writings on moral and ascetic themes, especially on the promotion of virginity as a Christian ideal. He was a strong advocate of self-denial and chastity, and under his encouragement many young women took vows of asceticism and devoted themselves to the full-time service of the church. Like a number of other late fourth-century leaders, he insisted upon celibacy for priests (see pp. 277–79) and urged Christian women who were widowed not to remarry but to give the remainder of their lives to the cause of Christ. In line with established traditions of ascetic discipline (see chap. 5), Ambrose regarded sexual relations, even within marriage, as a distraction from the life of the Spirit, and he preached the necessity of transcending what he saw as the perilous world of the flesh in pursuit of a higher state of purity in commitment to Christ.

Ambrose applied equally demanding standards to other areas of morality, including attitudes in regard to food, clothing, and material possessions, particularly for those who were called to serve in leadership positions. At the same time, his images of the ideal leader embraced a number of sociocultural stereotypes. One of his best known treatises is a work called *On Duties*, a manual on clerical ethics based upon a much-read text of the same name by the great Roman author Cicero (106–43 B.C.), and significantly influenced by Stoic thought. Ambrose urges his clergy to be models of good behavior and to be so in ways that implicitly convey a combination of old and new virtues. They are to show the best qualities of the classical Roman gentleman and, at the same time, the more stringent ethical standards of the servant of Christ. They are to walk, talk, and conduct themselves in a manner that will earn them social respect and admiration, but they are also to pursue humility, self-denial, and devotion to the service of others, displaying levels of dedication that society would never witness outside Christian circles.

Ambrose's spiritual vision was austere and uncompromising: the church was a community summoned to a life of holiness and witness, surrounded by a vicious world of evil forces, whose constant desire was to disrupt and oppose God's purposes for his people. These forces consisted variously of satanic temptations, false teachers, hostile politicians, and the beguiling voices of carnality. Initiation into the community of faith by baptism was, in Ambrose's presentation, a mystical privilege, and he impressed upon his catechumens the sense that they were favored with access to the deep things of God that the eyes of those without faith could never see.

Although his teaching was mostly derivative, Ambrose did contribute to the evolution of Western theology in a number of areas. He anticipated aspects of the understanding of original sin that would be expounded in the early fifth century by Augustine (see pp. 184–87). His depiction of the Eucharist spoke of a supernatural change taking place in the elements when the celebrant recited the dominical words, an idea that would be of considerable importance in medieval theology. His understanding of natural law, closely influenced by Stoic philosophy, would also prove quite seminal for later moral thought. Elsewhere in his ethical teaching, he anticipated later reflection (not least by Augustine, once again) on the principle that war may in certain circumstances be just and divinely sanctioned. In commending female asceticism, too, his emphasis on the example of the Virgin Mary helped to further the development of Marian veneration in the West (see further pp. 274–75).

Ambrose as Politician: The Success of the Nicene Faith

Ambrose's chief importance, though, lay in his ability to present the Nicene faith as the natural victor over every religious alternative, Christian as well as pagan. Yet in the early years of his ministry, the omens for success did not look good. He faced significant opposition from a sizable lobby of *homoian* antagonists in Milan. These dissidents refused to recognize his validity as their leader and met to worship in private, separate from the main church's services. In the late 370s Ambrose also upset prominent *homoian* bishops in Illyricum by intervening in an episcopal election in that region to ensure the success of a Nicene candidate. The offended parties seem to have made common cause with his opponents in Milan, and there were many keen to plot his downfall.

Ambrose's early forays into dogmatic theology did little to intimidate his enemies. In a work entitled *On the Faith*, released in two stages over the period 378–381[3] and addressed to the young Gratian (who had requested an exposition of catholic belief), he did not commend himself for his doctrinal acuity. His writing was at this stage unsophisticated and repetitive and relied heavily on rhetorical condemnation of all forms of Arianism as equally bad instead of offering a sustained engagement with the philosophical issues raised by his real target—*homoian* theology. Ambrose was not a great speculative theologian, and there were undoubtedly those on the other side who were more capable than he when it came to doctrinal discussion. As a sequel to his treatise *On the Faith*, in 381 he published a work entitled *On the Holy Spirit*. It was the first treatment of its kind in the West, but it did not progress much beyond a lengthy demonstration of the Spirit's essential divinity.

But Ambrose relied on other skills besides theological expertise. His efforts to win Gratian as an overt Nicene partisan involved arguing that the military disaster of Adrianople, the death of Valens, and the ensuing Gothic ravages of the Danubian provinces represented a divine judgment on those who had adopted and promoted Arian beliefs. The security of the empire was concomitant with loyalty to the true faith. In the volatile climate of the late 370s, this was a powerful claim, and it was one that Ambrose would continue to make in a variety of contexts over the years to come. Appealing to a strong traditional pride in the supremacy of Rome, he effectively equated sympathy for *homoian* theology with political treason.

In 381 the court of Gratian moved from Trier to Milan, and Ambrose acquired a degree of access to the ear of an emperor that none of his episcopal predecessors in the West had known. Though he was not always successful in his efforts to sway imperial decisions and his actions earned him opposition in some quarters, Ambrose proved a skillful lobbyist at court, and he often won support for the various causes on which he petitioned the authorities. His influence certainly paid dividends in church politics. At a council held at Aquileia on the Adriatic coast in September 381, he orchestrated the condemnation of his chief *homoian* critics in Illyricum, Palladius, bishop of Ratiaria, and Secundianus, bishop of Singidunum. Having persuaded Gratian that there was no need for Eastern bishops to attend the gathering (many of them had just recently attended the Council of Constantinople held in May that year), he surrounded himself with a group of staunchly loyal supporters from northern Italy and Gaul who were all too willing to come down hard on those who clung to *homoian* principles. Ambrose was able to follow the judgment up with appeals to both Gratian and Theodosius to make sure both Palladius and Secundianus were removed from their sees and to take action against others who were causing him trouble in his own territory.

Gratian never was entirely under Ambrose's sway, but he did show support for the Nicene faith. He also took a number of measures in open denigration of paganism. Some time between 379 and 382, Gratian formally declined the title of *Pontifex Maximus*. In 381 he withdrew state subsidies for traditional priestly cults including the cult of the Vestal Virgins, and the following year he again removed the Altar of Victory from the Senate-house in Rome (it had been restored by Julian after its removal by Constantius). He resisted appeals from eminent pagan senators that the decision be reversed. These were all crucial gestures, for they signaled Gratian's preparedness to take the policy of anti-paganism further than his predecessors had done. Neither Constantius nor Valentinian had interfered with the allowances for pagan priesthoods, and no previous Christian emperor had yet disavowed the status of "Chief Priest." Now one of the most potent symbolic trappings of the pagan past had been definitively discarded, never to be resurrected.

Gratian's reign, however, was short. In 383 he fell victim to a military rebellion led by a military commander (and another professing Nicene Christian), Magnus Maximus, and was murdered in Gaul by one of Maximus's subordinates. In the aftermath of the coup, Ambrose played an important role as a political mediator, going in person to Maximus to appeal for calm. Theodosius reluctantly agreed that Maximus could base himself in Trier and look after the Gallic provinces so long as he did not interfere with the authority of the boy-emperor Valentinian II in Milan. Ambrose, in return for his services, gained some limited leverage over Valentinian, whose mother, Justina, the obvious power behind the throne, was a committed supporter of *homoian* theology.

In 384 Ambrose succeeded in persuading Valentinian to refuse a legal petition from the distinguished Roman senator Symmachus that the Altar of Victory should be restored to the Senate-house. To give in to such a request, he argued, would be to give credence once again to the old gods, whose day had definitively passed. Symmachus mustered an eloquent and measured appeal in favor of religious tolerance and on behalf of the glory of Rome's traditions, and his case has gone down in history as something of a landmark attempt to represent the value of granting political freedom to diverse religious traditions. Ambrose, how-ever, was able to threaten the young emperor with dire consequences if he acceded to such reasoning, hinting darkly that any concession would be a betrayal of Christ so serious that it would incur excommunication from the church.

Despite successes such as these, the mid-380s still saw Ambrose in some serious difficulties. Justina and her allies at court made common cause with Ambrose's many *homoian* enemies in Milan, and demands were made that a church should be handed over to serve the needs of those who wished to worship according to *homoian* beliefs. Ambrose resolutely refused all such orders, even though they were backed up by legal sanction, for under the influence of one of his chief opponents, a former bishop from the Lower Danube named Auxentius, a law was passed insisting on freedom of worship for *homoian* believers. To yield public space to the Arians was, in Ambrose's mind, to afford them sym-bolic legitimacy, and this he could not stomach. No matter which of the various churches in the center of Milan was requested (and the *homoians* attempted to get more than one), none could be surrendered. No faithful bishop, Ambrose insisted, could surrender a "temple of God."[4]

At Easter 386, at the height of the crisis, Ambrose and his supporters staged a sit-in in one of the main churches in Milan while the building was blockaded by imperial troops. It was probably at this time that he introduced the practice of antiphonal congregational singing. It was a poignant time for such a highly charged vigil. The faithful sat in church singing their hymns and defying the authorities at real physical danger to themselves, while the forces of evil—in reality, the powers of law and order—prowled outside, ready to devour them. Ambrose's personal courage in the situation was real, though his public display of defiance reflected a brinkmanship that must have been calculated on the basis of inside knowledge of the mood at the imperial court. Whatever the case, his determination paid off. Valentinian and Justina backed down, alarmed at the prospect of serious public disorder and worried also that Maximus was likely to invade Italy. The court had been hopelessly outmaneuvered by the wave of popular support that Ambrose had managed to release.

In the immediate aftermath of the crisis, Ambrose sealed his success by dedicating a grand new cathedral in Milan[5] and then overseeing the discovery of some prominent martyr relics and their interment in the new building. The cult of the martyrs was increasingly powerful in the Western church, and the finding of these bones engendered considerable popular excitement; here, it was thought, was a sign of God's blessing on the bishop for his loyalty to the truth. The *homoians* never recovered their strength in Milan, and within a matter of months Valentinian and Justina fled to Thessalonica, another mission by Ambrose to Maximus having failed to diffuse the military tensions. The political situation remained perilous, but in the church the tide had turned. In Milan, the Nicene faith was going to win.

Ambrose and Theodosius

Faced with an invasion by Maximus, Theodosius put his political duty before his doctrinal affinities. In a swift and decisive campaign he headed to the West with a primarily barbarian army and defeated and killed Maximus near Aquileia. Valentinian was accompanied back to Milan, where he was reconciled with Ambrose before being dispatched to Gaul. Officially he was to rule the Gallic provinces; in reality, he had been moved out of the way. (He was found dead in 392, and there were rumors that his pagan military general, Arbogast, was behind his death, though he had probably taken his own life.) Theodosius took the remainder of the West under his direct control and until 391 based himself in Milan. At first Ambrose was hampered by a lack of diplomatic history with the new regime, but he used the political profile he had built up under Valentinian to impress on Theodosius that he was not to be trifled with as a spiritual leader.

At the end of 388, a riot occurred in the town of Callinicum on the Euphrates in which a Christian mob, led by the local bishop, plundered and burned down the local Jewish synagogue. Theodosius ordered the bishop to rebuild the synagogue at his and his church's expense. When Ambrose got wind of this judgment, he reacted sternly and wrote to Theodosius urging him to revoke his orders, on the grounds that no faithful Christian could be responsible for the construction of such a place of "idolatry." His letter[6] reflects some starkly anti-Semitic sentiment, which makes for shocking reading today. Theodosius is warned against the dangers of assisting the Jews, those guilty of rejecting the Messiah, to triumph over the church. In the end, Ambrose persuaded him not only to rescind the sentence on the guilty parties in Callinicum but to let the whole matter drop. Ambrose's biographers traditionally depicted the encounter as a confrontation between a daring episcopal Nathan and a chastened imperial David (cf. 2 Sam. 12:1–14). Certainly Ambrose was outspoken, but in reality Theodosius also discerned the political value of exercising clemency at the last, recognizing that it would win him the gratitude of catholic believers in Italy.

In 390, a still more shocking incident of public disorder in the East provided the setting for another confrontation between bishop and emperor. As the result of a riot and the assassination of a military commander in the garrison town of Thessalonica, brutal and severe punishment was exacted on the town's populace: as many as seven thousand residents of Thessalonica were killed in a massacre by the local troops. The majority were innocent of any offense, and the real ringleaders of the crimes for which the slaughter was revenge may well have escaped. Public opinion, inevitably, was outraged. Theodosius tried to distance himself from the atrocity, implying that it was an act of bloodlust carried out by an army stationed far from his immediate control. Probably it was, but he was obliged to bear overall responsibility. Ambrose wrote to him, warning that he would not be free to celebrate the Eucharist if the emperor appeared in his congregation. This was effectively a threat of excommunication, and Theodosius was obliged to do public penance in contrition for the events in Thessalonica.

Theodosius played his part, and was readmitted to communion by Ambrose at Christmas 390.

Ambrose's relations with Theodosius were in truth more complex than these famous incidents imply. Ambrose was unquestionably a consummate political operator who sought to exploit his advantages to the full in the interests of attaining maximum public influence. In an imperial capital, he was strategically placed to utilize the essential benefits of a Nicene emperor, both for the sake of his own standing and in order to confront his opponents with the triumph of his cause. Theodosius, for his part, was implicitly obliged by his professions of fidelity to the Nicene faith to pay attention to the bishop's authority. At the same time, it clearly suited both parties to present an image of a close bond between church and state. Each man needed the other for the marketing of a shared strategy. In reality, Ambrose's direct influence never was quite as secure as the public images suggested, but he was able to create the impression that he was an indispensable and incorruptible spiritual adviser on matters of religious policy. His carefully cultivated persona endeavored to combine the qualities of a traditional Roman man of affairs with the moral integrity and courage of an Old Testament prophet.

In a cosmopolitan city dominated by the extensive apparatus of an imperial court, Ambrose built up a community that could impress discerning eyes and ears. He constructed a number of new churches in Milan and decorated them in elaborate style, symbolizing the pervasive colonization of his city by the Nicene faith and the supplanting of traditional pagan images of civic identity. He sought to weed out from his staff those who were not loyal to him or in agreement with his doctrinal convictions, and by carefully forming a network of faithful subordinates he was able to spread the influence of his church not only within Milan but throughout the smaller, more fragile surrounding sees of northern Italy.

The success of Ambrose illustrates the degree to which the bishops of the fourth century had come to function as a new kind of imperial elite. They were political counselors, sponsors of particular causes with civil authorities, intermediaries between government and people, arbiters in financial disputes, and administrators of increasingly substantial ecclesiastical resources. Ambrose presided over a significant bureaucratic system with large charitable obligations and a responsibility to preserve local interests and traditions. He was a leader by nature, and the skills he had honed as an imperial bureaucrat were put to good use in the service of the church. Through the influence of figures such as

Ambrose, the Christian faith spread further among pagan intellectuals and prominent officials.

Theodosius's Legislation

It was under Theodosius, not Constantine, that Christianity definitively triumphed in political terms over the other religions of the Roman world. Under Theodosius's leadership the long, uneven process of Christianization that had gone on since the first quarter of the fourth century gathered a momentum that was never again to be reversed. Even so, it is important to note that mass conversions to Christ did not take place and to remember that, even at their most comprehensive, Theodosius's strategies were only capable of addressing public conventions and symbols, not private beliefs and values. Even when the emperor did attempt to legislate on private religious activity, he clearly could not force people into believing in anything, nor did he attempt to do so. In principle, Theodosius took no steps to stamp out intellectual belief in pagan deities or traditions as such; it was simply the outward practices that he sought to diminish.

The nature of Theodosius's own policies and the scope of his legislation also developed significantly over time. In the early years of his reign, certain outbreaks of violence against temples went on in the East, especially under a fiercely anti-pagan praetorian prefect named Cynegius, but during this period Theodosius himself continued to appoint pagans to high positions. In 384 he entrusted the education of his son Arcadius to the pagan orator Themistius, whom he had installed as urban prefect of Constantinople. When he went to the West to deal with Maximus, he left pagan officials with major responsibilities in the East, and when he visited Rome in 389 he granted honors to a number of eminent pagan senators. Such gestures were transparent enough, for Theodosius had no fear that non-Christians would any longer be capable of attaining the imperial office itself; if they were good at their jobs, they could safely be given whatever preferments he considered appropriate without any risk that they might upset a Christianized political system. Nonetheless, his willingness to continue to use and value pagan functionaries testifies to his initial desire to impose a religious policy that did not directly threaten individual pagans as such.

In the 390s the mood changed, and there were greater signs of intolerance. Whether the shift is attributable to the growing influence of Ambrose over Theodosius, or whether it derived from other political calculations, is hard to determine; it is unlikely that Ambrose's ascendancy is an adequate explanation in itself. At any rate, in February 391 Theodosius proclaimed a formal ban on all sacrifices, closing temples and stipulating financial fines for those of administrative class and above who persisted in observing pagan rites in public. It was the most comprehensive injunction ever framed against pagan cults, and it was theoretically the most significant moment in the legal history of Christianity in the empire since the time of Constantine. Some similar legislation against "superstition" and sacrifice had been attempted before under Constantius, but it had not been followed up with significant measures of enforcement. In Theodosius's case, the effects were much more substantial, for they relied less on threats of violent punishment and more on a strategic rooting out of the sponsorship of pagan religion by public officials.

Theodosius's legislation opened the door to unprecedented degrees of public hostility toward pagan temples. In Alexandria, the Serapeum, one of the most famous shrines in the Roman world and the home of a magnificent library, was destroyed by rioting Christians, urged on by the local bishop, Theophilus. Such vandalism was not sanctioned by the imperial authorities, but there was evidently little fear of retribution among the populace. Official orders were issued to avoid the wanton destruction of particularly splendid works of art, but in many cases they were ignored. Sometimes the apparent absence of divine judgment upon those who carried out the demolition encouraged people to convert from paganism. The year after the Serapeum was destroyed, Egypt was blessed with an unusually bountiful flooding of the Nile, guaranteeing exceptional fertility to the land; this was taken by many as a sign of favor by the Christian God compelling enough to produce a change of religious allegiance.

Where famous temples were spared destruction, they and the sacred lands surrounding them were often seized forcibly by the churches and reconsecrated as Christian sites. In areas of Asia Minor, Syria, Phoenicia, and Egypt, Christian bishops deployed marauding bands of monks or other hired muscle to appropriate pagan religious property and commit acts of plunder against secular aristocrats. These acts of violence continued long after Theodosius had passed from the scene; in Alexandria they reached their most shameful in 415 when Hypatia, a woman of considerable intellectual ability and a Neoplatonist teacher, was murdered by a Christian mob; her death went unpunished.

If Theodosius allowed lenient handling of those who perpetrated violence against pagans, he was more careful to safeguard the rights of Jews. In fact, the status of the Jews in the Roman world seems to have improved somewhat under his legislation. Christian attitudes to Jews in the fourth century had often been ugly, and things had not been helped by the Jews' willingness to cooperate with the apostate Julian. Under Theodosius's regime, however, Jews were deemed to be free to practice their faith without interference, and even if their missionary activities were resented and often bitterly opposed at a local level by Christian churchmen, they were not illegal. Synagogues were not to be treated as pagan temples were, and action against them was punished by law.

As the Callinicum incident showed, Theodosius's instinct was to require restoration from those responsible for vandalism of a Jewish sanctuary. Though he proved capable of being dissuaded by the impassioned rhetoric of Ambrose, his own views were clear. It was a great tragedy that he did not stick to them. The kind of scurrilous anti-Semitism found in Ambrose's arguments would intensify in the early years of the fifth century in several cities, most notoriously in Antioch, and it is conceivable that the achievement of Ambrose in forcing Theodosius to rescind the punishment on the guilty at Callinicum gave something of a boost to those who sought to push the boundaries of intolerance and oppression.

A further succession of edicts against paganism followed over the years from 391 onward. Public games and circus entertainments continued, as they had under Christian emperors all through the fourth century, but now they did so without the traditional cultic offerings. Measures were also taken to forbid regular circus games and theatrical performances on Sundays or on Christian festivals such as Easter and Pentecost. In November 392 Theodosius attempted to forbid the practice of pagan worship more extensively, including in private ceremonies. Nevertheless, the ban was limited in its application, and there was widespread flouting of the law. In many towns and cities, rituals including sacrifices continued clandestinely for generations to come, and in rural areas, as always, paganism remained firmly entrenched. The financial penalties prescribed for those who broke the law in Theodosius's time were probably rarely exacted before the sixth century.

Manichaeism

The last generation of the fourth century witnessed significant imperial measures not only against polytheism but also against other forms of religious belief. Among the most powerful religious forces of the era, and the one most vigorously opposed under Theodosius, was Manichaeism.

Founded in the third century by a cultivated and charismatic Syriac-speaking Babylonian teacher named Mani (ca. 216–276), Manichaeism purported to offer the final, universal religion. Mani himself was a convert from a version of Jewish Christianity, but his system drew heavily upon the traditional dualism of Persian Zoroastrianism and upon elements of Buddhist thought as well as upon radical Gnostic ideas. Mani styled himself the "apostle of Jesus Christ," but claimed to have abandoned the sect to which he had first belonged when he received certain special revelations of higher truths.

The Manichee myth posited a cosmic competition between two eternal principles, Light and Darkness. In a primordial battle, it was said, the kingdom of Light had been invaded by the kingdom of Darkness, but Darkness had been duped into swallowing particles of Light, and these particles were now imprisoned in the physical bodies of living things. The material world was the result of this conflict, and its history was the story of an ongoing contest between Light and Darkness. Religious teachers such as the Buddha, Zoroaster, the Hebrew prophets, and Jesus himself were sent to release the souls of Light from the captivity of their bodies, for by a process of knowledge (*gnosis*) the soul could be awakened to its divine origins and freed from its place in the corrupt realm of fleshly existence.

Mani himself had died a martyr's death during a resurgence of official Zoroastrianism in Persia, but the movement to which he had given rise had spread rapidly throughout Mesopotamia, Persia, Syria, Palestine, Egypt, and Africa, and within a few years of his death it had become a major force in a significant swath of the Eastern Roman world. It had been harshly persecuted under Diocletian as a Persian threat to Roman society, but it had continued to spread in large areas of the West. The Manichees were zealous missionaries, and their faith, often carried by mercantile traders, penetrated as far as India and China, where it would remain in various derivative guises until the late thirteenth or early fourteenth century.

There were two grades of Manichaeism. The higher grade was represented by "the Elect," who practiced a strict asceticism, shunning sexual activity. They followed a vegetarian diet and sought particularly to eat produce such as melons and cucumbers, which were believed to possess large quantities of Light particles. Most Manichees, however, were ordinary followers or "Hearers." They lived relatively normal lives, without such stringent self-denial. Their expectation was that when they died they would be reincarnated in some other human form, and their aspiration was to attain by a process of moral effort to the point where they might return as members of "the Elect" and eventually have their spirits freed from the cycle of struggle against the Darkness.[7]

Manichaeism proved a major challenge to the Christian churches both in the East and the West, and it was repeatedly proscribed in the later fourth century. The Romans readily associated its secret rites with black magic and moral crimes, and the Manichees were suspected of some of the same kinds of pernicious behavior of which Christians had once been accused. In an otherwise liberal regime, Valentinian I singled them out for hostile treatment, rendering their property liable to confiscation, and Gratian enacted legislation that treated them alongside the extreme Arians as undesirables and denied them freedom of worship. Further distinctly prohibitive measures followed under Theodosius, who believed the Manichees represented a menace to the vision of a secure catholic Christianity as the recognized faith of the empire. Despite all the efforts, however, there were still plenty of Manichees around.

Priscillian and His Followers

One of the grounds on which Manichaeism was particularly resented was its moral teaching. Manichaean conceptions of asceticism in particular posed a direct challenge to the impact of Christian images of self-denial. In one situation at least, the consequences of such rivalry were tragic. In the 370s, in southeastern Spain, a talented aristocrat named Priscillian had converted to Christianity and had devoted himself to the promotion of asceticism. The details of his teaching are not altogether certain, but it is clear that he influenced a considerable number of people to adopt a form of Christian lifestyle marked by self-denial and spiritual zeal, and he was keen to promote equality between men and women in the leadership of worship. Women certainly exercised a prominent role as prophetesses and moral exemplars in circles sympathetic to his ideas. Priscillian seems to have shown enthusiasm for noncanonical Scriptures such as the apocryphal *Acts* of the apostles and some kind of interest in mystical rituals, but his primary concern was with asceticism and the advocacy of a particular conception of holiness.

Some of the views associated with the Priscillianist movement were condemned at a council of Spanish and Gallic bishops in Saragossa in October 380, but Priscillian himself escaped censure, and in the following year his supporters were able to have him consecrated as bishop of Avila. Priscillian had many enemies, however, and he was soon forced to leave Spain for Bordeaux. There he attracted a further band of followers, especially among aristocratic women. Seeing the spread of his influence, his opponents appealed to Gratian to deal with him, alleging that he was a Manichee, apparently on account of his reputation for austerity. Priscillian emphatically denied that he had sympathies for Manichaean teaching, but in the highly charged and competitive religious atmosphere of the early 380s it was a powerful association for his critics to make. Gratian ruled formally that all heretics were be exiled, but Priscillian and his supporters refused to go away, and they endeavored to muster further support in Gaul and Italy. Though rebuffed by both Ambrose in Milan and Pope Damasus in Rome, they achieved some success in lobbying Macedonius, one of Gratian's top officials, and they were granted the right of existence as a movement.

After Gratian's fall, Maximus was encouraged by one of Priscillian's chief Spanish enemies, Ithacius, the erstwhile bishop of Ossonoba, to support further action against him, and at a council in Bordeaux in 384 Priscillian and his followers were again condemned, apparently as Manichees. Priscillian appealed directly to Maximus, but this time his foes accused him not of Manichaeism but of the more serious charge of practicing witchcraft or sorcery. Maximus handed matters over to his praetorian prefect, Evodius, and under his jurisdiction Priscillian and a number of his associates were found guilty. Despite appeals by Martin, bishop of Tours (on whom see further pp. 149–50), Priscillian and many of the condemned were executed and others were exiled.

The fate of Priscillian cast a dark shadow over the Western church: one Christian leader had been hounded to death by others for holding views that were considered unacceptable. Ambrose, who seems to have recognized, too late, the unreasonableness of the campaign against Priscillian, excommunicated his accusers, as did Siricius, Damasus's successor in Rome. Maximus sought to defend his handling of the affair by arguing that the Priscillianists had indeed been Manichees, but there was no good evidence for this; the slur of such connections had simply provided a pretext to get rid of Christians whose version of piety was controversial and challenging to accepted patterns. Priscillian may have been somewhat eccentric, but he was no Manichee.

Although action was taken against some of Priscillian's adversaries, this did not dampen the sense of outrage at the way in which he and his followers had been treated. Theodosius's legislation was firmly against Manichaeism, but Priscillianism experienced something of a revival, and in parts of Spain Priscillian became celebrated as a popular saint. Despite various other condemnations of his teachings both in Spain and in Rome over subsequent generations, genuine enthusiasm for his ideas continued among a dissident minority—fed, perhaps, by grassroots resentment of the growing wealth of the catholic church in Spain—until as late as the end of the sixth century.

The End of Theodosius's Reign

Following the death of Valentinian II in 392, the distrusted Arbogast (see pp. 109–10) sought to mollify Theodosius by nominating a new colleague for him in the West, a rhetorician and bureaucrat named Flavius Eugenius. Eugenius was nominally a Christian, but he had strong sympathies for traditional religion, and he sensed that there was potential political capital to be made out of siding with the sizable contingent of Roman traditionalists who were infuriated by Theodosius's legislation against paganism.

After an attempted negotiation with Theodosius had broken down, Eugenius's inclinations came to the fore, and the pagan senatorial aristocrats saw the chance to press their case. Eugenius invaded Italy in 393 and acceded to overtures to restore funds to pagan cults—though the resources came from his private wealth, not from state assets—and he agreed to restore the statue (if not the altar) of Victory to the Roman Senate-house. A number of pagan officials were appointed in Rome, and there was an effort to restore temples and reinstate traditional festivals. Pagan hopes were raised, and various oracles even prophesied the demise of Christianity. For all that Theodosius had done to devalue the "superstitions" of the past, it seemed that paganism was not yet moribund.

Non-Christian expectations were, however, short-lived. Eugenius and Arbogast were soundly defeated by Theodosius at the Battle of the Frigidus (modern Vipacco), between Sirmium and Aquileia, on 5 September 394, and Eugenius himself was captured and executed. The aftermath saw his supporters treated with clemency, but the battle had marked the defeat not only of a usurper but also of the pagan senatorial establishment that had sought to ally itself with the only conceivable challenger to Theodosius's state Christianity. Paganism continued, often tenaciously, but with the exception of a very brief resurgence in 408, it did so in private and without official approval.

When Theodosius died in Milan in January 395, Ambrose could hail him as a model Christian ruler and patron of a faith with a hold upon its world that was not to be shaken. In reality, the prospects were nowhere near as good as Ambrose claimed, and there were ominous signs of trouble brewing on the political horizon. Within a few years of Ambrose's own death in 397, the dream of a stable catholic empire in which he and Theodosius had invested would be shattered by major turmoil as the Western world fragmented under barbarian pressures and Rome itself fell to the Goths, whose religious affiliations lay elsewhere (see pp. 56–57, 296–302). Theodosius's sponsorship of the Nicene faith and his efforts to enhance Christianity's grip upon Roman society did not ultimately guarantee the security of the empire. Nevertheless, the advantages that Christians had obtained under his regime, when coupled with the disadvantages meted out to their opponents, meant that the churches entered the turbulent years of the early fifth century in a much stronger position than they might have done had political events unfolded similarly a generation earlier.

The Church of Rome

Our picture of the consolidation of the catholic faith in the West is not complete without considering the development of the church of Rome from the 360s onward. Rome and its bishops had benefited enormously from the benefactions of Constantine, but it was not until the second half of the fourth century that the see of Rome forged an identity that truly matched its political privileges with its aspirations to spiritual authority.

The context for the emergence of a definitively different style of Roman church was, not surprisingly, the doctrinal debates of the 350s. While Bishop Liberius was in exile in 355 for his resistance to Constantius, he was replaced by one of the deacons of the church, Felix. Felix proved very unpopular, and Constantius was faced with demonstrations in favor of Liberius and requests from aristocratic women that he be returned to his rightful place. Liberius himself was desperate to return, and after he had agreed to acquiesce in a compromise formula, he was allowed back in 358. Constantius's wish was that Liberius and Felix should share the leadership of the church between them. This was rejected by a sizable proportion of the Roman Christians, and the church split into two camps.

Felix died in November 365, and Liberius followed him the next year, but the division that had opened up in Rome only intensified. Some favored a supporter of Felix (and intermittent associate of Liberius) named Damasus as his successor; others favored a different candidate, a deacon called Ursinus, who had remained consistently loyal to Liberius. Matters came to a head in October 366 when public riots broke out, and a dreadful massacre took place in which 137 of Ursinus's supporters are said to have perished.[8] Pagan opinion was scandalized, for the killing had even taken place within a church building.[9] With political support, Damasus succeeded in gaining office, but the strife and bloodshed had cost his church dearly in terms of public image. Damasus was personally accused of responsibility for the deaths of his opponents, and he was said to have escaped condemnation only thanks to the mediation of rich friends who appealed directly to Valentinian I on his behalf.

Damasus

In a bid to compensate for his lack of credibility, Damasus set about magnifying the prestige of his office, and under his leadership (366–384) Rome's ecclesiastical status developed to an unprecedented degree. He spent vast sums on building up Rome's churches, constructing new edifices with the finest of materials and adorning them with splendid furnishings. The shrines of martyrs and previous bishops were developed and enriched with fine inscriptions and sonorous if amateurish epigrams. The practice of commemorating the saints in the liturgy of the church was extended. Damasus drew special attention to the apostolic origins of the Roman see and stressed that the splendor of Rome's past lay not so much in its imperial glories but in its Christian heritage; this was the city where Paul and Peter had been martyred for their faith and where their relics conveyed special spiritual eminence to the local church. By fusing the symbolic importance of his church and his city with the memory of the giants of sacred history, Damasus fashioned an image of Rome as the Christian center like no other. The process of directly identifying "Romanness" with Christianity, initiated by Constantine, was taken further than ever.

In the 380s Damasus took other steps to strengthen the authority of his church. In 380 he installed a new bishop, Acholius, in Thessalonica and treated him as his personal deputy in the provinces of the Balkans, thus staking a claim to a territory that fell under the jurisdiction of the church of Constantinople. At a council in Rome in 382 it was agreed that the primacy of Rome rested not on the decision of an ecclesiastical meeting—in spite of the decision made at the Council of Constantinople the previous year—but on its legitimate claim to have been founded by the apostle Peter.

Damasus sought to live in the style that he thought befitted his position as the head of such a church. Pagan critics noted his opulent manner; in a society familiar with the spectacle of the rich indulging themselves while the majority suffered regular economic hardships and shortages of food, Damasus's entertainments became notorious. He and his clergy were said to have a penchant for lavish feasting, fine clothes, and luxurious living, traveling around in carriages and outdoing the emperor himself in their pretensions to comfort and grandeur. Damasus allegedly cultivated the attentions of rich Roman ladies in particular and acquired a reputation for soliciting their wealth. His enemies called him "the ladies' ear-tickler" for his obsequious devotion to such sources of potential revenue, and his officials were said to have followed his example, enriching themselves as much as their church in the process. One wealthy pagan nobleman, Vettius Agorius Praetextatus, is said to have jested, "Make me bishop of Rome, and I'll become a Christian tomorrow!"[10] No doubt some of the pictures of the excesses were exaggerated, but to many onlookers the wealth and splendor that Damasus accumulated did nothing to dispel the rumors that he was a shady character from the start. No wonder, they thought, he had been prepared to stop at nothing, even mass murder, in order to win such treasures as his personal prize.

Damasus's devotion to worldly prestige brought him opponents at all levels of society, not only in Rome but farther afield. At the same time, it would be wrong to imagine that such social maneuvering had not already been a part of the church's life. From at least the third century, bishops all over the Christian world had endeavored to cultivate their status, power, and dignity, and the fourth century had only accelerated that process, particularly in the West, as increasing numbers of church-men came from higher social backgrounds, where they expected to be treated with formal respect and to belong at the natural heart of their society. Though Damasus himself was not from a significant family (his father was a priest), his behavior was, in one sense, simply an extension of an existing trend in the post-Constantinian empire.

It is equally true that the degree of enculturation of the church in higher-class Roman society that took place from the mid-fourth century onward contributed to the expansion of Christianity as a respectable option. As the church grew in the outward trappings of wealth and power, so it became a more attractive prospect for notable people. Damasus and his staff may have courted wealthy ladies to a degree that was palpably dangerous for the church's reputation, but at the same time such efforts provided an inroad for the Christian gospel into aristocratic households that might otherwise have seen little reason to be interested in the claims of Christian spokesmen.[11] In practice, the successes often stopped with the women; typically the men tended to remain pagan long after the women of the household had been converted. There was nevertheless a cumulative effect, for the children in turn came under the influences of Christian instruction at least from their mothers and aunts.

Damasus actively sought to suppress heresies, and he took a consistent line in opposing Arianism. His churches and monuments enriched the architecture of Rome, and he housed the archives of his see in new, secure premises. In spite of—or because of—the rumors about his clergy's worldliness, he urged his officials to pursue a path of moral commitment that included, for Damasus as for other churchmen such as Ambrose, a dedication to priestly celibacy as a vital part of the ritual purity to which those who presided at the Eucharist were believed to be called. As part of his preoccupation with the dignity of all things Roman, Damasus encouraged the use of Latin in the services of the Roman church—up to this time it was still standard for much of the liturgy in the city to be conducted in Greek, a practice that was inevitably alienating for the majority of people. Although Greek was not entirely supplanted for a long time, Damasus fostered an official transition to the vernacular in Roman worship.

One of Damasus's most important decisions was his choice of the individual to assist him as his secretary. He appointed a man in his midthirties whose career had already encountered controversy but whose gifts would ensure him a place as one of the greatest scholars in the history of early Christianity. Though this individual actually spent a good deal of his life in the East, was familiar with Eastern traditions, values, and practices, and employed a fair part of his time attacking Western opponents, his mind-set was fundamentally a Latin one. The nature and range of his work in Latin were unprecedented in the Western church, and it was on the West that he made his greatest impact.

Jerome

Hieronymus, or Jerome as we have come to know him, was born in an insignificant town, Stridon in Dalmatia, around 347. His parents were prosperous Christians, and they sent their son to Rome for his education. Jerome received a very thorough training in classical literature, language, and rhetoric, and the influence of secular authors remained deep within him for the rest of his days. After the completion of his studies, Jerome traveled widely. While in Gaul he developed a strong interest in monasticism, and he moved to Syria, where he lived as a hermit in the desert of Chalcis, east of Antioch. There he devoted himself to further

"Saint Jerome Reading," by Alvise Vivarini (ca. 1475/1480). Illustration from Samuel H. Kreiss Collection, National Gallery of Art, Washington, DC. Used by permission.

language study, particularly the acquisition of Hebrew. Jerome began to become a *vir trilinguis*—a person competent not only in Greek and Latin but also in Hebrew, a much scarcer tongue in Christian circles. After becoming embroiled in a number of quarrels with other hermits in the desert, he returned to Antioch, where he was ordained as a presbyter. He then embarked on further travels, and the years 380–381 saw him in Constantinople, where he was able to acquaint himself with the current controversies of Greek theology. At length he arrived in Rome, where he attracted the attention of Damasus.

Damasus was deeply impressed with Jerome's abilities as a writer and scholar, and he began to treat him as a primary dialogue partner and literary secretary. Alongside the regular duties that such a role entailed, Jerome was entrusted with a much more important task. Damasus commissioned him to undertake a new version of the Scriptures in Latin, in keeping with his plan to reinforce a "proper" Latin tradition. In the West, from the second century onward, a huge number of different versions of the Scriptures in Latin had come to be used, and the translations varied from region to region. The biblical text was not the same for believers in Gaul or Spain as it was for those in Italy, while in North Africa it was different again, and even within a small local area there were often many variant editions in circulation. As Jerome put it to Damasus, there were nearly as many textual forms in Latin as there were manuscripts of the Bible, and according to Augustine, writing some years later, just about anyone who fancied he had any ability in Greek had been prepared to have a go at translating the Scriptures.[12] The Latin of these versions was often colloquial and peculiar in both vocabulary and syntax, and a new common edition was sorely needed.

Jerome's first task was to create a standard text by collating the best versions of the existing Latin texts, and he began by working on the four Gospels. Naturally enough, this job involved comparing the Latin texts with the Greek original, and so in effect Jerome created a new synthesis that was partway to being a new translation, even though Damasus had not charged him with producing an entirely new translation as such. Jerome presented his new rendering of the Gospels to Damasus not long before the latter died in late 384.

Jerome's Bible

Jerome has traditionally been hailed as the creator of an entire Latin Bible, the "Vulgate," which was the standard (*vulgata*, "common") edition of the Scriptures in the West for centuries. The truth is, in fact, rather more complicated than this legend suggests. Although Jerome uses the term *vulgate* to refer to his own versions of the Scriptures—meaning that he intended them to be accessible to ordinary Christians, not just to scholars who could understand Greek and Hebrew—he did not single-handedly produce all or even most of what came to be known as the Vulgate Bible. It is unlikely, for one thing, that he translated the rest of the New Testament besides the Gospels, despite his claim to have done so. The texts of Acts, the Epistles, and Revelation, which have come to be part of the Vulgate collection, are probably the work of another reviser or revisers, whose identity remains elusive. What we call the Vulgate was not collated as a single entity until at least the sixth century. The oldest surviving manuscript of it, the *Codex Amiatinus*, was produced in Northumberland in England in the last years of the seventh century, but only in the ninth century did the new collection come to be regarded as a standard version in any serious sense, and attempts to standardize it went on for centuries after that.

What we can say, however, is that Jerome contributed more than anyone else to the process by which the Western Bible was standardized in the end, and he did so above all with his work not on the Christian but on the Jewish Scriptures. After he had completed his new version of the Gospels, he undertook a new edition of the Psalter from the Greek of the Septuagint. This translation was produced rapidly and shows some signs of crudeness. It has conventionally been associated with the "Roman Psalter," the version of the Psalms that was used in Rome until the time of Pope Pius V in the sixteenth century, but this identification is unreliable; Jerome's efforts may have contributed to that later text, but the Roman Psalter was not Jerome's work as such. A few years later, after he had left Rome and settled in the East, Jerome made another translation of the Psalms, this time using the text of the Septuagint as given in Origen's *Hexapla*.[13] This version became known as the "Gallican Psalter," as it was first accepted for use in the churches in Gaul.

Further work on other parts of the Old Testament convinced Jerome that any translation relying on only a Greek text was frankly not good enough; it was necessary to go back to the Hebrew original itself. Jerome was exceptionally well-equipped to take up this challenge, and he embarked on a completely new rendering of the Hebrew Scriptures. His knowledge of Hebrew, acquired at the cost of enormous personal dedication, surpassed that of any other figure in the early church, including Origen, and he put this expertise to extremely valuable use. Pursued intermittently, the task of translating the Hebrew Bible occupied about a decade and a half of his life, from 390–391 until 405–406. It included a third revision of the Psalter, based on the Hebrew, though this version never attained the liturgical popularity of its Gallican predecessor, which was incorporated into the Vulgate manuscripts in its stead and endorsed as the official text at the Council of Trent in the sixteenth century.

Jerome's return to the Hebrew of the Old Testament was groundbreaking in a variety of ways, not the least of which were its implications for the biblical Canon. The Septuagint translation included a number of books that were not part of the Hebrew Canon and that were rejected by non-Hellenistic Judaism.[14] In his early writings Jerome followed the usual Christian practice of quoting from these texts as equally scriptural, and at no time did he repudiate them as unworthy for the Christian church. However, he did come to argue that these books were to be regarded as "apocryphal," or of secondary status for the serious scholar, since they were not included in the Hebrew Canon.

Such claims were controversial. Jerome was sharply criticized by a number of his Christian contemporaries, among them Augustine, who argued that he was in danger of "Judaizing" in his apparent abandonment or relativizing of the Greek antecedents of the Bible as it had come to be known in the West. In reality, however, some of the polemic against Jerome's strategy was generated by ignorance: none of his opponents was in any position to engage with him on scholarly grounds when it came to knowledge of languages, and their reverence for the Greek Bible as uniquely inspired by God rested on the flimsy grounds of traditional usage rather than anything else. The church of the late fourth century remained dominated by Greek forms; it was Jerome's greatest gift to restore the importance of Christianity's Hebraic inheritance. His enthusiasm in this regard was not matched again in the West until the Reformation.

Biblical Scholar and Commentator

As part of his work as a biblical translator and textual critic, Jerome undertook extensive research into the content of the material on which he labored. He enquired into questions about the topography of important biblical sites, drawing upon knowledge acquired on his own travels in the Holy Land. Like many ancient scholars, he was also interested in the discussion of etymology, and he produced studies of the supposed meanings of Hebrew names, which were traditionally deemed to be of moral and spiritual import.

By far the largest part of his literary output, though, consisted of biblical commentaries, in which he sought to elucidate the meaning of the text of Scripture for his contemporaries. Jerome wrote commentaries on almost all the books of the Old Testament and on some of the New. Perhaps the most important of these are his studies on the Hebrew prophets, including a massive commentary on Isaiah and valuable treatments of the minor prophets, not least Daniel and Jonah. Jerome was the only author in the ancient church to write on all of the prophets, both major and minor.

Jerome's commentaries are not really verse-by-verse expositions such as we might expect today. Instead they offer comment on selected portions—verses or sections—of the text that Jerome felt required particular illumination. His works were often written at great speed, and some, like his commentary on Matthew's Gospel, were completed in a matter of days. As well as engaging in polemic from time to time (his commentary on Daniel spends some time refuting the arguments of the infamous pagan critic Porphyry), Jerome's studies reveal a large range of reading in both Christian and Jewish authorities. He placed considerable stress on literal, historical exegesis, but he was also enthusiastic about the possibilities of allegorical interpretation, often deriving his ideas from the influence of Origen (whom in his later years he came to criticize fiercely on doctrinal grounds). In addition, he was convinced that Jewish exegetical traditions were of importance for Christian understanding of the Hebrew Scriptures. Some of his knowledge in this area came secondhand from Origen, but a great deal of it seems to have been acquired by personal encounter with rabbinical wisdom.

The Moral Teacher

Jerome's years in Rome saw him involved in more than the beginnings of the biblical scholarship that would ultimately find him immersed in the Hebrew Scriptures. He wrote extensively on a variety of other subjects and promoted asceticism in particular. He formed close friendships with a number of aristocratic Christian women and studied the Bible and spiritual ideas with them, meeting in their homes. Among them were the rich widows Marcella, whose home was in the fashionable quarter of the Aventine (one of Rome's seven hills) and who was already well-known for her spiritual devotion, and Paula, a much younger woman than Marcella, two of whose daughters also came to belong in the same circle—Blesilla, aged around twenty and herself recently widowed, and Eustochium, still in her teens. Others included Asella, a widow of around fifty, and Lea, another widow and close friend of Marcella.

Over Paula and her daughters in particular Jerome came to exercise a powerful influence. To such women, he became a kind of personal tutor and counselor, encouraging them to withdraw in various ways from normal society and to distance themselves from the compromises of a Christianity that settled for respectability rather than consecration. Paula and her older companions already nursed such ideals, but it was harder for the young women. Blesilla was a vivacious girl who enjoyed an active social life and lavished attention on her clothes and her appearance. Jerome was determined that she and her sister (who proved much more readily malleable) were called upon to renounce such pleasures and live more and more like nuns, cherishing chastity, practicing fasting or simplicity in diet, deliberately neglecting their physical appearance, and consecrating themselves to a life of prayer and Bible study.

Jerome exhorted the women to sublimate sexual desires in particular and to avoid the company of married men and women. One of his most famous letters (*Epistle* 22) is addressed to Eustochium on the subject of virginity. It commends the Virgin Mary as the supreme exemplar of self-denial and quiet meditation, maintaining her piety on her own, away from the threatening forces of the world. Jerome's counsel was intended to be read not just by Eustochium herself but by a much wider public in the Roman church. In the same period Jerome also engaged in polemic against those in the church who held other views regarding sexuality. He wrote a treatise against Helvidius, a lay-theologian who taught that Mary had lived a normal married life after the birth of Jesus and held that marriage was therefore as high a state as celibacy.

In Helvidius's view, the "brothers" of Jesus mentioned in the New Testament (Matt. 12:46–47; Mark 3:31–32; 6:3; Luke 8:19–20; John 7:3, 5; Acts 1:14; 1 Cor. 9:5) were to be taken in the natural sense of the word, as other children born to Mary and Joseph. This was not only the most plausible construal historically; it had also been accepted by other teachers in the West, including Tertullian. Jerome, however, took fierce exception to it, as it undermined an alleged biblical support for the argument that celibacy was a superior way of life. In a passionate attack on Helvidius, he contended that Mary was a perpetual virgin and that the relatives of Jesus spoken of in Scripture were cousins—the sons of Mary the "mother of James the younger and of Joses" (Mark 15:40; 16:1), whom Jerome took to be the wife of Clopas and sister of Mary the mother of Jesus (cf. John 19:25). Jerome's argument prevailed, and his teaching became acknowledged as the official view of the Roman church, though it would be challenged by many in later years.[15]

For some, the pressure of Jerome's advice regarding self-denial proved too great. Blesilla suffered a nervous breakdown and died as a result of intensive fasting, and Paula collapsed at her funeral, eliciting considerable popular indignation at the lengths to which Jerome had encouraged his disciples to go. Jerome even rebuked Paula for showing excessive grief over Blesilla, who had, he insisted, been promoted to heaven as a spiritual heroine.

What got Jerome into real trouble, however, was not the effects of his advocacy of asceticism as such but his accompanying criticisms of his peers in the church. He issued scathing denunciations of the faults of the Roman clergy and penned bitingly satirical attacks on the extravagance and corruption of the Roman church and its "sham" Christians. Not surprisingly, such broadsides made him deeply unpopular with his colleagues, who saw it as paradoxical that while he preached ascetic virtues and denounced them for their worldliness, he enjoyed delicately close relations with his group of female patrons, especially Paula.

The Advent of Siricius: Jerome's Departure for the East

Jerome remained secure so long as Damasus was alive, but his fortunes changed after his patron's death. Damasus's successor, Siricius, was a hardheaded administrator whose years as bishop (384–399) would see the practical authority of the church of Rome enhanced still further, to the extent that its leader would not hesitate to issue direct orders to other Western churches, aping the edicts of imperial majesty in his "decretals" or letters of instruction to provincial authorities in Africa, Spain, and Gaul. As was made clear in the first of these decrees, a set of moral counsels addressed to Himerius, bishop of Tarragona in Spain, Siricius firmly endorsed the ideal of clerical celibacy, but he had little time for those he regarded as overly clever proponents of asceticism. Jerome was plainly in trouble. He was investigated and condemned for his personal behavior and effectively banished from Rome in 385.

Jerome was soon followed by a party of devoted women, led by Paula and Eustochium. They met up in Syria and traveled as a group to the Holy Land, where they visited a number of sacred sites, and to Egypt before finally settling in Bethlehem in 386. With the aid of Paula's wealth, two monasteries were set up—one for men, presided over by Jerome, the other for women, run by Paula. Jerome set out rules for both communities. He lived in this environment for the rest of his life, devoting himself to a program of study, writing, and teaching right up to his death in 420. He wrote extensively on a range of subjects besides scriptural exegesis, including lives of various Eastern hermits and a sort of "Who's Who and Who Was Who" of prominent Christians called *On Famous Men*, which contains its own share of caustic criticism as well as hagiographical reverence.

Jerome the Controversialist

One thing Jerome did not do when he settled in the East was leave controversy behind. His career reads as a catalog of disputes with other Christians over morals, doctrine, and biblical interpretation, and he left broken relationships everywhere. For many years Jerome was an ardent devotee of Origen, from whose exegesis, as we have noted, he appropriated a great deal, and he translated many of his homilies into Latin. In the last years of the fourth century, however, a bitter dispute broke out in the Eastern churches over Origen's teaching (see pp. 151–58), and Jerome changed his allegiances. He became violently and tendentiously opposed to "Origenism" and its influences.

One of Jerome's oldest friends, Rufinus, a scholarly monk from Aquileia whom he had met in Rome, took the opposite side, remaining loyal to Origen's memory. Rufinus had been based in a monastery in Jerusalem for some years, but in 397 he returned to Italy. In 398 he issued in Rome a new (and somewhat free) translation of Origen's *On First Principles*, accompanying it with a statement arguing that Origen's orthodoxy was not in doubt; he made bold to remark that Jerome had formerly been a zealous advocate of the Alexandrian's works. Jerome was incensed by both Rufinus's translation and his determined fidelity to Origen, and the ensuing years saw a fierce war between the two former associates, in which Jerome published his own literal translation of *On First Principles* to prove just how heretical Origen really was and played down his own earlier enthusiasm for his works. He went on to accuse Rufinus of fabrication of truth, heresy, and false translation, and he attacked his character in extremely intemperate language. The abuse even continued after Rufinus's death in 411.

Jerome was jealous of his scholarly abilities, and he did not suffer gladly those whose intellectual or literary efforts he regarded as substandard. Early in his career, he expressed some admiration for Ambrose's contributions on the subject of virginity, but this assessment soon gave way to scathing denunciations of Ambrose's lack of originality and poor style in his doctrinal and exegetical works. The criticisms were technically anonymous, but the target of Jerome's scorn, intentionally, was clear. To his credit, Ambrose never sought to respond in kind. More predictable attacks by Jerome were directed at opponents such as Jovinian, a former Italian monk who had become disillusioned with the ascetic life and sought to defend his change of mind on biblical grounds by arguing that all baptized believers occupied the same status. Celibacy was not superior to the married state, fasting brought no special reward, and those who were baptized were invulnerable to satanic temptation. Jovinian's reasoning was perceived by other churchmen besides Jerome as a threat to Christian moral endeavor and to the implicit superiority of the clergy in spiritual terms (both Ambrose and Augustine also attacked his ideas). But it was thanks to Jerome's impassioned assault on Jovinian's views that the ideal of self-denial was reinforced as an essential dimension of the Western clerical paradigm.

In 395 a priest from Aquitania named Vigilantius visited Bethlehem, and his stay ended in a quarrel over the validity of manifestations of popular devotion to the saints, such as all-night vigils and the veneration of relics. Years later, Jerome wrote a fierce critique of Vigilantius, accusing him of opposing the sacred principles of the cult of the martyrs, which had become so powerful in the churches of both East and West. In the last period of his life, Jerome, like many other prominent churchmen, became embroiled in attacking Pelagianism (see pp. 179–90), but he showed a greater ability to vilify his enemies personally than a capacity to grasp the doctrinal issues they were raising.

Jerome was a complex character. It is likely that many of the accusations he leveled at his foes reflected deep-seated insecurities and struggles within his own psyche. Scholars have suggested that this was especially true of his pursuit of asceticism, which was in no small measure a painful quest to conquer his own powerful sexual drives. It was certainly the case with his attitude to secular learning. In his famous letter to Eustochium, he narrates the story of a dream in which he was carried to heaven and turned away on the grounds that he was "not a Christian, but a Ciceronian."[16] He says that he vowed thereafter to devote himself to sacred texts rather than to the classics. For a period of years he did avoid quotations from classical literature, but in a later letter (*Epistle* 70) he proposed an accommodation whereby the much-loved books of his youth could be turned to good use provided they were appropriately sanitized of unsavory moral elements.

Jerome was profoundly attached to the literature of the classical world, and he found it extremely difficult to abandon its cultural legacy. Even his famous description of his dream is couched in prose heavily marked by classical influences. In the end, it is no surprise that, like several other highly cultivated Christians of his time, he came to contend that the best of the past could be taken over and revamped by the Christian scholar. (He also later mused that a vow made in a dream may not be binding.) But the tensions in his mind became famous: a large number of later European paintings depict Jerome in the wilderness, beating himself with a stone in a bid to drive from his breast the temptation to read classical literature.

The genius that made Jerome the scholar he was brought an arrogance and angularity with it, and he hardly looks the better for it. Jerome was a man of great irascibility and considerable humor, capable of both impressive generosity and startling malice. As an erudite student of the Scriptures, he was without rival in the ancient church, and his abilities as an exegete provided a model for generations of biblical interpreters. His sponsorship of asceticism, too, however intricately involved its psychological roots, was also a major force in the Christian world of his day. Whatever his obvious faults, Jerome was a figure of enormous gifts. Without his work in all its diversity, Western believers in particular would certainly in the longer term have been a great deal worse off culturally.

Jerome's commitment to ascetic ideals in particular raises an important question: why was it that the fourth and early fifth centuries proved such a significant period for the growth of asceticism among Christians more widely, not just in the West but also—indeed especially—in the East? To answer the question, we need to look more closely at the complex nature of the ascetic traditions of these times.

5

CHRISTIANS
AS ASCETICS

▼

Asceticism and Social Change

Asceticism had been a significant force in Christian circles from early times, and the second and third centuries had seen considerable development in the spirituality and theology of self-denial.[1] As the churches had expanded and become more entrenched in the cultural world of the Roman Empire, the images of such special devotion had become increasingly powerful. From the third century onward, ever greater numbers of Christians had found themselves drawn to ask if the benefits of social advancement had not come at an attendant cost in terms of moral distinctiveness and spiritual energy. This question had been implicit in most if not all of the major disputes about church purity and unity, such as those that had affected the churches in Rome and Carthage in the 250s, and it had certainly been present in the minds of those third-century Christians in Asia, Syria, and Egypt who had sought to commit themselves to lives of stricter dedication than their brothers and sisters in the churches at large.

It was in the fourth century in particular, however, that the drive towards asceticism really gathered momentum. The age in which persecution had remained a significant possibility had come to an end, and the privileging of Christians with wealth and status brought with it the very real risk that the church would settle into a mood of complacency and betray its calling to be different from the world around it. If the possibility of martyrdom was drastically reduced, the danger now lay, it seemed, in moral compromise. A combination of political change at the center and the escalation of regional traditions of spiritual rigorism, often as a result of the trials of the early years of the fourth century, generated new and widespread expressions of ascetic zeal.

These expressions varied greatly, and they were strongly shaped by their local contexts, but without the general shift in the climate within which all Christians existed in the Roman world they would not have appeared as they did. Nor, without the altered circumstances of the post-Constantinian scene, might the distinct ideas and practices of different kinds of asceticism have spread so rapidly from one setting to another. At the same time, in the changed environment of the fourth century, Christians would face increasingly vigorous competition from other belief systems that saw the privileging of this one faith as a serious threat to their prosperity.

Stoic and Pythagorean traditions[2] in particular also idealized the life of material simplicity, self-discipline, and contemplation, and educated readers were familiar with the literary celebration of pagan ascetics in works such as Porphyry's *Life* of Plotinus and the biography of Pythagoras produced by the great Syrian Neoplatonist philosopher, Iamblichus (ca. 250–326).[3] The images prized by these traditions represented an implicit challenge to the followers of Jesus to prove that they could outstrip their rivals in their dedication to austerity, and the depiction of ascetic virtues in pagan sources would significantly influence the characterizations of saintly morality in Christian writing.

Syria and Mesopotamia

The most fertile territory for asceticism in the early fourth century continued to be Syria and Mesopotamia, regions where the impulse to self-denial had already been strongly felt over several generations. The significance of the moral and spiritual influence of ascetics who lived either on or beyond the Eastern margins of the Roman world is another example of the degree to which our picture of Christian spirituality must include developments that went on far beyond the obvious centers of Mediterranean culture. The teaching of the most prominent writers of the early Syriac tradition, such as the orthodox leader Aphrahat (ca. 270–345), was not separatist as far as the mainstream church was concerned, but it placed a strong emphasis on consecration and sexual continence as characteristics of the baptized, whose commitment was to belong to Christ alone. The Syriac word for "ascetic," *idihaya*, can in fact be rendered as "single" or "alone" (the root of the Greek word *monachos*, "monk," is also *monos*, "single" or "alone," though the original sense of the word *monachos* itself is not clear).

For some of the believers from an eastern Syrian background, the cost of single-minded attachment to their Lord had been high. Until Diocletian's time, oppression at the hands of imperial authorities had in fact been limited in areas east of Antioch, but a number of Christians, both men and women, had been martyred in these regions during the Great Persecution. The Constantinian revolution, however, put a stop to that, and in 325 Nisibis, the chief city of Mesopotamia, was able to send its bishop, Jacob, to the Council of Nicaea. One of Jacob's followers, Ephrem (ca. 306–373), became the most famous writer in the Syriac church, and his theology was deeply shaped by ascetic principles.

Ephrem (traditionally known as "Ephrem the Syrian") was such a remarkable figure that he is worth pausing over in his own right. Born in Nisibis, he was appointed by Jacob as "interpreter" or "exegete" of the church there, a role that involved him in teaching and writing for the edification of the local Christians. After Nisibis was surrendered to the Persians in 363, Ephrem settled for the last years of his life in Edessa, where many of his extant works were produced. Ephrem wrote a good deal, and although matters are complicated by the existence of a large body of material falsely attributed to his name, a lot of his work does survive in the form of commentaries on biblical and other texts (such as Tatian's *Diatessaron*),[4] sermons, and hymns. All of this work is in Syriac, and a great deal is in verse. His writings provide a very important insight into the strategies of theological polemic and biblical interpretation in the context of Christianity at the (politically very turbulent) edge of the Eastern Roman world, and modern scholarship is only beginning to explore just how influential Ephrem was for the church at large.

It is for his hymns above all that Ephrem is justly celebrated. Often designed, as Ambrose's would be in the West, to inculcate catholic teaching against Arian and other errors, these compositions present a rich, incarnational theology, marveling at the mysterious grace of a God who condescends to become present in the confines of human form and lauding the process by which God restores humanity to its intended destiny of union with the divine nature. God is frequently described by Ephrem in striking feminine imagery, as is the case in other material deriving from Syria, such as the late-second-century *Odes of Solomon*, a series of short hymns only discovered in modern times.[5] Ephrem's hymnody became a core part of the liturgy in both the eastern and the western Syrian church. Among the most accomplished poetic achievements of the early Christian period, his compositions were widely translated and imitated, and they formed a vital influence on the emergence of later Byzantine liturgy.

Ephrem placed much importance on ascetic ideals and exemplars, especially on the consecrated virginity of Mary, the mother of Jesus. For Ephrem, chastity and holiness were one and the same thing, and truly dedicated believers were called to live an "angelic" existence, rising above the carnal commitments of this world on a path toward ultimate sanctification. At the same time, he did not unduly depreciate the material. The context of Ephrem's poetry was often sacramental, and he visualized the beauty and order of the natural world as symbolic of divine goodness. Though the life of the angels (cf. Luke 20:34–36) was the ideal, marriage and childbearing were also plainly necessary for the continuance of human existence. Appreciation of this paradox nevertheless did not prevent Ephrem from elevating sexual abstinence as the calling of the most spiritually minded. He himself was hailed as a paragon of ascetic sanctity, and the ideas and imagery expressed in his writings were assimilated all over the Greek East and (to a lesser extent) in the Latin West.

Farther west in Syria, where Hellenistic influences were much more potent, a wide variety of forms of asceticism developed in the fourth century. Some ascetics lived in communities, but many pursued a solitary existence as spiritual recluses, dedicated to cultivating their private relationship with God. These hermits (our English word comes from the Greek *eremites*, "desert-dweller") often adopted regimes of special austerity, donning chains, deliberately exposing their bodies to the extremes of a desert climate, almost starving themselves, and in some cases surviving on an animal's diet.

Some of them lived in stone towers and similar structures, and one in particular left behind the relative comforts of a monastery in order to spend the rest of his life on top of a column twelve to eighteen meters tall,[6] exposed to the elements, at Telanissus, in the desert northeast of Antioch. Simeon "the Stylite" or "column-dweller" (ca. 385–459) became famous throughout the Christian world and attracted a stream of

Remains of late-fifth-century basilica of St. Simeon "the Stylite" (Qalaat Semaan), built around his pillar at Telanissus in Syria. Illustration from Galen R. Frysinger. Used by permission.

pilgrims to witness his devotion.[7] Although many criticized his behavior as a perverted form of self-aggrandizement, he is said to have made a significant impression on many believers and converted numbers of pagans by his example. There were many other "stylites" who adopted similar practices in the East, in Egypt, and in Greece over the subsequent centuries.

The number of Syrian hermits grew considerably over the course of the fifth and sixth centuries. Many of the zealots were illiterate and could not meditate on biblical or other spiritual texts, but they gave themselves to a life of prayer and self-mortification. Women as well as men adopted practices designed to show their wholehearted dedication, and in significant ways asceticism offered women opportunities to break out of their traditional roles in society and pursue a path that, in its very independence, challenged conventional ideas of gender. The extremes of rigorism to which both men and women gave themselves strike most modern people as bizarre and superstitious. No doubt, for many of these ascetics, spirituality was a complex mix of Christian and non-Christian assumptions, and no doubt some were fanatics driven by a desire to become famous for the lengths to which they took their devotions as "fools for Christ's sake" (cf. 2 Corinthians 10–12). But many were presumably sincere in their quest to come closer to God by absenting themselves from the things of the world, even if the assumptions that underpinned that quest were open to objection in biblical terms.

Many ascetics endeavored to pursue their sense of vocation independently of the organized church. The most notorious of these were the so-called Messalians or "praying ones" (see pp. 89–90) of the late fourth and early fifth centuries,[8] who adopted an itinerant life, roughing it, and practicing a form of continual prayer to the Holy Spirit who, they believed, could enable them to transcend the desires of the flesh and attain a state of spiritual serenity. Though regarded as a challenge to the regular structures of ecclesiastical authority, especially in the Greek-speaking East, their emphasis on the Spirit's power exercised a certain attraction for some mainstream Christians as well.

Egypt

If Syria and Mesopotamia had provided the most productive soil for the growth of ascetic practice, the most influential *theology* of monasticism came from farther south, in Egypt. More than was the case almost anywhere else, Christianity in Egypt lived amid the juxtaposition of society and the desert, and the proximity of the wilderness to the main population bases clustered around the Nile confronted Egyptian Christians with a constant symbol of a wild, untamed region where tranquility might be sought, away from the pressures of organized society. The desert was visible everywhere, and the desert spoke of solitude.

This does not mean that Egyptian asceticism should be seen as a movement made up of individuals who rejected society simply because they had a natural bent towards retreat. The ascetics of Egypt were interested, rather, in constructing a new set of relations with society by demonstrating the capacity of the spiritual life to liberate from dependence on the usual patterns of human existence. The Egyptian churches had produced ascetics from quite early on, and the thought of teachers such as Origen had lent significant weight to the development of monastic spirituality in the region.[9]

Antony

The most famous of Egyptian ascetics was Antony (ca. 251–356), whose example was celebrated in a highly influential biography by Athanasius, written shortly after its hero's death. Athanasius's account presents Antony as an idealized Christian giant, and Athanasius undoubtedly has his own interests in mind in some of the points he makes about his subject's wisdom and his loyalty to episcopal authority, but his sketch presents a picture that can be broadly corroborated in other contemporary records.

According to Athanasius, Antony was born into a prosperous Christian family and was orphaned, along with a younger sister, at the age of eighteen. Around 270 he experienced a call to the ascetic life, and in obedience to Jesus's teaching he renounced his inheritance, placed his sister in the care of a community of virgins (whose lifestyle she subsequently adopted), and became a pupil of a village ascetic. After a period of spiritual struggle with the challenge to disengage from the world, during which he made visits to tombs on the edge of the wilderness where he is said to have wrestled with demons, he decided to move into the desert and become a solitary, away from the security of nearby company.

Antony lived for twenty years as a recluse in an abandoned fort at Pispir in Middle Egypt, after which he had some contacts with other Christians. He then determined to move still further into the eastern desert towards the Red Sea, to a place he designated his "Inner Mountain," in distinction from the "Outer Mountain" of Pispir. He continued to visit the latter base periodically to receive disciples and offer counsel to other ascetics, but most of his time was spent at the Inner Mountain, where he died at an advanced age in 356.[10] His move farther and farther into the desert symbolized his determination to confront the forces of evil and conquer their territory by establishing a spiritual oasis of peace, love, and discipline in the kind of wilderness realm in which Jesus himself had resisted the wiles of Satan in the temptation accounts of the Gospels (Matt. 4:1–11; Mark 1:12–13; Luke 4:1–13).

Antony became renowned as a teacher. Though he ended up living a solitary life, in his visits to the Outer Mountain he offered counsel, prayer, and sometimes spiritual healing to suppliants. A large number of sayings attributed to him (or in some cases about him) are preserved in a collection of desert monastic wisdom known as the *Apophthegmata patrum* ("The sayings of the fathers"). It was felt that those who lived close to God must speak with divine inspiration, and the words of wisdom uttered by such revered senior ascetics were avidly sought, both by less experienced monks and by travelers. Sages such as Antony tended to cherish silence as a spiritual virtue and yielded their counsel with some reluctance, but their prized sayings were eagerly written down and circulated in various editions.

Athanasius portrays his hero as illiterate, but Antony did correspond with other monks, Christians, and political figures. A handful of his letters survive in various fragmentary states and translations, though they were never as influential as Athanasius's *Life* or the sayings in the *Apophthegmata*. Antony's spirituality concentrated on the need to discern the seductive dangers of demonic forces—represented particularly by natural emotions such as fear, anger, and carnal desire—and to triumph over them by claiming the power of Christ in prayer and contemplation.

Anchorite Monasticism

Antony's influence as an exemplar of monasticism was enormous. Although Athanasius presents him as living in cooperation with the organized church's leaders, in practice Antony became synonymous with the principle of *anachoresis*, "withdrawal" or "retreat." Those who followed such a pattern were known as "anchorites." Antony was by no means the pioneer of the practice; there were thousands of other monks in the Egyptian desert living similar lives. In early-fifth-century texts such as the *Lausiac History* of Palladius (an educated Christian leader from Asia Minor who had visited various Egyptian monks in the late fourth century)[11] or the anonymous *History of the Monks of Egypt*, we can sense the sheer scale and the diversity of asceticism in the region.

Ordinarily many of the monks sought to follow a solitary existence, living in cells or isolated places, and giving themselves to a life of physical self-denial, continual repetitive prayer, and the recitation (rather than formal study) of Scripture. The need for food or sleep was often seen as a capitulation to the flesh and a distraction from spiritual duty, and prolonged deprivation induced hallucinations and trances in which "demons" such as seductive women might appear to test the resolution of the ascetic.

But not all anchorites were solitaries in a strict sense. Many of the monks of Lower Egypt, especially around the sites of Nitria, Kellia (literally "the cells"), and Scetis, adopted various forms of loose social organization, gathering around spiritual elders or meeting together sporadically for mutual encouragement. In some cases they had buildings and a church, and they would engage in shared industry or commercial activity in order to support themselves, on the grounds that if their physical needs were met they were better able to devote themselves to their spiritual vocation. Prominent figures in such circles included Amoun, Pambo, Macarius the Great, and another Macarius, of Alexandria.

Within the orbit of such teachers significant numbers of disciples gathered; they might live for the most part in their cells but come together from time to time for fellowship and to listen to the wisdom of their saintly mentor. Not all such devotees were men. Just as there were groups of female ascetics in the cities of Egypt, such as those to whom Antony entrusted his sister, so there were women anchorites, or "anchoresses," too. The sayings of a number of "desert mothers" (Ammas)—women such as Theodora and Sarah—as well as "desert fathers" (Abbas) are preserved in the *Apophthegmata* and in Palladius's *History*.

At Kellia, a highly educated former member of the Constantinopolitan church and convert to the ascetic life, Evagrius of Pontus (346–399), provided monasticism with a sophisticated exposition of spiritual teaching. Evagrius was able to link the influences of his background in the developed theology of Cappadocia and Constantinople with the practical piety of the desert, which he imbibed especially from Macarius the Great, and he was the first Christian monk to produce a significant amount of written work.

Heavily influenced by Origen, Evagrius analyzed the eight evil passions or "demons" that bedevil the would-be ascetic: gluttony, lust, avarice, dejection, anger, indifference or listlessness (*accidie*), vainglory, and pride. He believed these forces were apportioned around different compartments of the soul (according to a Platonist scheme of psychology) and could only be overcome by a process of spiritual contemplation, which advanced ultimately to the practice of "pure" or wordless prayer. In such an exalted state, he taught, the mind is free from any physical images of God that evil powers might instill. The perfect realization of self-denial was attainment of *apatheia*, "passionlessness." Such a condition had been advocated by Stoic philosophy as the state in which there is a proper apprehension of the nature of the world; Evagrius, however, saw it as a serenity and purity of heart that renders possible the exercise of truly spiritual love for God, untainted by earthly images.

When fierce controversy broke out in the last years of the fourth century about the validity of Origen's teaching (see pp. 151–53), Evagrius's ideas also became suspect to some, and sharp divisions occurred in Egypt (and Palestine) between those ascetics who favored Origenism and those who did not. But Evagrius's practical counsel on the spiritual life in the end survived the fray, and his work had great influence in Greek[12] and especially Syrian asceticism in the East. Through a visitor to Nitria, John Cassian (see pp. 150–51), it also traveled early to the West. Evagrius's impact on the monastic movement, both direct and indirect, was considerable, and in his explorations of spirituality and prayer an ascetic theology produced in Egypt had important consequences for the churches at large.

Pachomius: Coenobitic Monasticism

Not all Egyptian monasticism followed the anchorite pattern. Farther south, at Tabennisi in the Thebaid, another kind of ascetic existence was pioneered by Pachomius (ca. 290–346). Pachomius was a pagan convert to Christianity who had spent some years as an anchorite, attached to an ascetic teacher called Palamon, before becoming convinced that he was called to develop a different form of monastic life. He attempted to establish a system in which ascetics would live together rather than in isolation.

Initially, Pachomius seems to have met with little success, for there were some who sought to take advantage of his instinct to lead by example and who pursued their own interests; he soon discovered that it was not possible for his plan to work without a system of common rules that would ensure genuine unity among his monks. He set up a *coenobium* or "community" (he considered it a "fellowship," or *koinonia*) bound by a commitment to common ownership and rights, after the pattern of the early church fellowship described in Acts 2:42–47 (cf. also Acts 4:32–35). There was a strict code of discipline (Pachomius was a former soldier), presided over by a teaching superior. With this structure, the concept proved highly attractive, and within Pachomius's lifetime the community at Tabennisi numbered well over one thousand monks, with several thousand others spread around similar monasteries elsewhere in Egypt.

The lifestyle adopted by these ascetics was serious, but not nearly as severe as that of some of the anchorites. Compared with the rigors of many monastics, indeed, their regime was fairly liberal. They had beds to sleep on and regular, if frugal, meals. The monks lived together in small groups of cells or houses, and tasks such as cooking and laundry were shared among them. Though their lives were centered on twice-daily communal worship, the inmates also engaged in various handicrafts or trades and offered charity to the sick and to travelers. They nevertheless lived behind walls that symbolized their distinction from the world, and no one was allowed to join the community without rigorous prior assessment.[13] Pachomius's coenobitic model drew women as well as men, and separate communities were established for women in many areas. At one of the women's houses, Pachomius's sister, Mary, was in charge. Syncletica, the daughter of a prominent Alexandrian family, founded a community for women on the outskirts of her city and is celebrated in an anonymous fifth-century *Life*, reminiscent of Athanasius's portrait of Antony.

Palestine: Monasteries and *Lavrae*

In Palestine monasticism tended to grow in association with the holy sites, which were such powerful magnets for pilgrims in the fourth century (see pp. 21–22). In the early 380s an aristocratic lady from the Atlantic coast of Spain or Gaul wrote a diary of her travels in the East, which took in Egypt, Palestine, Edessa, and Asia Minor. Her name is given as Egeria, and she was perhaps a nun. Written in colloquial Latin, her work makes for compelling reading for a variety of reasons, not least for its detailed descriptions of Eastern Christian liturgy in the period; it is also notable for its testimony to the extent of monasticism.[14] Egeria's descriptions of holy places include references to monks at almost every site of pilgrimage from Sinai to Galilee. As we should expect, Jerusalem itself was the most important center, where ascetic communities grew up from Greek, Coptic, Georgian, and Armenian backgrounds. Often these communities included hostels for visiting pilgrims.

On the Mount of Olives, a community of ascetics was established in the later 370s by a wealthy Roman lady named Melania (ca. 342–410), who took up the spiritual life after being widowed at an early age. She was joined in Jerusalem by the young Rufinus of Aquileia (see p. 130), another educated convert to monasticism, who had met her in Egypt while on his own travels to visit the desert monks. Melania and the consecrated virgins who lived with her engaged in works of charity, providing hospitality for visitors and caring for the sick. In addition, Melania proved a devoted student of the Scriptures and of Christian authors, especially Origen. Towards the end of the fourth century she returned to Italy for a number of years (Rufinus had already gone back, following the outbreak of controversy concerning Origen's writings), but she was in Jerusalem once again in the last days of her life.

In Bethlehem, Melania's example was followed by the rich Roman widow, Paula, who financed Jerome's establishment of a male community and started an adjacent female community of her own, next to the reputed cave of the nativity (see p. 129). Even before their arrival, though, there was already a Greek *coenobium* in Bethlehem. The monasteries of Melania, Rufinus, Paula, and Jerome were centers of scholarly activity. Jerome and his disciples proved immensely dedicated students and copiers of texts, who not only wrote extensively but built up significant libraries and preserved important Christian literature in a volatile world in which documents were all too easily lost or destroyed in the midst of political upheavals. Rufinus was a historian of the church and of monasticism, an enthusiastic—if rather free—translator of Greek writers, and author of other works on the faith, including commentaries on Scripture and on the Apostles' Creed.

Melania's concern for self-denial, study, and charity was taken still further by her granddaughter, Melania the Younger (ca. 385–439). After two failed attempts to produce the progeny longed for by her family, at the age of twenty the younger Melania persuaded her rich husband, Pinianus, to live with her in celibacy as a brother rather than a husband. They abandoned their home in Rome and traveled in North Africa and Egypt, disbursing their enormous wealth as they went, before finally settling in Palestine. Their disposal of their property, which included vast estates in Western Europe and North Africa, outraged their families, and their determination to renounce their riches in the face of strong opposition testifies to the intensity of their convictions. After Pinianus's death, Melania founded another monastery on the Mount of Olives.[15]

In the Judean desert, a large number of male communities of ascetics developed over the course of the fourth to the sixth centuries, and again most of the pioneering figures came originally as pilgrims. The first prominent settler was Chariton, a native of Asia Minor who initiated a series of monastic settlements in the 320s or 330s. Chariton and his peers developed a distinctive form of asceticism: that of the *lavra*. The oldest form of *lavra* consisted of a central complex made up of a church and other buildings, such as a refectory, with individual cells scattered around at a distance. The cells were typically situated at intervals of about thirty-five meters from one another. The Greek *lavra* means "lane," and its usage for such settlements may derive from the fact that the cells were generally located on a path or ridge along the side of a ravine. The monks spent most of the time alone in their cells but came together for common prayers and meals. Their lifestyle was something in between the common life of the *coenobium* and the isolated existence of the desert hermits.

Judean desert asceticism was further expanded by the monks Euthymius (377–473) and his disciple Sabas (439–532), whose lives were described in detail by another monk who had experienced their regimes, Cyril, a native of Scythopolis (ca. 525–558).[16] Euthymius proposed the ethos of the *lavra* as the life to which the ascetic ought to aspire, but he conceded that the *coenobium* was an appropriate starting place for the would-be devotee. The fifth and sixth centuries saw the Palestinian monks drawn into a range of political and doctrinal disputes, not least the lingering differences over Origen's theology, and there were some sharp divisions between them. The monasteries of the desert declined in the Persian and Arab invasions of the seventh century.

Cappadocia: The Teaching of Basil

In Cappadocia the ascetic movement was shaped by a convergence of Greek theological ideas and Syrian monastic influences. As we noted in chapter 3 (see p. 84), Macrina, the sister of Basil and Gregory of Nyssa, persuaded her mother to set up a family ascetic commune on their estate near Caesarea in the late 350s, and her brother Naucratius lived there as a kind of hermit. By the time Macrina died in 380 there was a monastery for both men and women on the estate, and an important tradition of domestic asceticism pioneered by women was flourishing. Basil was directly influenced by this family context and also by his experiences of monasticism elsewhere.

Basil was friendly for a time with Eustathius, who became bishop of Sebaste in Pontus and promoted the establishment of a number of ascetic communities not far to the east of Cappadocia, and he shared Eustathius's enthusiasm for the ascetic life (though they came to disagree strongly about the status of the Holy Spirit; see p. 88). After traveling to holy sites in Syria, Mesopotamia, Palestine, and Egypt, Basil lived for a time with a few friends as a small monastic group on a picturesque family estate by the river Iris in Pontus where he wrote his first ascetic treatise, the *Moral Rules* (ca. 358–359), a collection of eighty principles supported by quotations from Scripture.

By the middle of the fourth century, significant tensions had begun to emerge between the increasing strength of ascetic groups and the regular life of the churches. Monasticism could attract dropouts from society, criminals on the run, and rebels with diverse economic or so-cial causes, and its practices could in various ways challenge the social, spiritual, and economic order of mainstream Christian existence. There was considerable polemic from clergy against those who wandered from place to place as mendicant ascetics without ever settling down to the challenge of living within the routines and disciplines of the of-ficial church. Athanasius's *Life of Antony* purposely presents its hero, by contrast, as a devotee of doctrinal conformity and as no rebel against the episcopate. By contrast, controversial groups such as the Messalians in the 380s and 390s were accused of neglecting the sacraments of the church in pursuit of their own spiritual fulfillment. Even when eremitic ascetics were thoroughly orthodox in their beliefs, they located their ideals somewhere other than in a regular liturgical system.

When Eustathius became bishop of Sebaste in 357, he sought to play down the distinction between the structures of monasticism and those directly under episcopal sway. The monks were given charitable duties to perform on behalf of the whole church.[17] Eustathius's approach was taken further by Basil when he became bishop of Caesarea in 370. Basil set about bringing the local monks directly under the control of the institutional church, and he criticized the extreme lengths to which some individuals were prepared to go in pursuit of a reputation for holiness. He thought such behavior gave asceticism a bad name and compromised the gospel imperative that bound every believer to love his or her neighbor as himself or herself. Basil prescribed a system of order in which asceticism was part of the organized life of the church and under episcopal authority.

Basil's *Asketikon*,[18] which went through various different editions, set out in question-and-answer form the principles upon which appropriate ascetic spirituality was to be based. Monks were not to meet for worship except under the authority of the bishop, and they were to shun individualistic displays of piety. The anchorite pattern was a failure to serve the world; holiness undoubtedly entailed the freeing of the spirit from the entanglements of the secular realm, but this must not mean a selfish neglect of the needs of the very society that the gospel was meant to reach. Nor were the gifts of the Spirit to be sought at the expense of the sacramental life of the church.

The upshot of Basil's teaching was twofold. First, and most obvious, the bishop was set firmly in control of monastic activity and was able to determine the ways in which the vocation to renounce the world was expressed in practice. Extreme fasting or ostentatious self-flagellation were not to be tolerated, and obedience to the bishop was all-important. Second, however, the influences of an ascetic Christianity were simultaneously incorporated into the larger life of the church. Basil's church included a hospital in which monks provided medical care, and set times of prayer and monastic choirs became more prominent in the regular liturgy. The work of relief for the poor and educational projects was also typically led by monks.

Scholars continue to debate which of these two principles—episcopal power or monastic assimilation—was in the end more important for the history of asceticism. Did the kind of rule proposed by Basil lend a necessary order to an otherwise fragmenting and individual-izing force, or did it minimize the distinctiveness of the ascetic life by co-opting it into the control of the episcopate? Did the assumption of ascetic spirituality bring a richness to the mainstream of the church's existence, or did it dampen the appeal of a quest for otherworldli-ness? The truth, perhaps, lies somewhere in the middle, but there is little doubt that monasticism in general was deeply affected by this late-fourth- and early-fifth-century drive to organization and sociality rather than spontaneity and individualism.

If monasticism was to represent an alternative way of life, it was to do so much more often within the parameters of episcopal catholicism than outside of them. Sometimes the consequences were positive, and the ascetic values injected an invigorating strain into the spiritual life of the church. In other cases, the results were much more ambiguous: in several parts of Egypt, Syria, and Asia Minor in the fourth and fifth centuries, bands of monks were variously mobilized as vigilantes, hired muscle in ecclesiastical disputes, protectors of refugee bishops (such as Athanasius), and destroyers of pagan shrines.

The Western Context

In the West, ascetic ideals were promoted in the churches of north-ern Italy by clergymen such as Eusebius, bishop of Vercelli from 340 to 371, who had visited Eastern monasteries while in exile from 355 to 362 and who established a monastery for himself and his clergy. In Milan, too, there was in Ambrose's time a monastery outside the city walls, presided over by a presbyter and subject to episcopal oversight. Female asceticism was prominently advocated by Ambrose, as we have seen (pp. 104–5). Ambrose was also a staunch enthusiast for clerical celibacy, and he insisted that his officials were either unmarried or else lived in continence with their wives if they had married prior to ordina-tion. In the rhetoric of Ambrose or of Jerome, whose vision was in this area very similar (see pp. 127–28), the renunciation of sexual activity and the prizing of virginity were the way to a serenity in which the flesh was held in subjection to the higher life of the spirit.

As Jerome discovered, the rigorous pursuit of such principles, espe-cially when combined with criticism of the comfortable lives of other Christians, could precipitate opposition and trouble just as much as admiration, and in the late fourth and early fifth centuries there were plenty of people both inside and outside the churches who thought of ascetics as mistaken extremists. Asceticism may often have provided an outlet for well-intentioned piety and provided, at least in its communal forms, a certain kind of fellowship and shared commitment for otherwise lonely individuals, but it also divided churches by presenting certain believers as more spiritual than others. Its effects were apparent at a wider level as well, for it could seriously disrupt social patterns, liberating women in particular from conventional roles or encouraging people to give away inherited family wealth. There is plenty of evidence that churchmen who promoted such expressions of devotion ran into serious hostility from the relatives of those who were moved to take their advice.

Nevertheless, monasticism was very well entrenched in the life of the Western churches. A number of monasteries existed in Rome in the late fourth century, and there was a strong interest in Eastern ideas and in reading Latin translations of works such as the *Life of Antony*. In North Africa, ascetic principles would be cherished and advocated by Augustine, to whom we shall turn in more detail in the next chapter. Augustine was himself affected by Eastern influences, though he also incorporated emphases of his own into his instructions on monasticism.

Paulinus of Nola

One of the most striking exemplars of asceticism in Italy in the late fourth and early fifth centuries was Paulinus (ca. 353–431), who became bishop of Nola in Campania, south of Rome. Born in Bordeaux, Paulinus was an aristocrat, a highly educated man with enormous wealth and landholdings and a former provincial governor of Campania. His Spanish wife, Therasia, was also wealthy. The couple's only child died in 389, and thereafter they began to divest themselves of their vast riches and pursue a joint calling to a consecrated Christian life. They were inspired by both Western and Eastern ascetic influences but also, in part, by a desire to escape a volatile political climate in Paulinus's sphere of duty as a public figure. Paulinus was ordained as a priest, and he and Therasia then returned to Nola in Campania, near the shrine of a popular saint, Felix, where they established a double monastery for men and women. He was consecrated bishop of Nola around 410, probably after the death of Therasia.

The regime in Paulinus's monastery seems to have been simple but by no means extreme. Both men and women adopted a distinctive style of dress, with trimmed hair for the men and veils for the women.[19] But

Paulinus retained sufficient wealth to finance the construction of an impressive church and a guesthouse/infirmary; he continued to have a staff of servants; and, while he endeavored to show restraint in diet, he kept up a cellar of good wine, had a very well-stocked library, and was free to travel regularly to Rome to visit his senatorial friends. Paulinus corresponded with a wide range of Christian and non-Christian peers, and he wrote urbane poetry that married biblical themes and the celebration of Christian saints with the styles and meters of classical Latin verse. The qualities of his writing continue to attract significant scholarly attention today. As an ascetic, he succeeded in combining the pursuit of piety and retreat from the world with the ideal life of a traditional gentleman scholar.

Martin of Tours

One of the figures who had influenced Paulinus in Gaul was Martin, bishop of Tours (ca. 315–397). Martin's life was rather different from Paulinus's. His character is described in hagiographical terms in a famous biography by one of his disciples, another gentleman scholar and friend of Paulinus named Sulpicius Severus (ca. 360–420).[20]

Born into a military family in Pannonia (on the border between modern-day Austria and Hungary) and brought up near Milan, Martin pursued a career in the imperial army. He was converted to Christianity and at some later date is reported to have had an encounter with a beggar to whom he gave half of his cloak. The beggar is said to have subsequently appeared to him in a vision as Christ, clothed in the fragment of his cloak, and Martin was inspired to abandon his military career and devote himself to a life of poverty. After a period of travels, around 360 he founded a hermitage at a place called Ligugé near Poitiers (he had earlier come to associate with Bishop Hilary). He attracted a group of disciples, who lived with him in a loosely organized commune. Having built up a reputation as a spiritual figure of remarkable depth, Martin was at length chosen, around 371, to become the bishop of Tours.

Martin had strong local support as bishop, but his open devotion to poverty and his inattention to his personal appearance were controversial among many of the prosperous bishops in Gaul and Spain. He established a further monastic community at Marmoutier, to the northeast of Tours. Its principles were similar to those followed at Ligugé, though the structure was tighter. From this base Martin engaged in active evangelism in the Loire and Seine Valleys, where there was still a strong attachment to paganism, and his methods are said to have included various miracles, healings, and spiritual signs. He experienced much success in his missionary work, building churches and other monasteries on the sites of former pagan shrines, and his endeavors played a major part in the spread of Christianity into the Gaulish countryside.

Sulpicius Severus presents Martin as the archetypal "holy man," whose sanctity and spiritual powers were in a class of their own. Although he was never called upon to lay down his life for his faith, Martin came to serve as one of the most renowned of all Western saints, and a flourishing cult in his honor grew up in Gaul.

John Cassian

Martin's version of asceticism may well have developed in relative independence of Eastern or Egyptian models. The same was not true in the other great center of monasticism in Gaul—Provence. Lérins, a small, rocky island off the coast near Cannes, was the base for a community organized by Honoratus (ca. 365–430), a former Gallic aristocrat who had experienced asceticism in the East and in Egypt. Honoratus's monastery drew a large number of converts and came to have a considerable influence throughout southern Gaul. Many of its monks went on to become bishops, and they in turn established monastic foundations in their dioceses.

Honoratus himself became bishop of Arles in his last years. While he was still in charge at Lérins, however, a monk named John Cassian arrived in Marseilles. Cassian was of Scythian origin, and he had become a monk at Bethlehem. He had traveled widely in Egypt, where he had been deeply impressed at Nitria by the teaching of Evagrius of Pontus but also by the methods bequeathed by Pachomius. At the height of the Origenist controversy, Cassian was forced to leave Egypt and move to Constantinople, where he spent a few years before heading west via Rome, finally settling at Marseilles.

Cassian sought to apply the values and practices of Egyptian monasticism to the situation of the West, and he organized communities at Marseilles for both men and women modeled on these principles. In his *Institutes*, he set out a detailed vision of the monastic life as an orderly rhythm of daily devotion and battle against the forces of the world and the flesh. His paradigm shows clear Pachomian influence. Cassian is concerned to present a system of community life that offers the most practicable option for those who desire to devote their lives entirely to

God but who are not sufficiently strong to be able to match the achievements of "the perfect" who can live alone in the desert. The solitary life continues to be seen as the ultimate ideal, but it is recognized that this ideal is not a possibility for all who would renounce the world.

In a work entitled *Conferences*, written in the later 420s, Cassian offered extensive spiritual teaching on the habits of the heart that the practical ascetic needed to cultivate. The text is presented as a series of discussions with desert fathers, and there is a great deal of Evagrian counsel on the avoidance of the eight chief sins and the quest for detachment from such corruption. Cassian's vision is, however, more directly biblical in tone: his ideal is not the Stoic-sounding *apatheia*, "passionlessness," but the expressly scriptural image of purity of heart (cf. Ps. 24:4; Matt. 5:8; 1 Tim. 1:5; 2 Tim. 2:22; 1 Pet. 1:22).

Cassian got himself embroiled in controversy for challenging aspects of the moral theology of Augustine (see pp. 187–88), and this cast something of a shadow over his reputation in some quarters. In Western tradition he has never been officially canonized as a saint. Nevertheless, his teaching on monasticism exercised a very great influence in the West. He conveyed some important aspects of the spirituality of the desert, but overall he brought to Western asceticism something akin to the order and discipline that Basil had promoted in Asia, and he shunned the charismatic sensationalism that attended some of the holy men in Gaul, especially Martin. Rather than being preoccupied with outward displays, Cassian concentrated on the interiority of spiritual devotion and the organization of a simple and unostentatious pattern of self-denial. His ideas proved deeply formative for the monasticism of Benedict of Nursia in the sixth century, as we shall see in chapter 12 (see pp. 322–24).[21]

The Origenist Controversy

Running through various stages in our account of Eastern monasticism has been reference to a major dispute of the later fourth and early fifth centuries concerning the orthodoxy of the writings of Origen. This dispute not only affected the ascetic movement; it also bedeviled relations between some of the major churches and involved some tragic elements in Christian behavior. Its divisive ramifications underscored the complexity of the relationship between theology, politics, and spirituality in this age and exposed the severe tensions that could exist between the interests of ecclesiastical and political power and the investments of ascetic faith.

The teaching of Origen was controversial in his own lifetime,[22] and it had been the subject of debate ever after. Defenses of his doctrine had been written by enthusiasts such as Gregory *Thaumatourgos*, Pamphilus, and Eusebius of Caesarea, and his works were still widely read and appreciated,[23] but suspicions and allegations lingered. In the mid-370s a vicious attack was launched by Epiphanius, bishop of Salamis in Cyprus (ca. 315–403), who was a determined campaigner against all kinds of heresies.[24] Origen was accused not only of teaching the preexistence of souls and the ultimate salvation of Satan but of interpreting the literal truth of Scripture in a spiritual fashion and thus, in particular, denying the doctrine of the resurrection of the flesh. There were undoubtedly grounds for a number of these criticisms in Origen's writings, and in themselves they were not new. What made Epiphanius's polemic especially significant was his reference to the influence of Origen among "certain Egyptian monks." Epiphanius had put his finger, quite deliberately, on a dispute that was emerging in Egyptian monasticism.

At Nitria and Kellia there was a group of four monks known as the "Tall Brothers," the most influential of whom was Ammonius, who all were strongly committed to Origen's teaching. It was to these circles that Evagrius of Pontus came when he arrived in Egypt, and through his work Origen's ideas were further popularized in the spiritual traditions of desert asceticism. Following in the line of Origen's Platonist conception of God as quintessentially spiritual and rational, Evagrius taught that the praying soul must transcend mental images of God as a being with physical form. To those who saw the incarnation as challenging this with its testimony that God had taken flesh, the Evagrian advocacy of "pure" or "imageless" prayer was a violation of the truth of the gospel of Christ. A quarrel arose between the "Anthropomorphites," who affirmed the relevance of the human shape of God in Christ for the practice of Christian devotion, and the "Origenists," who denied it. Sharp divisions emerged between the monks at Nitria, who favored the Evagrian line, and those at Scetis and elsewhere, who did not.

By this time, however, the dispute had spread much more widely, chiefly through the activities of Epiphanius. In 393–394, Epiphanius had visited Palestine, where he had provocatively preached against Origen's teaching, despite the fact that the bishop of Jerusalem, John, was a supporter of his ideas. He also persuaded Jerome, the former translator and admirer of Origen, that Origen's doctrine was erroneous, and Jerome turned into a bitter and tendentious opponent of Origen.

Jerome's erstwhile friend and fellow monk, Rufinus, remained loyal to Origen, and the ensuing years witnessed a vexatious dispute between the two former allies, fueled above all by Jerome's fury and abetted by his contacts in Rome (see p. 130).

In Egypt the Origenists initially enjoyed the support of the Alexandrian episcopate under Bishop Timothy (381–385) and his successor, Theophilus (385–412). Around late 399, however, Theophilus was confronted with a mass protest from Anthropomorphite monks, and he recognized that the majority in Egypt were on the anti-Origenist side. He abruptly switched his allegiance, and in 400 Origenism was condemned in Alexandria. By this time Evagrius was dead, but over the following years the monasteries of his supporters were sacked and the Tall Brothers and others (including the young John Cassian) were forced to flee abroad. Despite the efforts of Rufinus's associates to exonerate Origen in the West, the writings of Jerome and the overtures of Theophilus had persuaded the bishop of Rome, Anastasius, to issue a condemnation of "everything written in former days by Origen that is contrary to our faith."[25] Anastasius had stopped short of condemning Origen personally, but the censure of at least aspects of his teaching was significant. The rejection of Origenism was also officially upheld in Palestine and Syria.

Constantinople: John Chrysostom

The Tall Brothers made their way to Constantinople, where they put their side of the story to the imperial court, and in particular to the local bishop, John. John, later named *Chrysostomos*, "Golden-mouth," because of his abilities as a preacher, and hence traditionally known as "John Chrysostom," is one of the most significant figures in the story of the early church, but his career came to be fatally blighted by the machinations surrounding the Origenist controversy.

John was born in Antioch in the late 340s to a prosperous family, the son of a high-ranking official, and was well educated in philosophy and rhetoric under the renowned pagan teacher Libanius, whose lectures had also been attended by the young emperor Julian. After receiving baptism as a Christian, John began to study theology and asceticism. Drawn to a more extreme form of self-denial, he withdrew into the mountains outside Antioch, where he lived for four years with an elderly hermit and then for two years in more or less solitary confinement in a cave. His regime was so strict that he damaged his health (he suffered from a weak stomach

John Chrysostom. Illustration from
André Thevet, *Les Vrais Portraits et
Vies des Hommes Illustres* (Paris,
1584), Special Collections Library,
University of Michigan. Used by
permission.

ever after), and he returned for
a time to a secular career in
the civil service before being
ordained at Antioch as a deacon in 381 and then as a priest
in 386. He served the church
of Antioch for the next eleven
years, during which he built up
a reputation as an outstanding
preacher and teacher.

One of John's most fa-
mous series of homilies was
preached in 387, when the city mob of Antioch had rioted and destroyed
statues of the emperor Theodosius and his wife, and there was a threat
that there would be brutal retribution. John's preaching combined rebuke
for the violence of the crowd with reassurance of the fearful at a time of
crisis. A very large number of his sermons survive (almost a thousand in
all), recorded by stenographers, and although the chronology of many
of them is very hard to ascertain it is possible that a significant proportion of the extant texts stem from his years in Antioch. His preaching
presents a fascinating mixture of biblical exposition, attacks on heresy,[26]
exhortations to asceticism, and condemnations of contemporary mores,
not least the corruption of the rich and their neglect of the needy. In
397 Bishop Nectarius of Constantinople died, and after some dispute
surrounding the choice of a successor, John's name was put forward;
against his will, John was brought to Constantinople and installed as
bishop the following year.

John's attitude to the Origenist affair was complicated by a number
of factors. He had himself been trained in biblical exegesis by Diodore,
bishop of Tarsus (see pp. 196–97), who was an advocate of a literal interpretation of Scripture as opposed to the search for spiritual meaning
idealized by Origen, and although John's preaching does show some interest in allegorical and typological exegesis his preference on the whole
was for a straightforward historical reading of the biblical text. For all
his background in asceticism and his strong denunciation of Christian

compromises with the world, John was not especially enamored of the Evagrian elevation of a spirituality that transcended earthly realities. He was on good terms with monks who revered Origen's teaching, certainly, but he was not himself a partisan of the Origenist approach. His theology was self-consciously orthodox on the equality of the divine persons and the grace of Christ as Savior, and he had little or no interest in the speculative flights to which the Origenist tradition was prone.

Matters were further entangled by relations between Constantinople and Alexandria. Alexandria as well as Rome had resented the judgment of the Council of Constantinople in 381 that Constantinople possessed ecclesiastical precedence second only to Rome's, and when Nectarius had died, Theophilus of Alexandria had attempted to install his own candidate, a priest named Isidore, as Constantinople's new bishop in a bid to gain leverage over the see. In this Theophilus had failed, but he had managed to maintain reasonable relations with the new incumbent, John. If John now decided to sympathize with the Tall Brothers, this mood was bound to change. John was indeed impressed by the piety and sincerity of the Egyptian monks, and he offered them hospitality. The court decided meanwhile that there were charges to answer, and Theophilus was summoned from Alexandria.

For Theophilus, though, there were other forces at work. Since taking office as bishop, John had made a great many enemies in Constantinople. He had set about the moral reformation of his church, which under his easygoing predecessor had become very lax in its standards. His clerical order had been purged of unworthy candidates, and his congregations had been subjected to sharp denunciations of the shortcomings of those in positions of responsibility. John had annoyed members of his clergy by his condemnations of their financial greed, and he had offended visiting churchmen by his habit of dining frugally and alone, or offering only modest hospitality and support to those who sought his favor. Rumors abounded that he indulged in fine food and wine in secret, and though there was no evidence for such smears they did little to help his image. John had also annoyed the rich by his repeated condemnation of their luxurious living and neglect of the poor and by his claims that private property was a result of the fall; real wealth, he insisted, was to be found in sharing and in charity, not in hoarding one's treasures or engaging in obnoxious displays of personal affluence.

John had taken an angular and naïve approach to the reform of his church; tact was not his strong point, and although his outspoken manner had won him much support among ordinary people, he was resented in high places and among many in the prosperous elite of his city. He had interfered in ecclesiastical affairs outside his jurisdiction, and in 401 he had six Asian bishops deposed for "simony," or bribing their way into office (so named after the example of Simon Magus in Acts 8:18–24, who sought to obtain the gift of the Holy Spirit with money). This move did nothing for his reputation farther afield. He had also upset the empress Eudoxia, and it was she rather than her husband, Arcadius, who exercised the real power of the imperial throne. Eudoxia's relationship with John wavered between fearful respect and dangerous resentment; she had called upon him to baptize her only son, the future Theodosius II, and had made use of the bishop's authority for her own ends on a number of occasions. However, John had caused offense with his insinuations that she was complicit in a palace murder and with his thinly veiled reference to her as "Jezebel" for her seizure of a piece of property without consent (cf. 1 Kings 21).

When Theophilus arrived in Constantinople in the summer of 403, he was determined to exploit this ill-will to the full and to challenge John directly as a heretic. He had already tried to use Epiphanius to stir up charges of Origenism against John, and although this endeavor had not succeeded it had exposed the degree of opposition to John that existed in Constantinople and elsewhere. Having galvanized these forces by various underhand means, Theophilus decided to hold a synod of his own just across the Bosphorus at a villa on a country estate known as "the Oak," which was owned by a former official of Theodosius. This "Synod of the Oak" consisted of a number of Egyptian bishops and a group of John's opponents, and John was summoned to appear before them. When he refused, a sentence of deposition was pronounced against him. The existing resentment of John at court had only been intensified by his avoidance of the synod, and it was not surprising that the verdict was upheld by the emperor: John was ordered to go into exile.

John commanded significant support at a popular level, and in Constantinople there was a mass protest against his removal. Within hours he was able to return in triumph. Nevertheless, it was only a short time before his blunt speaking got him into trouble again. Once more he offended Eudoxia, comparing her this time to Herodias, the instigator of the execution of John the Baptist (Matt. 14:1–12; Mark 6:14–29). In June 404 he was exiled a second time, and on this occasion the order was enforced: he was sent to Cucusus in Armenia.

From there, sustained by the generosity of an aristocratic lady named Olympias who had established a monastery next to his church in Constantinople and with whom he was especially close, John kept up a correspondence with a wide network of supporters and appealed to a number of Western bishops for assistance. Many of his flock also traveled from Constantinople to see him. The government snubbed overtures from Rome and elsewhere, determined that John needed to be kept away from his see. It was decided that he should be moved to more remote quarters where he would not be so easily reached by his friends. In the heat of the summer of 407 he was taken on a dreadful expedition, on foot, to a more isolated place of custody on the eastern shore of the Black Sea. As the authorities almost certainly intended, the dreadful journey proved too much for him, and John died on the way through Pontus on 14 September 407.

Some of the reasons for the tragic end to John's career undoubtedly lay at his own door. No doubt if he had acted more judiciously and tempered his language he might have retained support not just from the crowd but also from the source that mattered most in strategic terms: the imperial court. John was a gifted preacher, biblical interpreter, and pastor of his church, whose impact upon the cosmopolitan world of the imperial capital was immense, but his inability to restrain the tongue in his "golden" mouth was his major undoing. Nevertheless, in terms of larger ecclesiastical affairs, it was primarily the dispute over Origenism that had precipitated his downfall. Had he taken a different stance with regard to the overtures of the Tall Brothers and the behavior of Theophilus, his fate would surely have been very different. John was not himself an Origenist, and it was a cruel twist that it was Origenism that had given his enemies their opportunity to get rid of him.

Theophilus's role in engineering much of John's trouble had obviously shown the Alexandrian bishop in a very bad light, and the years following John's death witnessed broken relations between Constantinople and Alexandria. There were also serious tensions with Rome, for Innocent, bishop of Rome (402–417), resolutely refused to recognize John's former enemies and badgered the new bishop of Constantinople, Atticus, to rehabilitate John's honor. There were few signs that Atticus was willing to comply, and for many years a large congregation of dissidents in Constantinople met independently of Atticus's church, backed by Rome. Healing only came in the late 420s, several years after Innocent's death, when a different bishop of Constantinople, Nestorius, persuaded a different bishop of Alexandria, Cyril—the nephew of Theophilus and at first an implacable resister of such pressure—to recognize that John was a worthy saint of the Constantinopolitan church. Only then did John's iconic status for subsequent Eastern Christianity gather pace.

Later Origenism and the Ascetic Movement

The fierce arguments surrounding Origenism did not go away with the demise of John Chrysostom. They continued to divide Egyptian and Palestinian monasticism as late as the sixth century, and they flared up with particular intensity in the 530s and 540s in Palestine. Whatever legitimate misgivings many Christians had about the orthodoxy of significant areas of Origen's doctrine, his influence came to dominate major swaths of both Eastern and Western asceticism for generations. Origenism was condemned on several occasions, especially at a council in Constantinople in 543 and at another, which came to be regarded as an ecumenical council, held to settle other issues, in the city in 553 (see pp. 229–31). Origen would always be regarded as an unavoidably significant author, but his teachings would only enjoy heavily qualified approval.

From the fourth century to the sixth, the quarrels over Origenism were about much more than the theology or practice of asceticism, but at every stage they were nevertheless deeply embedded in debates over the teaching and function of monastic traditions, and they reflected some of the major differences of opinion that existed with regard to the power of regular church authorities versus the power of monks. Origen's ideas did not become controversial as a result of the expansion of asceticism, but the manner in which asceticism developed, and its perceived threat in some quarters to the structures of mainstream church life and the exercise of episcopal control, undoubtedly affected the course that the Origenist disputes had taken from the 370s onward.

6

AUGUSTINE OF HIPPO

▼

Introducing Augustine

In the small town of Thagaste in the eastern part of Numidia (the modern Souk-Ahras in Algeria) on 13 November 354, a son was born to a pagan father and a Christian mother. He was named Augustine. His father, Patrick, a modest landowner and town councillor, had high ambitions that his son should receive the benefits of a good Roman education and make something of himself; his mother, Monnica, was a devout Christian, eager that her son should grow up to know and love God. Both influences would prove formative, though the tensions between secular intellectual formation and the claims of the Christian gospel would engender a long and painful struggle. For most of Augustine's youth, the pull of the world was stronger than the pull of Christ, but in the end it was to Christ that he gave his heart. What followed was a life of service, thought, and action that would profoundly affect the subsequent history of Christianity in Western society.

By the time Augustine was born, those who professed Christian faith probably made up a slight majority of the population of the Roman Empire. Augustine came from a region that already had long and rich traditions of Christian faith and witness, and he spent some time outside Africa in cities that also possessed unmistakable importance in Christian terms. He lived in an age in which there were many remarkable Christian leaders, scholars, and thinkers. Yet it is fair to say that no other individual in the period we are considering in this book would exercise a comparable degree of influence on later Western theology. If we would understand the development of the churches in the West as a whole, not only in the later fourth and early fifth centuries but ever after, Augustine and his world—a world that also included some redoubtable opponents of his ideas—deserve to be studied in some detail.

Confessions

Our knowledge of Augustine's intellectual and spiritual pilgrimage is conditioned inescapably by his own description in the first nine books of his *Confessions*, a text that deserves to be placed alongside some of the greatest works in all European literature. Addressed in prayer form to God and saturated with biblical idiom, Augustine's treatise involves "confession" in two senses: not just the acknowledgment of sins, but also the expression of praise and thanksgiving after the fashion of the psalmist pouring out his heart to God as creator, sustainer, and deliverer. Written in the period 397–401, and thus from a vantage point of mature consideration, *Confessions* is intended partly as a personal story, partly as a spiritual meditation, partly as a moral example for intellectuals interested in following in its author's footsteps in the spiritual life, and partly as a defense against a growing number of critics.

The *Confessions* offers some remarkable glimpses into Augustine's psychology and some brilliant insights into the nature of the human spirit more generally, but it is not an autobiography in any straightforward sense of the word.[1] We should not allow Augustine's stylish eloquence and carefully crafted self-presentation to beguile us into imagining that his text offers an account of his life exactly as it unfolded, and historians need to explore Augustine's journey not just in the light of his description here but also with reference to a wider range of material. Nevertheless, such other evidence is in the end fairly limited, and Augustine's own version of his life, from infancy to adulthood, from intellectual darkness to the light of Christ, from moral bondage to the freedom of the gospel, remains the most elaborate picture we have of his spiritual formation.

Like many children of one or more Christian parents in this period, Augustine was not baptized in his youth, and although he was registered as a catechumen and subjected to Christian teaching, he felt no strong attachment to the church. In his teens the attractions of sensual adventures seemed far more real, and at the age of seventeen he followed a standard convention by taking a concubine (a woman of low social status, her name is never revealed to us) with whom he lived faithfully for a number of years and with whom he had a son, Adeodatus ("Given by God"). A reading of a (now lost) work of Cicero called *Hortensius*, which spoke of the virtues of philosophical enquiry, encouraged him to think seriously about moral issues, but as his literary studies advanced he found himself unimpressed with the Christian Scriptures, whose style seemed to him crude and unsophisticated by comparison with the great classics of Roman literature. Augustine had done well in his schooling, and with the help of a wealthy patron he was enabled to continue his education at Carthage. He went on to become the equivalent of a modern-day university teacher, lecturing in rhetoric in Carthage (376–383) and in Rome (383–384).

Dissatisfied with Christianity, he was drawn instead to the Manichees. Manichaeism (see pp. 114–16) seemed to offer him a way of life based upon reason rather than mere assent to church authority. It criticized the apparent crudity of the Hebrew Scriptures, with their stories of polygamous patriarchs and their anthropomorphic images of God, and offered some stylish and splendidly illustrated literary traditions of its own in their place. It endeavored to ascend beyond the corrupting influences of the material world while retaining an attractive focus on the importance of a communitarian pursuit of virtue. Augustine became a "Hearer" or lower-level adherent, and remained with the movement for almost a decade. However, he gradually became disillusioned with this attachment too. The Manichees' pretensions to possess truth turned out to be less rational than they had at first appeared, their asceticism was not all that it claimed to be, and their dualistic cosmology did not satisfactorily account for the complexity of evil in metaphysical terms. Augustine sought answers from an acclaimed Manichee teacher, Faustus, but though he was impressed by Faustus personally he found his learning to be superficial and his arguments inadequate. He slid into a state of radical skepticism and uncertainty, doubting everything.

This was Augustine's mood around the time when he took up the municipal chair of rhetoric in Milan in 384, which had been secured for him in part through the influence of prominent friends. The post was a prestigious one, which brought the former small-town North African boy very good prospects, including a serious chance of attaining to a provincial governorship and senatorial status. Nevertheless, according to his own version of things, he had no inner peace. His personal turmoil was deepened by his reluctant agreement to give up his concubine in the interests of his career. His mother, who had followed him to Italy, had ambitions that he should contract a "good" marriage. At her instigation, he painfully parted from his mistress and became engaged to a young heiress, though their union would never take place.

Augustine tells us that two factors affected his life considerably at this time. One was the reading of what he calls "some books of the Platonists, translated from Greek into Latin."[2] We do not know exactly what these texts were, but it is probable that he read Latin translations of Plotinus's *Enneads* and perhaps also some material by Plotinus's disciple and popularizer, Porphyry.[3] The mystical Neoplatonism of Plotinus was popular among a number of Milan's leading intellectuals, and for some of them it sat perfectly well alongside Christian beliefs. As a disaffected Manichee, Augustine assumed that the attainment of true knowledge was impossible, but the Plotinian approach taught that the human mind could transcend the physical world and its transient images to reach a realm of pure spirit beyond. This framework offered Augustine an escape not only from anthropomorphic religion but also from the materialism of the Manichees.[4] If the true nature of reality is spiritual and all that exists is graded according to its proximity to goodness, then evil, or that which has turned most completely from the good and moved most fully towards nonbeing, is fundamentally a negative—the absence or privation of the good. Augustine could see himself as a spiritual being whose task it was to pursue the knowledge of the reality that was at one and the same time the basis of his existence and that which transcended him.

The other development that changed Augustine's life was his encounter with the ministry of his local bishop, Ambrose. In Ambrose, Augustine met a Christian intellectual worthy of respect. The style-conscious professor was impressed first by the bishop's rhetorical eloquence but then also, increasingly, by the aura of learning that characterized Ambrose's preaching. Ambrose's sermons were invested with Neoplatonist images, and although there is no direct evidence that Augustine absorbed his Platonism from Ambrose in particular, it is obvious that Ambrose's cultural register struck a chord. Above all, Augustine was impressed by Ambrose's ability to interpret the Scriptures. The Manichees had encouraged him in his inclination to dismiss the Jewish Scriptures as barbarous and inconsistent with Christianity in both moral and historical terms, but from Ambrose he learned that it was possible to read the Old Testament spiritually and allegorically. Contrary to the determinism of the Manichees, who taught that the elect are mysteriously predestined and that sin is a consequence of forces beyond human control, Ambrose exhorted Augustine to see good and evil as a matter of willed choice and to believe that the quest for truth and for God is one for which all humans are naturally inclined as a result of their creation in the image of God.

There were other forces urging Augustine in the same direction. He held consultations with a learned presbyter named Simplicianus, who had been Ambrose's own instructor (and who would eventually be his successor as bishop in Milan). Simplicianus was himself well versed in Platonism, and he doubtless encouraged Augustine to connect the Platonists' ideas with the teaching of the Christian gospel. Simplicianus told Augustine of the conversion in the 350s of another native of Africa, a prominent Platonist teacher in Rome, Marius Victorinus, who had created a storm by professing his faith publicly after his baptism. Marius Victorinus's recognition of the truth of Christianity and his preparedness to humble himself to its discipline evidently made an impression on Augustine.[5] From another friend Augustine also heard the story of how two young imperial officials had been moved to adopt celibacy by reading the *Life of Antony*.

Augustine tells us that all of these factors contributed to the final crisis of his will. His account of his conversion is very famous. Sitting in a friend's garden in Milan in August 386, worn out physically and mentally after his long inner struggle, he heard a voice "as of a child" calling, *Tolle, lege* ("Take, read"). Turning at random to the Christian Scriptures, he read Paul's words in Romans 13:13–14, which came to him as a summons to abandon the tendency to sexual license with which he had wrestled for years and "put on" Christ.[6] Augustine's description is intended to show that his conversion was an entirely rational process, in which he at last recognized the compelling truth of the one true God. He confesses that God had always been there, patiently and graciously calling to him all through his pilgrimage, and that his final surrender was an inevitable yielding to the beauty of the one who had wooed him all his days. Even in what he paints as his foolish flight from this destiny in the sensual indulgence of youth and in the proud search for other answers to his problems, he sees the magnetic splendor of the true God as the glory to which he was always being drawn.

The ultimate submission to this God and his moral demands was inevitably an emotionally charged affair in which Augustine had to repudiate the tawdry substitutes of worldly satisfaction and adopt the yoke of Christ. But in Augustine's mind, all of his life and all of the intellectual and moral struggles of his youth are to be read against the backdrop of the constant presence and attraction of God's existence. As he famously puts it at the outset of the *Confessions*: "You have made us for yourself, and our heart is restless until it finds its rest in you."[7] The vision of ascent bequeathed by Neoplatonism is translated into a story of the drawing power of a divine grace that compelled the mind, excited the spirit, and moved the will.

The Aftermath of Conversion

Augustine withdrew for a period to a friend's estate outside Milan in the small village of Cassiciacum. He was accompanied by his son, his mother, his brother, and some other friends. Together they discussed philosophical issues such as the nature of happiness, the basis of knowledge, the shape of providence, and the immortality of the soul. Augustine's thoughts continued to be deeply marked by Platonism and by the traditional intellectual concerns of a teacher of the liberal arts. His discussions with his friends, published in stylized form as a set of dialogues, breathe an air of Christian humanism and reveal their author's continuing idealization of conventional images of a life of contemplation. Augustine was convinced that his conversion meant the renunciation of his secular career and a path of self-denial. This conviction reflected his struggle to conquer his powerful sexual drive; it was also encouraged by his experience of the Platonized spirituality of Ambrose. In Ambrose's teaching, and in the bishop's own austere lifestyle, Augustine caught a vision of self-mastery that corresponded with his sense that the committed Christian existence was a calling to deny the flesh and pursue a path of spiritual ascent towards otherworldly union with God.

After receiving baptism from Ambrose at Easter 387, Augustine resolved to return to North Africa. He was delayed for a year in Rome, owing to a blockade of shipping caused by the civil war between Theodosius and Maximus. During this time his mother died, a moment of great grief for him. In these months he read about Eastern monasticism and became acquainted with Western imitations of these ideals. He had no desire to offer himself for the regular service of the church as a member of the clergy; his intention, instead, was to pursue an ascetic life amid a community of like-minded believers. Back in Thagaste, he lived for almost three years with a group of friends in a kind of lay-ascetic community, devoted to a life of prayer, fasting, study, and works of charity.

Over these years he studied the Scriptures and other texts and wrote extensively, focusing now less on the kinds of philosophical questions that had preoccupied him at Cassiciacum and more on expressly theological matters. He completed a number of works on biblical exegesis, the nature of the Christian faith, and Christian morals. Among the scriptural texts that he studied in some depth were Paul's Epistles, and from these he began to elaborate the first stages of what would become a very influential understanding of sin. At first Augustine was inclined to believe that the transition from a state of sin to a state of grace was a matter of human choice, but he soon came to believe that sin so powerfully incapacitates humanity that salvation can only be seen as a process of sheer, unmerited favor. Drawing upon existing African traditions and upon teaching, he had heard from Ambrose, he argued that the fall rendered human beings not only subject to death but incapable of exercising their wills in the right direction. Only by divine grace acting upon them are they enabled to recognize the truth and, more importantly, to reach out towards it.

Bishop of Hippo: Preacher, Pastor, Scholar

In 391, on a trip to the seaport of Hippo Regius (modern Annaba in Algeria) to visit an individual interested in joining his community at Thagaste, Augustine found himself reluctantly pressed into ordination as a presbyter by the aging local bishop, Valerius. In 395 he became

Valerius's coadjutor, and on Valerius's death the following year he assumed the office of sole bishop of Hippo.

Having previously lived in a lay community attached to the local church, as bishop Augustine took steps to establish his episcopal residence as an ascetic chapter-house and mini-seminary. Monastic ideals were the antidote to the

Augustine of Hippo. Illustration from André Thevet, *Les Vrais Portraits et Vies des Hommes Illustres* (Paris, 1584), Special Collections Library, University of Michigan. Used by permission.

treachery of human nature and the dangers of worldly encumbrances. His clergy were prescribed a *Rule* setting out the parameters of a shared life based upon charity and common ownership. They were committed to celibacy, but sexual purity in itself was not the primary concern of the community; the overriding aspiration was the recapturing of a social environment in which the sins of pride, individualism, and selfishness were overcome. *Concordia*, "harmony," was the key ideal, and in making this his emphasis Augustine added a distinctive dimension to the theology of monasticism. Inevitably, the reality was less exalted in practice than the rhetoric demanded, and Augustine's writings contain plenty of evidence of all-too-human problems that arose among the dedicated ones of Hippo. Nevertheless, the aim was for a community of altruism, intimacy, and dedication to standards different from those of the world outside.

The dream of pursuing a path of peace and intellectual contemplation lingered, but Augustine's life had already changed markedly after he had been ordained. As bishop he was under almost relentless pressure. He assumed the duties of teacher and pastor, minister of sacred rites, instructor of clergy, dispenser of charity, ecclesiastical administrator, judge, and intercessor. Preaching was a daily responsibility, and even before he succeeded Valerius he had already begun to build up a powerful reputation for his gifts in this area. Augustine combined a natural eloquence with an ability to communicate the truths of Scripture in simple language, accessible to the ordinary, largely illiterate people who made up his congregations. At the same time, as a former professor of rhetoric, he was equally capable of stimulating the educated. He was much in demand as a visiting preacher outside Hippo, especially in Carthage.

As a pastor, Augustine operated in a society in which, for all the advances that had been made in the social standing of Christianity, the customs, superstitions, and civic rituals of paganism remained widespread, and his congregation was still strongly affected by pagan values and assumptions. He ministered to those for whom the attractions of popular entertainments such as the theater, the games, and the shows were still considerable, and he had to labor to discourage his people from participating in activities in which the symbolism of pagan religion and the morals of a pre-Christian world continued to be heavily present. Like all who preached separation and the importance of heavenly mindedness, he knew failure as well as success in his efforts.

In addition to these commitments, Augustine was obliged to spend a great deal of his time arbitrating in civil disputes over matters of land, property, and debts. This was a task that had become standard for bishops by this time, but it was a tedious and burdensome business that he greatly resented. He also had to oversee donations and bequests to his church, organize (or take overall responsibility for the organization of) the distribution of alms to the needy, and mediate (often unsuccessfully) between his parishioners and civil authorities. His experiences and frustrations as a pastor and leader of people led him to trace an ever more critical analysis of human nature the more he felt himself confronted with the evidences of sinfulness in others and in himself.

In the midst of so many demands, Augustine managed to engage in an astonishing amount of scholarly activity. He may have deplored the degree to which his practical commitments were a distraction from intellectual pursuits, but it was by his pen that his most enduring influence was achieved. When Hippo was burned to the ground by the Goths in 431, the year after his death, Augustine's library miraculously escaped destruction, and it is thanks to this providence that so much of his literary legacy survives. He had spent his last years editing, annotating, and correcting his works, assuming a threefold division of books, letters, and treatises, but had never gotten beyond reviewing the books, which he counted to 232, spread over 93 works. His biographer, Possidius, enumerated 1,030 books, epistles, and treatises in all, but admitted that even this was not exhaustive.

Augustine compiled a vast array of works on philosophical, moral, and polemical subjects. He wrote on themes as diverse as the nature of language, the theory of rhythm, the good of marriage, and the burial of the dead, and his major texts reflect on issues that include human cognition, the functioning of memory, the nature of beauty, and the relationship between time and eternity. In terms of his philosophical context and cultural preoccupations, his world is very much the world of late antiquity, but his writings far transcend those limitations in the ways in which they address questions of perennial fascination and appeal to categories of thought that endure to this day.

Of the thousands of Augustine's sermons, a few hundred survive, though these and our collection of his letters have been augmented by important new discoveries in modern times. Some of his homilies, such as those on John's Gospel and on the Psalms, were collated into more-or-less self-contained pastoral treatises. His preaching made quite liberal use of spiritual interpretation of both the Hebrew Bible and the Gospels, but as a trained orator he also prized the clarity of import that came from the literal sense of Scripture. In a seminal work called *On Christian Doctrine*, Augustine explores the relationship between biblical

A Public Faith

exegesis, preaching, and secular culture. He saw the best of secular learning, including the skills of rhetoric, language, and historical research, as something that could be plundered by the Christian, but only in so far as it might facilitate the interpretation and communication of scriptural truth. Augustine actually commends abilities he did not possess, arguing that the biblical preacher ought to have a knowledge of Greek and Hebrew; he himself had only modest ability in Greek and no grasp of Hebrew at all.[8]

Doctrinally, Augustine sought to be a faithful devotee of the Nicene tradition, though handicapped by his poor knowledge of Greek he sometimes had limited awareness of the complexities of Eastern debates. He never wrote a work specifically on Christology, but his approach to Scripture was strongly Christ-centered in many respects. He concentrated on the redemptive, healing, and exemplary functions of the union of divinity and humanity in Christ, which secure deliverance and provide human beings with a knowledge of God that could never be attained by secular philosophy.

On the Trinity

Augustine's desire to defend catholic orthodoxy resulted in one of the most important of all his works, a massive study in fifteen books called *On the Trinity*. Produced over a period of about twenty years, from around 399 to 419, Augustine's treatise was the first truly substantial work of its kind in the West, far outstripping the efforts of previous Latin-language theologians, and it proved easily the most influential of all Western expositions of trinitarian theology. Augustine sought to repudiate Arian and Sabellian errors and to define the doctrine of God against any depreciation of either the Son or the Spirit as less than the Father. He endeavored to defend and elaborate an existing orthodox consensus that the three are one both in being and in operation. Whatever can be predicated of divinity can be predicated of each of the three, though there remains only one God.

When it comes to the conceptual language for expressing this reality, Augustine was, however, cautious. He appreciated that the terminology of "one *ousia*, three *hypostaseis*" had as its practical Western equivalent the formula that went back to Tertullian: "one *substantia*, three *personae*." But he preferred the term *essentia* to *substantia* as a proper equivalent to *ousia* and regarded the language of *personae*, "persons," as potentially overstating the plurality of the three. The Father, the Son, and the Holy Spirit are clearly three, but three *what*, if God is one? At this point, Augustine argues, human language fails, for they cannot be seen as three distinct individuals. If they are to be called "three persons," this is not because the designation is very suitable; it is only "in order to avoid saying nothing."[9]

The only way in which the three can be spoken of as distinct is by the language of "relations." They are all equally divine and equally eternal but are *related* to one another in particular ways. The Father is the Father because that is his relation to the Son; the Son is called Son because he is thus related to the Father. What of the Spirit? Augustine maintains that the Spirit is the "gift" of the Father's love to the Son and the Son's love to the Father, and so the Spirit is related to the Father and the Son as the bond of mutual love between them. Thus the three are distinct in terms of their "real or subsistent relations," but at the level of will, intention, and attributes they are one, and they act inseparably in all that they do.

Unlike the Cappadocians, who tended to speak of the Father as the "source" or "cause" of the Godhead, Augustine sees the Godhead in its unitary wholeness as the sole fountain of divinity. Within God's inner relations, the Holy Spirit proceeds not only from the Father but also from the Son (though Augustine can also concede that this procession occurs "principally" from the Father). A doctrine of the "double procession" of the Spirit was already established in the thinking of Western theologians, and Augustine did not mean to be controversial in affirming it; his primary concern was simply to underscore the unity of the Trinity. After Augustine, however, the Latin word *Filioque*, "and from the Son," came in the West to be inserted into the Niceno-Constantinopolitan Creed's description of the Spirit, so that it read: "And [we believe] in the Holy Spirit, who proceeds from the Father *and from the Son*." The insertion would be approved in the West at the Third Council of Toledo in Spain in 589 (see p. 339), and the altered creed would be very widely used by Western Christians in subsequent centuries, especially in the Frankish Empire. It eventually became an official part of the Roman liturgy in the early eleventh century.

The doctrine of "double procession" would be bitterly rejected, however, in the East from the seventh century. A number of Eastern theologians considered it vital to affirm that the Spirit proceeds "from the Father alone." The controversies to which the *Filioque* issue gave rise were enormous, and they contributed significantly to the great schism between the churches of the East and the West that took place around 1054. The divisions were about politics as well as theology, but there is no doubt that the doctrinal debates were of considerable weight. Despite many efforts to heal the breach over the centuries and a good deal of constructive discussion in modern times, the question of the procession of the Holy Spirit officially remains a point of division between Eastern and Western believers to this day.

It is nevertheless unfair to blame Augustine for initiating the entire dispute. However controversial things became in later centuries, Augustine's reasoning was in his own time quite conventional in the West. The problems arose not so much with the suggestions of Augustine's logic but with the later attempts in the West to change the creed unilaterally. To Eastern theologians these moves were not only evidence of theological error but a serious violation of ecumenicity and an attack on the sanctity of an agreed confessional tradition.

In the second half of *On the Trinity* (books 8–15), Augustine explores a variety of ways of illustrating trinitarian relations. If, according to Genesis 1:26–27, human beings are made in the image and likeness of God, then they are made in the image and likeness of the Trinity, and evidences of that trinitarian character ought to be clear in their human constitution. Augustine reasons that such evidence ought to be particularly apparent in the mind or soul, which he assumes most closely resembles the being of God. He identifies a range of what he calls "vestiges" (*vestigia*, "footprints" or "traces") of the Trinity in human psychology, including the tripartite structure of memory, understanding, and will. The *memory* embraces self-awareness and the subconscious and is the center of the personality. *Understanding* is a reflection of divine reason. *Will* is that which desires and reaches out to put into effect the joint intention of memory and understanding. In these three, Augustine sees a picture of the mind's created capacity to remember, know, and love God.

Augustine recognizes that his reasoning is speculative, and his expression of some of his ideas, albeit lengthy in nature, is quite tentative in tone. His thoughts are certainly strikingly creative, and they gave rise to a great deal of reflection in subsequent Western thought. Some modern theologians consider Augustine's thoughts to be highly questionable, because he appears to be seeking the image of the triune God in the human mind or soul without reference to the fact that humans are in reality *embodied* selves who need to be analyzed not in terms of isolated individualism but in relationship to others. In speaking of an inherent spiritual capacity to remember, know, and love God, Augustine is accused of presenting a rather Platonist vision of the ascent of the soul. Some have also argued that he looks for traces of revelation in the wrong places: should not divine revelation be primarily sought in Jesus

Christ, God's Son, and in the work of the Spirit of Jesus, rather than in the structures of human nature?

There are aspects of truth in some of these criticisms, but it is clear that Augustine's reflections need to be assessed within the context of his theology as a whole. More recent scholarship is concerned to emphasize the setting within which his ideas are located, both within *On the Trinity* itself and in his thinking overall. Augustine saw human nature as debased by sin and as bearing only a marred image of its intended glory: we are vitally dependent on the initiative of divine grace if we are ever to ascend to a right relationship with the triune Creator from whom we come. Augustine's logic is, in the end, far less Platonist and far more biblical in orientation than some of his critics have supposed.

Augustine the Controversialist

A great deal of Augustine's literary activity was generated by controversies. In his early years in Hippo, he wrote a number of works refuting the ideas of his former associates, the Manichees, arguing for the original goodness of creation, the reality of human free will, and the nature of evil as an absence of the good rather than a metaphysical necessity. In engaging with the Manichaean emphasis on the explanatory power of reason, he came to place increasing stress on the significance of faith as the starting point of religious knowledge and the apprehension of truth more generally. "Believe in order to understand," he famously enjoined his readers.

The necessity of faith was also sharpened for Augustine as he came to hold more and more that fallen human minds are naturally darkened by sin and incapable of breaking out of their own imprisonment by rational effort alone. In a condition of not only finitude but corruption there is no other way of access to God than by faith—and only God can grant that faith. Reason is never to be dismissed—it remains a gift that God intends us to use to discern truth and falsehood and right from wrong—but although complementary to faith in the life of the believer, it is always subordinate to the primary obligation to believe.

Donatism

If Manichaeism represented one enemy, there were other even more pressing sources of conflict in the North African environment. The primary one was Donatism. The movement that had begun in the early fourth century (see pp. 25–28) was by this time very strong all over North Africa. The Donatists' primary power base continued to be Numidia, but throughout North Africa, in the eastern as well as the western provinces, virtually every town and village had two Christian communities, each led by rival clergy. In a great many areas the Donatists constituted the majority church, with the result that the very labels "catholic" and "Donatist" were hotly contested. What existed in many places can only retrospectively be described as rivalry between "catholics" and "Donatists"; at the time, it amounted to rivalry between two groups of Christians, one more rigorist than the other, both of them claiming to represent the true traditions of the African faith.

Donatism had attracted significant numbers of educated and well-to-do people from the major population centers as well as rural areas, and many of the Donatist leaders were thoroughly cultivated individuals who wrote (and probably preached and led liturgy) in Latin. There were, it was true, other elements. From around 340 or so the Donatists were associated by their opponents with groups known as the "Circumcellions." The identity of these figures is not altogether clear, but they appear to have been a constituency of vagabonds who hung around rural martyr shrines (Augustine explains their name as deriving from *circum cellas*, "around the shrines"). They styled themselves as "soldiers" of Christ (*agonistici*)—zealous ascetics devoted simultaneously to the cause of self-denial and the righting of social injustices—but they existed outside the structures of regular, settled monasticism.

Supporting themselves by perhaps a combination of begging and seasonal agricultural labor, the Circumcellions claimed to represent the interests of the poor and the oppressed, urging the cancellation of debts and engaging in acts of vandalism against the persons and property of believers deemed responsible for economic inequalities. Their primary interest, though, lay in the cultivation of a reputation as uncompromising ascetics and in the pursuit of martyr status as champions of Christ's cause. Though they occasionally supported local revolts against Roman rule, as did some Donatist clergy (Donatus himself is said to have asked what the emperor had to do with the church), their protest was as much against "the world" and an allegedly compromised Christian community as it was against political systems as such.

On the whole, the activities of the Circumcellions were an embarrassment to a great many Donatists, whose social inclinations were towards the maintenance of respectability and whose religious devotion did not extend to displays of spectacular or subversive behavior. The active repression of the Circumcellions by the authorities at various stages, especially under the emperor Constans in 347–348, had only intensified the militants' claims to be replicating the courage of the martyrs whose memory they venerated. But to their critics they were crazed extremists, whose blatant provocation of the forces of law and order amounted to suicide rather than true obedience in the face of unmerited persecution.

Despite the hostility to Donatism from imperial authorities in the mid-fourth century, the movement had prospered under Julian and recovered some of the ground that had been lost in earlier repressions. When harassment and hostility were a reality, the Donatists could always put it down to their fidelity to truth and their determination to preserve a pure church. Donatus's successor in Carthage, Parmenian—who significantly was not a native African—had over the course of a lengthy term of office consolidated the rigorist churches into a well-entrenched network, and although his teaching had been subjected to some significant polemic by the catholic Bishop Optatus of Milevis in Numidia from the late 360s, the communities on whose behalf Parmenian spoke continued to flourish.

In the late 370s or early 380s, a gifted Donatist layman named Tyconius had produced an impressive manual on biblical interpretation known as the *Book of Rules*, which demonstrated the intellectual versatility of the more moderate tradition within Donatist theology. His work would in fact be absorbed and discussed by Augustine, despite its provenance, and Tyconius's principles for interpreting every part of Scripture as referring to Christ and to the church that is Christ's body became widely influential in later Western exegesis. Tyconius wrote other works besides, including a commentary on Revelation, though these have not survived,[10] and we are dependent on the evidence of the *Book of Rules* and on Augustine (who had his own reasons for emphasizing the degree to which the Donatists were divided among themselves) for our picture of his theology.

Tyconius's view of the spiritual character of the church was broader than the "official" Donatist position propounded by Parmenian. He seems to have depicted the church as a mixed body in which the true and false members may be distinguished only with reference to what may be seen of their will to obey Christ in practical conduct. Parmenian himself ruled that Tyconius's doctrine deviated from the Donatist line, and Tyconius was eventually excommunicated from the Donatist church, though he never joined the catholic side. Whatever the rights and wrongs of his ideas, and whatever the events of the 380s implied about the coexistence of different strands of thought within Donatism, his identification with the Donatist movement had symbolized the sophistication and cultural resilience that could be found within its ranks. Just as the physical dominance of Donatism was impossible to ignore in the presence of its churches, clergy, and congregations, neither could all of its thinkers be written off as theological lightweights.

Parmenian was still in office when Augustine arrived back in Thagaste in 388, but he died some time in the early 390s. Thereafter the rigorists began to become much more divided, owing to personality clashes, sharp differences of opinion, and splits between churches. Nevertheless, they were still a very significant presence, and in April 394 they could muster a council of 310 bishops at Bagai in southern Numidia (a Donatist stronghold) in order to crush a revolt that had arisen against the leadership of Parmenian's successor, Primianus, whose opponents had excommunicated him the previous year. Despite some serious opposition from churchmen such as Aurelius, the new catholic bishop of Carthage, Donatism showed no signs of losing ground.

The Donatists could not be condemned as heretics according to conventional understandings of that term, for they professed allegiance to the same Scriptures and upheld the same credal statements as their critics. Opponents such as Optatus of Milevis had to concede that they were orthodox on matters of christological and trinitarian doctrine and argued that their crime was not heresy but schism: they had broken off communion with their fellow believers, and in the judgment of the churches in Rome and the East they were not to be officially recognized. The problem was that the Donatists accused their rivals of just the same kinds of faults. They agreed that there could only be one true church, but as far as they were concerned they were precisely that: the people who had stood firm in the midst of persecutions and kept themselves pure from compromise. The clergy of the so-called "catholic" church were tainted by their complicity in sin and their lack of separation from corruption; their priestly offices were invalid, and the rites they administered were vitiated and ineffective. The Donatists maintained that they were in proper continuity with the church of the martyrs, and they appealed to the authority of Cyprian to legitimize their stern line on the seriousness of apostasy.

When Augustine became bishop of Hippo, he faced a society in which the Donatists were in a majority and their rivals nursed a strong sense of grievance at their social displacement and the insinuations that they were less spiritually committed. The two communities coexisted for the most part in an uneasy peace, but there was a good deal of ill-will, evidenced in sporadic displays of hostility and even violence. The need to find some way of dealing with the deadlock was, in Augustine's mind, an urgent, practical problem. He set about familiarizing himself with the substance of Donatist teaching and establishing the facts about the movement's history.

Dealing with Donatism

Having compiled evidence to his satisfaction regarding the deficiencies of the Donatists' views, Augustine attempted to engage in public debates with representatives of the Donatist churches—a tactic he had deployed with great success against the Manichees—but for the most part his Donatist opponents managed to evade such encounters. He started to develop instead a program of serious polemic, both in his preaching and his writing. He also endeavored to forestall Donatist denunciations of his catholic flock by placing great emphasis on the importance of moral integrity among his clergy and laity. If the claim was to be refuted that the catholics were not morally lax, it was necessary for leaders and people alike to be seen as serious about their obligations to holiness.

If we are to trust what he himself tells us later, Augustine was at first opposed to the use of imperial force to coerce his enemies into submission and was confident that with a sufficient resurgence of catholic vitality the force of Donatism would start to crack. Political oppression, he would later claim, tended to produce the wrong kinds of converts—those who switch allegiance as a matter of expediency rather than conviction—and his instinct was that it was better to appeal to intellectual persuasion and moral example than rely on the blunt instrument of imperial legislation. Gradually, however, he came to accept that coercion was the only way that a movement as vibrant as Donatism could be checked.

It was not difficult to invoke such power, for in 397–398 an unsuccessful rebellion in Mauretania, led by a military commander, Gildo, had been supported by some prominent Donatist clerics, particularly the highly influential Optatus of Thamugadi (Timgad), and the Donatists could thus be portrayed as rebels against Rome. The enthusiasm of a solid array of supportive catholic bishops meeting annually in Carthage from 397 encouraged Augustine that the time had come to call for serious official action against the Donatists. In 405 he successfully persuaded the government of the emperor Honorius to issue an "edict of unity" declaring the Donatists to be not just schismatics but heretics, and thus liable to severe punishment in law. Further measures followed in the succeeding years.

Initially the sanctions were only partially effective, and if anything there was an intensification of the activity of the Circumcellions, who reportedly engaged in acts of assault, theft, arson, and even murder. However, Augustine succeeded in persuading the authorities to set up a full legal enquiry, and a meeting of catholic and Donatist bishops was convened at Carthage in May 411. The records of the occasion, which survive in remarkably full detail, show 286 attenders on the catholic side, 285 on the Donatist; the former were led by Augustine, the latter by Petilian, bishop of Constantine (Cirta). In the chair was the local representative of imperial power, the tribune Marcellinus, a loyal catholic and friend of Augustine.

After fierce and tortuous debate, in which each party vigorously challenged the other's version of the historical roots of their disagreement, it was declared by Marcellinus that the catholics had proved their case; they, not the Donatists, constituted the true church of North Africa. In January of the following year, Honorius decreed the Donatist church to be illegal; its property was sequestered, its clergy exiled, and significant financial fines (their severity determined according to the social status of the deviant) were imposed on those who refused to enter the ranks of the official church. The repression that followed over the months and years ahead was harsh, particularly in the coastal regions of North Africa, where the forces of the law were stronger and in a position to act more decisively.[11]

Even so, Donatism did not disappear easily. Sporadic resistance continued over a period of a decade or so, both on the part of regular Donatist congregations and their clergy and through a flurry of Circumcellion outrages, and Augustine became ever more prepared to ask for and justify the use of force to deal with it. Coercion could even be presented as obedience to the Lord's command to "compel them to come in" (Luke 14:23 KJV). By the late 420s, though, the challenge of enforcing this principle was overshadowed by the threat of Vandal invasion from Spain. In 429 this threat was realized when the conquerors of Gaul and Spain, who espoused an Arian creed, crossed into North Africa (see further pp. 302–5). Catholics and Donatists alike were caught up in the ravages, and Christian leaders on all sides, including Augustine, agonized over whether they should resist or flee; both policies were adopted.

The Donatists survived, particularly in their Numidian heartland, long after the Vandals had prevailed and Augustine had passed to his rest in 430, and their presence endured even beyond the emperor Justinian's reconquest of the region in the 530s. As late as the end of the sixth century, we find complaints that the magistrates of North Africa were failing to enforce the legal proscription of Donatism. Only in the triumph of Islam in the seventh and eighth centuries would the Donatists eventually succumb to the forces ranged against them. The divisions that had deepened in earlier times had perhaps weakened the ability of Christians en bloc to resist the arrival of another faith in the longer term.

Augustine's claims that he came only reluctantly to accept the use of compulsion against the Donatists may or may not be true. Perhaps he subsequently felt a measure of regret over the degree of force that was used in the imposition of Honorius's laws and over the treatment meted out to those who had stuck to the Donatist line out of genuine principle; he certainly often argued for leniency in the punishment of the intransigent. Nevertheless, in the end he had not scrupled to exploit state authority to achieve his theological objectives, and he had tried to justify his strategy by a variety of means. He depicted the fate inflicted upon the Donatists as a matter of spiritual discipline, a harsh but necessary infliction laid upon them with a positive end in mind. He pointed out that some of those connected with the Donatists—the Circumcellions—were guilty of public outrages and needed to be stopped by tough means. Furthermore, the Donatists themselves had not been slow to appeal to the civil authorities when it suited them.

Augustine's attempts to defend his conduct may reflect his efforts to rationalize it to himself, though perhaps they hint at his growing sense of frustration with the sickness of human nature that, to him, could only be dealt with by such approaches. Sometimes, he argued, punishment and fear might move people to repentance in ways that love and patience do not. Some of his reasoning looks very much like special pleading, and certainly its possible applications were highly dangerous. In a post-Constantinian and post-Theodosian world, it was clearly all too easy for an influential churchman to mobilize the forces of law and order to enforce a particular ecclesiastical position. Whatever the complexities of Augustine's own case against the Donatists, his stance served ever after as an example to which some of the European churches' darker tacticians might appeal, and in the medieval, Reformation, and Counter-Reformation periods legitimacy would be sought for more than a few programs of brutal repression by citing Augustine's moves against the Donatists.

Church and Sacraments

Augustine's efforts to refute Donatist logic at a theological level provided a more constructive legacy. In a string of treatises spanning the last years of the fourth century and the first decade of the fifth, he challenged head-on the ideas of a series of prominent Donatist teachers, including Parmenian, Petilian, a grammarian called Cresconius, and Gaudentius, bishop of Bagai. As Augustine saw it, the root of the disagreement with Donatism lay in differing conceptions of the church. Was the catholic Christian community, as the Donatists maintained, an absolutely pure entity, or did it, as Augustine argued (and Tyconius, controversially, had recognized), contain a mixture of types, not just sociologically but morally as well?

According to Augustine, the parables of Jesus implied that the kingdom of God on earth includes both the wheat and the tares, both the good fish and the bad (Matt. 13:24–30, 36–43, 47–50), and only God can in the end separate them. Human attempts to differentiate were bound to fail and lead to schism, and this was a far worse sin than the crime that the original Donatists had so abhorred—the failure to resist persecution. The final dividing line between true believers and false must remain elusive in this world, however great the dangers. The holiness of the church consisted not in the intrinsic goodness of its members but in the holiness of the Christ whose body it is.

This reality, in turn, determined Augustine's construal of the legitimacy of the sacred rites dispensed by ministers. To the Donatists, baptism was valid only if carried out by a "pure" representative of a "pure" church. Rites administered by those who had failed to stand up and be counted in a time of persecution were tainted and ineffective. In this the Donatists could fairly appeal to Cyprian's teaching in the third century.[12] Augustine could, however, match such a strategy with the recollection of another important element of Cyprian's counsel: namely, that the schismatic who repents ought to be restored. Augustine could then argue, in a fashion much closer (in third-century terms) to the Roman theology of Stephen than to the actual inferences of Cyprian,[13] that the validity of a sacred rite rested not upon the merits of the individual who administered it but upon the merits of the Christ who had instituted it in the first place.

Medieval theologians would call this an *ex opere operato* (as opposed to an *ex opere operantis*) understanding of sacramental efficacy: it is not the personal standing of the minister that counts in the transmission of grace, but the performance in faith of the sacramental action itself. The *ex opere operato* view would become the most common Western position. Augustine's logic meant that he acknowledged the baptism administered by the Donatists to be *valid*, so long as it was carried out in the name of Christ and in obedience to the form that the Lord himself had prescribed.

However—and here he *was* closer to Cyprian's reasoning—he argued that in order for it to be an *effective* means of grace the recipient was obliged to be reconciled to the one catholic church, within which alone the Holy Spirit of Christ was to be found. So long as they remained in isolation from what could be claimed to be the catholic communion, the Donatists were bound to exist in a state of spiritual barrenness.

In reality, Augustine shared many of the Donatists' presuppositions about the importance of moral earnestness and resistance of the world's encroachments, and he consciously sought to connect his ideas with the emphases of the same indigenous traditions. In the end, however, his vision of the church was more inclusive. For all his convictions about the importance of Christian sanctification and about the intrinsic corruption of human nature, he was prepared to define catholicism as something that existed, mysteriously, in the tension between holiness and fallenness. In working out the implications of such a definition, he departed from as well as reaffirmed aspects of the North African tradition, and he bequeathed to the West a doctrine that was, overall, as much Roman as it was African. Nevertheless, it was in the precise context of an African struggle that what became the mainstream Western theology of the church and the sacraments was thought through at a deep level.

Pelagianism

In the years following the conference of Carthage in 411, Augustine found himself preoccupied with another doctrinal development of enormous importance: the influence of the movement we have come to call "Pelagianism." Pelagius (ca. 350–425) was probably British by birth, and if so he is the first British Christian author whose writings survive, but his background is of little if any importance because he passed the most momentous years of his life far from Britain, in the Mediterranean world, after arriving in Rome in the 380s. He had had a sound education in classical literature and philosophy, but though he is said by some contemporaries to have been a monk, he never belonged to any identifiable religious community and was never ordained as a priest. He did, however, have strong ascetic convictions and a passion for promoting holiness. Like Jerome, whose scathing denunciations of Rome's clergy precipitated his departure from the city in 385 (see pp. 127–29), he was shocked by the undisciplined and indulgent lives being lived by many Roman Christians, and he began to preach a message of urgent moral reform.

Pelagius's teaching attracted a number of prominent aristocratic believers, and although he faced some opposition he drew disciples and patrons from among the rich and educated classes in Rome. Among his most enthusiastic hearers were the powerful senatorial family of the Anicii, to whose household he came to act as a kind of personal chaplain. Over the last decade of the fourth century and the first decade of the fifth, he enjoyed a very favored place in Roman society, and his influence spread farther afield as well, to regions such as Sicily, where some of his wealthy followers owned country estates. At a time of political uncertainty, the ideals of ascetic detachment from a corrupt world struck a chord, and Pelagius's pleas for moral reformation and the pursuit of "real" Christianity over against merely external conformity sounded compelling to a social elite with conservative leanings.

Pelagius had no wish to be radical in doctrinal terms. A large body of written material survives under his name, and although it is difficult to tell which works are genuine and which are not, in the instances where the evidence of authenticity is clear-cut we see a figure who regarded himself as entirely orthodox on matters of christological and trinitarian belief. His commentaries on Paul's Epistles, and especially on Romans 5, directly challenged the understanding of original sin that Augustine would defend, but Pelagius made repeated appeals to the authority of respected Christian writers, including Augustine himself, on a range of other matters. His moralizing treatises were on the kinds of standard themes familiar to Christian readers, such as the virtues of constancy in adversity, the dangers of material riches, and the merits of virginity. Pelagius was a reformer whose views were to get him into serious trouble, but his intention never was to undermine the fundamental frameworks of Christian belief. His concern was simply to exhort believers to live better lives.

The theological substructure of his teaching proved highly controversial nonetheless. Pelagius argued that if Jesus had commanded his followers to be "perfect," like their heavenly Father (Matt. 5:48), perfection was both an obligation and a possibility. He was deeply opposed to pessimistic resignation in the face of the imperative to be moral, whether such defeatism came from Manichaean assumptions (which were widely held in Rome) that evil was an inevitable element in the material world, or—the more immediate danger in the context of the church—from what he regarded as excessively negative Christian views of human incapacity. He was greatly troubled by the theological teaching that humans are bound to sin because their nature is corrupt.

Several times in book 10 of his *Confessions*, Augustine prays to God, "Give what you command, and command what you will."[14] Pelagius thought such a prayer suggested that the believer was little more than a divine puppet, and it undermined the entire basis of moral effort. Unless sin and virtue are a matter of willed intention, he reasoned, there can be no ground for moral accountability. Human beings do not inherit a sinful nature that inclines them inevitably toward wrongdoing; rather, they learn to sin by the influence of bad examples and the effects of an environment that undermines the will's intention to resist evil and aspire to perfection.

As a result of political developments that we shall consider further in chapter 11, Rome fell to the Goths in 410, and Pelagius, like many others of the city's elite, sought refuge elsewhere. He and a group of his supporters made their way to North Africa. Foremost among his associates was a lawyer named Celestius, who proved to have a more combative temperament than his mentor. Pelagius moved on to Palestine not long afterwards, while Celestius remained in Carthage, where he thrust himself into local theological debates on the nature of the soul and the solidarity of the human race in the sin of Adam. Celestius came out with a string of outspoken allegations based on Pelagius's ideas: Adam did not become mortal as a result of sin, but was created mortal. The sin of Eve affected only Eve, not her offspring. Infants were born into the same state of innocence in which Adam existed prior to the fall. Baptism was necessary for salvation, but it was not a sign of the remission of sins but a symbol of sanctification. The law and the gospel were both alike capable of providing humans with the examples they needed in order to avoid sin. Christ was of course the supreme example, but there were other sinless beings prior to him.

For these claims, so baldly expressed, Celestius was denounced as a heretic by Paulinus, a deacon of Milan (and biographer of Ambrose) who happened to be in Carthage on church business, and Celestius's application to be ordained as a priest was refused. At a local council his views were condemned. When Augustine heard of Celestius's ideas around 412, he set about refuting them, arguing that the law prescribes what is morally necessary but only the Spirit of Christ can enable people to obey it. In a number of treatises and letters he further sought to rebut what he increasingly felt were dangerous notions concerning natural innocence and the role of grace in salvation. As he had done in earlier writings, he contended that human beings are not born with a clean sheet but in a state of culpability before God; only baptism, which ought to be administered in infancy, could deal with original sin.

For all that, Augustine's arguments thus far remained fairly moderate in tone. His primary concern was simply to assert the reality of evil as a universal disease and the consequent necessity of infant baptism to deal with its effects at the personal level. Celestius moved on to Ephesus, where he succeeded in persuading a more accommodating church community to accept him, and he was ordained there in 415.

Responding to Pelagian Ideas

Contradicting Pelagian ideas was not all that easy when some of the moral ideals that Pelagius and his allies sponsored were shared with existing principles of asceticism, and when respected, upper-class Christians who took holiness seriously, such as Paulinus of Nola and the young Melania and Pinianus (see pp. 148–49; 144), were impressed by Pelagius's personal sanctity. As late as 413, Augustine could write to Pelagius in courteous terms. However, the more he read Pelagius's writings, the more he became persuaded that the doctrine that underpinned his moral arguments was in error. Even so, tackling it was not simple, given the wide network of Pelagius's supporters and the social status of many of them. Problems ensued when Augustine sought to warn some members of the displaced Roman nobility of the dangers of following advice from Pelagius, as he did with Demetrias, a young woman from the rich Probi family who took vows of virginity in Carthage. Demetrias received counsel from a number of Christian writers, including Jerome as well as Pelagius, and Augustine did not endear himself to her family when he took it upon himself to caution that associations with Pelagius were undesirable.

Pelagius meanwhile had been received politely in a number of places in Palestine, including Jerusalem, but he ran into trouble for daring to criticize Jerome, who—in his usual forthright style—retorted that his misplaced confidence in the capacity of the human will was reminiscent of Origenism. By 415 Augustine was convinced that Pelagius's arguments deserved to be challenged directly. It was not just Pelagius's followers such as Celestius who posed a threat to catholic understandings of nature and grace with their claims that human beings could attain to a state of sinlessness; it was preeminently the teacher who had propagated such notions in the first place.

Augustine set about writing against Pelagius's views in passionate terms. He sent a young Spanish presbyter, Paulus Orosius, to Bethlehem to lay charges against the orthodoxy of Pelagius. However, supported by John, bishop of Jerusalem, and assisted by the indifference of other

Eastern bishops to a cause promoted by Jerome, Pelagius succeeded in defending himself, first in Jerusalem and then definitively at a provincial synod held in Diospolis (Lydda) in December of 415. After assuring the bishops that he distanced himself from some of Celestius's more extreme language and affirmed the necessity of divine grace for every moral achievement, Pelagius was completely exonerated.

In North Africa the acquittal of Pelagius was greeted with horror. Augustine was sure that the defendant had not been pressed to explain exactly how he understood grace to operate. In separate councils held at Milevis and Carthage in 416, the African bishops condemned both Pelagius and Celestius and sought to follow up their condemnation by appealing to Pope Innocent in Rome to excommunicate and anathematize them. In January 417 Innocent gave his consent to do so if they did not recant their views, and Augustine hoped that the case against Pelagianism was closed. However, Innocent died on 12 March 417, leaving his edict unfulfilled, and his successor, Zosimus, was lobbied in person by Celestius, who impressed him with his high moral ideals. The African bishops stuck to their guns, and a furious phase of pamphleteering ensued as Augustine and his supporters sought to whip up widespread antagonism toward Pelagius and Celestius and ensure the downfall that Innocent had decreed for them.

The Roman church was sharply divided. In the spring of 418 there was a riot in Rome in which the ringleaders happened to be Pelagians, and the emperor Honorius (who was based at Ravenna) ordered the expulsion of all Pelagians from the city; their teaching was to be regarded as a threat to the peace. On 1 May 418 a further council of bishops met at Carthage and reaffirmed their denunciation of Pelagius, Celestius, and their followers. This time Pope Zosimus elected to give in to the pressure, and in a circular letter known as the *Tractoria*, sent around all the principal sees of both the West and the East, he confirmed the findings of the Council of Carthage, upheld the decision of Pope Innocent, and called for assent to an anti-Pelagian statement on the nature of human sin and guilt.

A group of south Italian churchmen led by Julian, bishop of the small town of Eclanum (modern-day Mirabella) in Apulia (ca. 386–454), refused to comply with Zosimus's injunction and were deposed from their sees. Pelagius himself disappeared from sight not long afterwards and probably died in the East some time around 420. Julian, in exile in the East, continued to fight Pelagius's doctrinal cause, and the last decade of Augustine's life witnessed a prolonged and acrimonious dispute between Augustine and Julian on the substance of Pelagian teaching on sin, grace, free will, and sexuality. Julian was a dialectical theologian of some ability, and he saw himself as defending the essential importance of moral endeavor against the negativity of Augustine's doctrine of evil and what he perceived as its fatalistic implications for Christian ethics.

Nature, Sin, and Grace

Over the course of his polemic against Pelagius and then Julian, Augustine elaborated an ever more pessimistic portrayal of the effects of evil in creation. According to Romans 5:12, he argued, the entire human race fell in Adam. Adam's sin was committed by one who was capable of resisting evil, and therefore it was especially heinous. Augustine claimed that in the story of Genesis 3 sin has sexual associations: in the immediate aftermath of eating the forbidden fruit, Adam and Eve sense for the first time that they are naked and attempt to cover themselves (Gen. 3:6–7). He thus proposed that Adam's guilt is transmitted biologically to all his descendants, through every generation of humanity, in the act of procreation. Since the time of the fall, there has been in sexual intercourse even within marriage an inevitable element of "concupiscence" or lust, which overcomes reason or the exercise of will over carnal passions. Human beings, thus conceived in sin (cf. Ps. 51:5), are naturally helpless to remedy their condition before God.

Seeing baptism as remitting the guilt of original sin, Augustine contends that if no one is born innocent, it is necessary to baptize newborn infants; even if they have not yet committed any *actual* sins, children inherit a debased nature and are guilty on that account. Babies who die unbaptized are consigned to a state of judgment, albeit a milder one than the hell deserved by mature sinners.[15] After baptism, people of course still sin, and they remain constantly in need of God's grace; of themselves, they are incapable of doing anything that is not at some level tainted by sin. The pursuit of holiness in obedience to Christ is the believer's vital obligation and true delight, but talk of perfection assumes a hopelessly naïve assessment of the human condition.

Augustine describes humanity as a "mass of perdition," utterly dependent on grace for salvation. But it is clear that some are saved and others are not. On what basis is this so? Augustine argues that God chooses or, in biblical terms, "elects" certain individuals and not others; all justly deserve damnation in hell, but some are elected for salvation while others are passed by and left to the fate their guilt warrants. At an early stage in his theological thinking, Augustine tentatively held to the idea that election was grounded in divine foreknowledge of human choice, but in working out his arguments against Pelagianism he came to believe that the basis for God's choice is entirely mysterious; people have been chosen before the foundation of the world not because God foresaw anything of superior value in them or any intrinsic potential (which would be the basis for a concept of human merit), but simply because God was pleased to be gracious to them. To the charge that this implies an arbitrary or unfair scheme of salvation, Augustine's response is that since all are undeserving, God shows mercy if even one is spared.

What, though, of human freedom? In some passages Augustine speaks of divine grace as preparing the human will to cooperate with God, but overall his contention is that grace is an irresistible power: if God has elected to save someone, that person will be saved. This does not mean, however, that in such a case God coerces the human will into doing what it does not desire; rather, the individual is presented with the sheer beauty and desirability of God, and his or her will is enabled to achieve what it desires to do but cannot achieve of itself—to reach out in love to its maker. In this way, in the terms of the prayer of book 10 of the *Confessions*, God "gives what he commands." Grace is not the denial of freedom, but the empowering of otherwise impotent creatures to achieve it. Perseverance in faith to the end of life, reflected in a Christian character and the doing of good works, is the demonstration that grace is operative in one's life and that God's electing purpose is fulfilled.

The foundations upon which Augustine's polemic against Pelagianism rested were undoubtedly open to dispute at a number of points. Romans 5:12 in Augustine's Latin Bible stated that all sinned "in Adam." However, according to the original Greek, the verse might more appropriately be translated "*because of* Adam" all sinned. This may render other construals possible besides Augustine's—including, perhaps, the idea of an innate *proclivity* to sin *as a result of* Adam's sin as opposed to an inherited *culpability for* Adam's sin as such. However, there had been others in the West who had treated the verse's theological import in quite similar terms to Augustine's, including an unidentified Pauline commentator of the late fourth century known to us as "Ambrosiaster" (since his works, which were in many ways remarkably sophisticated studies of Paul's Epistles, were for a long time wrongly circulated under the name of Ambrose of Milan). Concepts of hereditary guilt were present in both Ambrosiaster and Ambrose.

One of the assumptions upon which, in Ambrosiaster at least, such ideas seemed to depend was in the West as old as Tertullian—the notion that human beings derive not only their bodies but also their souls from their parents (a view that has come to be known as "Traducianism," from the Latin *tradux*, a "shoot" or "sprout"). Many theologians have found it difficult to justify such a concept biblically, seeing it as betraying a crudely materialistic view of the soul, and the majority position historically has been the so-called "creationist" one that each individual soul is a new, direct work of God. Augustine himself was in fact undecided about which of these positions he favored. After a good deal of reflection and consultation, he ended up with something of a compromise: a fresh soul is created by God in the case of each new life, but this soul is tainted by sin at the moment of its conjunction with the body in its fetal existence.

Augustine's continued insistence on baptism as the means by which the ensuing guilt of original sin is remitted is clearly questionable in terms of the New Testament's theology of baptism, and it can easily lead to a superstitious understanding of infant baptism as constituting in itself an automatic guarantee of final salvation. Such mistaken ideas may have been some way from Augustine's own intentions, but they have bedeviled many Western churches over the centuries and are hardly nonexistent today.

Overall, it is obvious that Augustine's reasoning was strongly affected by his own spiritual experience. He had struggled long and painfully with his own sexual urges, and his association of sexual desire with guilt is in part a reflection of that inner battle. He also of course lived in a context in which virginity, celibacy, and continence were widely prized Christian ideals, and his own teaching on asceticism evinces assumptions that were by no means uncommon in his time, even if he gave his own particular slant to many of them. There is much more to the scriptural picture of sexuality than Augustine implies and much more to a biblical view of bodiliness than might be suggested by some of the ideas on renunciation and self-denial that were prevalent in his age.

Nevertheless, it would be wrong to imagine—as too many of his casual critics in the modern world have done—that Augustine's views of sexuality were entirely negative. Unlike the great majority of the church fathers,[16] Augustine did *not* in fact regard sex as the direct result of the fall or assume that Adam and Eve had in paradise lived a virginal or sexless existence. He believed that sexual relations existed prior to the fall, and this conviction was fundamental to his conception of marriage, which was far more positive overall than the views we find in such writers as Jerome. As far as Augustine was concerned, marriage was indeed a blessing, ordained by God for the purposes of human fellowship and the rearing of stable families. That said, Augustine's close association of sex with concupiscence and his ideal that even within marriage libido was to be deployed only for the purposes of procreation clearly did derive from a misreading of biblical teaching and from the influence of non-Christian traditions of austerity.

Opposition to Augustine's Arguments

As far as Julian was concerned, at any rate, the influences of Augustine's background on his thought were all too clear—and they consisted not so much in his private struggles with sexual desire as in his former associations with Manichaeism. Julian believed Augustine had been affected more deeply than he knew by the antimaterialism and predestinarianism of Manichaean theology, and his teaching was, as Pelagius had feared, fatal to ethical effort. It seemed as if all one could do was accept the reality of inevitable sinfulness and never be sure whether salvation was a possibility or not, since all depended on an inscrutable process of election in which some had been chosen and others passed by. Augustine's position appeared to his opponents to turn human beings into automata, to demean the goodness of creation, and to trivialize the obligation to pursue holiness.

Despite the official condemnation of Pelagianism by Pope Zosimus and the maintenance of the same line under his successors Boniface (418–422) and—with greater firmness still—Celestine (422–432), sympathy for at least aspects of Pelagian thinking remained widespread in various parts of the West, stretching from North Africa to Britain (on the latter, see pp. 351–52). There was a strong current of feeling, especially in monastic circles, that Augustine had gone too far in his theology of predestination and had undermined human responsibility altogether. In the late 420s a group of monks at Hadrumetum to the southeast of Carthage received a vigorous reply from Augustine when they proposed a certain softening of his presentation of human incapacity and irresistible grace, and elements in southern Gaul were met with the same treatment when they similarly questioned the orthodoxy of Augustine's teaching, suggesting that it left no room for human free will. John Cassian and his monastic associates around Marseilles argued that while grace is necessary for salvation, free will is presupposed in the gospel invitation. When God discerns the first signs of a human response, grace is infused into the soul to enable the will genuinely to reach out and do that which by itself it cannot do.

The debate went on well after Augustine's and Cassian's deaths. The Gaulish view has sometimes been dubbed "semi-Pelagianism," implying that it was a deliberate attempt to find a middle way between the Augustinian and the Pelagian positions, but in fact it stemmed from an effort to disown Pelagius's doctrine while at the same time avoiding the full ramifications of Augustine's final stance on predestination. The suggestions made by John Cassian were vigorously attacked by the staunch Augustinian layman, Prosper of Aquitaine (ca. 390–463), who set out an uncompromising defense of Augustine's teaching—though Prosper later tempered his views markedly and accepted a much more significant role for free will.

Pelagius and Celestius had made a notable impact in the East, and the Eastern theology of original sin, while quite undeserving of the name "Pelagian" as conventionally understood, never would be the Augustinian one. Eastern theology would continue to talk not of hereditary guilt but of mortality, and would grant greater scope to the cooperation of the will in the realization of salvation. Indeed, there would be far less emphasis on "grace" as such in much of the Eastern tradition and more stress on the direct role of the Holy Spirit in uniting the soul to God. Officially, though, Pelagian teaching remained condemned in the East as well as the West. Celestius found some sympathy from the patriarch Nestorius in Constantinople, but this alliance did Nestorius no favors in his own theological troubles (see pp. 199–208), and both men were condemned at the Council of Ephesus in 431.

In the West, the controversy in Gaul rumbled on for some time—well into the sixth century, in fact. The course of the debates there was considerably affected by the growing prestige of Lérins and Arles as key ecclesiastical centers, well capable of writing their own theological agendas. Writers such as Faustus, a former monk of Lérins who became bishop of Riez in Provence in the 450s, argued that Augustine's theology rightly challenged Pelagianism but downplayed free will. Augustinian theology still remained widely favored, but even where the so-called semi-Pelagian perspective was officially condemned—as it was at the second Council of Orange in 529 under the influence of the loyal Augustinian, Caesarius, bishop of Arles (see pp. 319–22)—the position adopted stopped well short of some of Augustine's language and specifically repudiated the notion that some human beings are predestined to damnation.[17] As the churchmen of Gaul were by then increasingly preoccupied with more immediate challenges from Burgundian and Visigothic Arianism, the technicalities of the debate about grace seemed a somewhat less serious matter.

The Legacy of the Pelagian Controversy

The Pelagian controversy was undoubtedly complicated by misunderstandings on both sides. Pelagius never did want to deny the crucial need for grace, and Augustine never wanted to minimize the importance of holiness. Pelagius did not advocate unalloyed human autonomy or a do-it-yourself system of salvation, and Augustine did not wish to suggest that human beings are devoid of personal responsibility. Both men would have been distinctly uncomfortable with views that later came to be justified with appeal to their names.

The dispute between the two traditions was shaped as it was because of political as well as ecclesiastical circumstances. If Rome had not fallen and Pelagius and his allies had not traveled to North Africa and the East, the affair might never have assumed the significance that it did. If the African church had not succeeded in securing the condemnation of Pelagian doctrine, Augustine might never have worked out quite the same synthesis on sin, grace, and election. Whatever the historical contingencies of the context, though, and whatever real difficulties attend aspects of his thought, Augustine's encounter with Pelagianism produced some of the West's most enduring theological emphases.

Augustine recognized that the issues at stake in his disputes with the Pelagians lay at the heart of the Christian faith. Is grace simply the presentation of an option or the facilitating of a freely willed response; or is it the free action of God upon an otherwise helpless creaturely condition? Is sinful behavior merely the result of a corrupt environment, or is it an inevitable part of our natural state, from the effects of which we cannot extricate ourselves? Is Jesus only an example to which humans choose to respond, or has God acted decisively in him to bring about a state of affairs that we are incapable of achieving for ourselves? Is final salvation a matter of human effort, albeit enabled by God, or is it entirely secured by God's sovereign choice?

Augustine argued that there could be no halfway house between these options. Either human beings are completely free to be sinless or they are not; either they are capable of pleasing God or they are not; either they are naturally in a position to keep on to the end or they are not. Augustine's own experience had convinced him that humans have an inbuilt bias to sin—or, in Pauline terms, a "law" that works within them (Rom. 7:23–24), inclining them to behave contrary to God's will and contrary also to their own highest ideals. A theology of divine-human cooperation can very easily become, in the final analysis, a theology of human merit, for to say that God recognizes some potential or desire in the human is to say that God identifies some prior cause to be merciful, and thus to say that grace is not unconditional. The glory of salvation, Augustine insisted, is that it is from first to last an undeserved gift.

The moral optimism of much Western liberal theology from the eighteenth century onward has assumed an essentially Pelagian reading of human nature. Yet when we consider the dreadful crimes of which supposedly enlightened, sophisticated people have been capable in the modern world, Augustine's general construal of the human condition can sound not so much pessimistic as realistic. Few today might wish to endorse all the details of Augustine's reasoning, but the sobering realities to which he points us are perhaps not so easily dismissed as some have supposed.

The City of God

One final area of Augustine's contribution to subsequent Christian thinking is worth noticing. In the years after the fall of Rome in 410, Augustine, like most Christians, was obliged to reflect on the degree to which the changed political situation of his world reflected the purposes of God in history. For generations, believers had assumed that they were living in "Christian times," and the Roman world had been seen as God's chosen means to achieve the expansion of the gospel and realize the kingdom of God on earth. The emperor had been God's representative, charged with the role of preserving this realm from military threat and political anarchy and thus enabling the churches to flourish and put down ever deeper and more expansive roots in society. Now that world had collapsed, and Rome, the "eternal" city, privileged with a church established by the chief apostles, was overrun by barbarians—many of whom were nominally Christian at that (see pp. 296–300). Where was God's providence in all of this?

As had so often happened in lesser crises in the past, pagan intellectuals blamed the disaster directly on the Christians. It was because the traditional gods had been neglected that Rome had fallen; the true protectors whose patronage had made Rome great had been offended as never before by the actions of the Christians and their naïve political sponsors. A number of Christian responses were forthcoming,[18] but none was as substantial as Augustine's. In a massive work called *The City of God*, produced in stages between 413 and 426, he set out a vast defense of Christianity and a statement of its role in the world.

In the first part of the work (books 1–10), Augustine seeks to answer the charges of the pagan thinkers in an expansive critique of Roman religion and philosophy. Drawing extensively on pagan sources, he argues that Rome never had been immune from barbarian attacks and that this climactic crisis was not the result of enmity on the part of Rome's old deities, who were nothing more than elevated mortals; it was, in practical terms, a consequence of Rome's abuse of others, for which the true God had visited in judgment. For far too long Rome had failed to uphold justice and righteousness and had brutally oppressed other peoples; its downfall was God's condemnation of these evils and God's sign that the gospel was not only for the peoples of the Roman world but for all peoples, including the barbarians.[19]

In the remainder of *The City of God* (books 11–22), Augustine discusses the nature of human society and presents the story of history as a tale of two cities—a divine city and an earthly city, the city of God and the city of the world. The city of God is made up of those whom God has chosen for salvation—those whose desire is, accordingly, not for temporal goods but for God and for obedience to his commands to treat all with justice, love, and compassion. The city of the world consists of those who have turned away from God—those whose goal is to pursue their own selfish purposes irrespective of God's laws.

It is important to appreciate that these two cities do not simply represent, in Augustine's vision, the spiritual and the physical, or church and state. Augustine pictures his two realms as intertwined in time, and the city of God is distinguished from the city of the world in a manner that is invisible to human eyes. The city of the world is not identical with any single earthly empire, whether that of Rome, Babylon, Egypt, or any other power; it is the totality of worldly society in which the love of self rather than the love of God is the governing ideology. The city of God is not simply the catholic church as experienced in the world but a community of the elect, people whose love is for God, not self. The number of its members is known only to God. It is his prerogative to separate the good and the bad at the last.

In the light of this logic, Augustine views the Roman Empire as more or less neutral in theological terms; it is neither directly synonymous with the city of the world nor is it to be equated with the kingdom of God. It is simply one stage in the flux of history, through all of which God is working to bring about the circumstances in which the elect will enter into the fullness of the salvation for which they have been purposed since before the foundation of the world. The empire has happened to be an element in the temporal context in which God's redemptive plan is effected, and it is one that has had both virtues and vices. Earthly rulers have a duty to govern responsibly, promote justice and equity, and avoid oppression; the Roman imperial system succeeded in these respects in varying ways. Christians also have a duty to play their part in civic terms by participating in political life, upholding good order, and engaging where necessary in just wars in defense of their society. But all human systems are corrupt, and believers should not confuse the Roman Empire, or any other realm, with a divine dominion.

The fall of Rome, for Augustine, did not represent the end of God's world but only a part of the realization of God's real purpose in history to bring about a kingdom that will never disappear. Augustine's vision of this consummation is speculative in certain respects. He surmises, for example, that time, development, and communication as we know it—by means of words and signs—will be no more in heaven. Nevertheless, he does appeal to biblical imagery for his picture of the world to come; however contemplative its activity, God's kingdom will be a place inhabited by physically embodied beings, not ethereal souls.

The City of God represents a remarkable fusion of a number of Augustine's key emphases. From the rationale of his polemic against Donatism, and from his reading of Tyconius in particular, he develops a picture of the church as a mixed society. In tandem with his opposition to Pelagianism, he presents the theology of election as central to the understanding not only of the nature of the church but of all history. Along the way he offers wide-ranging reflections on matters of philosophy, law, and politics. His treatise is part apologetic, part polemic, and part political analysis and philosophy of history. Nothing quite like it in scope or style has ever been produced elsewhere, either in the early church or since. In the end, the labyrinthine scale and dense texture of the work make it a daunting read for many people today. In his own time, however, Augustine offered his readers not only an appraisal of their political circumstances but a distinctive assessment of the nature of creaturely existence in a world marred by sin but promised transformation by grace.

Looking Back on Augustine

Augustine's towering gifts and his genius for originality brought him both veneration and contempt, in his own day and ever since. The fifth and sixth centuries saw the enshrining of his teaching on sin and grace, and virtually all medieval and Reformation Christian thought was deeply influenced in one way or another by his ideas on the church and salvation. At the same time, the critical reactions that his views encountered in his own lifetime have never gone away, and in the modern world in particular his opinions have been heavily assaulted in many quarters, both inside and outside the churches.

The history of Augustinian theology undoubtedly has its dark sides, and some of the criticisms directed at the complex traditions to which Augustine's ideas gave rise have been inevitable. Yet the creativity and acuity of Augustine's intellect are such that we perhaps pass by the wisdom of Augustine himself at our peril. He is often far more interesting and far more balanced in his arguments than are the writers who have sought to interpret him or speak in his name. As has been remarked more than once, those who have most dismissed Augustine's ideas have all too often been those who have read him least. Augustine was in every sense a Christian of late antiquity, but for those who are prepared to give his thought the hard work it deserves, he can seem a remarkably modern figure too, whose questions and insights resonate in powerful ways with concerns that continue to intrigue the human spirit today. In the dramatic story of God's church in history, Augustine has played one of the most influential parts.

7

FURTHER REFLECTION
ON CHRIST

▼

Theological Debate in the East

In the years when theology was developing in maturity in the West, plenty of very important doctrinal thinking was still going on in the East. Greek theologians continued to reflect on the issues that the Arian controversies had thrown up and to argue about the implications of some of the strategies that had been adopted in the refutation of Arian ideas. Even where there was strong agreement that Arian theologies were in error, there were enduring debates among Eastern church leaders and intellectuals about how the divinity of Christ was best described. How could it be said that Christ was fully equal to God without undermining his humanity, and how could the integrity of his humanity be affirmed without compromising the claim that God was genuinely present in him?

Questions such as these were obviously not to be found on the lips of all believers, and as always the majority of Christians continued to live out their faith in their own ways regardless of the complex intellectual affairs that preoccupied clergy and scholars. Nevertheless, the

195

overall direction in which the churches of the Eastern Mediterranean world would travel over the later fourth and fifth centuries was in reality significantly determined by the course of theological discussion about just such matters.

Alexandria and Antioch

As we saw in chapter 3, the debate over Christ's divinity had produced in some quarters of the Alexandrian tradition a potential truncation of his humanity. Apollinaris believed Christ was one nature and one *hypostasis*, and in him the place of a normal human mind was taken by the Word. This language was vigorously opposed by many in the 370s and conclusively rejected at the Council of Constantinople in 381 as undermining the reality of Christ's humanity and weakening his status as Savior. Some of the sharpest criticism of Apollinaris's extreme version of Alexandrian Christology came from the church in Antioch. The reasoning of Antiochene churchmen was rooted in a somewhat different approach to theology and Scripture, and in fact Apollinaris himself had in part been driven to argue as he had because of his objection to aspects of the Antiochene tradition.

The most important pioneering figure among the Antiochene thinkers was Diodore, a presbyter of Antioch who served as bishop of Tarsus from 378 until his death around 390. While still in Antioch, Diodore had run a kind of Christian school in which he offered instruction in biblical interpretation, theology, and the practice of asceticism. John Chrysostom was one of his pupils. Diodore concentrated on the historical exegesis of Scripture rather than following the tendency to allegorize that had long been a part of the Alexandrian tradition.[1] The difference in hermeneutical styles between Antioch and Alexandria should not be overstated, since both schools in practice combined a variety of interpretative techniques, and it is certainly too simplistic to suppose that all Antiochenes took an entirely literal or historical approach to biblical texts while their Alexandrian peers were interested only in allegory. Nevertheless, it is true that Antiochene theologians were particularly keen on historical readings of Scripture, and for them this yielded a moralizing approach to the Word of God as the story of God's promises and actions in the world. The historical interpretation of the Bible presented the reader with stark obligations to practical holiness and self-denial; in the case of the Gospels, it also encouraged a construal of Jesus's life that stressed the reality of his moral choices as a human being.

It is a little difficult to ascertain the details of Diodore's theology since our evidence is in fragmentary form, but the outlines of his position on the person of Christ are clear enough. Diodore repudiated understandings of Christ that in his view jeopardized the Savior's role as a moral exemplar. He resisted the logic of the Alexandrian school that the Word should be seen as the direct subject of the experiences of the incarnate Lord. The one who was born, ate, drank, developed as a human being, suffered, died, and was raised was the human son of Mary, not the Word, for the Word is by nature immortal and unchangeable. Christ lived a perfect human life, but the Word was not mixed or confused with his flesh; it was as a man that Jesus fulfilled the moral requirements of God and triumphed over evil.

In Diodore's opinion, Alexandrian views of Christ ended up confusing or mingling the divinity and the humanity of the incarnate one by rendering his human nature utterly subject to the initiative of the Word. Christ was certainly divine, and there could be no room for any kind of Arian reduction of the fullness of his divinity, but his divinity and his humanity needed in a vital sense to be kept distinct. Diodore seems to have taken exception to a traditional way of describing Mary the mother of Jesus as the *Theotokos*, the one who "bears God." Though this title had been in use since the third century, he believed it was inadequate in itself, for it implied just the kind of conflation of divinity and humanity that was so objectionable, and it was no surprise that it was much favored by supporters of Apollinaris. If Mary was the "God-bearer," she must also, with equal weight, be called the "man-bearer" (*anthropotokos*).

From what we can tell, Diodore did not succeed in explaining what it might actually mean to preserve the independent integrity of both the humanity and the divinity of Christ. Things were given a greater degree of clarity, however, by one of his most gifted pupils, Theodore (ca. 350–428). Like John Chrysostom, he was a student not only of Diodore but also of the great pagan orator, Libanius. After serving as a presbyter in Antioch, in 392 Theodore became bishop of Mopsuestia on the Cilician plain east of Tarsus, where his skills as a preacher and exegete earned him the designation "the Interpreter," and his impressive scriptural commentaries and writings on doctrine brought him a wide readership.

Theodore's theology was essentially based upon a conviction quite similar to Athanasius's—that creation, left to itself, slips away into nonexistence and that only divine action can disrupt the creaturely problem of corruption and death. Unlike Athanasius, however, Theodore focused on God's saving action as moral rather than ontological. What happens in the incarnation and saving work of Christ is not so much that the condition of the world is transformed in the here and now, but that the world witnesses to a life lived in perfect obedience to God. Christ confronts us with a supreme moral example that we may follow, in the expectation that the condition of all things will be revolutionized in the age to come. Redemption depends utterly on the authenticity of Christ's response to the will of God as a man. In him there was a perfect coincidence between his human will and the will of the God he called Father. His resurrection confirmed that his life and death guaranteed the final destruction of the present age and opened up a path to a new world.

What Theodore offered, then, was what has been labeled by some modern scholars a "Word-man" Christology, as distinct from the "Word-flesh" model of Alexandrian theology. In the Alexandrian approach, the incarnation was thought of as the Word's assumption of human nature ("flesh") as a whole; in this Antiochene teaching, the incarnation was pictured as the union of the Word with a specific human being. The "Word-flesh" and "Word-man" terminology may be misleading if it is taken to suggest (as it too often has been) that the Antiochenes were concerned primarily to emphasize the full humanity of Jesus whereas the Alexandrians were so preoccupied with the divinity of the Word that they paid only lip service to his humanity. In reality, both traditions were keen to confess that the Son of God had indeed become incarnate, and it is important not to force the Christologies of particular thinkers into rigid categories that exaggerate their differences or oversimplify the subtleties of their teaching. Nonetheless, there were somewhat different conceptions of what needed to be underscored in saying that the Word had entered into human space and time for the purposes of salvation. Like Diodore, Theodore was convinced that the Alexandrian approach led to a conflation of divinity and humanity in Christ. The union of divinity and humanity in him did not in any way compromise or weaken the completeness or the normality of his human nature. In fact, the incarnate Christ could be seen as a conjunction of two watertight compartments—a divine nature and a human nature.

On the face of it, it almost appeared as if in Theodore's account there were *two* "persons" (Greek *prosopa*) in Christ, one divine and one human. Theodore insisted, however, that divinity and humanity came together in *one* concrete "person" (*prosopon*), the "person of the union," solely by the good pleasure of God. There is a Word who assumes and a man who is assumed, and each is perfectly represented in Christ. Instead of the Word as the all-determining subject, there is a mutual concurrence of two complete and unimpaired subjects, a divine and a human, into a single being by grace. The human experiences of Christ—his growth, his limitations in knowledge, his physical needs, his temptations, and his sufferings—are attributable to his humanity, not to the divine Word, for if the Word is divine, he remains of necessity invulnerable and impassible.

To say anything else, Theodore reasoned, was either to compromise Christ's full humanity, as Apollinaris had done, or to compromise his divinity, as Arius had done. In the incarnate one there are two complete natures, and his humanity cannot be absorbed into his divinity any more than his divinity can be reduced to the level of his humanity.

Nestorius

In the same year that Theodore died, 428, another individual from the church of Antioch was appointed bishop of Constantinople. Nestorius (d. 451), who had probably been one of Theodore's pupils, was a former monk with a reputation as a dedicated ascetic and an outstanding preacher. Like John Chrysostom before him, he was determined to reform the church in the imperial capital, and he had a passion to root out heresies of various kinds. However, he soon found himself embroiled in controversy for his own theological views.

One of Nestorius's priests, a chaplain named Anastasius whom he had brought with him from Antioch, incurred public criticism for his objection to the use of the title *Theotokos* for Mary. Nestorius fully supported Anastasius, and he rebuked one of the leading priests of Constantinople, Proclus (who had earlier been defeated in his attempt to win the episcopal chair in the city),[2] for his deployment of the term. Like Diodore and Theodore, Nestorius regarded the designation as synonymous with Apollinarianism, and to him it was inappropriate, certainly on its own, however genuine the devotion to Mary that lay behind it. Mary was *anthropotokos*, the "man-bearer," or, perhaps better, *Christotokos*, the "Christ-bearer." To speak of her as *Theotokos*, without further qualification, was to dissolve the distinction between the two natures of Christ and to undermine his humanity in particular.

Nestorius's aim was to say much the same as his Antiochene predecessors, but his use of language was careless. He may have been prepared to countenance, under pressure, a qualified use of the title *Theotokos* in conjunction with other specifications of the nature of the one whom Mary had borne, but his instinctive hostility to the term seemed suspicious. It sounded to some as if he took Christ to be *only* a man and not to be divine as well. Was Nestorius effectively going back to the old heresy of the adoptionists and saying that Christ was just a human being who happened to be specially inspired by God or adopted into relationship with him as his Son?

News of Nestorius's teaching reached the ears of Cyril, the bishop of Alexandria (ca. 380–444), and the ensuing course of christological debate in the fifth century and beyond was dramatically affected by the way in which Cyril chose to respond.

Cyril of Alexandria

Cyril had been bishop in Alexandria since 412, when he had succeeded his uncle, Theophilus. Like Theophilus, he had always nursed an instinctive resentment of the see of Constantinople, which he regarded as an upstart ecclesiastical establishment, dating only from the fourth century and not from an apostolic foundation, as Alexandria itself claimed to be. The growth in Constantinople's prestige and territorial authority and the confirmation of its privileges in the council held there in 381 were very sore points indeed in Alexandria. Theophilus's behavior towards John Chrysostom had amply demonstrated this (see pp. 155–57), and Cyril himself had for several years upheld his uncle's refusal to vindicate John's memory. When Nestorius had come to power in Constantinople, Cyril had in the end reluctantly agreed to rehabilitate John by inserting his name into the "diptychs" or list of saints recited in his church during the liturgy of the Eucharist, but his spirit of cooperation was soon to be changed by his reaction to Nestorius's behavior.

Cyril's years as a bishop had already been marked by plenty of controversy. He too had been determined to stamp out heresy and to consolidate the authority of his church in its immediate society, and he had had to face down considerable opposition from the start. His election in 412 had been disputed, and he had had to resist political pressure and popular unrest in order to secure his position. In the years that followed he had made himself thoroughly unpopular with many in Egypt by his suppression of dissidents, not only within but outside the bounds of the church; he had also treated Jews very roughly[3] and had shown a marked intolerance towards pagans. His incitement of intolerance had reached its darkest hour in 415 when the distinguished Neoplatonist teacher Hypatia was set upon and murdered by a Christian mob, with apparently no attempted intervention on the part of the bishop. Her death was heard of with horror in Constantinople, and the news naturally did little to quell fears about Cyril's tactics.

Other controversial incidents had continued in Alexandria in the ensuing years, and though none was quite so appalling as the killing of Hypatia, Cyril's abrasive style continued to bring him enemies. His confidence seemed to have been undiminished all the same, and he was already engaged in some of the writing that would ultimately win him much fame, including work on a refutation of the arguments of the apostate emperor Julian against Christianity. Cyril was a highly prolific author, who wrote extensively on Scripture as well as theology. The largest part of his literary output consisted of biblical commentaries; many of these are now lost, but a number survive either in their original Greek form or in ancient translations. Cyril's style was diffuse and rhetorically impassioned, but he was a thinker of penetrating insight and deep spiritual conviction. A staunch follower of Athanasius's theology and a proud representative of a distinguished tradition of Christian culture, Cyril saw no reason to yield to anyone in presenting his faith as the only viable option for his social and intellectual world. It is possible to exaggerate the fierceness of Cyril's temperament and to overlook his considerable significance as a theologian and teacher, but it is undoubtedly the case that his manner of operating was often ruthless, and even allowing for the volatility of the times, his methods of dealing with those who disagreed with him can hardly be defended.

Toward the end of 428, a group of four Alexandrian citizens complained to the emperor Theodosius II that they had been mistreated by Cyril. The emperor referred the matter to his local bishop, Nestorius. This inevitably provoked Cyril's ire. Cyril refused to accept the right of Constantinople to sit in judgment on his conduct, and he launched into an attack on Nestorius on the basis of what he had heard about his doctrinal views. Cyril was a very capable theologian and biblical expositor, but he was also a thoroughly unscrupulous propagandist, and he exploited every opportunity to besmirch Nestorius. Writing to his own monks in Egypt warning them of the dangers of false teaching, he seized the chance to jibe obliquely at Nestorius's reluctance to accept the *Theotokos*. When Nestorius expressed offense that he had been implicitly accused of denying the deity of Christ, something that he had not the least desire to do, Cyril remonstrated that it was he, Nestorius, who had caused the problem in the first place, and that all he had to do was affirm the *Theotokos* in order to allay fears.

In reality, it was Cyril who was most guilty of stirring up these fears by using accessories in Constantinople to foster an atmosphere of hostility towards Nestorius as a blasphemer against the Savior's divinity, and by alerting the bishop of Rome, Celestine, to what was being preached in Constantinople. It was not particularly difficult to whip up opposition in Constantinople, for Nestorius had made enemies through his outspoken denunciations of contemporary social mores. Nevertheless, Nestorius continued to enjoy the favor of the emperor Theodosius II, so there was as yet a limit to what Cyril's overtures or the machinations of his allies could achieve.

Early in 430 Cyril wrote another letter to Nestorius. Its argument became one of the most significant documents in the Christology of the fifth-century church. Cyril claimed, with some pertinence, that the term *Theotokos* was a logical correlate of Mary's status as the human mother of the one who, according to the Nicene faith, was on earth "the Word of God, begotten of the substance of God the Father." If Nestorius was not prepared to recognize that, surely he was calling into question the credal affirmation of the divinity of the incarnate Son. Cyril acknowledged that the distinction between the divine and the human natures of Christ was not abolished by their union, but he insisted that the two sides nevertheless come together as a single personal entity. The eternal Word united with himself, in his own *hypostasis*, a body and a rational soul, and thus became human.

Cyril was careful to avoid a charge of Apollinarianism by stressing that the humanity of Christ was complete and that Jesus possessed a rational soul or mind. But he insisted fundamentally that the Word was not united to an independent human being but rather "became flesh"—and so, however mysteriously, the Word, though intrinsically impassible and eternal, might be said to have suffered and died when Jesus was crucified. Talk of the Word as growing, developing, being vulnerable, and so on was not just a concession to popular thought but an essential part of what it meant to confess that the Word became incarnate. If the Word was the subject of the incarnate Christ, and the Word was God, Cyril argued, then Mary genuinely had to be described as the mother of God, or the "God-bearer"; to say anything less was to misunderstand the nature of Christ as a single divine-human being.

When Nestorius replied to Cyril's second letter, he made bold to rebuke him for failing to understand the tradition of Nicaea. The credal phrase, "one Lord Jesus Christ, his only-begotten Son," revealed, he argued, that the fathers of the council deliberately placed side by side the names that belong to both natures, and they were careful not to attribute the human experiences of Christ directly to his divinity. Christ is one, but certain things that he says and does are to be attributed to his divinity and certain other things to his humanity. In short, Nestorius adduced a classic Antiochene Christology of two distinct natures.

Cyril continued to foment opposition to Nestorius. He wrote letters to prominent members of the imperial court in Constantinople complaining in thinly veiled terms about Nestorius's beliefs, and he sought to play on the tensions that existed between Theodosius's elder sister, Pulcheria, who disapproved of Nestorius, and his wife, Eudoxia, who favored him. More significantly, he also sent a copy of his second letter to Nestorius to Celestine, who was already none too well disposed toward his colleague in Constantinople for his favorable treatment of Pelagian churchmen who had been excommunicated by Rome (see p. 188). Celestine replied by assuring Cyril that a Roman synod had considered the grounds of his objection to Nestorius's teaching and had determined that Nestorius must be commanded to alter his views or face condemnation. Nestorius was to be allowed just ten days from receipt of Cyril's letter to recant his views and confess the faith as held in Rome and Alexandria or else be excommunicated.

Actually Nestorius was given more time; the injunction did not reach him until November 430, despite having been written in August. It was accompanied by a third epistle from Cyril that vigorously condemned the core elements of the Antiochene approach to Christology and contended that Nestorius must abjure his erroneous interpretation of the Creed of Nicaea. This time Cyril showed Nestorius no quarter whatsoever and insisted that he acknowledge the error of his ways. Cyril summed up his argument in Twelve Anathemas of falsehood concerning the person of Christ, and he demanded that Nestorius give his word that he dissented from every one of them. Among the "falsehoods" to be denied was the characteristically Antiochene emphasis on the distinction between the two natures.

Nestorius was called upon to confess that the Word is the subject of the incarnate one and that it was wrong to ascribe certain actions or expressions to his humanity instead of his divinity. Nestorius had to be prepared to affirm that the Word "suffered in the flesh," and to accept that the Word was able voluntarily to restrain his powers in order to live within the confines of humanity. Cyril's intemperate language in this letter potentially raised problems for far more Christian confessors than just Nestorius, and his anathemas were undesirable in several respects, for his own position, while classically Alexandrian, seemed to tread perilously close to the extremes of Apollinaris in stating that while the Word suffered in the flesh, he remained impassible in the process—a claim that appeared to undermine his humanity.

The Council of Ephesus

By the time Nestorius received Cyril's letter and the papal judgment, Theodosius had decided to summon a council of churchmen to meet at Ephesus at Pentecost the following year, 431, to try to settle the dispute. Nestorius was assured of strong support from the Syrian bishops, led by his friend John of Antioch, and he was confident that Cyril's Twelve Anathemas were sufficiently dangerous to swing the tide of episcopal opinion in favor of the Antiochene alternative.

However, things did not go as Nestorius and his allies expected. First, the Syrians were delayed in arriving in Ephesus as a result of bad weather.[4] The local bishop, Memnon, was deeply hostile to Nestorius, and he supported the ploy of Cyril to get the council under way in any case, on the pretext that Nestorius himself was present and that things had been delayed already. The emperor's representative, the military commander Candidian, tried in vain to defer the proceedings, and for his efforts he was accused of favoring Nestorius. In the absence of the Syrian churchmen, Cyril's position was bolstered by the activities of a large number of monks, variously imported from Egypt or supplied by Memnon, who terrorized his opponents.

More significant than the physical threats from Cyril's monastic partisans and the efforts of his episcopal colleagues from Egypt was the widespread hostility to the Antiochene Christology felt by a large majority of the bishops of Asia Minor as well as the resentment of the prestige of both Antioch and Constantinople, Nestorius's church, by the representatives of other sees in their regions. Constantinople's status was naturally disliked in Ephesus and elsewhere; Antioch's power chafed on sensibilities in Jerusalem, where Bishop Juvenal was convinced that his see deserved to be recognized as the leading episcopate in the East.

Cyril was able to capitalize on these feelings and, further, to spread fear of Nestorius at a popular level by claiming disreputably that Nestorius taught a Christ who was only a specially inspired man. For many ordinary believers, Nestorius's alleged views were easily demonized: for those who instinctively pictured Christ as God in human form and who thought of themselves as worshiping his incorruptible flesh in the Eucharist, the prospect of a Savior who was not intrinsically divine was a genuinely loathsome thought. In reality, this was not at all what Nestorius taught, but his resistance to the language of the *Theotokos* and his insistence on a distinction between the humanity of Christ and the inviolable majesty of God were readily turned into much more sinister claims.

In this climate of overwhelming resentment and distortion of ideas, Nestorius refused to recognize the council's legitimacy and declined to appear before it. By the time the Syrian bishops arrived, Cyril had engineered the condemnation of Nestorius for contempt of ecclesiastical authority, and word was sent to Celestine that he had been duly excommunicated. The Syrians, however (numbering forty-three as opposed to the two hundred or so bishops of Cyril's council), proceeded to convene their own synod at which they in turn declared Cyril and Memnon to be deposed for having held an invalid assembly. When emissaries finally arrived from Rome,[5] they sided with Cyril, according to Celestine's instructions, and gave the sanction of the bishop of Rome to the legitimacy of Nestorius's condemnation. Cyril's assembly was reconvened, and now it was officially said to be the third great "ecumenical" council. The findings of the synod of the Antiochenes were formally dismissed without further discussion, and various decisions were made to reinforce the disapproval of the Syrians and to reward the supporters of Cyril.

The two parties of Cyril and John of Antioch anathematized each other, and both sides lobbied the emperor. In considerable confusion, Theodosius endorsed the condemnations of all three of the protagonists of Ephesus—Cyril, Memnon, and Nestorius—on the apparent assumption that the decisions of the separate ecclesiastical gatherings had been made by a single council. A period of tortuous negotiation then ensued, in which Cyril spent vast sums on bribes to petition influential members of the court. Cyril and Memnon managed to extricate themselves from custody and return to their sees, officially acquitted. Nestorius was allowed by Theodosius to retire to his monastery at Antioch. It was assumed that he had resigned his see, though this was not his intention. In any event, he had neither the will nor the resources with which to maneuver his way out of his predicament, and he was obliged to accept his fate. A successor to him was appointed, one Maximian, a weak character who was acceptable to the pro-Cyrillines.

With Nestorius himself removed from the forefront of the fray, Cyril was somewhat more amenable to making his peace with John of Antioch and his supporters. Both sides needed to compromise, however: the Antiochenes would have to abandon their support for Nestorius and accept his official condemnation, and Cyril would have to agree to let go of his insistence on the Twelve Anathemas stipulated in his third letter to Nestorius. For Cyril, the potential climbdown was greater, but under pressure from Theodosius he responded positively to an invitation to reach a settlement.

The Formulary of Reunion

In 433 Cyril put his signature to a statement that became known as the Formulary of Reunion. This document had first been drafted by the prominent Syrian theologian, Theodoret, bishop of Cyrrhus, a town to the north of Antioch (ca. 393–460). It was essentially Antiochene in tone and declared Christ to be a "union of two natures," consisting of "perfect God and perfect man . . . , of one substance with the Father in his Godhead, and of one substance with us in his humanity."

This was in principle similar to the kind of formula that Nestorius himself could have endorsed: the incarnate Christ is one person in whom two distinct natures are combined. The statement went beyond the terms of its original form to affirm that Mary was indeed to be confessed as the *Theotokos* on the grounds that the union of the two natures, while "unconfused," is genuine. It also proposed—directly contrary to Cyril's contention in the fourth of the Twelve Anathemas—that certain New Testament texts could be understood to refer to the "one person," while others referred to one or other of the "two natures."

Most Antiochenes except for Nestorius and some of his staunchest advocates, above all the formidable Theodoret, had in fact never had serious difficulty with the *Theotokos* in any case, and so, in theological terms at least, little was being given up on their side. The statement secured the very insistence on the two natures that had always been the Antiochene preoccupation. For Cyril, on the other hand, the Formulary represented quite a significant concession. No longer was he insisting on the divine Word as the subject of the flesh of Christ or on the impossibility of distinguishing the words and deeds of Christ according to his divinity on the one hand and his humanity on the other. Cyril's more zealous partisans were outraged that he had accepted such a compromise, and he sought to reassure them that he understood the "union of two natures" to be akin to the union that exists between two technically separate entities, "body" and "soul," in any human being; while the mind might logically differentiate these entities, there is in reality only one "nature" subsequent to their union.[6]

The Formulary of Reunion, agreed under a strong measure of political influence, brought a degree of peace between the Antiochenes and the Alexandrians while John and Cyril were alive. There was nevertheless a significant amount of discontent. Cyril continued to gloss his acquiescence in a largely Antiochene statement by deliberately stressing the singleness as opposed to the duality of which it spoke, but his efforts did not satisfy those who felt that the all-important emphasis on the oneness of the divine Word's saving action had been compromised. On the Antiochene side, too, there was some serious unease—not because of the overall thrust of the Formulary's theology, but because of the way in which Nestorius personally had been betrayed. Even before the passing of John and Cyril, there were problems. Cyril might argue that he had not in fact withdrawn any of his previous teaching; at the same time, in large parts of Syria, Armenia, and Persia there was enduring and passionate support for the Antiochene doctrine as a package quite distinct from the views of Cyril.

Theodoret continued to speak out against Cyril's ideas, and there was widespread reverence for the theology of Theodore, Nestorius's great mentor, whose teaching was particularly championed by Ibas, bishop of Edessa.[7] Cyril meddled actively to try to dissuade the Armenian churches from their sympathies, abetted in this task by the agencies of Proclus, the successor of Maximian at Constantinople, who wrote a lengthy letter to the Armenians interpreting the Formulary of Reunion in a plainly Cyrilline direction. Theodore was not condemned by name, but it was hinted in the strongest terms that the theological trajectory to which Antiochene Christology belonged was in error. The incarnation was the coming into flesh of "the divine Word, one of the Trinity," not a union of the Word with an independent man.

By the later 440s, few of the figures at the forefront of the dispute remained. John of Antioch died in 441, Cyril in 444, and Proclus in 446. In Rome, Sixtus III, who had succeeded Celestine in 432 and ratified the settlement of 433, had died in 440 and been replaced by Leo (I). Nestorius himself outlived most of his immediate enemies and all but Theodoret among his prominent advocates. In 435 his writings had been condemned and in 437 he had been banished to Egypt, but he survived until around 451, after spending his last years in the desert, where he suffered a good deal.

While in exile, Nestorius sought to defend his orthodoxy in a series of letters and tracts, of which for the most part only fragments are extant today. One more substantial item from this legacy, however, was a collection of his ideas that survives under a later cryptic title, *The Book of Heracleides*. A Syriac version of the text was discovered only in the late nineteenth century; the manuscript was destroyed in Kurdistan during the First World War, but copies had already been made and published in 1910. If Nestorius's arguments in this work are to be taken at face value, it is clear that his theology never had been what it was alleged to be. His assertive style of churchmanship and forceful denunciation of the views of his opponents had not helped his cause, but in doctrinal terms it seems Nestorius never was a "Nestorian," in the sense that he never taught, as his enemies alleged, a doctrine of a schizoid Christ, composed of two distinct persons, nor had he suggested that Jesus was merely a man taken into special relationship with God. By the standards of the christological consensus that came to be settled upon around the time of his death, Nestorius could probably have been accommodated within the bounds of orthodoxy.

The Dispute Reopens: Other Personalities

Such accommodation was not Nestorius's fate; but the efforts in defense of his position ensured that his views continued to enjoy a significant amount of support among traditionalist Antiochenes in the later 440s, and the differences that had crystallized between Alexandria and Antioch in the light of his teaching were not to go away. It took only the passing of the main protagonists from the two camps for relationships to become seriously frayed once more. Cyril was succeeded in Alexandria by Dioscorus. Dioscorus was at first widely welcomed as a change from Cyril: he seemed to be a modest and sane man who would not jeopardize relations with other sees. Even Theodoret had high hopes of his good sense. However, Alexandria's new leader turned out to be a ruthless and devious character with a passionate determination to assert the influence of his see and to root out support for Nestorius wherever he believed it to exist.

Dioscorus's strategy was facilitated by the character of some of his major contemporaries in the East. In Antioch, John's successor was his nephew Domnus, who proved a weak leader, very much in submission to Theodoret. In Constantinople, Proclus was replaced by Flavian, who was well-meaning but of a somewhat retiring temperament. Flavian's loyalties lay with the "Word-flesh" approach to Christology, but he was keen to uphold the Formulary of Reunion as a basis for maintaining the peace between those of more radical views on either side of him. In the midst of it all, the emperor Theodosius II was singularly indecisive; always prey to competing and changing forces in his court, he was by the late 440s guided by a chief official named Chrysaphius, for whose power and cunning Flavian was no match. Chrysaphius was influenced by a senior monastic abbot or "archimandrite" in Constantinople,[8] Eutyches, who was a great enthusiast for Cyril's theology and a fierce opponent of what he regarded as the Nestorian tendencies implicit in a Christology of two natures.

From 446 onward, Dioscorus interfered in Antiochene territory in a bid to stamp out Nestorianism. He succeeded in removing (on technical grounds) Irenaeus, bishop of Tyre, a committed Antiochene and former fierce critic of Cyril whom Domnus had installed. In addition to the obvious embarrassment caused to Domnus, further complaints were stirred up against Theodoret, who was obliged to write in defense of his doctrine. Theodoret published a lengthy and cleverly crafted attack on Alexandrian Christology entitled *Eranistes* or "Collector" (implying that the typical Cyrilline theologian constructed his opinions by collecting all kinds of heretical ideas into a pastiche of false doctrine). The work consists of three dialogues with an imaginary Cyrilline opponent, whom Theodoret accuses of confusing the natures of Christ and thus rendering the Godhead itself liable to change, adulteration, and suffering. Theodoret's arguments are skillfully assembled and carefully supported by both scriptural citations and quotations from traditional authorities.

However, the axis of forces at work against the theology Theodoret was seeking to defend was considerable. Dioscorus was driven not only by hostility to Nestorianism but also by a strong antipathy to Antiochene attempts to claim that the church of Antioch, as allegedly founded by the apostle Peter, was a more prestigious see than Alexandria, which was supposed to have been established by Mark. Dioscorus also had influential contacts. One of his associates was Eutyches, the great admirer of Cyril, with whom he had corresponded in earlier years. He also had close connections with the powerful Chrysaphius. In the spring of 448 the alliance of Dioscorus, Chrysaphius, and Eutyches resulted in an imperial edict preventing Theodoret from convening conciliar gatherings and confining him to his own diocese.

Eutyches and Flavian

That same year, Eutyches provocatively attacked the soundness of those who spoke of "two natures after the union," arguing instead that the humanity of Christ was absorbed by his divinity. The Word was made flesh, but his human nature was not "of the same substance" as ours; it was taken up into the one nature of the divine Word. The Formulary of Reunion, Eutyches claimed, was an unworthy addition to the Creed of Nicaea as a doctrinal standard. Eutyches's teaching was, on the face of it, self-consciously Cyrilline in orientation. Cyril himself had spoken of "one nature of the divine Word incarnate." By leaving out the term *incarnate*, however, Eutyches was implying that he saw the divine Word as utterly dominant, and in denying that the humanity of Christ was consubstantial with ours and criticizing the two-natures language of the Formulary, he seemed to leave little room for ambiguity. He believed there were indeed two natures *before* the union of Word and flesh, but only one *after*.

Eutyches was accused of heresy before Flavian by Eusebius, bishop of Dorylaeum. Eusebius had attacked Nestorius nearly twenty years earlier as a young lawyer in Constantinople, and he remained strongly opposed to all sympathy for Nestorius, but he was concerned that Eutyches was guilty of going too far in the opposite direction and confounding the two natures altogether. At a local synod in Constantinople in November 448, Eutyches was condemned for teaching an Apollinarian reduction of the full humanity of Christ. Eutyches protested that his trial had not been conducted fairly, and he conveyed his complaints not only to the bishops of Alexandria and Jerusalem but also to Rome.

Unsurprisingly, Dioscorus sided entirely with Eutyches and accused Flavian of requiring some test other than the Creed of Nicaea as a determinant of orthodoxy, despite the decision at Ephesus in 431 that no such supplementary requirement could be made. Flavian in turn reported his problems also to Leo in Rome. Theodosius, influenced by Chrysaphius and annoyed by reports of disturbances in Edessa as a result of the teaching of Bishop Ibas, made it clear that he had no confidence in Flavian's ability to handle the dispute and decided to call another council to meet at Ephesus in August 449 with judicial powers to settle the matter between Flavian and Eutyches. Dioscorus was to preside.

A Second Council in Ephesus, and Leo's *Tome*

The odds were stacked firmly against Flavian. With Dioscorus in charge, supported by a very strong representation of pro-Alexandrian bishops and a group of faithful monks ready to make their presence known; with the most capable of the obvious countervoices, Theodoret, silenced; and with the emperor himself on his side, things were bound to go Eutyches's way. Leo was invited to attend from Rome, but he had already dithered over how to handle the joint appeals to him by Flavian and Eutyches. Leo's initial instincts had been that Flavian, like most bishops of Constantinople, had probably been acting above himself and that Eutyches was probably more foolish than he was heretical. After acquainting himself with the details of Eutyches's trial, Leo realized that Eutyches definitely was in error; nevertheless, he still declined to attend the council: instead he would send three legates and a statement of doctrine, addressed to Flavian, which could be read to the council.

Leo's *Tome* (as it came to be known, from the Greek *tomos*, "booklet"), written in characteristically elegant prose, was unoriginal in content and reflected established assumptions of Western Christology, but it spelled out a firm denunciation of Eutyches's ideas. It was quite wrong to speak of "one nature after the union" or to deny that the humanity of Christ was consubstantial with regular human nature. If Christ was not truly one of us, if he did not genuinely "take our nature and make it his own" by "receiving the reality of his body from the body of the Virgin," he could not have conquered the sin and death that afflict the human condition. For human salvation to have been secured, Leo contended, there needed to be a union, by divine grace, of two distinct natures. The incarnate Christ was "complete in what belongs to him, complete in what belongs to us." There could be no possibility that his humanity was abridged, though it was possible to speak of the attributes of each nature applying to the other on account of their union in the one person. Eutyches had got things quite the wrong way around; the truth was not that there were two natures before the union and one after, but rather that there was one nature before and two after.

Leo's *Tome* demonstrated the way in which Western Christology was capable of holding together aspects of both of the main streams of Eastern thought, but in the context of the late 440s its message was abundantly clear. As far as the church of Rome was concerned, Eutyches, no matter how much powerful support he had, was in the wrong and was to be called upon to renounce his error. Leo's effort, however, did Flavian no good. The legates from Rome were received at the council and given seats of honor, but they were never allowed to read out their bishop's communiqué. Flavian and his supporters were refused permission to speak in their own defense. Eutyches was exonerated and reinstated, and Flavian and Eusebius of Dorylaeum were deemed to have violated the stipulations of Ephesus by treating assent to the Formulary of Reunion as a test of orthodoxy; they were therefore to be deposed. The Formulary, and with it the language of two natures after the union, was abandoned.

Dioscorus used violence, intimidation, and corruption to get his way. Flavian himself was physically assaulted and never recovered from the treatment he received; he died on the way to an enforced exile not long afterwards. Dioscorus sealed his victory by securing the deposal of Theodoret, Ibas, and Domnus. Others similarly perceived to be guilty of Nestorianism, including Eusebius of Dorylaeum, also fell in the aftermath, and in November 449 a former protégé of Cyril's, and recently Dioscurus's representative in Constantinople,[9] one Anatolius, was installed as Flavian's successor in the capital.

By this time Leo had already heard of the proceedings at Ephesus, and he was outraged. He denounced the assembly as a "den of robbers" (*latrocinium*), and relayed to the emperor that a Roman synod had reached the same conclusions. Besieged with appeals from Flavian, Eusebius, and Theodoret, Leo wrote to the emperor requesting that another council be called, and he sought the support of Theodosius's sister, Pulcheria, to bring this about. He also attempted to negotiate with Anatolius. But Theodosius remained satisfied with the outcome of Ephesus, "robber council" or no, and although Pulcheria's influence was beginning to challenge the position of Chrysaphius at court, little as yet could be done to reverse the advantage that the Alexandrians had achieved.

However, everything was to change in the summer of 450. After sustaining a bad fall from his horse, Theodosius died on 28 July. Pulcheria took over the government, and she took as her consort a former Thracian general and senator named Marcian. The new regime brought a change in ecclesiastical politics. Pulcheria and Marcian were determined to reestablish good relations between Constantinople and Rome, amid a turbulent climate of barbarian invasions. This meant a reversal of the theological stance of Theodosius's last period. Chrysaphius was executed, and Eutyches was sent into exile. Flavian's remains were brought back to Constantinople, and the honor of his memory was restored by the insertion of his name among the honored saints mentioned in the Eucharist. Leo continued to negotiate with Anatolius—in a series of maneuvers that all came down to competing claims about the relative status of the two sees—and was hopeful that agreement could be reached between them.

Marcian was determined to exercise control and have matters settled once and for all, and in the end he called a general council to meet at Nicaea in September of 451. The venue was shifted to Chalcedon, just across the Bosphorus from Constantinople, and proceedings did not begin until 8 October.

The Council of Chalcedon

The assembly met in fifteen sessions and went on until 10 November. It was attended by over five hundred bishops.[10] The overwhelming majority were from the East; the West was represented by just two emissaries from the church in Rome and two bishops from Africa. The proceedings were firmly controlled by Pulcheria's imperial commissioners, and most of the sessions were chaired by laymen. Dioscorus was tried for his conduct at the "robber council" and found guilty of acting illegally; though defiant to the last, he was deposed, and the proceedings of 449 were overturned. Some of Dioscorus's former allies, such as Juvenal of Jerusalem, deserted him and were allowed to keep their positions. Juvenal was rewarded by the council's recognition of his see as having jurisdiction over the whole of Palestine, though he would find there was much opposition to this when he returned home.[11] Theodoret and Ibas were restored to their offices on the condition that they at last disowned Nestorius, who was denounced as a heretic.

The most important achievement of the council was, however, the statement of faith that it issued. It was clear from early on that Marcian and Pulcheria, through their officials, were keen that a new confessional formula should be promulgated, and although there was much unease and dissension about the process, the bishops were obliged to come up with something by way of a settlement to the doctrinal controversies of the past years. It was necessary that the language of the statement should expressly draw on existing positions with which all might concur. It was agreed that the statements of Nicaea in 325 and Constantinople in 381 should be endorsed without qualification, and the teaching of Ephesus in 431 was also reaffirmed. These councils were jointly recognized as being of ecumenical authority for the whole church.

But what of the more recent wrangles? Leo's *Tome* was read and, after some debate, approved as orthodox, but it was proposed that Leo's teaching was essentially in line with Cyril's, whose authority was treated as of fundamental importance. Cyril's repudiation of Nestorianism was the key to his emphasis on the oneness of Christ, and Nestorianism needed to be proscribed without any ambiguity. Many of the Greek bishops were reluctant to go further than this, since any new statement about the formal relationship of the singleness and the duality in Christ was only likely to perpetuate division. Nevertheless, the imperial authorities were determined to secure more than just an effective acknowledgment of Leo's mediating language. After much negotiation and discussion, the council produced the following new confession of faith:

> Therefore, following the holy fathers, we confess and all with one voice teach our Lord Jesus Christ to be one and the same Son, the same perfect in Godhead, the same perfect in manhood, truly God and truly man, the same consisting of a rational soul and a body, of one substance with the Father as concerning the Godhead, the same of one substance with us as

concerning the manhood, like us in all things apart from sin; begotten of the Father before the ages as concerning the Godhead, the same in the last days, for us and for our salvation, born of the Virgin Mary, the *Theotokos*, as concerning the manhood, one and the same Christ, Son, Lord, Only-begotten, acknowledged in two natures, without confusion, without change, without division, without separation; the distinction of the natures being in no way abolished because of the union but rather the characteristic property of each nature being preserved and concurring into one person (*prosopon*) and one subsistence (*hypostasis*), not as if Christ were parted or divided into two persons (*prosopa*), but one and the same Son and Only-begotten God, Word, Lord, Jesus Christ; just as the prophets from the beginning spoke concerning him, and our Lord Jesus Christ instructed us, and the creed of the fathers has handed down to us.

The language of the formula was drawn from various sources. The description of Christ as "perfect in Godhead, the same perfect in manhood . . . of one substance with the Father as concerning the Godhead, . . . of one substance with us as concerning the manhood" came from the Formulary of Reunion. The clause, "the distinction of the natures being in no way abolished because of the union," derived from Cyril's second letter to Nestorius. The claim that "the characteristic property of each nature" is "preserved" and that together these qualities can be thought of as "concurring into one person and one subsistence" originated in Leo's *Tome*. The Cyrilline stress on the oneness of the incarnate Word was deliberately asserted in the repetition of "one and the same" and "the same," and the *Theotokos* was also affirmed. At the same time, the reference to Christ's "rational soul" ruled out an Apollinarian understanding of the Word's subjecthood as in any way lessening the integrity of his humanity; his human nature was firmly stated, against Eutyches's teaching, to be consubstantial with ours.

The most contentious clause was the phrase "in two natures," which came from Leo's Western context. Some of the churchmen preferred to say "*out of* or *from* [*ek*] two natures" rather than "*in* [*en*] two natures," but there were fears in some quarters, especially among the Roman delegates, that this risked the danger of Eutyches's position, for he had spoken of "one *from* [*ek*] two." By saying that Christ is "acknowledged *in* two natures," the formula implied that he is recognized as *having* two natures. The entailments of the union of these natures were specified in four negative clauses (in the original Greek, four single adverbs): "without confusion, without change, without division, without separation." The first two affirmed, in Antiochene style, the reality of the twofoldness even in union; the second two made it equally clear that there could be no

Nestorian splitting apart of the natures so as to constitute two distinct persons. The formula thus endeavored to affirm, with the traditional Alexandrian approach, the unity of the one Lord Jesus Christ while also, under Antiochene influence, shunning any idea of a conflation between the Savior's divinity and his humanity.

The Council of Chalcedon attempted to set out the parameters within which the mystery of the incarnation could be spoken of, and in some sense to settle the conflicts that had divided the churches so unhelpfully for so long, especially in the East. Its language was nevertheless destined to run into difficulties immediately. To some of the more zealous Antiochenes, there was concern that the distinction between the essential qualities of the two natures was not being affirmed strongly enough. On the other side, and of still greater significance in the longer term, there was opposition from thoroughgoing Alexandrians. To them, far too much was in fact being given away to the Antiochene approach. If Christ was not "from two natures" but "acknowledged in two natures" then, whatever caveats were entered about an absence of "division" or "separation" and however much it was said that the incarnate one represents a single "person" and "subsistence," the uniqueness of the divine Word enfleshed seemed to be compromised.

The formula was rejected by a significant number of Christians in Egypt in particular and by others from elsewhere in the East as well, especially in Palestine and Syria. These believers cherished Cyril's depiction of the incarnate Christ as existing in "one nature," and were convinced that Chalcedon had betrayed the reality of the fleshly existence of divinity on earth. The political and intellectual history of the Eastern churches in the later fifth, sixth, and seventh centuries is in great measure the story of diverse attempts—all, in the end, futile—to achieve a settlement that would restore unity between those who accepted Chalcedon and those to whom its teaching appeared to be in serious error.

8

ARGUING OVER CHALCEDON: DIVISION AND EXPANSION

▼

Recognizing Chalcedon

The agreement reached by the delegates at the Council of Chalcedon ran into problems straightaway. In the first place, there were significant difficulties surrounding the council's practical enactments. As at previous councils, a series of canons had been issued. Twenty-seven in number, they were primarily concerned with church order and with the discipline of officials, but among their prescriptions were some controversial judgments concerning ecclesiastical authority. The see of Constantinople was recognized to have the right to act as a court of appeals against the decisions of provincial bishops. A twenty-eighth canon had also been added, which reaffirmed the contested decision of the Council of Constantinople in 381 that the "new Rome," like the old, possessed ecclesiastical primacy because of its imperial status. It had further been specified that the bishop of Constantinople had direct jurisdiction over the major metropolitan dioceses of Pontus, Asia, and Thrace, and over the churches outside the empire that were associated with them.

The Roman legates protested strongly at this, appealing to the sixth canon of Nicaea, which had named Rome, Alexandria, and Antioch as the three primary sees, though that decision had been passed prior to the existence of Constantinople as a city. It was quite unacceptable to Pope Leo that the authority of Rome should be deemed to depend upon secular political prestige rather than upon the eminence of an apostolic foundation. Although the emperor Marcian officially declared the decrees of the council to be law, Leo proceeded to annul the twenty-eighth canon, protesting against it (and Constantinople's Bishop Anatolius) in the strongest terms. Despite the obvious risk entailed for church relations, he refused to ratify the doctrinal statement of Chalcedon until 453.

Leo had no quarrel with the council's theology; his delay in granting formal recognition to its pronouncements stemmed from his resistance to the further aggrandizement of Constantinople. Others, however, had far more deep-seated objections to the details agreed upon at Chalcedon, and it was in the specifics of the council's Christology that the most enduring problems lay. It soon became clear that, as had been the case at Nicaea in 325, there were differing interpretations of the council's confessional formula even among those who had signed it. The delegates had recorded their approval of Cyril's letters to Nestorius and to the Antiochenes, but they had not clarified which particular letters were in mind. Among even fairly moderate Cyrillines it was claimed that this statement included approval of Cyril's third letter, with its notorious Twelve Anathemas (see p. 203). If this was the case, then the duality of which the formula spoke when it referred to the union of both a divine and a human nature in the incarnate Christ was clearly to be construed in a distinctly limited fashion.

"Monophysite" Opposition

Much more significant still was the opposition of those who would have no truck whatsoever with any specification of two natures in Christ after the union. They protested furiously against what they regarded as the dangerous imposition of a divisive statement about the dignity of their Lord's earthly existence. Fierce passions were aroused in Egypt, Palestine, and Syria in particular, where such so-called "Monophysite" feelings were most powerful.

It must be stressed that the label "Monophysite" was not a self-description of those who took this position. To them, the term was an offensive nickname used by their opponents, who failed to appreciate the precision of the point being made about the relationship of divinity and humanity in the incarnate Lord. The dissenters insisted they were *not* saying what Euytches had been held to say—namely that the single nature of the incarnate Word was of some other substance than the humanity that the rest of us share. No, their claim was that in the coming together of divinity and humanity the union was so close that there was, thereafter, "one nature out of two." To say anything less, they argued, was to diminish the full reality of the incarnation and to commit the error for which Nestorius had been condemned at Ephesus in 431.[1]

In Alexandria, as in Rome, there was also strong resentment of Chalcedon's privileging of Constantinople, but it was the council's two-natures doctrine that provided the most serious focal point for anger. Feelings were stirred by many of the Egyptian monks in particular, who were deeply hostile to Chalcedon's language, and the troubles that ensued between opponents and defenders of the council went on for years. The successor of Dioscorus (see p. 208) as patriarch of Alexandria, Proterius, who endorsed Chalcedon, was killed in a public riot in March 457. He was replaced by a passionate opponent of the formula, Timothy Aelurus, who had been pushed into prominence by the monks in the aftermath of the emperor Marcian's death a few weeks earlier.[2] Timothy protested to Marcian's successor, the emperor Leo (not to be confused with Pope Leo), that Chalcedon was in error and that its statement could not be accepted by the church of Alexandria; a new council should be called to annul the findings of 451.

Timothy's views were too extreme to be practicable, and the emperor yielded to the advice to send him into exile. The see of Alexandria was filled in turn by another Timothy, Timothy Salafaciolus,[3] who was a Chalcedonian by conviction, but the ousted patriarch continued to enjoy the support of a substantial majority in his church, and he engaged in an active program of writing to further his views. Timothy Salafaciolus was obliged to defer to "Monophysite" sensibilities in a number of respects, not least as a result of the strong feelings generated by the monks, and he protested formally to Constantinople that he could not accept the claim of Chalcedon about the place of "new Rome." The status of Chalcedon's pronouncements remained a highly contentious cause in Egypt for years.

Significant tensions began to open up between the regions where the "Monophysites" were strongest and churches in other contexts, especially the church of Rome. Even where there was clear loyalty to the Christology of Chalcedon, there was much resentment of the place that the council had given to the see of Constantinople. The opponents of Chalcedon could scarcely be ignored, for their numerical strength and their devotion to their cause were both considerable. The Roman world was already living in very volatile times, with serious pressures from barbarian powers in both sectors of the empire, and conventional political structures in many quarters had effectively entered upon an age of terminal decline.

In the mid-470s the emperor Zeno was temporarily ousted in a palace coup, and his usurper Basiliscus deemed it politically expedient to show favor to the anti-Chalcedonians throughout the East. Timothy Aelurus was allowed to return to Alexandria, where he remained as a rival bishop, unrecognized by Rome, until his death in 477. Another prominent "Monophysite," Peter the Fuller, was installed in Antioch. Bishops were invited to endorse a statement denouncing Chalcedon's formula. These policies were reversed when Zeno recaptured control in 476, and Peter and other churchmen of similar persuasion were deposed, but the troubles persisted in several Eastern churches, and there were major disputes over rival candidates in both Alexandria and Antioch in particular over the coming years.

Zeno's *Henotikon* and the Acacian Schism

In Constantinople, the able Bishop Acacius (471–489) was torn between loyalty to Rome and the pressure to appease his brethren in other areas of the East. He was increasingly convinced that the latter cause was more important. In the summer of 482 he persuaded the emperor Zeno to issue a circular letter to the churches of Alexandria, Egypt, and Cyrenaica aimed at restoring unity between Alexandria and Constantinople and within Egypt itself, where there were tensions not only between pro- and anti-Chalcedonians in general but also between various strains of anti-Chalcedonianism.

The document, drafted in close cooperation with Acacius, became known as the *Henotikon*, or "instrument of unity," and was issued on the emperor's own authority, without any council or synod having taken place. It condemned both Nestorius and Eutyches, expressly sanctioned Cyril's Twelve Anathemas, and declared Christ to be "one and not two." The wording carefully made no reference to "natures" at all. The essential authority in Christology was said to be the teaching of the Niceno-Constantinopolitan tradition, and a curse was pronounced on any contrary doctrine, "whether taught at Chalcedon or at any other synod."

The *Henotikon* was signed by the "Monophysite" leaders in Alexandria and Antioch, who secured recognition from the emperor in return for their cooperation, and on the surface a measure of unity was secured. Almost all of the anti-Chalcedonians' demands had been met, though Chalcedon itself had not been set aside. For many of the more assertive "Monophysites," however, this was not enough; for them, it definitely *was* necessary to repudiate Chalcedon formally. In Alexandria, the pro-*Henotikon* bishop, Peter Mongos,[4] faced strong opposition from a lobby of intense opponents of Chalcedon, who regarded him—with some reason—as a traitor to their cause. He had to rely on support from Constantinople in order to stay in office.

On the Chalcedonian side, for obviously different reasons, the reaction was sharper still. Zeno's document did imply that the Chalcedonian formula was suspect, and this was unacceptable. It also hinted, without expressly saying so, that one of Chalcedon's critical influences, Leo's *Tome*, which had been a particular bone of contention among "Monophysites," was to be rejected. In Rome, this was a major cause of offense. Acacius had not consulted Rome about his intention to establish relations with the opponents of Chalcedon, and he proved downright evasive in his treatment of Roman emissaries. Rome had not helped its cause by backing the Chalcedonians in both Alexandria and Antioch—supporting individuals who were politically unacceptable and making noises about the authority of the see of Peter. In the end, a Roman synod under Pope Felix excommunicated Acacius on 28 July 484, and in an angry communication to the emperor Zeno instructed him not to interfere in affairs that bishops alone ought to settle.

The split that opened up between Rome and Constantinople, known to history as the "Acacian schism," lasted for a generation, enduring long after Acacius's passing and throughout the tenures of several other Roman leaders after Felix. The causes of the schism were obviously heavily mixed up with church politics as well as doctrine, and the *Henotikon* was not the single spark that ignited the problem but only one of a number of contributing factors, the most serious of which were the rivalries between the two sees. For historical reasons, the hostility was strongest on the Roman side, not the Eastern, though even some of Felix's supporters felt that he went too far in demanding a complete capitulation by Constantinople. Nevertheless, the persistence of the rupture for so long also testifies to the strength of the conviction in Constantinople, both political and ecclesiastical, that stability in the East ultimately mattered more than good relations with Rome and the

West, where barbarian control of one sort or another was already the order of the day.

Distinct Theological Traditions Intensify

These years saw the various theologies of the East settle into increasingly established forms, as church leaders and thinkers concentrated on justifying and elaborating their respective convictions. There was no greater measure of consensus, despite intermittent attempts to make moves toward healing the divisions.

The diversity was considerable. There were some who nursed grievances predating Chalcedon. They felt that Nestorius had been badly treated and that the Council of Ephesus in 431 and all that had followed from it had betrayed the distinction between the two natures of Christ. To their opponents, these believers were simply "Nestorians," and they deserved to be squashed. In 489 the Christian school at Edessa was forced to close because of its alleged Nestorian tendencies. In reality, the affinities of those in this tradition were essentially for conventional Antiochene teaching in the mold of Theodore; nevertheless, they tended to adopt different phraseology to that advocated by Chalcedon, and they were deeply ambivalent about Chalcedon's success in guarding against the collapse of the two natures. The political climate only encouraged their belief that imperial policy was bent on appeasing the "Monophysites." There was a movement of determinedly Antiochene Christians further East, beyond their traditional heartland in Syria into Persia, and especially to Nisibis.

Figures such as Barsumas (d. before 496), bishop of Nisibis, were strong enthusiasts for the theology of Theodore, and the writings of Diodore and Theodore were preserved in Persian as well as in Syriac as a result of their popularity in this context. Another important thinker in the same environment was Narsai (d. ca. 503), a teacher from Edessa who established a school in Nisibis in Barsumas's time and exercised a significant influence as a spiritual instructor, biblical commentator, and hymn-writer.[5] Persian Christianity already had long-standing traditions of its own in spirituality, asceticism, liturgy, and organization, and its leaders had taken no part in the great councils. By the late fifth century, the Christians of Persia were keen to distance themselves farther from the Roman world in the interests of their own political well-being, for when Persia was at war with Rome there was almost always persecution from the Persian authorities. A devotion to Antiochene Christology over against the formulae of imperial Christianity assisted in the Persian effort to forge a separate ecclesiastical identity, though it obviously increased the gap between the churches in Persia and believers elsewhere who espoused other positions.

The fears that imperial policy supported an accommodation with those who denied any doctrine of two natures were well-founded. Under the emperor Anastasius (491–518), tolerance was the order of the day, and the *Henotikon* was seen as the best way of promoting unity in the East, despite the severe problems that had arisen with the West. The separatist Antiochenes in Mesopotamia might be thankful that they were outside of the imperial territory; for convinced Chalcedonians within the Roman Empire, circumstances were more immediately depressing. Anti-Chalcedonian theology of one kind or another flourished.

The most sophisticated exposition of a single-nature approach came in the work of Severus (ca. 486–538), patriarch of Antioch from 512. Severus was an ardent devotee of the theology of Cyril. Although he agreed with the condemnation of Eutyches and had no time for those who devalued the humanity of Christ, he was vigorously opposed to the language of two natures after the union; "out of" the two dimensions of divinity and humanity had come the one incarnate nature of the divine Word, a single nature activated by a single "energy." Severus was highly unpopular in many areas of Hellenistic western Syria, but his work was in equal measure influential farther east, in the Syriac-speaking regions, where he received loyal support from prominent churchmen such as Philoxenus of Hierapolis (ca. 440–523).[6]

There were also other types of "Monophysitism" besides that of Severus and his network of allies. One of Severus's friends, Julian, bishop of Halicarnassus in Caria (d. after 518), the most influential single-nature theologian in western Asia Minor, came to take a harder line on the implications of the incarnation. Julian espoused the view that the flesh of Christ was, strictly speaking, incorruptible (*aphthartos*) from the first moment of its conception and that the sufferings of Christ's earthly existence were attributable to his freely willed choice to be vulnerable for the sake of others. This view was challenged by Severus, who insisted that incorruptibility did not characterize the flesh of Christ until after his resurrection. Sharp disputes broke out between "Monophysites" who positioned themselves on opposing sides on this question: the "Severans" accused the "Julianists" of adopting a form of Docetism, while their antagonists in turn labeled them "worshipers of the corruptible." "Monophysite" theology in general came to be characterized by the coexistence of what might be called a more moderate stream, which held to the Severan tradition, and a more radical group, who followed the Julianist line.

In the church in Constantinople there was still a strong current of opposition to expressly single-nature logic, in spite of all the problems that bedeviled relations with the pro-Chalcedonian church of Rome. The objections sometimes manifested themselves in disputes over matters of liturgical practice. Prior to Chalcedon, it had become standard in many churches to use a refrain known as the *Trisagion* ("thrice holy") in worship. It ran: "Holy God, Holy and Strong, Holy and Immortal, have mercy upon us." In some quarters, especially in Syria, parts of Asia, and Egypt, the language was seen as an acclamation of Christ rather than of the Trinity, and in Antioch the phrase "who was crucified for us" was added after "Holy and Immortal." This was supported by many "Monophysites" but fiercely opposed by many devotees of Chalcedon, who felt that the addition blurred the distinction between the two natures of Christ and implied that God the Trinity rather than the human Jesus was crucified. An attempt, supported by Anastasius,[7] to use the emended *Trisagion* in a service in Constantinople in 512 resulted in a public riot.

The End of Schism

When Anastasius was succeeded by the elderly Justin in 518, there was a sharp reversal of his tolerant religious policy. Justin's roots were in the West; he was Latin-speaking and loyal to Rome; he was also influenced in a Chalcedonian direction by his gifted nephew, Justinian, who in practice ran his affairs. Moves had already been made by the most recent bishop of Rome, Hormisdas (514–523), to rebuild relations with Constantinople, though under Anastasius these had not progressed very far. With Justin's support, Hormisdas's initiatives now bore fruit, and in 519 the bishop of Constantinople, John, and a significant contingent of Eastern bishops signed a formula condemning Acacius, accepting Chalcedon and Leo's *Tome*, and acknowledging the importance of Rome's authority. The *Henotikon* was abandoned, and the schism between Rome and Constantinople that had endured since the early 480s was over.

Many convinced "Monophysite" churchmen, regardless of their particular stripe, were in trouble. Both Julian and Severus were deposed, and other figures also had to take refuge elsewhere, typically in Alexandria. Severus remained in exile for most of the rest of his life until his death in 538, at first issuing counsel by letter to his many followers, and then granting his blessing to the establishment of distinct, non-Chalcedonian clerical structures in the East from around 530.

Justinian and the Quest for Unity

Under the long reign of the emperor Justinian (527–565), there was a concerted effort to reunify East and West politically and to recover the splendor of the former Roman world, which, as we shall see in chapter 11, had by then been very severely eroded by the power of barbarian peoples. By the early sixth century, the sway of the emperor in Constantinople was restricted largely to the territories bordering the Mediterranean. In the West, control lay in the hands of various barbarian rulers, and even if a number of these purported to govern on behalf of the emperor, in reality the Western provinces were no longer under Constantinople's authority. In the East itself there were mounting pressures from Germanic peoples to the north and especially from the might of the Persian Empire to the East, the foe that had been Rome's major thorn in the flesh for centuries.

We shall return to Justinian and his political and cultural policies in chapter 12; here we shall simply note the relationship between his overarching imperial strategy and his efforts to secure doctrinal stability. Like his uncle, Justinian was a Latin speaker with a pride in his Western inheritance; he was also a Greek thinker with a deep awareness of the theological and cultural traditions of the East. He could simultaneously appeal to the Western symbolism of Rome's historical glory while devoting himself to enhancing the prestige of a Greek-speaking Byzantine world. The restoration of the West was critical, but the center of the revived empire would lie not in the old Rome but in Constantinople. One of the most vital expressions of unity would be the witness of a common religious alignment. In the West it was necessary to revive the status of the catholic faith against the Arianism of barbarian rulers; in the East the preservation of the same orthodox creed and the championing of a shared conception of Christ's incarnate glory would demarcate the empire of light from the darkness of its threatening neighbors.

As far as Justinian was concerned, there was an essential connection between the reinstatement of the traditional honor of the Roman Empire and the consolidation of a single, orthodox faith. He accepted the fact that the clergy and monks of the church were the obvious representatives of ecclesiastical authority, but he equally considered that his personal responsibilities as emperor extended not only to affairs of state and the general protection of church privileges but also to the promotion of right belief. He did not hesitate to become closely involved in theological debates, using his own knowledge of the Scriptures and of the history of doctrine to advise the clergy's most senior figures directly on what they should do.

Here, however, Justinian was subject to conflicting inclinations. As had already been clear in his influence in the government of Justin, he himself was by instinct strongly in favor of Chalcedon, which he saw as crucial to his objectives of winning back the West. His empress, Theodora (d. 548), on the other hand, a former actress who played a dominant role in his regime and greatly influenced his policies, was firmly pro-"Monophysite" in her sympathies. Justinian's religious strategy was accordingly marked by a number of twists and turns, driven by a fundamental desire to accommodate the sensibilities of both the Chalcedonians and their opponents. The former may have enjoyed the privilege of Justinian's genuine sympathies, and they would in the end be the recipients of his strongest—and most controversial—patronage, but the latter were far too significant to be ignored, especially amid political circumstances that mandated a search for unity in the East.

Theological Protagonists

By the early 530s the single-nature tradition was a very strong force in the East, political attempts at containment notwithstanding. A distinct "Monophysite" church, with its own clergy and monks and its own liturgy, had now definitively emerged in eastern Syria and in various areas throughout Asia Minor, pioneered particularly by John of Tella, with the endorsement of the exiled Severus. In Egypt, too, the power struggle within the churches had continued, and the Alexandrian patriarchate was in the hands of a "Monophysite" leader, Timothy III. Even in Constantinople itself there was some sympathy for single-nature teaching at a popular level if not among the official clergy, and many convinced "Monophysite" churchmen and monks both in the capital and elsewhere were given shelter and support by Theodora.

Anti-Chalcedonian theology received serious intellectual representation as well. An unidentified Syrian writer, strongly influenced by the great Neoplatonist philosopher Plotinus and the work of a later Athenian teacher of Platonism called Proclus (ca. 410–485), had published early in the sixth century some works of mystical theology under the name of Dionysius, one of the two named converts of the apostle Paul in Athens (Acts 17:34).

The writings of this "pseudo-Dionysius," as modern scholars have come to designate him, were deeply marked by pagan Greek understandings of moral progress and the conception of spirit as pure intelligence, but they were also reflective of a mild form of "Monophysitism." In time they came to be prized as the authentic writings of the biblical Dionysius by Chalcedonians also, and they greatly influenced the evolution of later mystical theology in many mainstream quarters in both the East and the West. They were first used, however, by "Monophysite" believers. Another important "Monophysite" scholar was John Philoponus (ca. 490–570), a gifted Platonist teacher in Alexandria who wrote learned commentaries on Aristotle as well as carefully crafted discussions of Christian doctrine.

At the same time, there was also serious intellectual weight on the Chalcedonian side. A number of thinkers in the East took up the defense of Chalcedon in ways that revealed impressive theological acumen and creativity. Back in the last years of Anastasius's reign, a theologian called John the Grammarian had sought to argue that the teaching of Chalcedon was in fact entirely consonant with the logic of Cyril, whose work had of course been so influential on the emergence of "Monophysite" thought, especially in its more moderate forms. Some decades later, a monk known to us as Leontius of Jerusalem developed similar arguments, reinforcing the case by claiming, in accordance with Cyrilline reasoning, that the humanity of Christ possesses no independent reality of its own but is real only in union with the divine Word.[8] The human nature of Christ, Leontius argued, is hypostatic, or personally real, only *in* the Word. In itself, the humanity of Christ has no personal subsistence; its reality comes from its subsistence *in* the divine person of the Word. It can thus be said to be at one and the same time "anhypostatic" (not personally real in itself) and "enhypostatic" (personally real *in* [*en-hypostasis*] the person or *hypostasis* of the Word).

Modern scholarship has sometimes labeled such arguments "Neo-Chalcedonian," but the designation is misleading, for the aim of such thinkers as Leontius was not to modify Chalcedon but to defend it in Cyrilline terms by stressing the identity of the one *hypostasis* of the incarnate one with the second person of the Trinity. As a reading of the formula of 451, their proposals had good claims to plausibility. Their reasoning, typically developed in lengthy technical debates with their opponents, adduced a solid intellectual case for the possibility of being faithful to Chalcedon while retaining Cyril's emphasis on the subject-hood of the Word in the incarnation. Other uses of *anhypostatic* and *enhypostatic* terminology were developed by other Chalcedonians, including another Leontius, known to us as Leontius of Byzantium,[9] a monk from Palestine who took an active part in the disputes concerning the person of Christ in Constantinople in the 530s and 540s and wrote a series of tracts on christological topics. In defending Chalcedon in *enhypostatic* terms, this Leontius emphasized primarily the concrete reality of the humanity of Christ rather than the grounding of that humanity precisely "in" the Word as such. He believed that it was necessary to assert a thoroughly authentic union of divinity and humanity in Christ over against the equal dangers of Nestorianism on the one hand and Eutychianism on the other.

The difficulties Justinian faced in getting even the friends, never mind the foes, of Chalcedon to agree was illustrated by a dispute over the correct way to speak of the suffering of the Son of God. Some Christians in the East favored a phrase that said that "one of the Trinity suffered in the flesh," or "one of the Trinity was crucified." Such language had been used as early as the 430s, in deliberate evocation of Cyril's teaching that "God the Word suffered in the flesh" and in order to emphasize the *Theotokos*. It was, however, rejected by many who claimed to be loyal to the letter of Chalcedon on the grounds that it allegedly conflated the two natures of Christ. As far as they were concerned, Chalcedon's insistence that there is no confusion of divinity and humanity in the incarnate one ruled out the possibility that one of the divine persons could be said to have been involved so directly in the most costly aspects of Jesus's human experience. The language in question smacked of "Theopaschitism"—the idea that God suffers—and in so doing it violated traditional assumptions that divinity as such must necessarily be above all possibility of suffering. In short, the claim that one of the Trinity was crucified reflected a "Monophysite" error.

Many theologians today would argue that this kind of resistance to divine vulnerability derived from Greek philosophical rather than biblical conceptions of God. It can be argued plausibly that in taking flesh and dwelling among us God the Son did elect to become personally weak and helpless in the world. Though divine transcendence of the contingencies of creation cannot have been compromised, part of the mystery of the incarnation is that in Christ God did enter personally into the experience of creaturely suffering and brokenness. This degree of immersion in the conditions of a fallen world need not be at odds with the affirmation that the divinity and the humanity of Christ each have their own integrity, because his humanity may be said to have existed in the world at all only in so far as it was assumed and actualized by the second person of the Trinity.

Justinian himself did not consider the contested phraseology to be at odds with the logic of Chalcedon, and he apparently hoped that by sanctioning it he might win over the devotees of a single-nature position. In the aftermath of a debate between representatives of both sides over a range of matters in 532, he issued an edict in March 533 that endorsed the status of the four Councils of Nicaea, Constantinople, Ephesus, and Chalcedon, stressed the *Theotokos*, and affirmed the "Theopaschite" formula (Leo's *Tome* was not mentioned, and Nestorianism was again repudiated). The edict at length received backing from Rome, controversially, but a number of Chalcedonians in the East were offended by the inclusion of the Theopaschite language. Others, those who read Chalcedon in a strongly Cyrilline fashion, would argue differently, supporting the Theopaschite formula as entirely consonant with the explicit Chalcedonian claim that it was "one and the same Son" who experienced all that the incarnate Christ experienced. Theologically they had a very good case, and their position would in the end win out, but there was plenty of hostility from other Chalcedonians whose stress lay more on the distinction between the two natures.

If Christians who supported Chalcedon could not agree among themselves, there was certainly no chance that those of "Monophysite" sympathies would, for their part, give approval to any edict that reaffirmed Chalcedon. It would take something more than this to bring divided believers together.

The "Three Chapters" and the Second Council of Constantinople

In the early 540s Justinian tried a different tack. The defenders of Chalcedon were active, but so too were their opponents, and their strength showed no signs whatever of abating. In Justinian's mind, the quest to reconcile the various parties was given a particular urgency by ominous signs of judgment in the world, especially the effects of a terrible plague that ravaged the empire in 541–543, killing perhaps a quarter of the population of the East and almost taking the emperor's own life.[10] When he recovered from his affliction, Justinian had to deal with a vast array of administrative, economic, and military needs generated by the crisis. He also had to face the fact that the "Monophysite" church had prospered in the midst of the troubles, thanks in part to the fact that Theodora's hand had effectively rested on the helm of government while he was laid aside.

In the opinion of many "Monophysites," one of the great objections to Chalcedon was that the council had not condemned the views of

Antiochene leaders who were, in their eyes, guilty of Nestorianism. The consolidation of Antiochene doctrine in the areas influenced by the eastern Syrian and Persian churches seemed to them to confirm the error that had been made. Persian Christianity in particular was extremely active in missionary terms, and the views of Theodore, if not Nestorius, traveled far to the south and east. Writing before the middle of the sixth century, a strongly Antiochene, if not expressly Nestorian, merchant from Alexandria known to us as Cosmas Indicopleustes (Cosmas "the Indian navigator")[11] wrote a work entitled *Christian Topography* in defense of the reliability of the Bible as a source of information on the natural world, and in it he mentioned the presence of similar believers as far away as southern India and Sri Lanka. Certainly this faith would be carried by missionaries and traders well beyond central Asia into Indo-China, and there were also later some evidences of comparable teaching in parts of Africa and even in Rome. To the most committed critics of such doctrine, the early signs of this very wide diffusion of unqualified two-natures theology pointed back to fifth-century mistakes.

In a bid to appease those who felt that Chalcedon had treated far too lightly churchmen who were complicit in Nestorius's falsehood, Justinian was persuaded to repudiate a list of objectionable teachings by Theodore of Mopsuestia, Theodoret, and Ibas of Edessa. The person and works of Theodore, the writings of Theodoret against Cyril, and a letter of Ibas addressed to one Mari of Nisibis were condemned as "Three Chapters" of error, tarred with the dreadful brush of Nestorianism. At Rome, Pope Vigilius (537–555) was deeply reluctant to acquiesce in this, as a condemnation of these prominent exponents of a two-natures Christology seemed to make no sense in combination with a continued affirmation of the Chalcedonian formula. Summoned to the East by imperial authority and subjected to serious pressure, Vigilius consented, but for this he was in turn disowned by the Chalcedonians of Jerusalem and Alexandria and personally excommunicated by the church in North Africa, and in 551 he withdrew his approval. There were significant tensions all around, and Justinian determined to call a new council to meet in Constantinople in May 553 to settle the affair.

The gathering became known as the fifth "ecumenical" council, though much of the West was thinly represented, and Vigilius himself and his closest supporters refused to attend. Instead Vigilius drew up a statement that distanced him from some of Theodore's teachings but refused to condemn Theodore himself. In his absence, however, he was humiliated by Justinian, who revealed his vacillations over the previous years and had his name removed from the diptychs (signaling that he was severing communion with Vigilius personally, though not with the church of Rome in its entirety). The council anathematized the Three Chapters in its final session. Vigilius, for his part, changed his mind yet again the following year and wrote a document repudiating the Three Chapters. This won him a reprieve from Justinian, but his actions came too late to redeem him in the West, where there were a number of temporary schisms between Rome and other churches. Vigilius died on his way home to Italy in 555. His successor, Pelagius I (555–561), was fiercely opposed to the condemnation of the Three Chapters, but he was induced by Justinian to uphold the council's authority despite enduring Western opposition.

Constantinople represented Justinian's effort to bring together an endorsement of Chalcedon with a repudiation of some of the ideas that were most obnoxious to "Monophysite" ears. It espoused the essentially Cyrilline line that while the incarnate Christ consisted of two natures, his human nature was only real insofar as the divine Word assumed it and made it his own. The subject of the incarnation was the Word, condescending to live a human existence. It also anathematized those who denied that Christ, who was crucified in the flesh, was one of the Trinity. Justinian's hope was that these affirmations might afford a solution to the divisions. Inevitably, however, the attempt failed. Even quite mild "Monophysites" could have no truck with an agreement that did not shun the notion of two natures after the union, however the union was said to function.

As a putative political settlement, the council served not to reconcile but to harden the distinctions, and the feelings were only made worse by the tortuous maneuvering and manipulating that went on concerning the stance of Rome. Unlike the four previous general councils, Constantinople did not issue any canons, though among its decisions was a condemnation of Origenism, which had again flared up in Palestine in the early 540s and caused further significant divisions in an already highly charged doctrinal climate.

"Monophysite" Expansion and Consolidation

Justinian resorted to increasingly firm methods to bring the advocates of the single-nature teaching into line. The cause was, however, anything but straightforward. "Monophysitism" continued to spread and deepen in its impact, assisted by energetic missionaries and dedicated leaders. Despite strong opposition from Chalcedonians, the charismatic Syrian leader Jacob Baradaeus (ca. 500–578) had already begun to engage in a highly successful program of clandestine expansion[12] that extended a thriving "Monophysite" church not only within Syria but in large areas of Asia Minor and the Aegean.

Jacob saw Justinian's policies as threatening the integrity of the anti-Chalcedonian tradition, and he labored not only to spread the faith among potential converts but also to win over existing Christians to a single-nature position. He ordained presbyters to lead the newly formed communities of dissenters, many of which were based initially around monasteries, and galvanized their activities with the assistance of enthusiastic supporters. The consequences of Jacob's industry were remarkable, and the non-Chalcedonian Syrian believers, who broke with the patriarchate in Antioch and came to have an episcopal succession of their own, began to be described as the Jacobites in honor of his influence. Their descendants, who remain strongly represented in the Middle East and in southern India (there are further constituencies in Western Europe and the Americas), are known as the Syrian Orthodox Church. In India a significant proportion of the modern-day "Thomas Christians" of Malabar espouse this tradition.[13] They represent one of the most educated and spiritually active Christian communities in the country and have engaged in a great deal of missionary work in Africa and Asia.

In Egypt a majority of Copts naturally favored a strongly Cyrilline faith. They felt that Chalcedon did not safeguard the concerns of such a position overall, the arguments of its putative Cyrilline defenders notwithstanding, and support for the formula of 451 continued to be a minority position, despite the official professions of Alexandria's bishops. Those bishops in Egypt and Syria who remained in communion with the Chalcedonianism of the imperial see in Constantinople came to be known as Melchites, from a Greek version of the Syriac word *malkaya*, "imperial," but the majority took a different line, and their influence was considerable.

In the Nile Valley, heading south toward northern Sudan, the kingdom of Nubia was evangelized by mainly "Monophysite" missionaries in the 540s,[14] and within a generation the three Nubian territories of Nobatia, Makuria, and Alodia were officially Christian, following the conversion of their rulers. In Nobatia at least, and probably more widely, the theology adopted was "Monophysite." Chalcedonian critics claimed that this was a result of determined interference by the empress Theodora, who saw to it that the major program of evangelism in the region was undertaken by preachers opposed to Chalcedon. It is difficult to know whether such contentions should be taken seriously, but there is no doubt that the Christianity that spread in Nubia was indeed "Monophysite" in doctrine. In Ethiopia, where the kingdom of Aksum became an important Christian territory in the first half of the sixth century under King Kaleb, there were strong historical links both with the Coptic church and with Syria,[15] and there was also a marked predominance of "Monophysite" conviction.

Armenia had been the first country officially to embrace the Christian faith at a national level (see p. 42), but its church had not been represented at Chalcedon. Armenian Christianity had been led by some very impressive figures over the course of the fourth and early fifth centuries. The Armenian patriarch or "Catholicos" until about 373 was Nerses, a direct descendant of Gregory "the Illuminator," the "apostle" of Armenia. Nerses had been a vigorous organizer and moral reformer whose outspoken condemnation of royal sins had finally brought about his liquidation by the authorities. His son, Isaac the Great (c. 350–438), had won metropolitan status for the Armenian patriarchate from Constantinople and independence from the authority of the church of Caesarea in Cappadocia, and together with a coadjutor named Mesrob (c. 361–439), he had done a great deal to foster a rich Armenian Christian literature and hymnody.[16]

At councils in Dvin in 506 and 555, the leaders of the Armenian churches firmly repudiated two-natures language. At the second council, the Armenian bishops allied themselves with the non-Chalcedonian Syrians and definitively condemned the imperial church as doctrinally corrupt. The original kingdom of Armenia had been carved up between the Roman and Persian Empires from the late fourth century, with the eastern part subject to Persia, and it is probable that the Armenian Christians' opposition to Chalcedon did not simply reflect theological conviction but also their desire to distance themselves from the Roman world and to escape the lingering effects of Constantinople's dominance.

In 506 the Armenians had been supported in their opposition to two-natures theology by the churches of Georgia (or "Iberia" as it was known in Greek) in the southern Caucasus to the northeast of the Black Sea. Christianity in Georgia had spread in the fourth century, thanks in particular—according to an influential tradition at least—to the witness of Nino, a female slave from Cappadocia who converted the Georgian queen and her household around 350. In the fifth century and the early years of the sixth, a number of the Georgian Christian leaders were noted for their commitment to monasticism. They also included some strong critics of Chalcedon. From around 519–520, however, the churches in the region became increasingly keen to assert their independence from

Armenia in turn, and they eventually reestablished communion with Constantinople.

For all that Justinian achieved, it was clear that he could not secure doctrinal unity in his empire. His own determined loyalties to Chalcedon had been ever more strongly expressed, not least after Theodora's death and in the light of the obvious depth of antagonism to the single-nature teaching in the West, though in his last days he had given some support to a view of the incorruptibility of Christ's flesh that was not far from the teaching of the erstwhile anti-Chalcedonian Julian. In the end, however, Justinian's efforts to deal with the "Monophysites" by persecution rather than negotiation served only to intensify their convictions, and the divisions in Syria and Egypt in particular were only deepened by the use of force. As it became more and more painfully clear to the Christians in these regions that the emperor was against them, so too they became increasingly detached from the imperial government and less and less concerned about remaining within the Roman world. In an already volatile time, with mounting pressure from Persia and early signs of trouble from the Arabs, political disintegration was accelerated by doctrinal divisions.

The serious military difficulties that confronted Justinian's imperial successors in the resurgence of diverse barbarian pressures and the escalation of military challenges in the East rendered the quest for ecclesiastical stability all the more important in political terms, though all the less likely in reality. In the face of successive invasions, the vital strategic significance—or military vulnerability—of many of the areas where "Monophysitism" was most dominant made reconciliation with their dissident believers especially desirable, for as vast amounts of imperial territory in the East began to follow the earlier fate of the West and fall to other powers, the security of what remained became all the more precious. Some further attempts were made to secure confessional consensus, again often driven as much by political interests as by spiritual convictions, but by now the chasms were far too serious to be bridged by pragmatic accommodations, and the enemies of the empire were not slow to exploit the tensions for their own ends.

Monothelites and Dyothelites

The emperor Heraclius (610–641) was the founder of a new dynasty of Byzantine rulers and a capable strategist whose policies managed, against all the odds, to recover a remarkable amount of ground against the Persians. Under his reign the proposal was advanced that while the incarnate Christ had two natures, he possessed only a single principle of activity or a single mode of "energy." This view was supported in the early 630s by Sergius, Heraclius's patriarch in Constantinople, and it received initial endorsement by Pope Honorius in Rome, but it was utterly unacceptable to most convinced Chalcedonians, and it was strongly opposed in particular by Sophronius, bishop of Jerusalem. Honorius, who probably did not understand all that was at stake in the discussion, spoke unguardedly of not just a single "energy" but a single "will" in Christ. The language of a single "will" was advanced in a statement issued by Heraclius in 638 (known as the *Ekthesis*, the Greek for "statement"),[17] and this was accepted by Eastern churchmen meeting in Constantinople in 638–639.

However, this thinking was widely repudiated in the following years as a betrayal of the two-natures teaching of Chalcedon. If there were two natures after the union, most Chalcedonian Christians reasoned, this means that the incarnate Christ must be said to have possessed two *wills*, one divine and one human. The references in John's Gospel to the Son coming not to do his own will but the will of the Father who sent him (John 4:34; 5:30; 6:38), or Jesus's prayer in the Garden of Gethsemane—"Not my will, but yours be done" (Luke 22:42; cf. Matt. 26:39; Mark 14:36)—seemed to suggest not a "single-will" or "Monothelite" position but a "two-will" or "Dyothelite" interpretation.[18] Monothelitism appeared to hint directly at "Monophysitism," and it was no surprise that the idea found particular favor in the parts of the East where the single-nature theology was most cherished. Admittedly, some of the more zealous Cyrilline Chalcedonians were also supportive of it—a fact that almost certainly influenced subsequent imperial thinking. But most in the avowedly two-natures camp were against it, especially in the West, where resistance would be very firm indeed in the years to come. So contentious was the issue that in a bid to promote peace an edict was promulgated (known as the *Typos* or "Rule") by the emperor Constans II (641–668) abrogating the *Ekthesis* and banning all reference to any number of wills or operations in Christ.

In Rome, Pope Martin I (649–653) proved a firm opponent of the Monothelite stance, and both the single-will teaching and the legal order forbidding discussion of it were condemned at a council of mainly Western bishops held in the Lateran basilica in 649. Resistance was especially strong in the North African church, where a number of local synods had already condemned the single-will position and declared the imperial policy to be heresy. Martin in particular reaped the consequences of his bold defiance: he was removed from office, brutally treated by the authorities, and banished to the Crimea, where he died of his sufferings in 655.

Martin was the last of the bishops of Rome to be venerated as a martyr, but he was not the last person to suffer for his adherence to a theology of two-wills in Christ. Monothelitism encountered its most able intellectual opponent in the gifted Byzantine monk, theologian, and ascetic writer, Maximus "the Confessor" (ca. 580–662). Maximus presented the logic of Chalcedon's reference to two natures after the union as offering at one and the same time a profound affirmation of human nature and a demonstration of divine redemptive power. In a remarkably creative fashion, Maximus was able to underscore the authenticity of Jesus's humanity, with its real choices and temptations, while also asserting that his human nature existed as it did precisely because it was the humanity of the Son of God. In becoming incarnate, the Word became all that humans are, yet he did so in his own unique way as a divine person, and thus it was that his human willing, while utterly genuine, was consonant with the will of God. Maximus thought that such a conception facilitated a vision of salvation as a mystical union between God and creation in which the integrity of the human is fully respected. To be saved is to be "divinized," and such a union with God, so far from being an obliteration of the dignity of created beings, is in fact the realization of creation's true destiny.

Maximus was responsible for mobilizing a good deal of the fiercest hostility to Monothelitism in the 640s, both in the East and in the West. In the end he paid a terrible price for his resistance to imperial demands to abandon his loyalties and comply with the *Typos* edict. Having already been arrested and sentenced to exile for his views, in 661 he was again interrogated by the authorities in Constantinople and tortured. It is said that his tongue and his right hand—the instruments by which he had waged his doctrinal war—were cut off. He died in exile of his wounds the following year, tragically forgotten even by most of the churchmen who had agreed with him. Only in retrospect did he earn the title "Confessor" in recognition of his preparedness to suffer for his convictions.

The Dyothelite position that Maximus had championed finally prevailed at another council held in Constantinople in 680–681, the third in the city and the sixth of the general councils. The gathering took place at the behest of the emperor Constantine IV Pogonatus, who was convinced that the Monothelite stance was no longer very useful politically, as a large proportion of "Monophysites" were to be found in areas that had in any case fallen to Arab control from the late 630s onward and looked as if they would remain that way. The proceedings at Constantinople were dominated by the envoys of the church of Rome, who relayed the findings of a recent Roman synod strongly affirming the Dyothelite view.

The council essentially reproduced the language of Chalcedon, with an additional clarification about the necessity of two wills. No mention was made of Maximus, and no canons were issued. It was declared that in Christ "there are two natural wills and modes of operation ["energies"], without division, without change, without separation, without confusion." It was also said, however, that there is no tension in the psychology of the sinless one: "His human will follows, without any resistance or reluctance but in subjection, his divine and omnipotent will." As far as official orthodoxy was concerned, Chalcedon's formula was to be understood ever after in a Dyothelite fashion.

Looking Back to Chalcedon

By the end of the seventh century, there was plainly very little prospect of reconciling the friends and foes of Chalcedon. In effect, at least two kinds of orthodoxy had evolved in the East. One was the orthodoxy of the main Byzantine church, headed up by the four patriarchates of Constantinople, Alexandria, Antioch, and Jerusalem, which remained in communion with the churches of the West. All of these believers adhered to Chalcedon and officially to the further qualifications of its emphases as specified at Constantinople in 553 and 680–681.[19]

The other kind of orthodoxy was the position of a smaller but still very significant body of dissenters: the Armenians, the Copts, the Ethiopians, and a large number of Syrians. They repudiated altogether the language of "in two natures" as violating the uniqueness of the incarnate Word and naturally also shunned the sixth- and seventh-century efforts to elaborate upon this teaching. While some limited progress had at times been made in discussion between the most Cyrilline members of the first group and the most moderate members of the second, in the end the differences between the two constituencies were too great, and the outcome of the Monothelite/Dyothelite dispute appeared to seal the division in their perspectives beyond all doubt.

Alongside both of these groups there was also, still farther to the east and the south but with a presence in other quarters as well, a significant constituency wedded to yet another position. They equally thought of themselves as maintaining the true faith, and they acknowledged the Christ of Nicaea. But they rejected the definition of Ephesus in 431

and the designation of Mary as the *Theotokos*, and they were not enthusiastic about Chalcedon. Their strong preference was for the traditions of Antioch, Nisibis, and Edessa, and that, to their fellow believers,
rendered them "Nestorians," even though—as was true of Nestorius
himself—their theology was not at all what it was held to be in that
respect. This "Church of the East," as it came to be known (also styled
in modern times the Assyrian Church of the East) had produced some
very gifted leaders, teachers, and spiritual thinkers. They included not
only such earlier figures as Barsumas and Narsai but also the theologian Babai the Great (d. 628), who composed a work on the union of
divinity and humanity in Christ, and a clutch of monastic writers whose
works proved of enduring attraction, such as Sahdona (fl. mid-seventh
century) and Isaac of Nineveh (d. ca. 700).

If the Council of Chalcedon had been designed to promote unity, then,
it had clearly failed, and all the efforts to find a basis of reconciliation
over more than two centuries, whether by dialogue and appeasement or
by edict and coercion, had come to nothing. The use of persecution in
particular had only intensified convictions, and political developments
had further exacerbated the differences. Further ominous changes had
also been afoot, the consequences of which would in the long term cause
the divisions between Christians to pale into insignificance.

The Rise of Islam

Alongside the Byzantine and Persian Empires existed another group
of peoples, the Arabs, who occupied the steppes and the desert zone that
bordered the battleground of the two great powers. Arab tribesmen had
been subject to both Jewish and Christian influences for centuries as a
result of trading and missionary contacts, and since the fourth century
a good number of sheikhs in northern and central Arabia in particular had been committed believers, who devoted rich resources to the
establishing of Christian monasteries and the promotion of Christian
piety and learning in the oasis cities that dotted their vast, arid land.
The structures of Arab Christianity are not entirely clear, but there
were undoubtedly clans that prided themselves on their devotion to the
Christian God and saw their faith as an integral part of their identity
over against tribes that followed other religions.

Around the year 570, in the city of Mecca in the Hijâz, midway along
the western side of the Arabian peninsula, was born to merchant parents a son, Mohammad. We know little about his early life, but at the

age of forty he began to experience religious visions, which as far as he was concerned confirmed that there was only one true God (in Arabic, *Allah*). He believed he was called to proclaim the truth of this God as the one who transcended the religious diversity of his world; the same God who had spoken through Moses, in Jesus, and by the mouth of countless other prophets had now communicated directly and definitively with this one prophet. Mohammad gained some converts in Mecca, but in 622 he and his followers moved north to the city of Medina, where they settled as a group. The date of their *hijra* or "flight" would come to mark the beginning of a new calendar, the point at which a new people had been established.

Mohammad and his disciples were an armed group much like any other, except that they were set on spreading their conviction that God had spoken to Mohammad and called him to summon all his Arab countrymen to turn from their idolatrous ways and recognize that they were the descendants of Abraham through Ishmael. In 630 Mohammad and his companions returned to Mecca, where they cleansed the *Ka'aba*, the shrine on the spot where Abraham was believed to have sacrificed to the one true God, and thus they symbolically restored the place to its original religious glory by invoking the blessing of Abraham's God. Mecca became the spiritual center of the movement and the *Ka'aba* its holiest shrine.

Mohammad continued to receive visions intermittently and dramatically from 610 until his death in 632. The words he spoke during these visions were said not to be his own; it was claimed that he was reciting the word of God. Sequences of the recitations were carefully memorized by his followers and passed on by skilled reciters throughout the Arab world, which had evolved a very rich classical language through the exchanges of its storytellers, poets, and scholars. The sayings were not written down in any substantial or sequential fashion until a generation after Mohammad's death, when they came to form the book known to us as the *Qur'ân*, which in Arabic means "reading." Here, it was claimed, was the final inspired rendering of the voice of the one true God. The Arabic language in which the reading was conveyed was deemed to be vital, and for centuries there would be no officially permitted translations of the *Qur'ân*.

To the will of this God, all needed to submit. "Islam," the name adopted by the new faith, and "Muslim," the word used to describe one who espoused it, were rooted in the same Arabic letters for "submission," "surrender," or "trust." Those who followed the multiple gods of pagan faiths were ignorant of the true God or willfully rejected him; all who had ever trusted in one transcendent deity were "Muslims" in reality, even if they called themselves Jews or Christians. As far as the followers of Mohammad were concerned, Jews and Christians had apostatized from or distorted the messages given to them by Moses and Jesus. In the case of the Christians, all of the energy spent upon defining the divinity of Christ one way or another was a dreadful error, for Jesus himself, it was said, had never claimed to be divine.

The new movement progressed with astonishing rapidity. Mohammad's companions were convinced that God was on their side and that they were fighting a holy war to defend his honor, demonstrate the rightness of their cause, and save their fellow Arabs from divine judgment. They swiftly captured the towns and cities of the Arabian Peninsula. Under the Caliphs, the "successors" who served as the political leaders of the movement over the generations after Mohammad and his Companions, the Arabs pressed on across a vast swath of Asia Minor. Within a hundred years of Mohammad's death, the territory in which the faith of his followers was represented would stretch from central Asia across Egypt and North Africa to the Atlantic coast of Spain, from Baghdad to Cordoba, embracing huge areas that had long included key centers of Christian witness.

It is a mistake to think that the initial Arab conquests forced Christians into relinquishing their faith, or to imagine that an Arabic society was established comparable in any real sense to the Muslim world of today. The physical presence of Islam in the seventh century was overwhelmingly concentrated in or around cities, and in many areas Christian elites continued to hold sway. For a long time, Jews and Christians were not physically coerced into abandoning their beliefs, unlike the devotees of pagan religions, who faced a choice between Islam or death. Fellow monotheists of the Muslims became subject to certain conditions, chiefly liability to a special tax, but they were granted freedom of worship and indeed legal protection, and there was a great deal of social, intellectual, and economic contact between Christians and Muslims. Sometimes, as in the case of former Persian territories, Muslim rulers proved more generous to Christians than their predecessors had been, and in many parts of the East Christians actually welcomed the arrival of Islam in political terms. Statistically, Islam remained for a long time a minority faith in the regions that the Arabs had taken, and widespread conversions to Islam and the development of a thoroughgoing Islamic social culture did not take place until the Middle Ages. Nevertheless, the first seeds of the process that would eventually generate these results had been sown.

Divided Christians

The story of Islam's spread and its long-term consequences for Christianity in both the East and the West will be followed up in the next volume in this series. Suffice it to say here that in the seventh century the bitter divisions that existed among Eastern Christians in particular did little to assist in the maintenance of a cohesive witness in the face of the Arab advance. Confronted with a common challenge, many believers continued to insist that the heart of the gospel was at stake in their own particular doctrinal position. The loss of regions such as Syria and Egypt to the Byzantine Empire served only to harden the distinctions between the churches in these territories and their Byzantine counterparts, as the Christians in these areas were no longer subject to imperial influence or control. The upheavals in the political landscape also significantly reduced the size and influence of the ancient patriarchates of Alexandria and Antioch in terms of the Christian church as a whole.

Ecclesiastical as well as civil structures reflected the degree to which the world in which all Eastern Christians lived was a fragmenting and uncertain place. Chalcedon was upheld as the benchmark for right confession of Christ in the imperial Byzantine realm, and there was thus in principle a shared faith between a majority of Christians in the East and the believers of the West, for whom the council had been essentially uncontroversial all along. Nevertheless, the nature of the orthodoxy that had prevailed in the East was primarily delineated by political boundaries, and outside of these limits there were many with very different views who equally thought of themselves as faithful to the gospel.

And so it continued to be. The primary churches of Armenia, Syria, Egypt, and Ethiopia still officially reject Chalcedon to this day, yet they also contend that they are faithful to the true teachings of apostolic Christianity as interpreted by the great theologians of the early centuries. They are often described, accordingly, as the Oriental Orthodox Churches in order to distinguish them from the Eastern Orthodox, whose roots lie in the Byzantine world.[20] In modern times there have been various contacts at senior levels between these different bodies, and talks have also taken place with the Roman Catholic Church. A number of declarations of common convictions have been issued that seem to offer some hope for the future, but officially the divisions over Chalcedon persist. The loyally Antiochene Church of the East, which has suffered much depletion, fragmentation, and trouble over the centuries, also continues to be ambivalent if not expressly hostile towards the confession of 451.

The subsequent history of all of these traditions lies outside of our boundaries in this book. In each case, it makes for fascinating reading, and all of the non-Chalcedonian branches of the church went on to produce some remarkable Christians whose witness amid many political and social difficulties over the centuries—not least the challenge posed by more militant forms of Islam—was often outstanding. Those who endorse Chalcedon today should not forget that it was through the efforts of non-Chalcedonian Christians that the gospel was spread in significant areas of Asia, Indo-China, and Africa, and many of the believers who came from these traditions proved to be outstanding exemplars of holiness, spiritual zeal, and commitment to Christ, who were prepared to pay the ultimate price for their faith under assault from their enemies.

At another level, it is worth remembering that it is to the Syriac, Coptic, and Ethiopian churches that we owe the survival of versions of works such as Nestorius's *Book of Heracleides*, as well as some very important copies of Christian and Jewish sacred texts.[21] In Armenia it was thanks to scholarly Christian leaders such as Mesrob that the nation acquired an alphabet as well as precious translations of the Scriptures, hymns, and many other theological treatises. In all of these contexts, distinctive liturgical and spiritual traditions of often great power and beauty evolved directly as a result of relative independence from other influences.

In the longer term, a separatist mentality was in no sense confined to those who resisted Chalcedon. A shared attachment to Chalcedon was not enough to prevent further, much more serious, divisions between the mainstream Orthodox churches of the East and the Christians of the West in later times. From the ninth century onward the old differences between Rome and Constantinople escalated, fueled by other doctrinal, liturgical, and political issues, not least the question of whether the Western churches could possibly be allowed to alter the Niceno-Constantinopolitan Creed to say that the Holy Spirit proceeds not only from the Father but also from the Son (see p. 169); for the Eastern Orthodox, they certainly could not. These differences would climax in the great schism in the eleventh century, which technically still divides the dominant Christian traditions of East and West today, despite many political and ecclesiastical efforts in the cause of restoring unity.

Chalcedon Today

What, then, of the lasting validity of Chalcedon itself? Notwithstanding the very notable importance of the churches that still dissent from it, for a majority of Christians in the world today its formula remains an official part of orthodox tradition and a reference point against which proper confession of the status of Christ may usefully be measured. Yet, to judge from history at least, Chalcedon has clearly served to divide as well as to unite, and in the period with which we have been concerned in this chapter its teaching obviously contributed to problems that weakened the testimony of at least parts of the Christian cause in a critical age of political upheaval. In remarkable ways, the divisions did not inhibit Christian expansion and growth in many contexts, and those with very divergent views are all part of the rich tapestry of the church's story. Even so, this fact can hardly justify the historical fragmentation, far less legitimize the continuation of divisions on these ancient grounds today. If this is what Chalcedon produced, what are we to make of such a complex legacy?

As a theological statement, Chalcedon's declaration has been subjected to some heavy criticism over the past two centuries, most of it generated by representatives of Western traditions that officially uphold its teaching. Chalcedon has been accused of presenting a very abstract, metaphysical Christ rather than the living Jesus of the Gospels; its language is preoccupied with categories such as "substance," "natures," and "persons" rather than with the biblical depictions of the dynamics of Jesus's actual existence in the world. It is also said that its definition of the relationship between divinity and humanity is essentially negative rather than positive: it speaks of what does *not* happen in the coming together of the two natures (they exist "without confusion, without change, without division, without separation") but does not really address the fundamental question of how these two dimensions can actually be deemed to be one.

Over against such criticisms, and various further refinements of them, defenders of Chalcedon's status as a doctrinal statement of lasting importance point out that the council never did attempt to *explain* the incarnation so much as to set out the necessary parameters within which the mystery of the person of Christ must be confessed. It says all that can safely *be* said about a wonder that transcends human understanding, and it does so with equal caution all around, compromising neither the closeness nor the distinction between the two aspects of the incarnate one. Any "explanation" of how divinity and humanity can uniquely coexist in a single historical individual is of necessity impossible, and in stressing the negative as well as the positive aspects of the union of natures the formula invites believers frankly to acknowledge this fact. In seeking to safeguard both the divinity and the humanity of

Christ and to specify that this is what it means for God the Son to live a human life, Chalcedon spells out with impressive clarity and precision the broad basis of what needs to be affirmed by believers in every age, while allowing a variety of interpretations of its logic. Mystery is not "solved"; it is simply summarized in some essential ways.

The debate between the critics and the defenders of Chalcedon is likely to go on. Some who are skeptical about the value of the formula today are willing to concede that its claims may have had a certain validity in their own time; others who think that the council led to regrettable divisions in history nevertheless feel that its confession represents a well-crafted account of what continues to matter for a majority of believers, and that Chalcedon's place in Christian tradition is much too important to be set aside. Some claim that all such dogmatic summaries in any age are mistaken attempts to stamp a political uniformity on Christian belief; others argue that while confessional statements may be right and proper as expressions of a believing consensus, this particular one either fails to capture what must be said or is couched in language that is inaccessible to most Christians today.

Whatever may be said on both sides of this argument, the history of debate over Chalcedon should at least have taught us this: faith's claims about the person of Christ will always be challenging to reason, so long as reason insists upon assuming that divinity and humanity are inherently incompatible categories. To confess that God is present in the world in the person of the man Jesus is to acknowledge that natural ways of thinking are simply wrong; according to faith, God truly was and is in Christ in this astonishing and unparalleled fashion. In electing to come to us this way, Chalcedonian Christians insist, God has radically subverted our human expectations and redefined our distorted conceptions of both divinity and humanity. Chalcedon's carefully balanced combination of positive and negative language, and its insistence both on the priority of divine action in salvation and on the concrete reality of Jesus's humanity, surely do reflect vital Christian contentions in every age. If believers today dismiss Chalcedon too quickly or abandon its claims altogether, they may well be cutting themselves off from a rich inheritance of shared witness to the one they too call Lord.

On the other hand, there can be no doubt that the council's confession has indeed served to divide Christians in unfortunate ways. While it has become a venerable part of a widely held confessional tradition, its teaching has not found favor with many whose doctrinal instincts can in no way be deemed heretical by the standards of earlier conciliar orthodoxy. All of these believers have shared the conviction that God the Son was incarnate in the person of Jesus of Nazareth, and none of them has wanted to diminish either the divinity or the humanity of Christ. The same is true of their heirs. As modern dialogue has shown, those whose traditions have been opposed to Chalcedon are still today frequently driven by many of the same convictions as their interlocutors. The nature of the disagreement lies not in what "orthodoxy" means, exactly, but in how to pin down the details of its implications. In the central area of the incarnation, no one wishes to get things wrong.

In so far as Chalcedon's place lies within tradition rather than Scripture, most Christians would agree, it should in principle be open to some kind of reconsideration. However, the role of ecumenical conciliar authority and the degree to which the legacy of such authority can be tampered with are also subjects of enduring dispute, depending upon differing conceptions within Christian traditions as to how divine revelation takes place and what the nature of the church is as a body led by the Spirit of God. Any possible reappraisal is additionally rendered more difficult with time, given the weight of the investments that accrue on both sides and given the fact that the debate is not only about intellectual differences but bound up with political and ethnic divisions and tensions between long-established organizational structures. To deal with doctrinal problems seriously may mean some serious practical costs on all sides—costs that Christians have often proved reluctant to face.

If Chalcedon is to continue to matter, it is perhaps best to see it in terms that have been much discussed in modern theology—as not so much an *end* but a *beginning*. Just as Chalcedon did not bring to an end the christological debates of the early Christian period, so it should not foreclose further reflection, exploration, and dialogue today—either among the majority of believers whose traditions continue to connect them with it officially to one degree or another, or among those who continue to reject its authority. No word about Jesus the Christ can ever be the last, and every fresh acknowledgment of faith will generate new meditation upon the wonder of who he is today as well as who he was yesterday. Some of that reflection certainly has to be undertaken with reference to the great milestones of Christian confession in the past, and Chalcedon is undoubtedly one of these, as its critics as well as its enthusiasts are increasingly willing to acknowledge. In this way, whether the language of Chalcedon is retained or not, its affirmations may act as a *beginning* by stimulating further thinking and the acknowledgment of fundamental assumptions held by followers of Jesus everywhere.

It is unlikely that modern thinking about Christ can long avoid the kinds of complexities with which believers grappled in the early

Christian centuries, but engagement with the issues that Chalcedon sought to address need not presuppose that everything has already been said, or that divisions, however complex, are incapable of being healed. One thing is clear: if Jesus Christ is who Christians say he is—"God with us" in a way that does not undermine either divinity or humanity or their coming together in the single, concrete reality of his existence—then he will always transcend all human efforts to understand or describe him, whether at Chalcedon or anywhere else.

9

CHRISTIAN WORSHIP

▼

Everyday Faith

At this stage in our story it is worth taking a detour from our primary narrative to consider some of the more practical aspects of Christian life and witness as they had evolved over the course of the period from the fourth century onward. However crucial the issues that have occupied us in the preceding chapters, we must remember that the practice of Christian faith always involved far more than the activities of the scholars and politicians whose personalities dominate our literary sources. The overwhelming majority of believers clearly did not take part in the debates of councils and synods about matters of doctrine, and most did not read the works of apologetics or polemics produced by the church's great thinkers. The effects of Christian witness and expansion in society were felt not just in the transformation of political structures or the outward symbolism of official pronouncements, but in the testimony of ordinary lives lived amid the realities of an everyday social world. As far as most followers of Christ were concerned, spiritual development took place in the dynamics of daily Christian obedience and through participation in the rhythms of worship and ritual that lay at the heart of the life they shared with their brothers and sisters in Christ.

In the following two chapters we shall look at some of the ways in which Christians worshiped and the manner in which their communities were organized and led over the course of the fourth, fifth, and sixth centuries. Here too, however, we need to bear in mind that growth took place as much through personal contact, the sharing of experience, and the expression of practical Christianity at mundane levels as it did through formal proclamation or ceremony in the context of official church activities. While the story of grassroots piety in these centuries remains largely unknown and the names of most ordinary believers are confined to the mists of history, the primary work of the Christian community in late antiquity—as in every subsequent age—went on in the discipleship of just such persons, living out their faith within their regular social environments.

The Effects of Statistical Growth

It would be quite wrong to suppose that the post-Constantinian world saw thousands of people flocking into the churches in an urgent desire to commit their lives to Jesus Christ, but the period from the fourth century onward had certainly witnessed sizable numbers seeking to join the visible ranks of the Christian community. In the political climate of a Roman world where Christianity was a favored faith, it had become all the more necessary to ensure that the implications of Christian profession were properly understood. Statistical growth of a kind not encountered previously was all very well, but it had significant dangers as well. Individuals might have a variety of reasons for attaching themselves to the Christian cause, not all of which suggested genuine conviction. Profession of Christianity might be a way of furthering career prospects, a means to economic or political advantage, or a strategy for social maneuvering. People might claim to believe in order to please relatives or superiors, or as a way of obtaining a marriage partner, or to win the favor of a particular individual or family.

In a bid to address these realities, programs of catechesis, renunciation, and scrutiny that had evolved over the second and third centuries had been significantly extended, with the result that the process of initiation into the church had become all the more elaborate. Such developments reflected the efforts of the Christian community to preserve its moral and spiritual integrity amid the radical social changes of the times.

Initiation as Mystical Process

We are fortunate to possess some impressive literary evidence of the kinds of systems that emerged as a result of this process of initiation. One particularly striking example comes from the East and the church in Jerusalem. Prior to Helena's visit to Jerusalem in 326 (see p. 21), the see of Jerusalem had not been regarded as especially significant, but in the wake of her pilgrimage and the construction of new churches there and elsewhere in the Holy Land by Constantine the city had attained a far higher prominence. As believers flocked to Palestine from all over the Roman world, the church of Jerusalem grew enormously in prestige, and its customs and liturgical practices in turn became extremely influential elsewhere as visitors carried back with them their experiences of its rituals. It also in turn absorbed some of the patterns represented by its patrons. Jerusalem was both a launching pad and a meeting place for a wide range of liturgical conventions.

Some time around 350, Cyril (ca. 315–387), who had recently become bishop of Jerusalem, delivered a series of catechetical lectures to candidates for baptism in his church. It began with a *Procatechesis*, or introductory lecture to catechumens, delivered in the presence of the whole church prior to Lent, stressing the gravity of the step the candidates were about to take and emphasizing the need for repentance and due preparation. This was followed by eighteen sessions of instruction during Lent addressed to the *photizomenoi*, or "those to be enlightened," which explained the essentials of the faith as understood in the Jerusalem church.

Attached to the text of these lectures we have a group of five *Mystagogical Catecheses*, delivered during Easter week to the *neophotistoi*, "neophytes" or "newly illuminated." These cover the nature of the sacraments: the first three are on baptism, the last two on the Eucharist. Some scholars think that these five homilies were not composed by Cyril but by his successor, John, who became bishop of Jerusalem in 387. If they were given by Cyril, they certainly date from the end of his episcopate and must therefore be seen as stemming from a different context than the lectures that precede them in our collection. But even if they are not by Cyril, they almost certainly reflect teaching that is close to his.

The lectures, and especially the *Mystagogical Catecheses*, offer a remarkable glimpse into liturgical practice in Jerusalem. Baptism was seen in dramatic terms as an awesome privilege, and those who were officially on their way toward receiving it were already set apart from other catechumens. Christian spirituality borrowed from the ideas of the pagan mystery religions of Greece and the East, and the final steps of entry into the church were characterized as a deeply mysterious transition, which needed to be preceded by due ceremony and hedged about with considerable secrecy. Such notions had some roots in earlier Christian teaching, especially in later-second- and early-third-century conceptions of catechesis, but they were developed considerably in the fourth century. It was seen as important that baptismal candidates should not know all the details of what was going to happen to them, and the air of uncertainty and wonder heightened the psychological impact of the process.

Those about to be enlightened were warned that they must not disclose what they were about to learn or betray the secrets of the "deep things of God" even to the ordinary catechumens, far less to their unconverted neighbors. The maintenance of reverence and holy silence was vital, and only once candidates had received baptism and celebrated the Eucharist were they given an exposition of the spiritual meaning of these rites. The language of mystery was specifically used of the baptismal actions, and "mystagogy" described the teaching that followed initiation. In later times, such an emphasis on the concealment of the inner details of the faith from the prying eyes of the unworthy, whether nonbelievers or ordinary catechumens, would be labeled the *disciplina arcani*, the "discipline of the secret."[1]

In Cyril's church, the candidates for baptism assembled in the vestibule of the baptistery. Facing the west, they stretched out their hands and formally renounced the devil. Turning to the east, they solemnly professed faith in God as Trinity and in the one baptism of repentance. Passing into the inner chamber, they removed their clothes and were anointed with oil. They were then led by the hand into "the sacred pool," where they again professed their faith and were immersed three times. Anointed once more with oil, they donned white garments and were led as neophytes back into the main church, carrying lighted tapers as they went. They then received their first communion.

The whole process was deliberately dramatic and laced with symbolism. Baptism was seen as regenerative and essential to salvation, as a cleansing from sins and a bestowal of the gift of the Holy Spirit. The font contained the waters of death, in which sins were symbolically laid to rest, and the waters of life, in which the gift of eternal life was conveyed. The Pauline theology of dying and rising with Christ (especially Rom. 6:3–11; Col. 2:12–15) dominated the imagery of initiation, and the entire sequence of participation was seen as a symbolic identification with Jesus himself: it was a baptism into his death for sins, and into his resurrection as a decisive victory over evil and as the pledge of eternal life. The threefold immersion spoke of the three days of Jesus's sojourn in the grave between the cross and resurrection. The postbaptismal anointing symbolized the seal of the Spirit of Christ and the confirmation of the neophyte as henceforth an instrument of the Lord; the white garments and the lighted tapers signified the light of the risen Christ now shed upon those who had previously lived in darkness.

Comparable stress on the sacred mysteries of Christian initiation and the awe-inspiring rites that attended them is to be found in other major writers of the later fourth and early fifth centuries. Alongside Cyril's lectures, we have baptismal homilies by John Chrysostom in Antioch, Ambrose in Milan, and Theodore in Mopsuestia. The depictions of the baptismal process by these leaders clearly do not describe practices that would have been observed in all churches, and many local variations were also to be found, but through the evidence of such sermons it is possible to reconstruct certain broad patterns at least.

Easter was overwhelmingly the preferred time for baptism, and the season of Lent was used for prebaptismal catechesis. Moral instruction was always a vital element of the process, and public scrutinies were taken particularly seriously in Rome and North Africa. In the churches as a whole, the doctrinal teaching given to those enrolled for baptism also became somewhat more substantial than it had been in earlier generations, and the bishop's lectures were generally in the form of a commentary on a particular creed. If in earlier times baptismal confession had been characterized more by interrogatory forms—with the bishop asking candidates, "Do you believe in . . . ?"—by the fourth century it had come to take a much more declaratory nature, with the candidates themselves professing allegiance to the fundamentals of the faith.

The profession was generally tripartite in structure, confessing the three persons of the God into whose name baptism was about to take place. Naturally, initiates were not expected to offer any kind of systematic analysis of the nature of God as Trinity, but they were meant to be able to articulate key elements of the truth about God's character as Creator, Redeemer, and Sanctifier. Such a declaratory creed was known as a "symbol" (Greek *symbolon*, Latin *symbolum*), a confessional token or even password for full membership in the community of believers. Formally "delivered" or "handed over" by the bishop, it was to be committed to memory and then "rendered back" or recited by the candidates in public as part of the baptismal liturgy. The twofold process was known in Latin as *traditio symboli* and *redditio symboli*. The solemn delivery, memorizing, and rehearsal of the creed contributed to the mystery of the initiation process. Only those who were proceeding to baptism were given the creed, and even then it was kept secret from them until the later stages of their preparation.

The conventions of baptismal confession also contributed to the growing importance of credal forms as not just summaries of basic truths but tests of orthodoxy. Traditionally the symbols passed on to candidates were local affairs, synopses of the essentials of the faith as understood in the church in question. There was probably no insistence on absolute perfection in verbal recitation, so long as a knowledge of the basic content was evident. In the midst of the doctrinal controversies of the fourth century, however, precise wording came to matter very much. What sort of Christ were candidates confessing—one who was fully "consubstantial" with God the Father, or one who was "like" God in some looser sense? What kind of Holy Spirit was being affirmed—one who was truly divine, or one who was some lesser agent of God's purposes? As the arguments over Nicene theology intensified and expanded, Nicene phraseology became more and more prominent in local creeds.

The Creed of Nicaea was widely used in Eastern catechesis, while the formulary that we call "the Nicene Creed," which came to function as the standard baptismal pattern in the Eastern churches, may have originated as a local creed used in the church of Constantinople (see pp. 97–98). In the West the so-called "Apostles' Creed" similarly emerged out of an earlier baptismal form, conventionally designated by scholars the "Old Roman Creed."[2] Local creeds continued to exist widely, but there tended to be family resemblances between verbal forms in particular geographical areas. Overall, there was a growing trend toward standardization and stability of language, rooted in the belief that baptism needed to be accompanied by formal assent to normative summaries of truth that Christians in general should endorse.[3]

Besides the teaching aspect of the baptismal process, other elements were widespread in initiation ceremonies in both the East and the West. The removal of clothes before baptism, the blessing of the baptismal water, profession of faith on immersion, and the donning of white garments after baptism were all very common features. Specific rites for the renunciation of evil (in Greek, *apotaxis*), the act of "adherence" or professing allegiance to Christ (in Greek, *syntaxis*), and anointing both before and after baptism came to be observed. Prebaptismal anointing was variously seen as a form of exorcism or a sign of preparation for combat with the devil. In Syria the candidate's head was typically anointed separately from the body; the first implied a mark of new ownership by Christ, the second suggested adornment with a new garment of immortality.

Postbaptismal chrismation was often simply an anointing of the head, though in other cases, such as in Cyril's Jerusalem, it involved not only the head but also the ears, nose, and chest, with each gesture symbolizing a particular dimension of the blessings of grace. In northern Italy, Ambrose attests to the ritual practice of washing the feet of the newly baptized (*pedilavium*), in imitation of the actions of Jesus in John 13:1–17. In Ambrose's day this was not done in Rome, but it would become a part of Easter-week liturgy in many churches, not only in the West but also in the East. The mystagogical teaching presented to the newly baptized gave elaborate spiritual interpretations to all of the ritual actions, offering typological and allegorical renderings of biblical texts to expound the significance of what they had experienced. Often the homilies delivered to neophytes were attended by the rest of the faithful; the late fourth-century Spanish pilgrim Egeria (see p. 143) describes how in the church in Jerusalem both the catechetical lectures and the postbaptismal sermons were heard by the members of the church as well as by the new initiates.

Baptism of the Young

From the later second century if not before,[4] baptism had been applied not only to adults but also to young children. There had been opponents to this practice, but in the third century it was widely found, particularly in North Africa and other parts of the West. In the fourth century, the custom had spread rapidly.

The ages at which children were baptized varied a good deal: in some cases, baptism took place with babies who were only a few days old; in others, children were nine or older. In a world in which infant mortality rates remained very high, various Christian teachers had already suggested that babies should be baptized as young as possible; both Cyprian and Origen had argued this way in the third century.[5] Gregory of Nazianzus, on the other hand, considered that around three was the optimum age; he wrote that at this age children "can take in something of the mystery and answer [the questions put to them], and even if they do not as yet understand fully, they can nevertheless retain some impression."[6] Gregory may have had optimistic ideas of a three-year-old's capacities, but he was clearly concerned that children should in principle be capable of answering for themselves rather than relying on adult sponsors in order to be baptized.

In the fifth century, in the course of his tortuous disputes with the Pelagians, Augustine had developed an explicit theological defense of infant baptism. Personal belief on the part of the child was not necessary for baptism, he had argued; rather, the child became the recipient of grace through the belief of those who answered on his or her behalf. If baptism remitted the guilt of original sin, and babies were affected by the effects of this original sin even before they had committed any actual sins, it was important that they should be baptized as soon as possible. If they died unbaptized, they would be damned, though the degree of their punishment would deservedly be much lighter than that bestowed upon older people. "Emergency" baptisms were frequently carried out by presbyters in cases where babies might die before the bishop could arrive. On the assumption that baptism was essential for spiritual regeneration and that its validity lay formally in the performance of the rite, infant baptism became the norm in most churches, not only in the West but also in the East.

The ceremonies that attended the baptism of babies and children were generally comparable to those for mature candidates, and rituals such as anointing remained standard; weak or ill infants were, however, spared immersion and were usually sprinkled with water instead. Often children went on to receive the Eucharist as soon as possible after their baptism, and in the East communion typically followed immediately, even for the very young. There were, however, many variations to such conventions. In the church of Rome and elsewhere, it was thought desirable for children to go through a process of catechesis before being baptized, unless they were in imminent danger of death. They would be enrolled as catechumens at an early age and given exorcism and instruction during Lent prior to being baptized at Easter. In a large number of cases, they were clearly too young to understand what they were being told, but it was considered important that they at least in theory acknowledged the truth prior to initiation.

The solemnity of baptism as a moral commitment led many individuals to defer being baptized until later in life. A remarkable number of children of Christian homes, including those of such prominent churchmen as Basil, Gregory of Nazianzus, John Chrysostom, Ambrose, Jerome, and Augustine, did not receive baptism in their childhood. Other converts, such as the emperor Constantine himself, were baptized at the end of their days. To be enrolled as a catechumen was one thing; to take the final step of baptismal initiation was another.

Baptism and Sealing

The number of candidates for baptism had increased so dramatically in the fourth century that bishops could not baptize them all in person, and baptism was frequently administered by presbyters. This was certainly the case with emergency baptisms; it also applied in missionary environments, and in some churches presbyters might even perform the rites in the presence of the bishop. Episcopal authority was nevertheless considered important for anointing in particular. In Eastern churches it was common for the oil used in anointing to be consecrated by the bishop, even if it was then applied by presbyters. In the church of Rome presbyters were allowed to baptize with their bishop's authority, but they were not permitted to bestow postbaptismal anointing on the brow of candidates; such "sealing" with the Spirit was expressly held to be the bishop's prerogative alone.

Initially the consequences of such a distinction were not very significant, since those who had been baptized would often receive this second anointing soon afterward, and might even take their first communion before this occurred. Over time, however, the differentiation of baptism and sealing became greater in the Western churches. In circumstances such as those in fifth-century Gaul, where dioceses were much larger and episcopal authority was spread much more thinly than it was in central Italy, the gap between baptism and "confirmation" grew much longer, and the second became an entirely separate rite performed at a later stage in life when an opportunity arose to present oneself before the bishop. In medieval times, confirmation would often be refused by bishops for moral reasons or neglected altogether by professing believers who felt that the degree of commitment it symbolized was unnecessary or undesirable.

The Liturgy of the Eucharist

The sense of awe that surrounded baptism was closely connected with the solemnity of the rite of the Eucharist to which it granted admission. In order to impress upon worshipers the holiness of participation in the body and blood of Christ, the eucharistic liturgy became a good deal more formal and elaborate. The images drew upon ideas that had already developed significantly between apostolic times and the fourth century, such as the sense that the eucharistic rite was not just a sacred feast of communion but a holy sacrifice or offering designed to bring honor to God by spiritually representing the perfect oblation of Christ himself.[7] Such concepts were expanded as part of an overall inculcation of wonder and reverence in worship, and the Eucharist was depicted as a profound mystery, whose spiritual depths were far too holy and tremendous to be trifled with or made known to the unworthy.

There was much need for such an emphasis on the majesty of the occasion. Congregations were no longer made up primarily of the truly committed but embraced many who seem to have had little sense of what worship was about. The demeanor of people in churches elicited frequent criticism from Christian leaders; noise and chattering were common during the services, and there were complaints about young people engaging in pranks and petty thieves picking the pockets of worshipers. Disruptive behavior was not confined to wilder elements from outside the church; some of the faithful themselves were chided for gossiping and acting in irreverent fashion during the liturgy as the Scriptures were read and expounded or the prayers were offered.

In order to deal with these problems, the Eucharist increasingly came to be presented as a mysterious sacred drama, and styles of liturgical action were developed to emphasize the seriousness and profundity of what was taking place. Such notes had of course been sounded since early times, but in the fourth century they became more necessary than ever before. Worshipers needed to appreciate that they were in the presence of Almighty God and that the Christ whose broken body and shed blood were symbolized in the thanksgiving was also divine in his being. Just as the catechetical teaching stressed the holiness of the sacrifice that was offered in the Eucharist and the importance of approaching it with fear and trembling, so too the prayers, hymns, and procedures that took place within the service were designed to instill awe and reverence.

The eucharistic prayer would typically make it clear at the outset that what was about to take place was utterly sacred. The elements of the Eucharist were seen not only as symbols of Christ but as holy food to nourish the soul and as objects of mysterious spiritual power, which conveyed a range of blessings to the recipient: they sanctified the body and might protect it against evil and sickness. Practical advice on the appropriate spirit of reception might take the following form:

> When you come forward, then, do not come with your arms extended or your fingers parted. Make your left hand a throne for your right, since your right hand is about to welcome a king. Cup your palm and receive in it the body of Christ, saying in response *Amen*. Then carefully bless your eyes with a touch of the holy body, and consume it, taking care not to drop a particle of it. For to lose any of it is like losing part of your own

body. . . . After you have partaken of Christ's body, approach also the cup of
his blood. Do not stretch out your hands for it, but bow and say *Amen* to
show your homage and reverence, and sanctify yourself by partaking also
of Christ's blood. And while the moisture is still on your lips, touch it with
your hands and bless your eyes, forehead, and other organs of sense.[8]

Christians had always believed that the taking of the bread and the
cup represented a genuine participation in the body and blood of Christ,
and symbolic interpretations of the eucharistic elements continued.
However, the more "realistic" construals that had been found in some
earlier authorities also became increasingly common. Bishops warned
their hearers that it was wrong to suppose the emblems, placed upon the
altar of the eucharistic sacrifice, were nothing more than bread and wine.
The action of the celebrant was seen as involving not only remembrance
and thanksgiving but the *consecration* of the bread and wine.

Consecration

Different views were taken as to how this consecration took place. In
the East there was a strong emphasis on the *epiclesis* or invocation of
divine power. In earlier times, such invocation had been mainly understood as a request for divine blessing upon the worshipers who were
about to receive the elements. While the appeal for blessing of participants remained, there was now more of a sense that God was being
implored to act directly upon the elements themselves and to bestow
upon them the special status that would fulfill the holy purposes for
which they were intended.

Sometimes the prayer asked that the second person of the Trinity, the
Logos, should be sent to achieve this task. This is evident in a prayer traditionally (although somewhat dubiously) ascribed to Serapion, bishop
of Thmuis, the friend of Athanasius (see p. 87), which includes the
petition: "Let your holy Word come on this bread, O God of truth, that
the bread may become body of the Word; and on this cup, that the cup
may become blood of the Truth." Invocation of the Word continued
to be common in some traditions of Egyptian liturgy in particular. In
general, however, it was not God the Son but God the Holy Spirit who
was invoked, and the eucharistic prayers of a great many Eastern bishops tended to take this form. The *epiclesis* was increasingly seen as a
request that the Spirit would not only bless the bread and wine but, in
a mysterious way, cause them to *become* the body and blood of Christ.
Such an idea is already clear in the prayer regarding the Word attributed

to Serapion; with reference to the Spirit, it can be paralleled widely in Cyril of Jerusalem, John Chrysostom, and others.

In Western churches, on the other hand, the consecration of the elements was held to take place not through invocation of the Holy Spirit but as the celebrant recited the words of Christ ("This is my body . . .") from the institutional narrative. Ambrose puts it this way:

> How can something which is bread be the body of Christ? Well, by what words is the consecration effected, and whose words are they? The words of the Lord Jesus. All that is said before are the words of the priest: praise is offered to God, prayer is offered up, petitions are made for the people, for kings, and for all others. But when the moment comes for bringing the most holy sacrament into being, the priest does not use his own words any longer: he uses the words of Christ. It is Christ's word, therefore, that brings this sacrament into being.[9]

While Ambrose possibly also had a prayer to the Spirit to bless the offering of the Eucharist, on the whole Western liturgies did not see *epiclesis* of the Spirit as the means by which the elements were consecrated. From the fourth century onward, this distinction would be a major liturgical difference between Western and Eastern churches. In general, the West had been much slower than the East in evolving its own liturgical styles—at Rome in particular, the Eucharist was still performed in Greek until the time of Damasus—but as a distinctly Latin rite emerged, its difference in this area was notable. Both the East and the West were increasingly prone to speak of a change occurring in the eucharistic elements, but the West regarded this as something that happened in the solemn recitation of Christ's words, while the East would continue to invest great significance in the appeal to the Holy Spirit. Forms of appeal to the Spirit can certainly be traced in some Western patterns, but the traditional Roman rite contained no reference to the Spirit, and it was only in much later times that prayers of *epiclesis* were routinely added to Western liturgies.

Eucharistic Prayers

Whatever differences had begun to emerge between the East and the West, the fourth century had also witnessed a growing standardization of eucharistic prayers in the churches as a whole. Recognizing the importance of liturgical forms as media of sound doctrine, bishops became keen to use patterns that spoke appropriately of the divinity of Christ

and the Holy Spirit so that believers understood the true character of
the triune God they were worshiping. Eucharistic worship both in the
East and the West typically continued to take the form of a dialogue
between the leader and the congregation, beginning thus:

> The Lord be with you.
> And with your spirit.
> Lift up your hearts.[10]
> We lift them to the Lord.
> Let us give thanks to the Lord.
> It is right and fitting.[11]

This exchange would then lead into praise of the glory of God as seen
in creation and redemption. It was common for this to climax in a hymn
known in Latin as the *Sanctus*, based upon the angelic cry in Isaiah 6:3,
"Holy, holy, holy . . ." (a formula also found in some Jewish synagogue
prayers and already employed by Christians in earlier times), though
the *Sanctus* took longer to become established in the Western Eucharist
than it did in the East. In the sixth century a further hymn was added,
Benedictus qui venit, "Blessed is he who comes in the name of the Lord,"
from Matthew 21:9. The institutional narrative would usually be read,[12]
and the words of Jesus on eating and drinking in remembrance of him
would be quoted. God would be asked to accept the offering of thanksgiving or spiritual sacrifice by the assembled company, and other inter-
cessions would be made for the church. Very often these prayers were
seen as embracing all of the faithful, the dead as well as the living, and it
became common to name departed saints and martyrs in them. In a great
many churches, the Lord's Prayer would be recited by the congregation.
Finally there would be a doxology, ascribing praise to God.

While specific traditions were cherished in particular contexts, many
of these patterns traveled from place to place, leading to a fair degree of
cross-fertilization between different churches. Major archetypes included
the Antiochene or West Syrian tradition (classically known as the liturgy
of St. Basil and St. John Chrysostom), the Alexandrian tradition (the
liturgy of St. Mark), and the Roman tradition (the Roman canon). While
each undoubtedly has its distinctives, study of their classical textual
forms reveals that a broadly similar sequence of *anaphora* or "offering"
prayer was observed across a wide geographical spread of Christianity.
Much evolution in liturgy continued over subsequent centuries, but
already by the early fifth century there was a strong discouragement
of innovation on the part of individual clergy. The solemnity of giving

thanks tended to be marked best by the dignity of standard rhythms, and improvisation represented a sort of violation of the sacred routine.

Discerning the Drama

The sense of drama in eucharistic activity was captured not only in physical rituals and verbal forms but in the interpretation of the process in preaching. Theodore of Mopsuestia portrays the whole liturgy as an allegory of Jesus's suffering, death, and resurrection—a dramatic reenactment of the foundational elements in the Christian story of salvation. Each gesture and stage represented a vital aspect in that narrative. The carrying of the bread and wine to the altar symbolized Jesus being led to his passion; the spreading of cloths was a reminder of the winding-sheets or grave clothes in which Jesus was wrapped; the invocation of the Holy Spirit represented the moment at which the crucified one was raised from the dead to bestow his grace and power upon his people; and the solemn breaking of bread spoke of the appearances of the risen Christ, who invited the faithful to come and feed upon him.

By the later fourth century the Eucharist was celebrated not only on Sundays but daily in many major churches, yet its solemnity was taken no less seriously. The reality was that the more awe-inspiring and mysterious the Eucharist was rendered, the more a distance was created between ordinary believers and the real purpose for which the ritual had originally been given—the privilege of remembering Christ and sharing in him regardless of social distinctions or degrees of spiritual achievement. Bishops such as John Chrysostom, who placed such importance upon the moral character necessary for the reception of the rite, could produce the opposite results to those they intended. In advising people who were guilty of serious sins to leave the service prior to the Eucharist, the commendable aim was to encourage them to examine themselves and amend their lives. In practice, however, many of the hearers simply chose not to participate in the Eucharist at all, at least not on a regular basis; some took communion only once a year. The unfortunate consequence was that numbers of churchgoers came to regard participation as something that was incidental to faith—a view that was plainly at odds with the earliest Christian practice.

Such ideas were fostered by a widening of the gulf between clergy and laity. Some considered the Eucharist to be something that the clergy carried out on their behalf, at which they themselves did not necessarily need to be present. Church leaders denounced the practice of leaving before communion but in the end could do little to prevent it. In order to ensure that those who were leaving at least did so in an orderly manner, various rites of dismissal came to be added to the liturgy. Believers who did receive communion were also sent away afterwards with a formal blessing by the celebrant. Whether before or after the communion, it was this practice of dismissal that in the West led to the Latin name *missa* (a word also used for the dismissal of soldiers from a parade) or "mass" being applied to the service of the Eucharist itself.

As we saw in chapter 6, theological reflection on the nature of both baptism and the Eucharist had expanded considerably in the fifth century, when Augustine expounded these ceremonies as "signs of sacred things" or "visible words," which convey divine grace to those who receive them. Such definitions would generate endless further discussion of their own in medieval, Reformation, and later thought, but whatever their details they undoubtedly evoked established elements of earlier Christian thinking. For Tertullian, back in the early third century, the rites of baptism and communion could legitimately be called "sacraments" because they were means by which believers participated in the mystery of Christ (rendering the Greek *mysterion* with the Latin *sacramentum*). They were also evocative of the *sacramentum* or "sacred oath" of allegiance taken by Roman soldiers.

To receive baptism was to demonstrate publicly one's initial commitment to Christ, and to be sealed with the sign of the cross was to receive the standard under which the fight of faith was to be fought. To take communion was to maintain one's pledge to be part of the army of Christ's warriors and to anticipate his assured triumph over all his enemies. As Augustine himself insisted, sacramental participation lay at the heart of the Christian life, and any marginalizing of its importance as a means of grace was a serious violation of the basic principles of Christian existence.

Daily Prayer

The recognition of Christianity in the fourth century also meant that the patterns of daily prayer that had evolved over previous centuries could become a public as well as a private aspect of Christian piety. By the third century, it was normal for most believers to observe prayer several times each day: a threefold (9:00 a.m., 12:00 noon, and 3:00 p.m.) or fivefold (these three plus early morning and evening) sequence of prayer was common. Such rhythms were now no longer only for the individual believer or the Christian family to keep in private or at home; they were part of the churches' daily liturgy, enacted in an official, publicly visible capacity. Two in particular, the morning and evening prayers, came to be communal activities led by the clergy.

The "cathedral" office, as scholars call it, was seen as an offering of praise and intercession by the whole church—a priestly service involving a range of ministries on behalf of the believing community and the world in which it was set.[13] Psalms featured prominently. In the morning, Psalms 148–150 were widely used; Psalms 51 and 63 were also favorites. In the evening, Psalm 141 was standard in much of the East, as was the Greek hymn *Phos hilaron*, traditionally sung at the lighting of lamps;[14] Psalm 105 was common in the West. The psalms and hymns preferred in a particular context tended to remain constant from day to day. Prayers were said for the church and for society at large. Incense, symbolic of the offering of prayer (cf. Ps. 141:2; Rev. 8:3–5), was in use in a number of major churches in the late fourth century, though its usage in worship did not become widespread until the seventh century. The ceremonial lighting of candles was already quite common in the fourth century; the use of lighted tapers in baptismal ceremonies probably had roots in the initiation practices of classical mystery religions, which, as we have noted, had some influence upon the understanding of the Christian sacramental drama.

One form of prayer that became very widespread was the "litany" (Greek *litaneia*, "supplication"), which seems to have originated in Antioch and spread to Constantinople, from where it traveled to Rome and the West. Litanies consisted of a series of petitions said, or sometimes sung, by a leader, either a priest or a deacon (diaconal litanies were especially common in the East), to which the congregation would give fixed responses. One short response in particular came to have especially wide use: the Greek words *Kyrie Eleeson*, "Lord, have mercy" (usually rendered *Kyrie Eleison*). This Eastern prayer was incorporated into Latin liturgies of the Eucharist by the later fifth century, with the Greek untranslated.

At the end of the sixth century, when the Roman eucharistic liturgy was revised in various ways under Gregory the Great (see pp. 332–38), the *Kyrie Eleison* would be recognized as a vital element in the mass, overriding other petitions in significance; Gregory also attests that the supplementary petition, *Christe Eleison*, "Christ, have mercy," was normal in Rome, though it was not found in the East. Over later centuries these prayers would be organized into a range of formal patterns, such as a ninefold recitation of the *Kyrie Eleison* and a threefold recitation of the *Christe Eleison*, and elaborate styles would be devised for setting them to music.

The expansion of asceticism in the fourth century had also yielded significant liturgical developments. "Monastic" prayer had its roots not so much in corporate praise and intercession as in ceaseless meditation as an element in a quest for spiritual perfection. The solitary contemplatives of the desert in Egypt and Syria had always concentrated on maintaining a continual vigil of prayer in pursuit of special intimacy with God, but more communal forms of asceticism were also dedicated to the cultivation of a higher degree of meditation than was possible for believers occupied in the workaday world. Monastics of most kinds shared a specially deep devotion to the Psalms and to the Scriptures in general, often reciting very long stretches of material in a single session, and their commitment to prayer involved strenuous patterns of contemplation and silent petition as well as audible worship. The systems of offices developed by figures such as Basil and John Cassian aspired to make worship a constant activity.

As monasteries came to be located not only in isolated places but also in the vicinity of towns and cities, and as more and more members of the clergy had themselves experienced the ascetic life in one form or another prior to their careers as ecclesiastical leaders, the patterns of monastic prayer increasingly came to influence the practices of the church at large.

Cathedral liturgy in a number of churches expanded to accommodate a greater number of offices, and laity as well as clergy were exhorted to give due devotion to daily worship. By the turn of the fifth and sixth centuries, the church in Rome had devised a scheme in which the Psalter was recited in its entirety over the course of a week, and the reading of Psalm 119, the longest psalm, was structured around the services at the third, sixth, and ninth hours of the day. In other places patterns were often simpler, and a smaller range of psalms was employed, but the chanting or singing of scriptural material typically followed some kind of ordered cycle, and it was officially regarded as a course of meditation as well as a matter of instruction or praise. Worshipers were also encouraged to cultivate their private prayer lives outside of the regular church services, and the examples of the ascetics were often cited as an inspiration.

The proximity of monasteries to urban churches and the transference of some personnel between the two contexts meant that ideas traveled in the other direction as well, and monastic prayer also absorbed more mainstream practices. In the monastic *Rule* of Benedict of Nursia, drawn up around 540 (see pp. 322–24), the office for morning prayer was essentially similar to the service of the cathedral church, with the same psalms used each morning, whereas the pattern for evening prayer was typically monastic in style, following an ordered weekly cycle of psalms. Benedict's system also incorporated "responsories," or responsive chants of scriptural texts, "antiphons," or scriptural verses recited in alternate fashion before and after the psalms and hymns, and a fixed course of biblical readings.

Further fusions of cathedral and monastic approaches in subsequent generations ensured that by medieval times there was widespread observance of a pattern that included most or all of the following offices: Mattins (Latin *matutinus*, "of the morning") and Lauds (from the repetition of the Latin *laudate*, "praise," in Psalms 148–150) in the early morning (the Greek name for both was *Orthros*, "dawn"); Terce (Latin *tertius*, "third") at the third hour, or 9:00 a.m.; Sext (Latin *sextus*, "sixth") at the sixth hour, or 12:00 noon; None (Latin *nonus*, "ninth") at the ninth hour, or 3:00 p.m.; and Vespers (Latin *vesper*, "evening") in the evening. The additional offices of Prime (Latin *primus*, "first"), observed at the first hour or 6:00 a.m., and Compline (Latin *completorium*, "completion"; the equivalent Greek version was known as the *Apodeipnon*, "after supper"), said at the completion of the day, before retiring for the night, were also very common.[15] Though many variations existed, and the content of the services in terms of scriptural texts and sung material evinced some diversity from context to context, a broadly similar approach was shared by both regular clergy and monastics.

Hymns

Sung praise had always been important to Christians, and the development of the liturgy of daily prayer fostered the use of song in worship. As had always been the case, the Psalms were especially cherished, and they continued to be a pervasive feature of Christian praise everywhere. Other compositions were of growing significance, but most of these still had a strongly scriptural flavor. The later fourth-century document known as the *Apostolic Constitutions*[16] refers to a Greek version of a hymn that would be known in Latin as the *Gloria in Excelsis* ("Glory be to God on high"). Essentially a Christian version of the kind of language of praise to be found in the Psalms, it was used in the East in the morning office, and in the early sixth century it would be introduced into the Eucharist in the West. A shorter form of doxology consisting of an ascription of praise to each of the persons of the Trinity, the *Gloria Patri* ("Glory be to the Father. . ."), also came into use in the fourth century. Overall there was an enduring favor for "canticles" or "odes" taken from the Bible. The Magnificat, the song of praise sung by the Virgin Mary in Luke 1:46–55 ("My soul magnifies the Lord . . ."), was variously sung in both morning and evening liturgies in the East and the West, as was the Benedictus ("Blessed be the Lord . . ."), Zachariah's thanksgiving at the birth of his son, John the Baptist (Luke 1:68–79). The Nunc Dimittis ("Now let your servant depart . . ."), Simeon's prayer in Luke 2:29–32, was in widespread use, especially in the evening (a Greek version is mentioned in the *Apostolic Constitutions*). Other biblical songs, such as those of Moses (Exod. 15:1–18; Deut. 32:1–43), Hannah (1 Sam. 2:1–10), and Isaiah (Isa. 26:1–21), were used especially in the East, and the *Benedicite* ("Bless the Lord . . ."), based upon a song of praise put into the mouths of the three young Hebrew exiles, Shadrach, Meshach, and Abednego (Daniel 3), in an apocryphal book of Scripture (*The Song of the Three Children*) was popular both in the East and the West.

Alongside these expressly scriptural forms, however, hymns of other kinds had become more common, especially as media of doctrinal instruction. Amid the theological turmoil of the fourth-century debates about the nature of the incarnation and the theology of the Trinity, both Arians and Nicenes had used song to further their ideas. As we saw in chapter 5, Ephrem the Syrian had made striking contributions to hymnody with his celebrations of the glory of Christ, the presence of God in the world, and the nature of human salvation. Ephrem's writings greatly influenced other authors and were translated into Armenian, Greek, Latin, and other tongues. Greek hymns had also been produced by other talented writers such as Gregory of Nazianzus. Congregational hymn-singing had been promoted by teachers such as John Chrysostom in Constantinople, and it had been developed with especially notable effect by Ambrose in Milan (see pp. 103–4, 109). The hymns of Ambrose had a very powerful impact in the West, and it became very common to imitate his techniques, with the result that large numbers of hymns came to be attributed falsely to his personal authorship.

One of the most impressive of Western hymn-writers was a Spanish poet named Aurelius Prudentius Clemens, or Prudentius for short (ca. 348–410). Prudentius had spent much of his life as a civil administrator, but in his retirement years he devoted himself to spiritual exercises and to a range of writing on Christian themes. He combined great artistic talent with deep commitment to the truth of his faith, and he wrote some remarkable verse on the divinity of Christ, the origin of evil, and other theological subjects. His *Psychomachia* ("The Struggle of the Soul"), a lengthy allegory in which the trials and temptations of the Christian soul represent the challenges faced by the church in the world, exercised an enormous influence on later Western authors, especially in the use of personification to depict spiritual vices and virtues. Prudentius wrote a large number of lyrical poems in classical meters, excerpts from which came to be widely cited in collections of hymns. Though composed in Latin, they were given Greek titles, following a long-standing convention in Roman literature. The *Cathemerinon* ("The Daily Round") was a group of twelve hymns mostly intended for daily use;[17] the *Peristephanon* ("On Martyrs' Crowns") consists of fourteen compositions in praise of various Spanish and Italian martyrs.

The fifth-century Latin poet Caelius Sedulius, of whose life little is known, produced an epic on the gospel of Christ (which he also translated into prose) and a number of hymns, two of which survive today.[18] Perhaps the most gifted of Latin hymn-writers, however, was Venantius Fortunatus (ca. 540–601), a north Italian poet who settled in Poitiers, where he became bishop late in life. Fortunatus wrote over three hundred poetic compositions of considerable aesthetic and spiritual quality, including hymns, elegies, epigrams, epitaphs, panegyrics, and other works. His most famous hymns were on the subject of the cross of Christ and were written for the occasion of the presentation of an alleged relic of the true cross at a new convent in Poitiers, founded by a pious Merovingian queen, Radegund, in 561. Two of them in particular—"The royal banners forward go" (*Vexilla Regis*) and "Sing, my tongue, the glorious battle" (*Pangue, Lingua*)—were incorporated into the later Western liturgy of Passiontide and endure in a number of hymnals to this day.

The most celebrated of all early Latin hymns is of uncertain origin. The Te Deum, in praise of God the Father and God the Son, was written not in verse but in rhythmical prose. It has been linked with a number of different writers, including Niceta, bishop of Remesiana (ca. 335–414), a missionary among the Goths on the Danube frontier in the later fourth century. A ninth-century legend claimed that it was composed by Ambrose for the baptism of Augustine, but this is purely imaginary. The true origin of the work remains unclear. It may have links to a Paschal Vigil liturgy, perhaps dating from the third century. Whatever its roots, it was already very much in use in the West in the sixth century, and it came to be a regular part of the office of Mattins.

There were some who argued that praise ought to be confined to the language of Scripture, and in the sixth century there would be official pronouncements in certain circles against the use of nonbiblical poetic compositions in worship. Nothing, however, could curb the instinct of Christians to express their devotion and their doctrine in verse forms. In the Eastern churches, short doctrinal hymns known as *troparia* ("stanzas") flourished, and a Syrian writer named Romanos would become famous in Constantinople around the middle years of the sixth century as a composer of *kontakia*, extensive metrical sermons set to music, on themes from the life of Jesus.[19] One stanza would be sung by a soloist with a following refrain by a choir. The most famous example of a *kontakion* is an acrostic hymn in twenty-four stanzas known as the *Akathistos* (in Greek "not sitting," since it was sung standing), composed in honor of the Virgin Mary. It was not written by Romanos, but its author was probably influenced by him. Such compositions would become very popular in the East during the seventh and eighth centuries, and the *Akathistos* is still sung today in Eastern Orthodox churches during Lent.

Music

About the actual music of Christian worship we know a lot less than we might wish. So far as we can tell, singing remained unaccompanied virtually everywhere, but an absence of instruments certainly did not mean that the aesthetic qualities of worship were treated lightly. It is clear that increasing effort was put into the music of liturgy, whether the forms of praise were directly biblical or other compositions. The psalmody of the office was generally led by a reader or singer—a junior official and sometimes quite a young boy, who would either intone the text as a solo or lead worshipers in a responsive fashion. Choirs were to be found widely from the later fourth century, and in the larger urban churches they could be of considerable size.

As it had doubtless always done, singing could move worshipers considerably, sometimes to a degree that individual participants found troubling. Augustine was deeply affected by the praise of the Milanese church in the early days of his faith, and he was afraid that on occasion the music mattered more to him than the words.[20] Others, including many of his contemporaries in the church in North Africa, shared such concerns and advocated the speaking rather than the chanting of scriptural material. On the whole, however, it was acknowledged that music, treated reverently, enhanced rather than detracted from worship, and Augustine himself disagreed with those who argued for its removal.

In the East, in the Syrian churches and in areas such as Cappadocia, antiphonal singing was common, and it is highly likely that Ambrose's hymns were also sung this way. The practices of the major churches in general tended to affect styles in smaller centers. At the end of the sixth century in Rome, Gregory the Great would do a great deal to emphasize the dignity of liturgy, and the style of singing developed there would profoundly influence patterns elsewhere in the West; in later times it would become standard to refer to the Roman style as "Gregorian chant," though in reality the high medieval forms of plainsong evolved far beyond anything that might have been found in Gregory's church.

Christian intellectuals continued to accept the ancient convention that the science of *musica* was one of the liberal arts, and those who upheld the legitimacy of such secular studies as preparatory for spiritual learning granted enquiry into *musica* a relevant place in Christian education. *Musica* in this sense was not music theory as we might think of it today but the study of mathematical relations between sounds and the elaboration of tonal systems. Augustine wrote a treatise on this subject not long after his conversion, which offered a blend of Christian and Neoplatonist thinking on the theory of rhythm and meter. Other later Western authors such as Boethius (see pp. 312–13) and Cassiodorus (see pp. 324–25) would also recognize the validity of such reflection and seek to apply their ideas to the sacred music of their time. Formal musical notation would not develop until the ninth century, but the architectonic systems of the Middle Ages had their roots in a synthesis of Christian music with mathematical speculations on rhythm and harmony that stretched back into classical antiquity.

10

ORGANIZATION, MINISTRY, AND SYMBOLISM

▼

Sunday

As well as inspiring further developments in liturgical forms, the fourth century had also contributed to the formalizing of the special times set aside for Christian worship and devotion. In 321, Constantine had closed the imperial law-courts on Sundays for all purposes other than the emancipation of slaves and enjoined an abstention from work in general on Sundays, though farm labor was excluded. Constantine's avowed aim was to encourage respect for the sun rather than to facilitate Christian worship, but his legislation had marked the first official recognition of Sunday as a day of rest as well as the day on which Christians gathered to remember their Lord and celebrate his resurrection.

Sunday had increasingly come to be seen not only as the main occasion for Christian assembly, thanksgiving, and praise but also as a time to be taken away from normal daily pursuits. In gathering together in conscious detachment from regular activities—bringing their gifts, offering their worship, and submitting themselves to the authority of God's Word—believers were encouraged to think of themselves as making

269

manifest the true nature of the church. During the rest of the week they were dispersed in the world, going about their diverse tasks; on this day they came together as one, publicly different from those around them, to experience the special presence of their Lord in their midst and to pledge their hope for the coming of his kingdom.

For many Christians, especially those of lower or average socioeconomic status, the freedom not to work on Sundays remained severely limited or nonexistent, but there was a growing sense that in so far as it could be, the Lord's Day was to be treated as special, and worshipers were exhorted to avoid activities that were inappropriate to the day of their main weekly devotions. Such principles had already begun to be enunciated prior to Constantine, but they had gathered further momentum over the course of the fourth century, and many churchmen issued fierce denunciations of believers giving themselves to worldly entertainments on Sundays.

The influence of bishops close to those in authority sometimes helped to generate civil laws prohibiting such activities in the later fourth, fifth, and sixth centuries, but on the whole theatrical shows, games, and races continued, and Christian leaders had to contend with the fact that not all of their flock were enthusiastic about relinquishing popular amusements in the interests of spiritual duties. The extent to which Sunday was obviously not uniformly kept as a day of piety can be gauged in the escalating penalties prescribed in early medieval legislation for nonattendance at church and the pursuit of improper business on the Lord's Day.

Sacred Seasons

The Council of Nicaea had formally resolved the dispute over the dating of Easter by decreeing that the Pasch fell on the first Sunday following the first full moon after the spring equinox. This was generally accepted, though there were some who continued to dissent from the principle that Easter should always be observed on a Sunday, and Quartodeciman believers were to be found in parts of the East well into the fifth century.

There were also enduring differences over the way in which the spring equinox was to be calculated. In the third century an Alexandrian scholar named Anatolius (d. ca. 282), who became bishop of Laodicea, had worked out a nineteen-year cycle based upon Jewish ways of reckoning the date of the Passover.[1] Different versions of the nineteen-year cycle were used in Alexandria and Constantinople until the sixth century, while Rome, along with a number of other Western churches, for quite a long time preferred to follow an alternative eighty-four-year cycle (though a nineteen-year pattern may have been followed by the church of Milan as early as the 360s). The nineteen-year system gradually prevailed in the West, and it was finally accepted by Rome in the early sixth century.[2] Nevertheless, Rome's transference to the nineteen-year model would still cause some significant problems more than a century later, when Roman traditions clashed with the sensibilities of other Western Christians who insisted in operating upon a different basis (see pp. 387–88).

Easter was widely recognized as the main season for baptism and as a festival for which all believers ought to prepare by the exercise of fasting and spiritual discipline. The fourth century saw a growth in the observance of a period of Lent as a time when baptismal candidates reached the final stages of their preparation for initiation and the faithful practiced self-denial in commemoration of their Lord. The duration of this pre-Paschal fast still varied a good deal from church to church. At the beginning of the fourth century, a forty-day fast in imitation of Jesus's example (Matt. 4:1–11; Mark 1:12–13; Luke 4:1–13)[3] was common in the West, but many Eastern churches confined themselves to a shorter period of fasting over the seven days prior to Easter.

When Athanasius had been exiled to the West in the 330s, he had been struck by the greater dedication shown by Western believers with regard to Lenten observance, and on his return to the East he encouraged the adoption of the forty-day scheme there also. Even once the extended Lenten season became generally standard, however, there were many different ways of reckoning its obligations. In the East, Lent lasted for seven weeks, but in most churches Saturdays as well as Sundays were considered exempt from fasting (with the exception of the Saturday prior to Easter Sunday). In the West, a six-week fast was kept that included Saturdays. With the apparent exception of the church in Jerusalem, it was a long time before a Lenten observance over an actual total of forty days was widespread; in the West it probably was not found until the seventh century. Prior to that, diverse local customs persisted, and the number *forty* was often treated as symbolic rather than literal.

The specially sacred days of Easter were naturally the three days of Friday, Saturday, and Sunday, but it had also become normal to mark an entire Holy Week leading up to Easter. The practice seems to have begun in Jerusalem and to have spread as a consequence of pilgrimage. Devout believers could indulge their desire to reenact in liturgical form the climactic events of Jesus's life. When Egeria had visited Jerusalem in the early 380s, she had witnessed not only the familiar patterns of the Paschal Vigil and the baptism of catechumens but also a ritual procession with palms on the Sunday before Easter, a service on Good Friday that included a veneration of an alleged relic of Christ's cross, and, in a church built on the spot where the Upper Room was believed to have been located, a commemoration of the risen Lord's appearances to his disciples.

The observance of Palm Sunday and the veneration of a crucifix, if not a relic of the true cross, had both spread to other churches, not least in the West. The liturgical details varied somewhat according to location, and certain customs that would become classical (such as the blessing of palms) did not evolve until much later, but many of the main elements of the traditional Holy Week were already well established by the later fourth century, including the celebration of the Thursday before Easter as the day on which Jesus washed his disciples' feet and instituted the Eucharist.[4]

The period of fifty days following Easter continued to be regarded as a time of celebration. Fasting was not permitted, and there was no kneeling for prayer; both of these rules are found in the canons of the Council of Nicaea. Prior to the fourth century, little emphasis seems to have been placed on the fact that the outpouring of the Holy Spirit had occurred on the fiftieth day itself, but Pentecost had now come to be marked as another special season, second only to Easter in its importance for believers. By the later fourth century, the ascension of the risen Jesus into heaven as described in Acts 1:9 was also being widely observed, typically with a solemn procession and in Jerusalem with an expedition to the Mount of Olives. The ascension had in some cases been celebrated in conjunction with Pentecost, but it became standard to mark it instead on the fortieth day after Easter, in accordance with Luke's chronology that the risen Jesus had appeared to his disciples and taught them over a forty-day period (Acts 1:3). In some churches, particularly in the West, the significance of the day of ascension led to a resumption of regular fasting after this time, even though fasting was not supposed to take place during Pentecost.

The earliest evidence for the celebration of 25 December as the festival of the birth of Jesus is to be found in a list of Roman bishops compiled in 354, which mentions the days that were treated as significant in Rome in the year 336. It is not clear why 25 December was chosen, and various theories have been proposed to account for it. One theory is that since the date was also that of the winter solstice in the Julian calendar and the occasion of a popular pagan feast in honor of the birthday of the Sun-god, the intention was to demonstrate that Christ was the true Sun of Righteousness who alone deserved to be worshiped on that day. After Constantine, associations of Christ and the sun were very common, and there was conceivably a concern to ween people away from pagan celebrations by providing them with a Christian substitute that evoked aspects of the same imagery while representing the truth of the gospel. Such deliberate syncretism certainly occurred with other aspects of pagan symbolism in the fourth-century churches, not least in Rome.

Another possibility, already discussed in some early Christian authors, is that 25 December was arrived at by a particular way of reckoning the duration of Jesus's life. It was believed in some quarters that the length of Jesus's life must have been an exact number of years, and that the date on which he died must therefore have been the same date on which he was conceived. On the calculation that he died on 25 March and that his conception also took place on such a date, his birth was assumed to have occurred exactly nine months later, on 25 December. Whatever the truth of the matter, commemoration of the nativity of Christ had come to be seen by many church leaders in the fourth century as an important way of underscoring the reality of the incarnation and of affirming the full deity of the Son of God over against lesser views of his status.

In the East the feast of Epiphany on 6 January had traditionally had associations with the birth of Jesus, though it also commemorated his baptism. Initially Eastern Christians continued to treat Epiphany as more important than Christmas, but gradually 25 December grew in significance in the East as well as the West, and by the middle of the fifth century it was well-established. The church in Jerusalem was slower to adopt 25 December as special, not recognizing it as the Feast of the Nativity until 549, and the church in Armenia continues to this day to hold to 6 January as its celebration of the incarnation. For the most part, however, 25 December was accepted.

As Christmas had evolved, the significance of Epiphany had developed in some measure along with it. Not only had 6 January long been associated with the nativity, but it was especially connected with the baptism of Jesus. These links continued, especially in the East, but in Rome and North Africa it was associated much more with the manifestation of Christ to the Gentiles in the context of the visit of the Magi (Matt. 2:1–12) and with other events such as the turning of water into wine at the wedding at Cana (John 2:1–11). While Eastern ritual included a solemn blessing of water on this day and other Western churches made dominant reference to the baptism of Jesus, Roman and North African liturgy emphasized the main significance of 6 January as a commemoration of the time of the appearance of salvation to the Gentiles.

The Cult of the Saints

One of the most striking features in the life of the churches in the fourth century and beyond was the expansion of the cult of the saints. In the earliest Christian churches, the description "saints" had been applied to believers in general, but early Christian thinking had also absorbed Jewish traditions that regarded certain people, particularly martyrs, as specially holy. For generations now Christian martyrs had been invested with special degrees of sanctity and attributed with solemn powers to intercede with God on behalf of "ordinary" believers. Martyr feasts had been treated as sacred "birthdays," when the victims of cruelty or oppression had entered into their new life in heaven.[5]

All of these conventions continued with vigor: veneration of martyrs' graves became more important than ever, and relics were cherished, traded, and bequeathed by the pious as sacred possessions with wonder-working powers. As pilgrimage became increasingly common, so cults traveled, and practices were further shared by Christians exiled from their own churches in times of turmoil. Saints' days grew significantly in importance, and a great many individuals who had originally been of only fairly local fame came to be venerated in churches far afield from their original contexts. Many of the great poetic compositions of authors such as Paulinus of Nola[6] and Prudentius (see pp. 265–66) were produced in honor of the saints, and other literary accounts of martyrs' acts were very fashionable. The popular power of cultic practices was immense.

The category of the saints included not only martyrs but other believers deemed to be specially sanctified and favored by God, including confessors, virgins, and particular spiritual teachers. In imitation of biblical ideas of a heavenly register of the elect, the names of living as well as departed heroes and heroines were given in lists recited by a deacon in the liturgy of the Eucharist (the "diptychs");[7] as we have seen illustrated at a number of points in preceding chapters, deliberate exclusion of a name from such a list was seen as sign of solemn judgment upon the person in question. Biblical exemplars had also come to feature with increased prominence, and days were set aside to mark their significance. Old Testament figures and New Testament apostles were all widely commemorated. The most important exemplar, however, was the Virgin Mary, whose status as the most exalted of all the saints had developed considerably from the fourth century onward.

Veneration of Mary

The passions aroused in the early fifth century over the title of Mary as *Theotokos* indicated the degree to which Mary was already being venerated very highly; if she was indeed worthy of the title, as the Councils of Ephesus and Chalcedon affirmed, such devotion was bound to increase. A Feast of the Annunciation, commemorating the declaration of the angel Gabriel to Mary that she would become the mother of Christ (Luke 1:26–38), was being celebrated on 25 March in some churches in the sixth century. Mary's death was also marked in a variety of ways. As early as the later fourth century there had been talk of Mary having been bodily assumed into heaven on her death, and by the end of the sixth century a Feast of the Assumption was being kept on 18 January in some places and 15 August in others; the latter date would prevail, by imperial authority.[8]

These and other feasts of Mary would continue to grow in importance over subsequent centuries, and the announcement of new feast days was often connected to the dedication of churches in Mary's honor. Claims developed that certainly elevated Mary far beyond anything that the New Testament itself could warrant. In the East, where the cult of Mary was especially strong, she was celebrated as the "Queen of heaven," the protectress of cities, and the guardian of the empire. In a number of instances there were clear associations with the traditions of pagan mother-goddess religions.

"Octave" Feasts

Some Christian feasts were marked not only on the day on which they occurred but also over the week afterwards. The practice probably grew out of Old Testament ritual (cf., e.g., Lev. 23:36), and it offered an obvious way of extending the celebrations that took place at the dedication of new churches and shrines. In liturgical usage, an "octave" was the eighth day after a feast day, which by inclusive reckoning always fell on the same day of the week as the feast itself. On this day the feast was officially brought to an end with a particular ritual. Major festivals including Easter, Pentecost, and, in the East, Epiphany were afforded such "octave" status. In due course, the style would also be applied to the feasts of major saints such as the apostles Peter and Paul.

Structures of Ministry

The structure of the clerical offices continued to reflect the main roles that had evolved by the third century,[9] but there was a great deal of variety in the practices of individual churches and regions. Major churches had come to envisage a sequence of orders through which their servants had to pass, akin to the succession of posts held by an administrator or politician in the secular world. The higher offices were those of deacon, presbyter, and bishop, but there was no uniformity with regard to the number of lower grades. Subdeacons, acolytes, exorcists, readers, and doorkeepers were all common in larger churches, but the enumeration and ranking of such roles varied a good deal. Rules were laid down in local synods as well as at larger councils.

Classification of orders tended to be tied increasingly to the degree to which officials were licensed to engage in sacramental activity; the highest offices, those of presbyter and bishop, were widely believed to be such because those who held them were authorized to carry out sacerdotal functions, especially the consecration of the Eucharist. Deacons could not actually consecrate the bread and wine, but they participated closely in the administration of the eucharistic liturgy and thus were also of special importance. So too were subdeacons, who prepared the sacred vessels and removed them after use. Subdeacons represented the bridge between the higher and the lower orders, and in some cases they came to be treated as part of the higher tier of clergy.

Within each order there were also gradations. Some senior presbyters were known as "archpriests," and "archdeacons" had existed from earlier times. Seniority was conferred either by years of experience or by special recognition from the bishop, who might consider particular liturgical, managerial, or secretarial responsibilities to merit a more exalted rank. Numbers of archpriests in particular churches varied. In sixth-century Gaul archpriests acted as overseers of rural clergy and existed in large numbers; in Spain, on the other hand, there was still only a single archpriest in each episcopal church. Archdeacons might assume considerable powers as the vicars of their bishops with responsibility for matters of clerical discipline and the stewardship of assets, and in situations such as that in Gaul they eclipsed archpriests in importance.

Ecclesiastical legislation and the decretals of popes such as Siricius (see p. 129) and Zosimus (see p. 183), proposed a variety of rules regarding the ages at which offices could be held. The overall drift was to raise thresholds beyond what had been accepted in earlier periods, in a bid to ensure that officials were sufficiently mature and appropriately prepared to assume the responsibilities that went with the higher orders. In general, the minimum age for an acolyte or subdeacon was twenty-one; for a deacon, twenty-five; and for a priest, thirty years. The most commonly mentioned age for admission to the episcopate was forty-five. Exceptions to all these principles were, however, widespread, and in a great many cases individuals were elevated to the highest offices at other ages or without having completed a regular path through the ranks. In Athanasius's day, a bishop might be just thirty, and Athanasius himself had been consecrated, controversially, just short of this age. Ambrose had become a bishop in his midthirties, after being baptized and raised through the various grades of the clergy within the space of a single week. In the church of Rome it was not at all unusual for bishops to be sought from among the ranks of the deacons and for men to be elevated to the episcopate who had never held the priesthood at all. The Roman diaconate in particular enjoyed a remarkable degree of prestige, and in the late fourth century at least it effectively outshone the status of the city's presbyters in popular estimation.

Clerical Celibacy

The growth of the ideal of clerical celibacy was connected with the joint influences of asceticism and the elevation of the mystical status of the sacraments. Fourth-century Western churchmen such as Damasus, Siricius, Jerome, and Ambrose regarded celibacy as a necessity for those who administered the sacraments: such abstinence guaranteed ritual purity, ensuring that the sacrifice of the Eucharist was offered by those who were "undefiled" physically as well as spiritually. Comparable assumptions about ceremonial integrity were common in other religions, and pagan priests were similarly supposed to abstain from sexual intercourse prior to offering sacrifices. Such notions came to have a powerful influence in Christianity, not least through the authority of Rome. Many church leaders, especially in the East but also in rural areas more widely, preferred to maintain only temporary periods of continence prior to the sacrament, but for those who celebrated the Eucharist daily this was not enough, and a constant state of celibacy was seen as essential.

Such rules were held to apply not only to bishops and presbyters but also to deacons, and in the fifth century, in Rome and North Africa at least, to subdeacons.

A great number of clergy nevertheless remained married, and candidates who had been married at an earlier age frequently presented themselves for service to the church. Legislation such as the thirty-third canon of the Council of Elvira in the early years of the fourth century[10] had required married bishops, presbyters, and deacons to live in continence, treating their wives as their sisters. Similar prescriptions were frequent in later generations, as chastity was increasingly prized by ascetically minded teachers. Theologians such as Jerome, Ambrose, and Augustine were accused of denigrating marriage in their teaching that continence was a necessarily superior state to normal marital relations and suggesting that sexual intercourse was closely associated with the transmission of sin.

It is clear from the preaching and writing of many churchmen that exhortations to married clergy to remain continent often fell upon deaf ears, and there were also very widespread problems with single clergy who fell into temptation or behaved hypocritically. Many supposedly celibate priests and deacons lived with women who were neither their wives nor any other form of blood relative.[11] The arrangement had obvious dangers, and it was condemned repeatedly by church councils and bishops, who demanded that their subordinates avoid all suspicion of double standards. Another problem created by celibacy was the situation in which enthusiastic married men sought to put away their wives in order to pursue a spiritual vocation. Such action was prohibited by law in the fifth century.

Practices differed a great deal between the East and the West. In the major Greek churches it was accepted that presbyters and deacons could be married prior to ordination, though bishops were selected from among the celibate. In the West there was a much stronger demand for complete celibacy throughout the higher orders and an insistence that junior officials who aspired to reach these upper levels needed to be prepared from a young age to renounce marriage altogether. With the spread in monasticism, a good many bishops tended to come from ascetic backgrounds in any event, as would be the case with Gregory the Great (see p. 332). For all the idealization of celibacy, however, there were always a great many exceptions to the rules, and even in the West there were quite a number of individuals who rose to episcopal status as married men in the sixth century and beyond. The degree to which papal decrees and ecclesiastical legislation continued to insist upon total continence among those in higher orders indicates just how widespread the violations of the laws on celibacy were.

Bishops

If the authority of bishops increased significantly with the changes in the church's social status, so too did the challenges that surrounded their appointment. The will of the people could frequently be overruled by the desires of other bishops from neighboring churches, whose collective consent to the consecration of any candidate was vital. In some cases pressure from the laity was strong enough to force an outcome contrary to the wishes of other leaders, but more often it was up to external bishops to indicate which person they were prepared to consecrate, and such decisions were of course not always popular. The processes of approval were often directly affected by political machinations, including interference from civil powers, especially in strategic sees.

Some bishops came to enjoy considerable prestige and social privileges, and they earned significantly higher stipends than other clergy. Ceremonial forms of address traditionally used for civil officials were applied to bishops, and particular reverence was held to be due to those in the primary sees. From the sixth century onward the bishops of Rome, Alexandria, Antioch, Constantinople, and Jerusalem were officially addressed as "patriarch." The title "pope" (Greek *pap[p]as*, Latin *papa*, "father") had been traditionally used of bishops quite generally, and in the East of the bishop of Alexandria in particular; from the fifth and sixth centuries it gradually came to be applied in the West especially to the bishop of Rome, though it also continued to be used of others until the Middle Ages. Rome's claims to special status were of course part of a process that had been under way for a very long time, and already in the early fourth century the bishop of Rome was being addressed on some occasions as "most glorious," a description which in secular parlance denoted very distinguished rank.

The temporal rewards of episcopal office were invariably commensurate with the status of the church in question, and church leaders in smaller towns were inevitably presented with much more modest advantages than those in the most prestigious sees. The contrast between the style of figures such as Damasus and the way of life followed by rural bishops was remarked upon by Christians and non-Christians alike. At the same time, when leading bishops did display a deliberately frugal manner or stress their support for ascetic principles, they could always be criticized for being uncouth, mean, or inhospitable, as John Chrysostom was in Constantinople. The challenges of acting as overseer of charity, political manager, and humble pastor all at once were considerable, and it was all too easy to be accused of getting things wrong one way or another.

Bishops needed a range of skills, and in a great many areas it was very difficult to find candidates who were suitably educated to undertake the full spectrum of responsibilities. While the overall social status of senior clergy had been raised markedly after Constantine, with figures such as Ambrose coming from obviously privileged backgrounds, many ordinary clergy continued to hail from poor economic contexts in which the educational opportunities available to them had been distinctly limited. The more learned and socially polished leaders still often had their work cut out for them to inculcate appropriate habits of study, communication skills, and pastoral sensitivity among their subordinates. Clerical morality could pose alarming challenges, not only in matters of sexual ethics but in other areas as well; bishops continued for generations to warn their staff against such habits as engaging in commercial business in their spare time, courting legacies from rich parishioners, or going in for worldly entertainments such as hunting or frequenting drunken dinner-parties.

As we have seen so often, bishops might face not only significant doctrinal divisions within their communities but interference from magistrates or other political agents, including direct meddling by rulers. Such external manipulation appeared to ease in certain respects after the official demise of Arianism at an imperial level, but the age of barbarian upheavals and the enduring christological debates of the fifth and sixth centuries continued to see churchmen subjected to many demands, and there were many who paid a very severe price, including giving their lives, for resistance to the imperatives of their political masters. If some occupied privileged roles as spiritual confidants or intellectual counselors of civil authorities, many more were regarded as far too trivial in status to be anything other than pawns in the games of social, bureaucratic, or military power. The most notable churchmen might emerge as the cherished patrons and benefactors of their communities, but not all were so successful, especially those who served in the frontier zones of Christian evangelism, far away from the opportunities afforded by life in the major centers.

Talented individuals might be understandably reluctant to expose themselves to the demands that episcopal life entailed. Some worried that the intellectual and social costs of accepting office would be excessively high and feared that service to the church would spell the end of any personal tranquility.[12] Being a bishop meant far more than teaching and leading the faithful on their spiritual pathway; it also involved such tedious tasks as settling petty civil disputes and dealing with local social problems—or, when things became really bad, organizing food supplies for a community struck by famine, or arranging the defense of a town against a mob of brutal invaders. Sometimes formal dissent regarding one's nomination as a bishop might be little more than an expression of modesty, but some were genuinely none too keen to take on the burdens.

Through it all, however, there were undoubtedly thousands of churchmen who served faithfully and with enormous dedication and whose place both in their churches and in their wider communities was of strategic significance for the furtherance of the faith. The fourth, fifth, and sixth centuries produced some outstanding preachers, whose commitment to the exposition of the Scriptures and the instruction of their people was extremely impressive and whose personal piety and sense of the holiness of their calling might well put many modern Christians to shame.[13] In terms of social action, the practices of many bishops were less radical in reality than their rhetoric suggested—they might roundly denounce such evils as abuse of the poor, the practice of usury, or the ill-treatment of slaves, yet sometimes do little to seek to overturn the socioeconomic structures upon which the injustices of the rich and powerful depended. Nevertheless, in a world in which the needs were truly enormous, the work of almsgiving, care of the sick, and protection of the weak that was undertaken by the churches was considerable. Failures in duty and abuses of privilege were doubtless abundant, but there were also great achievements, and the inherent conservatism that affected a lot of clergy was continually challenged by the moral earnestness of the ascetic movement.

Clerical Dress

By and large, Christian leaders had not worn special dress in the early centuries, except perhaps on occasions such as major feasts. While there is evidence that some Christians endeavored to wear their best clothes when they went to church, the majority of ordinary people would have had little if any choice in what they wore, and in a lot of cases their leaders were not much better off. From the fourth century onward, some clergy had gradually begun to adopt more impressive styles as a consequence of the growing wealth and social status of their churches. Sometimes rich individuals or political patrons gave gifts of special clothing to Christian communities, and such garments might be worn on significant occasions.

However, there was in general nothing specifically *clerical* about clerical dress. Not until later times did forms of clothing convey anything distinctively ecclesiastical or priestly about the wearer; in the fourth, fifth, and sixth centuries they continued to reflect the conventions of secular society. Impressive, long overtunics of wool or linen such as the "dalmatic" in the West were representative of upper-class styles in late ancient society. Preferences for (or avoidance of) certain colors and materials generally derived from existing ways of thinking. Sometimes there were symbolic associations, with white tunics donned by the newly baptized, or bright linen worn by the bishop at the baptismal liturgy representing the purity and light of the new life into which the initiates were entering. Ostentatious attire was widely condemned by Christian moralists, and many clerics adopted deliberately simple or plain styles.[14]

If the elevation of bishops to an elite social status meant that the insignia of social prominence were gradually assumed, it was not until later that more elaborate styles of clerical garb evolved, with bishops donning staffs, miters, and rings, or wearing particular symbols on their clothing. One exception that began earlier was the wearing of the *pallium*, a band of white wool decorated with crosses and worn around the shoulders. This seems to have become a hallmark of a metropolitan bishop from the late fourth century onward; later it came to be associated especially with the authority of Rome, being worn by the pope and by bishops directly sanctioned with his approval.

Defining Episcopal Status

The process of defining "metropolitan" episcopal status continued to be a complicated one long after the first formal reference to the issue in the fourth canon of the Council of Nicaea, and there were many tensions between the chief sees or patriarchates and other large churches; relations between Rome and other Western churches were notably problematic. Patriarchs and then metropolitans came to be designated as "archbishops" and "primates" to signify their senior status. Beneath metropolitan bishops were those with powers only within their own "diocese." This Greek word was used of an administrative unit in the Roman Empire and came into Western Christian usage in the fourth century to mean much the same as it does in its modern ecclesiastical usage. Over time, a group of such dioceses together typically came to be known as a "province," another term from civil organization.

The traditional word for the territory immediately subject to a regular bishop had been "parish" (Greek *paroikia*, Latin *parochia*, "district"), but from the later fourth century onward "parish" started to be used of component parts of a diocese, delegated by the bishop to presbyters. Diocesan bishops might be assisted in their duties by coadjutors, who in turn were often their successors in the see. In some regions, especially in Asia Minor, the title of *chorepiskopos* ("rural bishop" in Greek) came to be applied in the fourth century to bishops of country areas; such an official was regarded as of episcopal rank, and he had powers to ordain junior clergy, but he remained very much subject to the authority of his diocesan bishop, whom he might represent at formal gatherings. The number and functions of *chorepiskopoi* were both curtailed within the same period.

Collegiality and Orthodoxy

One of the key assumptions in theological reflection on episcopacy from the third century was the concept of "collegiality"—the idea that when bishops met in a synod or council they constituted more than a collection of individuals but formed a body with composite spiritual authority. This was one of the reasons why the joint endorsement of bishops was so important in the case of ordinations, and it was also implicit in the perception that the doctrinal and disciplinary rulings of councils had special significance that transcended the importance of individuals' opinions.

The so-called "ecumenical" councils of the church only acquired this status by political sanction, and retrospectively. In reality they were often not very "ecumenical" at all in their makeup; the West was generally much less represented than the East, and there were a number of gatherings whose ultimate significance was lower which more genuinely reflected diversity of episcopal background. Councils tended to acquire authority according to the degree of political impetus or manipulation behind them and the extent to which their judgments were accepted in practice. The arguments of those who participated in the decision-making generally made much of appeals to tradition and invoked the authority of revered teachers and their works. There was also a cumulative effect in conciliar prestige, with one council affirming the findings of another. However ambiguous its origins, the designation of the great councils as "ecumenical" or "general" came to carry great weight, and the long-term importance of these milestones in theological tradition would be very significant.

For all the considerable divisions in the churches, there was a long-standing conviction among Christian leaders that unity was desirable and that in principle at least there was a basic set of assumptions upon which true believers ought to be able to agree. The delineation of such a rule of faith never had been easy or uncontroversial,[15] but it was undoubtedly an important quest. Vincent, a monk of Lérins in the fifth century, argued that truth was to be identified in that which had been believed "everywhere, always, and by all,"[16] suggesting that traditions that did not conform to this principle were to be rejected as false. Vincent did not hold that doctrine was incapable of developing, but he saw this development as an organic process in which a core Christian identity was maintained regardless of the diversities of circumstances and forms in which belief was expressed.

The fact that the context of Vincent's own arguments was polemical—he participated in the opposition to Augustine's teaching in Gaul in the early 430s (see pp. 187–88)—testifies to the complexity of the challenge of pinpointing the essentials of an orthodox faith. Nevertheless, Vincent's proposal of a logic of catholicity offered an enduringly useful way of approaching the task, and his definition came to be much cited, becoming known as the "Vincentian canon."

The Ministry of Women

Over the course of the second and third centuries, women had come to exercise far less visible roles in ministry than had been the case in apostolic times, and in the fourth century and beyond the official face of the churches was overwhelmingly male.[17] Though some scholars have pointed to a few exceptions, the formal functions of the churches were predominantly carried out by men, and in the vast majority of places women did not occupy the major clerical positions. Where women did engage in tasks such as preaching or administering the Eucharist, their actions were mostly regarded as irregular or as valid only for distinctly limited constituencies, chiefly of other women.

Women continued to serve in diaconal roles, particularly in the churches of the East, but commission to the work of a *deaconess* (the word itself only originates in the fourth century) was not seen as comparable to ordination to the male diaconate. Female deacons were sometimes regarded with suspicion by men as usurpers of male prerogatives in ministry, and in a number of cases they clearly did exceed their designated authority. The female diaconate declined in importance as a consequence of such fears, and it would also suffer as a result of the spread of infant baptism; as fewer adult women overall were baptized, fewer female deacons were needed to attend at initiation. In the West, where such ministry had been much slower to develop in the first place, the office of female deacons was abolished by councils in Gaul in the sixth century.

As it had always done, asceticism offered women significant opportunities to express their piety with a degree of independence from male authority. Since ordination was not a necessary qualification for pursuit of a higher spiritual life, women were able to attain to roles in this area that were not open to them in the regular ministries of the churches. Some types of female asceticism clearly were subject in the end to episcopal control—such as the kind of consecrated virginity to be found so prominently in major churches such as Rome, Milan, and Antioch, or in the lot of the widows who devoted their precious resources and energies to the work of such communities—and many of the ways in which such commitment was celebrated reflected male ideals of submissiveness and anonymity for women. In other contexts, however, such as those of the desert mothers or the leaders of female monastic communities, women lived lives of relative emancipation, and their roles as spiritual exemplars were of genuine significance for Christians generally, not least for other women living within more conventional social surroundings.

The degree to which women were afforded a place in a particular movement within the churches was sometimes seen as evidence of that movement's soundness, and concerns that women were too prominent were used as a reason for squashing certain developments as dangerous, as was the case with Priscillianism (see pp. 116–18). Many of the greatest heroines in more approved circles, such as the older Melania or Paula (see p. 143), tend to be defined in the sources with reference to their proximity to men. In terms of a vision of marriage, Christian elevation of the virgin over the bride was decidedly disruptive of conventional patterns of social existence, and it was also vigorously opposed by many non-Christian traditionalists in late Roman society, who saw it as a serious threat to the structures of marriage and child-rearing in their world. In the end, however, the rhetorical idealization of the holy woman could be presented by Christian communicators as a new model of moral authenticity: here was a woman who actually did evoke conservative ideals of female chastity and sobriety, but did so in ways that took these ideals to a new level.

Others were won over by pragmatic considerations. Women who opted for consecrated virginity rather than marriage saved their families the burden of having to meet expensive dowry payments. While there were certainly objections in some households when daughters expressed a desire to devote themselves to the church, by no means were all parents opposed to their girls taking such a step. Indeed, it became not at all unusual for girls to have the ascetic life chosen for them at an early age; betrothal to Christ became the expression of a new kind of arranged marriage. Given Christians' deep hostility to traditional Roman practices such as the exposure of children and abortion, many Christian families included far more girls than could easily be provided for when it came to dowries, and dedication of daughters to the church might help to alleviate a practical problem. In all of these ways, the growth of female asceticism represented a force for social change.

There is no doubt that women frequently served as the primary messengers of Christianity in their households, and it was often through their efforts that their husbands or other male relatives were converted. If their zeal caused alarm in some instances—especially where the wealth of a rich household was eroded as a consequence of charitable activities or where the prospect of children to continue a family line was jeopardized by sexual continence[18]—it was nevertheless through the work of such women that the faith was spread and good was achieved. Unmarried as well as married women were also of strategic importance in this respect; women such as Macrina were clearly individuals of considerable spiritual eminence and theological vision, whose impact within their families and communities was of great significance. However restricted the possibilities at the level of official ministry, the commitment of women continued to be—as it always had been and always would be—vital to the cause of the Christian gospel.

Church Architecture

Christians had possessed recognized church buildings in many parts of the Roman world by the end of the third century, but their property had remained vulnerable to appropriation by the authorities, and during the Great Persecution a large number of places of worship had been seized or destroyed by imperial forces. With the conversion of Constantine, the churches had acquired an official character physically as well as symbolically, and unmistakable edifices had appeared in the main streets of the empire's cities and towns. Although in some places Christians had continued to meet in private houses until well into the fourth century,[19] in the Roman world as a whole a new physical reality had been witnessed—the presence of obvious places of worship, reflective of imperial favor and a new kind of social confidence.

Constantine's extensive Christian building program, stretching from the old Rome to the new, to the Holy Land, and elsewhere, had manifested his determination to go far beyond making up the losses that Christians had suffered in the persecutions and to make it abundantly clear that their faith now enjoyed imperial patronage. The architectural paradigm for Constantine's churches was the basilica, an existing Roman type of assembly hall designed to accommodate large numbers of people for civic or military functions. The Roman model was altered in various respects, but its generous proportions and its unmistakable character as a public style of architecture were well suited to Constantine's purposes, and the adaptation of a classical form to Christian usage signaled the visible enthronement of the Christian faith.

There was a fair degree of local variation in the planning of Christian basilicas, and no single pattern dominated prior to the middle of the fourth century. Gradually, however, a classical form had emerged, influenced in particular by the style used in Constantine's Church of St. John Lateran in Rome, completed in 319–320. The Lateran basilica consisted of a rectangular hall with five aisles, measuring seventy-five meters by fifty-five meters, with a semicircular niche or apse opening off one of the shorter sides. A conventional basilica typically comprised a central nave flanked by two, or sometimes four, aisles separated by columns. The roof of the central hall was higher than the roofs of the side sections. Light came from windows set high in the walls of the central hall above the columns, a system that provided the archetype for what would later be called "clerestories" ("clear stories"). Earlier basilicas typically had their apse on the western end of the building, but it later became standard to orient the basilica to the east, towards the rising sun, in symbolism of the resurrection. It also became common to include a lateral hallway or *narthex* at the front of the nave, with between three and five doors. In many cases there was an additional atrium or forecourt outside this.

Styles varied in accordance with local experimentation, and many basilicas were altered and added to over time, but the essentials of the Constantinian basilica were widely followed. In the West it became the standard form—its popularity doubtless enhanced by the enthusiasm

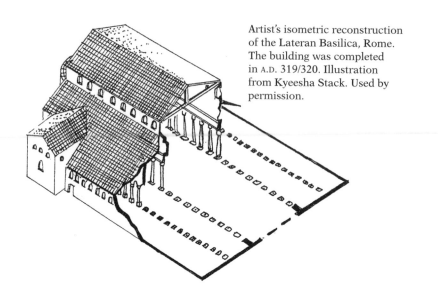

Artist's isometric reconstruction
of the Lateran Basilica, Rome.
The building was completed
in A.D. 319/320. Illustration
from Kyeesha Stack. Used by
permission.

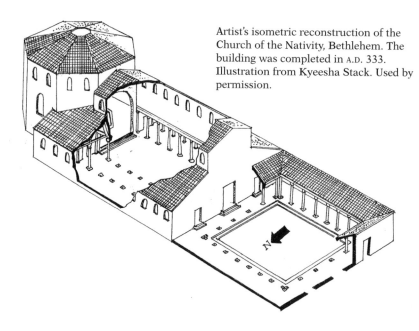

Artist's isometric reconstruction of the
Church of the Nativity, Bethlehem. The
building was completed in A.D. 333.
Illustration from Kyeesha Stack. Used by
permission.

The domed basilica of Hagia/Sancta Sophia, Constantinople, as it exists in Istanbul today. The church was converted into a mosque by the Turks in the fifteenth century. Illustration from Alan Ingram. Used by permission.

of pilgrims who had visited some of the great churches in Rome and in the Holy Land. The Constantinian basilicas in the Holy Land were of course typically erected on sites associated with the life of Jesus. This often meant that the central sacred point of these buildings was a memorial shrine. In the Church of the Nativity in Bethlehem, for example, the apse was replaced by an octagonal room commemorating the believed birthplace of Jesus, and in the Church of the Holy Sepulchre in Jerusalem the apse was linked to a rotunda via a portico.

Such fashions were mostly confined to special sites or to churches sacred to the memory of martyrs, and they were probably engendered by Roman traditions of combining central-plan and temple architecture. Martyr shrines (*martyria*) could be square, round, or octagonal to emphasize the location in which the holy relics lay. In Syria and Mesopotamia centralized designs became the norm, and they were gradually combined with the rectangular basilica form to create monumental domed churches. The most famous example is the magnificent basilica of Hagia/Sancta Sophia (Church of the Holy Wisdom) in Constantinople (see p. 23).

The emergence of the basilican church was significant not only in architectural terms. It had been influenced by, and had in turn reinforced, the growing distinction between clergy and laity. The apse was reserved for the clergy, and at its center sat the bishop on a raised throne. A stone altar or table was permanently set up at the front of the apse for the celebration of the Eucharist, and underneath it might often be saints' relics. The bishop and his attendants would process from the apse to this area during the liturgy, where they would preside while the congregation listened and observed. Catechumens, baptismal candidates, and penitents preparing for reconciliation were restricted to the narthex or porch area at the rear of the nave.

In some buildings the separation of clergy and people was further accentuated; at St. Peter's in Rome, a transverse hall or transept crossed the church between the nave and the apse, formally dividing the two. The transept served not only as the clerical space during the liturgy but also as a memorial shrine on what was believed to be the site of the martyrdom of Peter. In Syria basilicas tended to have their doors not on the end of the nave but on one of its longer sides, and sometimes there were separate entrances for clergy and laity or for men and women.

Older "houses of the church" on private estates and "halls of the church" of one kind or another continued to be used alongside basilicas as late as the fifth century. In other instances buildings such as baths, libraries, and covered markets were adapted to become vaguely basilican in form. This was especially common practice in the East. In addition, Christians from the late fourth century had begun to take over pagan temples and turn them into Christian sanctuaries, particularly in the aftermath of Theodosius's legislation banning pagan cultic practices (see pp. 112–14). In the fifth century the Parthenon at Athens, the Pantheon at Rome, and the temple of Apollo at Daphne were all converted in this fashion.

In some cases, conversion of a pagan temple meant significant destruction first in the requisitioning of the site for the purposes of erecting a new edifice, but architectural features from the former building might find their way into its successor. The magnificent double basilica of the Church of Mary in Ephesus was constructed out of the spoils of a pagan temple complex destroyed by Christians around 400. Similar processes happened to Jewish synagogues as well, such as at Stobi in northern Macedonia, where a Jewish meeting place was demolished and then used to rebuild a church; some of its old elements and inscriptions were redeployed in the new structure.

By the early fifth century, basilicas in the Aegean were somewhat different from those in the West: more square than rectangular, and often with a cruciform transept. Often the structures around the church were remodeled and assumed into a complex of ecclesiastical buildings, such as a hospital or a residence for the bishop. Christian building projects such as these pointedly revolutionized the physical landscape of ancient cities, demonstrating the vital place of the church in the public spaces of urban society.

Christian Art

If architecture had been profoundly affected by the conversion of Constantine, so too had art. As they had done for generations,[20] Christians symbolized their convictions in the decoration of jewelry, furniture, tableware, and everyday domestic items, but visual expressions of faith were no longer confined to a predominantly private world. Now they were able to flourish on a much larger scale.

Basilicas established through imperial beneficence were lavishly decorated on the inside. Murals covered an enlarged repertoire of biblical themes, including the Israelites' crossing of the Red Sea, and some of the older Christian iconographic motifs, such as the depiction of Christ as the Good Shepherd, tended to be replaced with more triumphant images, such as scenes of Christ enthroned in glory or giving the law to his apostles. Traditional Roman details such as birds, flowers, grapes, and harvest scenes continued, but they were intertwined with increasingly regal portraiture of Christ. Some churches, especially those established close to the supposed sites of martyrdoms (or the graves of martyrs) or synonymous with the cultic veneration of particular saints, also had pictures of their Christian heroes and heroines.

In addition to paintings there were mosaics, used very widely on walls, floors, and ceilings. From Aquileia in northern Italy we have an early-fourth-century floor mosaic depicting the Jonah story and an image of the Good Shepherd, and in the churches of North Africa there were multiple depictions of the apostles, the Virgin Mary, and other biblical exemplars. The growth in veneration of Mary in particular provided a major opportunity for art, and many striking churches were dedicated in Mary's honor, such as Sancta Maria Maggiore in Rome, which was built in the 430s and adorned with elaborate mosaics and a triumphal arch. Besides paintings and mosaics, churches also had decorative hangings, altar cloths, and candelabras, and there were significant ivory carvings on important furniture such as bishops' chairs and items such as boxes, book covers, and diptychs. Communities claiming apostolic origins often prized particular items that were said to go back to their founders, and episcopal thrones on which Peter, James, and other early Christian leaders were supposed to have sat were cherished in sees such as Rome and Jerusalem.

However pervasive, the practice of decorating churches was also controversial with some. Even before an imperial church building program had begun, the Council of Elvira had already issued a canon expressing disapproval of mural paintings in churches, albeit without any specification of what the offending images might be. When Eusebius of Caesarea was contacted in the late 320s by the sister of Constantine asking for a picture of Christ (she imagined a true likeness would be likelier to be found in Palestine), he responded firmly that while such images were for sale widely to visiting pilgrims, they were quite inappropriate, and those who fashioned portraits or statues of Jesus could not be true Christians. Later in the fourth century Epiphanius of Salamis fought a passionate campaign to have similar images removed from Palestinian churches, but in the end he was unsuccessful.

Disapproval did nothing to stop practices inspired by a combination of popular piety and decorative flair. Paulinus of Nola felt the need to defend the presence of pictures in his church on the grounds that they provided valuable visual instruction for his congregation. In an age when so many ordinary worshipers remained illiterate, art could convey lessons that in written form remained locked up beyond the reach of the lowliest believers. Augustine and others were concerned that veneration of saints sometimes bordered on worship of them, but images of many kinds were ubiquitous, and they undoubtedly performed functions that were positive for some. Outside of church, private individuals possessed statues of figures such as Jonah, Daniel, and Christ the Good Shepherd, and other Christian sculptures could be found in public places on fountains and other examples of civic architecture. In Caesarea Philippi, a bronze statue representing Jesus and the woman with the issue of blood existed in the fourth century, erected near a building said to have been the woman's home.[21]

The full flowering of Christian art is to be seen in the late Roman and early Byzantine periods, and particularly under Justinian. By this time Christian art and architecture no longer constituted an alternative to secular forms. Whether a building or an object was "Christian" depended more on its provenance, patronage, and usage than on a distinctively Christian iconographic style. Buildings and artifacts were

The church of San Vitale, Ravenna, as it exists today. The original building was completed in A.D. 546–548. Illustration from Michael Gaddis. Used by permission.

expressions of the social prestige, wealth, and political entrenchment of the churches. Edifices such as the great church of San Vitale in Ravenna, which was funded by a wealthy banker, became centers of pilgrimage as travelers flocked to admire their artistic glories and look for spiritual blessing from their saints, and this in turn greatly added to the wealth and prestige of their endowments.

The gradual replacement of the ancient scroll with the parchment *codex* or bound book in Christian circles from the second century had provided a particular opportunity for artistic expression, and in the late fifth and sixth centuries the practice began of illustrating these texts with small paintings, typically done with egg tempera and defined with gold and silver inks. The work was carried out in many different parts of the empire, not least in Egypt and Syria. Splendid sixth-century examples include the forty-eight surviving leaves of a codex of Genesis in Vienna, executed on rich, purple-stained parchment to stress the value of the book, which was perhaps designed for an imperial recipient. They contain remarkable miniature depictions of Noah's ark and of Rebecca and Eliezer at the well (Genesis 24).

A codex of the Gospels kept in the Italian city of Rossano, made up of excerpts from Matthew and Mark, illustrates many scenes from the life of Jesus, including the raising of Lazarus and the trial before Pilate. One of the earliest surviving depictions of the crucifixion is to be found on a Syriac Gospel codex written by a late-sixth-century scribe called Rabbula,[22] which may draw on images produced for pilgrims to the Holy Land. The remarkable art produced in such literary contexts offers further testimony to the way in which the expression of Christian faith lay at the heart of the sophisticated cultural achievements of the Byzantine world.

From Justinian onward, religious images came to occupy the status of traditional imperial statues. Justinian set up a huge statue of Christ over the main gate of his palace in Constantinople, and from the late seventh century a depiction of Christ appeared on imperial coinage. Icons or pictures representing Christ, biblical characters, and Christian saints became a pervasive feature of popular piety. The note of disapproval heard in earlier times from figures such as Epiphanius of Salamis continued to resound in some quarters, and in the eighth century it would lead to a systematic attempt to destroy such images on the grounds that they amounted to idolatry and conflated biblical theology with conventions associated with pagan deities. Thousands of believers would refuse to relinquish their patterns of devotion, and there would be fierce debates over the implications of the incarnation, the goodness of the material world, and the nature of Christian worship. Persecution would be used to secure imperial policy, but large numbers of Eastern Christians, especially monks, were prepared to face death rather than destroy their icons.

The course of the "iconoclastic controversies," which endured for a century and a half, can be followed up in the next volume in this series. The disputes were lengthy and bitter, and they would sharply divide the Byzantine world, contributing to a growing gulf between the emperors of the East, who favored iconoclasm, and the bishops of Rome, who did not. In practical terms, however, their effect would merely be to encourage devotion to icons among ordinary believers, and the veneration of icons would become an essential element in both the public and the private worship of the Byzantine church.

11

CHRISTIANS
AND BARBARIANS:
THE CHURCHES IN A
CHANGING WORLD

▼

Rome and the Barbarians

The christological debates and ecclesiastical developments that occupied
us in chapters 7 and 8 went on against the backdrop of a political world
that had changed dramatically since the days of Christianity's most
impressive social advances in the fourth century. Successive waves of
barbarian invasions in the West had begun to reconfigure the boundaries
and structures of an administrative order that had lasted for centuries
and to reshape the appearance of the Roman imperial system in ways
that would never be undone. The origins of the changes lay partly in
migrations and struggles for land that first arose outside of Roman
territory, but they came to have a massive impact on the stability and
complexion of the Roman Empire and in turn to affect the progress of
Christianity throughout a great deal of Europe, Africa, and the East.

295

In central and eastern Europe, beyond Roman frontiers, there were two main categories of non-Roman peoples. On the one hand were the fairly settled groups whose territories bordered the empire: peoples such as the Goths, Vandals, Sueves, Franks, and Saxons. All of these groups spoke versions of Germanic languages and practiced essentially stable forms of agriculture. On the other hand were the nomadic peoples who originated farther to the East such as the Alans and Huns, non-Germanic tribes from the steppes of Asia who lived a pastoral existence and had little experience of settled farming. The Romans considered both of these constituencies to be "barbarians," though the patterns of life practiced by some of the Germanic peoples were at heart not so different from those that went on in provincial Roman territories, minus the regulatory codes of Roman law and bureaucracy, and it was the nomadic Asians whose character was more alien to the Roman mind-set. Both groups sought land and new opportunities, and those closest to the imperial borders looked on the empire in particular as a realm of wealth, civilization, and opportunity.

The desires for land and a share in the benefits of imperial prosperity were nothing new: similar pressures from barbarian peoples had presented major challenges for Roman frontier security for centuries. In the later fourth century, however, the effects on imperial stability were greater than ever before, and for a variety of socioeconomic and military reasons the Romans were unable to cope with the scale of the problem. The implications in turn for the churches were very significant. It is not possible to follow the Christian story in the fifth, sixth, and seventh centuries, either in the West or in the East, unless we appreciate something of the conditions in which hundreds of thousands of believers were placed due to developments that went on around them in the dramatic shifts of power and social conditions that took place in their wider political world.

The Goths

In the early 370s, the largest of the nomadic peoples to the East, the Huns, began to move towards the West, into the territory of the eastern Gothic kingdoms. The reasons for their movement are not very clear. The Huns were accompanied by contingents of the Alans, Iranian wanderers who occupied the region east of the river Don, who were forced into alliance with them. Between them these peoples attacked Gothic dominions that covered a vast expanse of territory to the north and west of the Black Sea, compelling the major tribal groups among the eastern Goths, the Greuthungi and the Tervingi, who were incapable of resisting their onslaught, to head farther and farther to the south.

By 376 thousands of Goths had congregated as refugees on the north bank of the Lower Danube, and in desperation they appealed to the emperor Valens for asylum. Valens had already recognized an opportunity to expand his source of military recruits and extend his taxation revenues by accepting such people, and he allowed the Tervingi to cross the Danube and settle on specially designated territory. The Greuthungi were, however, kept out of the deal, as the Romans followed their usual policy of trying to break up dangerous confederations of barbarian forces. Among the terms of the settlement with the Tervingi was probably the condition that the newcomers had formally to embrace Valens's *homoian* Arian Christianity. As the *homoian* Christian creed had already been spread among large numbers of other Goths through the activities of Ulfila and other missionaries (see pp. 56–57), the formal adoption of this profession presumably did not seem a major imposition, and even if the Tervingi saw no need for it, it was a small price to pay in return for security.

Both inside and outside the empire, however, the Goths greatly distrusted the Romans, and it was not long before fighting broke out. The Goths began to plunder far and wide, while the Romans, preoccupied with war to the east over Armenia, had inadequate resources with which to respond. The climax was the catastrophic battle of Adrianople in 378, which saw the destruction of two-thirds of Valens's army and the death of the emperor himself. Theodosius succeeded in settling the Gothic war by a combination of military campaign and diplomacy, assisted in 381 by some effective operations from the forces of Gratian. In October 382 a peace agreement was finalized, probably with both the Greuthungi and the Tervingi. The Goths were given imperial land on which to settle and farm in security between the river Danube and the Balkan mountains in northern Dacia and Thrace. They were to be exempt from taxation and have the right to manage their own affairs and observe their own laws—a concession from normal Roman policy. In return, they would undertake military service for Rome, guarding their own local frontier along the Lower Danube, and no single Gothic leader would be recognized as an official client-king.

Roman public opinion felt a good deal of unease with this compromise, but a stability of sorts had been secured, and it was certainly not the first time that the Goths had been used by Rome militarily and rewarded with land for their services. Gothic leaders enjoyed favorable relations with Theodosius, and significant numbers of Goths performed military service both in the crushing of Maximus's revolt in 387 and in the defeat of the usurper Eugenius in 392–394 (see p. 118). There were nevertheless serious problems festering underneath. Sporadic revolts occurred, and there were grave—and probably well-founded—suspicions among the Goths that Theodosius's policy aimed at eroding their manpower by making them bear the brunt of his greatest military escapades, not least that of the Battle of the Frigidus, when as many as ten thousand Goths were slain in the crushing of Eugenius's forces. The dangers of his pragmatism would not be contained for long.

In the last months of his reign, Theodosius made the decision to divide his realm between his two young sons: after his death, the older son, Arcadius, age seventeen, would rule the East, while the younger, Honorius, age ten, would be allocated the West. Arcadius was under the guardianship of the praetorian prefect, Rufinus; a Vandal general, Stilicho, was appointed regent over Honorius. Stilicho claimed that Theodosius on his deathbed in 395 also designated him guardian to Arcadius, and it was clear that his ambition was to control both West and East. Stilicho's claims were hotly contested in the East, and the two courts argued especially over the question of which side controlled Illyricum, the vital strategic territory that covered Dalmatia and the western Balkans and formed an important source of military recruits.

The Goths recognized that they had a chance to make their feelings known. A major revolt occurred, led by Alaric, a Gothic commander of obscure origin who had played some part in earlier troubles and subsequently emerged as the most powerful leader among the Goths settled under the treaty of 382. Supported by a powerful force of followers, Alaric was able to stand up to Roman armies under Stilicho, the de facto ruler of the West, in 395 and 397, and to exploit the weaknesses in imperial policy created by the intrigues between the courts of the West and the East. Over a period of years he consistently demanded annual cash payments for his followers and a generalship for himself, contrary to the terms of the peace of 382, which refused recognition of any individual leader. Stilicho, intent on his own political ambitions to control the entire empire, variously attempted to negotiate with him, defeat him, and buy him off. According to circumstances, Alaric was intermittently recognized as *magister militum*, "Master of Soldiers," opposed by force, and envisaged as a useful ally. The many twists and turns in Stilicho's handling of the situation, when seen through Eastern eyes, contributed greatly to the disintegrating relations between Constantinople and the West.

In 408 Stilicho was deposed in a coup organized by the advisers of the young Honorius. Alaric, realizing that he was going to make no further progress in the East, turned his attentions to the West and invaded Italy. Large numbers of slaves and barbarian auxiliary forces went over to his side, swelling his army significantly. He marched on Rome and blockaded the city, threatening to sack it unless he received a vast quantity of plunder. As conditions in the city worsened, with starvation and hardship widespread, the terrified authorities gave in to his demands, and the siege was lifted. However, the Western government, based at Ravenna, delayed the ratification of a formal settlement, and in 409 Alaric marched on Rome once again.

After stalled negotiations, the imposition of a temporary puppet regime in Rome, varying demands for gold, a generalship, corn supplies, and land for his troops, Alaric finally lost patience with the authorities at Ravenna, and on 24 August 410 he gave orders to his men to sack the city. In a three-day rampage they plundered the historic citadel of the empire. Besides widespread looting, there was fairly significant loss of life, and women were raped by Gothic soldiers. For the first time in eight hundred years, Rome had been taken by a foreign enemy.

Dealing with Rome's Fall

The shock waves reverberated around the empire, and Christians too had to face up to the reality that, as Jerome put it, "the city which captured the whole world is itself captured."[1] Christians as well as non-Christians were among the victims, and Jerome and other believers wept at the loss of old friends. For people hearing of the disaster in far-flung places, the news seemed to foreshadow the end of the world. Yet, as pagan critics of Christianity took pains to point out, the calamity that had befallen the supposedly Eternal City had been caused not by the devotees of some outlandish foreign religion but by those who were officially Christian. Some of the Gothic troops came from the survivors of a failed invasion of Italy by a pagan Gothic leader called Radagaisus a few years earlier, but at least a large proportion of Alaric's forces would have been nominally Christian, having embraced the *homoian* creed. It had not stopped them from behaving in an outrageous fashion.

Those who hated Christianity were not slow to stress these facts. Not for the first time, Christians were accused of treacherous conduct and of incurring the judgment of the old gods with their spurious beliefs and values. Already, during the crisis in 408, Pope Innocent I had resisted appeals to reinstate public sacrifices in a bid to appease the gods (though he had turned a blind eye to private pagan offerings). To the traditional pagan religionist, and there were still many in Roman society, it was because of the cultural entrenchment of the Christians' faith and their flagrant indifference to the honor of other deities that Rome had now been unable to withstand its attackers. The Christians also seemed to be symbolically implicated in some measure, whether they liked it or not, in the crimes of the raiders. Pope Innocent himself had conveniently been away from the city when the Goths poured in, having gone off to Ravenna supposedly to negotiate a truce—unsuccessfully of course—between Honorius and the enemy. His motives were in fact genuine, and to Christians his absence from the strife was providential; to others, however, it looked like a shameless act of escapism.

It was no wonder that figures such as Augustine felt it necessary to respond to the charges that Christians were responsible, directly or indirectly, for Rome's fall (see pp. 190–92).[2] What could be said for Christianity and about the purposes of God in history if some so-called Christians could do such things to others? In reality, as Augustine was quick to note, the Goths had been sufficiently Christianized to spare those who took refuge in church buildings, even if they did not hesitate to ransack the buildings themselves for their treasures. Their heretical faith may have been reprehensible and their general violence inexcusable, but it was the very Christianity that was so reproached by the pagans, Augustine reasoned, that had mitigated the worst instincts of the Goths' savagery. A good deal of this logic was special pleading, for the invaders had not scrupled to wreak plenty of destruction on Christian property and, as Augustine also conceded, consecrated Christian virgins as well as other women had suffered violation at their hands.

Even so, for all the momentous psychological impact, the very real suffering, and the flood of refugees that it produced, the fall of Rome was not quite as significant as it seemed to be in political terms. Alaric had been driven to sack the city only as a last resort, frustrated by the failure of his other policies. While these policies were obviously bound up with personal greed and ambition, they were more especially concerned with the winning of guaranteed land, peace, and security for his people. Alaric wanted a powerful role for himself as the supreme military commander in the West, but he also sought a legitimacy for the Goths. Rome had been ravaged only when diplomacy had failed and patience had been exhausted. The Romans had calculated, quite rightly, that Alaric was not to be trusted, but in the end they had been unable to resist the scale of his threat.

Nonetheless, despite the catastrophe that had befallen Rome, the overall outcome of the situation was inconclusive. Rome was in any event no longer the primary political center in the West, and the Western court was relatively safe behind the marshes at Ravenna. No meaningful settlement followed. Alaric marched farther south, contemplated but did not complete an attack on Sicily with a view to invading North Africa, and died of disease before the end of 410. Control of the Goths passed to his brother-in-law, Athaulf, who elected to lead his followers into Gaul, where he adopted a similar strategy of combining force, persuasion, and meddling in other imperial intrigues, including the sponsoring of political usurpers, in order to secure the best possible terms for his people.

In the end, no agreement was reached in Athaulf's lifetime. The Goths came under renewed pressure from Constantius, the leading general of Honorius, and were driven into Spain. Intrigue, feuding, and political murder confounded their chances of coordinated leadership in response, and peace was at length agreed with Rome by the Gothic king Wallia in 416. Wallia was succeeded by Theoderic I in 417–418, who concluded another treaty with the Romans, which at last produced a period of stability. The Goths were given fertile land in the Garonne Valley in Aquitania, from Toulouse to Bordeaux, which satisfied them at last in their lengthy quest for economic self-sufficiency. In the years ahead a large number of them fought on Rome's behalf. The most ambitious dreams of Alaric and his successor had been defeated, but an essential part of what the Goths had been seeking over two generations had been achieved: they had at last settled in a territory of their own under a king who was officially recognized by Rome.

As far as the churches were concerned, the migrations of the Goths and the upheavals wrought in the West had brought trial and suffering for many ordinary believers, and the fall of Rome in particular had engendered some soul-searching among more serious Christian thinkers about the purposes of God in world events. The Goths' activities may have had nothing to do with religious causes, but the demise of Rome at the hands of nominally Christian forces threw into relief once more the differences between the catholicism officially favored by the imperial authorities and the enduring strength of the Arian faith espoused by numbers of the invaders. The conflict of Roman and barbarian had long been presented by some Christians as a contest between true believers and heretics, but it could not plausibly be depicted as a warfare between believers and pagans.

To the enemies of Christianity, the destruction caused by the Goths only showed how socially dangerous the Christians really were, and for believers there was a necessary job to be done in distancing the moral entailments of the gospel from the violent actions of those who also called themselves Christians but whose real interests were material, economic, and political. Roman Christians also had to learn to live alongside the Goths and to reach their own accommodations with changed social circumstances. Even as these concerns were addressed, there were other issues to confront as well. The turmoil not only exposed the gulfs that existed between very different construals of appropriate Christian behavior; it also precipitated a diffusion of diverse Christian ideas. It was in no small measure through the exodus of refugees from Rome that Pelagianism in particular spread so widely around other parts of the Mediterranean world. In all of these ways, the effects of the Gothic migrations were significant for the circumstances in which the churches found themselves in the early fifth century.

The Vandals

In the meantime there had been other major incursions into the empire, with still more serious long-term consequences. On 31 December 406 the Rhine had frozen over, and many tens of thousands of other Germanic peoples, Vandals and Sueves, had crossed over into Gaul, joined by several thousand Alans. The most prominent among them were the Vandals, made up of two main groups, the Asdings and the Silings. It is not clear whether all of these groups had also been driven westwards by pressure from the Huns, but the likelihood is strong. Whatever the causes of their movement, its effects on the Western empire and on its churches were considerable.

The invaders advanced more or less unimpeded across Gaul, and numerous towns and cities fell into their hands. There were fears for a time that they might cross the Channel and enter Britain, but instead they turned to the south and made for the Pyrenees and Spain. Much of the Gallic countryside was turned, in the words of one contemporary, into a vast "funeral pyre."[3] The Vandals in particular became a byword for wanton violence and destruction—"vandalism"—virtually everywhere they went. Yet, as with the Goths, a large proportion of them had nominally been converted to Christianity as a result of earlier waves of evangelism, probably led by the Goths themselves. They too had embraced a *homoian* Arian faith, and they remained deeply committed to this position; they saw it as a further way of differentiating themselves from the creed of their imperial enemies. Even so, Christians as well as non-Christians suffered at the point of their swords and in the flames of their fires.

All the while, Stilicho was preoccupied with Alaric and with his own political schemes, and matters were further complicated by other problems in the West. In 406 the Roman forces stationed in Britain had nominated a number of different candidates as their preferred emperor, and the last of these, a soldier with the auspicious name of Constantine, crossed the Channel to Gaul early in 407 with a determination to establish his claims. He set up a base at Arles and extended his power both to the east and the west, towards both the Alps and the Pyrenees. By 409 the Vandals, Sueves, and Alans had crossed into Spain, and the Gallic provinces were increasingly fragmenting and slipping away from the control of the imperial court in Ravenna. Honorius's general, Constantius, was able to spearhead the defeat of Constantine's rebellion by 411 and regain a degree of authority in southern Gaul, but the achievement came at the cost of accommodating the Goths as allies and using them to fight against the new wave of invaders.

The Sueves began to establish an independent kingdom of their own in Galicia in northwestern Spain, where they would manage to maintain a position for almost two centuries despite some significant pressure from the Goths. The Vandals, however, accompanied by what remained of the Alans, pressed on further south, making instinctively for Africa, the granary of Europe and by nature the richest region in the Western world. In the spring of 429, led by Geiseric (their ruler from 428 to 477), they crossed the Straits of Gibraltar. By the following year they had advanced along the coast from city to city through Mauretania and Numidia and were besieging Hippo in Augustine's last days. Within a few years they had gained control of a large swath of imperial North Africa, and in 439 they seized Carthage itself.

From this base this previously inland people became the strongest maritime power in the western Mediterranean, able to cause major problems for shipping and control the progress of vital trade in corn, oil, and other commodities between Africa and Europe. All the while the Western authorities were weak in their attempts to deal with the crisis, and even ambitious efforts from the East failed to achieve success. The Vandals' dominance of the seas caused major shortages in Italy and enabled them to launch an attack on Rome in 455, when Pope Leo managed to plead with Geiseric's forces to show some restraint in their treatment of the city; looting was impossible to prevent, but at least Rome was spared wholesale massacre and destruction.

In North Africa, a great deal of the Vandals' fierce energies went into the attempt to impose their Arian faith. The policy was launched under Geiseric and taken still further under his successor, Huneric (477–484). Catholic clergy were exiled, monasteries were dissolved, and serious pressure was brought to bear on Christians who resisted the demand for conformity. Some did comply; others fled; many suffered severely for their defiance. Refugees included both clergy and laity; the latter were typically members of the landowning class who had been dispossessed of their property. They found sympathy from fellow believers abroad, and everywhere they went they took the stories of the Vandals' atrocities with them. Some of the most important Christian literature from African writers of the later fifth century was produced by the victims of the Vandals' attempts at doctrinal totalitarianism. Among such works were the writings of churchmen in exile, such as Victor of Vita, who wrote a valuable history of the persecution while removed from his church in the late 480s. Vigilius, bishop of Thapsus, was banished by Huneric in 484 and fled to Constantinople, where he produced a number of texts in defense of orthodox doctrine, though most of these do not survive.

Under the Vandal rulers Gunthamund (484–496) and Thrasamund (496–523) there was less violence, but Arianism continued to be pushed strongly, and catholic believers continued to experience problems on one account or another.[4] In the early years of the sixth century the scholarly Augustinian Fulgentius, bishop of Ruspe, suffered a fate common to many earlier catholic leaders and was banished to Sardinia for championing Nicene teaching; in exile he wrote various tracts against Arian and Pelagian views. He was, however, allowed to return to Africa under Thrasamund's somewhat more tolerant successor, Hilderic (523–530), who reversed the policy of hostility to catholic bishops and allowed catholic believers to meet publicly for worship once again.

Hilderic was unpopular as a ruler with the Vandals themselves, and he was deposed in 530. He appealed to Constantinople for help, and in 533–534 that help proved decisive. The Vandals' pirate state was finally crushed by Justinian's general Belisarius (see pp. 325–27). The efforts of its rulers to stamp out catholicism had not succeeded. There had been strong popular resistance, a powerful core of determined clergy, and genuine intellectual and spiritual strength on the Nicene side. The Vandals' policies had caused enormous upheaval and many difficulties for the orthodox Christians of the region, but in the long run their actions had contributed to some important sharing of personal contacts, doctrinal ideas, and spiritual teaching between North Africa and other churches in the West. Many of the banished clergy and monks in particular made significant contributions to the life of churches in Spain, Gaul, and Italy.

The Huns

Another prominent barbarian challenge to Rome's dominion came from the Huns, whose movements had precipitated many of the other migrations into the Roman Empire. Although there had been missionary outreach to the Huns from some churches, with initiatives from John Chrysostom and others, on the whole they remained, unlike the Goths and the Vandals, unaffected by Christianity. To both Romans and Goths they were legendary for their cruelty, destruction, and disregard of any concern even for women and children or those who took refuge in church buildings. They raided large areas of the Danubian provinces in the last years of the fourth century and the first quarter of the fifth, and caused particular devastation in the East, in Cappadocia, Armenia, and Syria.

These raids were serious enough, but when the warlord Attila rose to power in the 430s, the diverse tribes of the Huns came together as never before. Under Attila's leadership, Hunnic society became better organized, more stable, and wealthier, and in its increased state of cohesion it posed a formidable military threat to Rome. In the 440s Attila launched a further series of attacks on the empire. The Huns invaded the Balkans, and although they were stoutly resisted by the local peoples they succeeded in ravaging significant tracts of territory. By 451 they were able to enter Gaul. They were successfully repulsed by the able military commander Aetius and a force of allied Goths, but in 452 they broke through into Italy and pillaged, plundered, and intimidated all over the north of the country. They are said to have been dissuaded from sacking Rome itself by the agencies of Pope Leo (whose representations, as we have seen, also served to lessen the effects of the Vandals' destruction three years later). The reality was, however, that the further the Huns ventured from their traditional territory on the northern steppes, the less secure they were militarily, for their tactics depended on a reliable supply of horses and the appropriate terrain on which to use them. It was probably this fact rather than Leo's overtures that inclined them towards showing leniency to the city of Rome.

Translated into the terms of modern geography, Attila's conquests stretched all the way from the Caucasus to France in the west and Denmark in the north. Roman policies for dealing with him ranged between resistance and appeasement, depending on the shifting calculations of those in authority. In the early 450s the emperor Marcian was determined to fight him, but the prospects were not good. In the end, circumstances intervened. Attila died suddenly in 453 after a drinking bout at his wedding to the latest in his series of wives. His sons divided his dominions among themselves, but they soon began to quarrel, and their armies fell prey to uprisings from their subject peoples, encouraged in their mutiny by the Romans. Attila's empire collapsed the following year.

The consequences for the churches in all this had been the usual grim ones brought about by military turmoil—destruction of property; the rape, ill-treatment, and killing of innocent people; economic difficulties; and general hardship. The invasions in Gaul and Italy also served to identify many Christian bishops as heroes of resistance, leading their communities in ways that the civil authorities failed to do. In many places they galvanized their people into staying put in their own areas and by their preaching and example urged courage in the face of terrifying odds. Often, of course, their exhortations to trust in God seemed to be expressions of wishful thinking, since devastation, looting, and terror occurred in any case. At the same time, where any leniency was shown by the barbarians, it was naturally attributed to episcopal entreaties. Frequently the real reasons lay in more prosaic military exigencies; nevertheless, the symbolic role of clergy in checking societal breakdown was often quite important and helped to reinforce the image of churchmen as sponsors of a measure of local stability amid all the changes taking place in the larger political world.

In any event, however gratuitous the violence and injustice, the Huns had no interest in trying to crush Christians in particular. Christians certainly suffered a great deal at their hands, but the Huns' real objectives lay in the pursuit of land, wealth, and status, and they were unconcerned about the religious beliefs of their victims. The power of the Huns, relatively short-lived though it proved to be, caused much chaos and difficulty for believers and undoubtedly contributed to the overall demise of the Roman Empire, but it had little long-term impact on the spread of Christianity.

Salvian

Some Christians saw the upheavals wrought by barbarian invasions, whatever their source, as a judgment on the Roman world for its decadence and corruption. Attila appears in various Christian sources as the "Scourge of God," an instrument of divine vengeance in evil days. Salvian (c. 400–480), a presbyter of the church in Marseilles in the middle of the fifth century, extended some similar images to the age of the barbarians more generally. He painted a dark picture of the vices and injustices of a society that had, as he saw it, lapsed from the high ideals of its Roman past, a world in which bureaucratic incompetence, financial embezzlement, and sensual indulgence were rife. It was even possible to contrast some of the better moral qualities of the invaders with the delinquencies of supposedly civilized society.

Salvian's denunciations were not only directed at the wider world: they were also aimed at the churches. He regarded Christians too, not least their leaders, as greatly tainted by worldliness. Too many churchmen sought office for the sake of social status and as a possible way of holding on to their own conservative social values. Salvian believed the providence of God in allowing sore trials to befall the professing community was a clarion call to believers to wake up to the imperatives of holiness, faith, and purity of life.

Barbarian Kingdoms and the Churches

By the later fifth century, two "supergroups" of Gothic peoples had emerged. The first consisted of the Visigoths, who had settled in Aquitania. They had gradually expanded their dominions farther to the south, both west and east, and under King Euric (466–484) they were a powerful, independent kingdom, taking over the great imperial centers of Provence and the Auvergne, and acquiring in the 470s most of Spain, with the exception of the territory of the Sueves. Much of the time they had been keen to win over the elites of Gallo-Roman society by a mixture of diplomacy, cooperation, and respect for Roman law, but they had increasingly been prepared to seize land by force, and their expansion into Spain in particular had been carried out by the sword.

Even where the means of takeover were peaceful, it was necessary for rich landowners to be prepared to give over a large slice (generally two-thirds) of their estates to the new arrivals as "guests." Such annexations of territory inevitably brought protests from senatorial

grandees who suddenly found themselves dispossessed of vast proportions of their assets, but the Western court at Ravenna, presided over
by a succession of short-lived emperors, was more or less powerless
to deal with the source of the problem, and the distributions of land
were in any case formally grounded in legal agreements. Most of the
imperial political power lay in the hands of military leaders who were
barbarians themselves.

Other significant Germanic people groups also pressed their advantages. The Burgundians, an east German group, suffered badly under the
Huns and were resettled within the empire in eastern Gaul around the
Rhone Valley, in an area roughly covering the French-speaking part of
modern Switzerland and the southern stretches of the French Jura, an
important strategic region that controlled a number of the main routes
between Italy and southern Gaul. To the north, the pagan Franks held
powerful sway over a good deal of territory beyond the Loire. Other
long-term troublemakers for Rome, the eclectic west German tribes of
the Alamanni ("Men from everywhere"), continued to prove problematic
with their raids around the Rhine Valley and into Alsace. The Visigoths
remained enthusiasts for Arian doctrine, and Arianism was also espoused
by the Burgundians. The Sueves vacillated between credal alignments,
according to political circumstances. The Franks and the Alamanni
were as yet predominantly pagan.

Under the Visigoths, intermittent persecutions of catholic churches
took place in the south and east of Gaul and in Spain; some orthodox
bishops were not replaced when they died, and a number of new Arian
sees were established. Inevitably, catholic clergy became synonymous
with the power of Rome and with the preservation of existing structures,
and as such they were often seen as fair game for harassment by their
Visigothic masters. Many clergy did indeed collaborate actively with
traditional authorities in resisting Visigothic objectives, and could not
claim immunity if they encountered trouble on account of it. On the
other hand, the Visigoths also came to see that bishops might be usefully
deployed as go-betweens with the imperial powers, capable of putting
the cause of the new rulers to the old.

Plenty of ordinary people in regions such as Aquitania saw the
Visigoths as welcome deliverers from the Romans politically, even if
they were heretical in their beliefs, and the Visigoths gradually appreciated that where they showed respect for church property and
for catholic leaders the interests of social fusion could be advanced.
In the end, the resentment that did exist on doctrinal grounds was
much stronger on the catholic side than it was on the part of the

Visigoths, and much of the time there was a fair measure of religious freedom, even if confessional differences in the end kept the Goths and their subjects culturally distinct. Overall, catholic Christians suffered far more at the hands of the Vandals than they did under Germanic Arianism.

Something of the condition of the catholic church in southern Gaul can be seen from the letters of Sidonius Apollinaris (ca. 430–486), a patriotic Gallo-Roman aristocrat who became bishop of Clermont in 470. A talented poet and champion of classical culture, Sidonius agreed to become bishop in the hope that he might spearhead successful resistance to Visigothic takeover in the Auvergne. His example illustrates the degree to which conservative-minded nobles could look on episcopal office as a possible basis upon which to preserve traditional values and ensure a reasonable way of life in a world with much less security and fewer openings for the representatives of the old elites. Sidonius's hopes, however, were not realized, and he experienced exile and imprisonment.

After his reinstatement in 476, Sidonius spent most of his remaining years collating his correspondence with other Gallic leaders. These included figures such as Faustus, bishop of Riez, one of the leading intellectuals in the Gallic church; Lupus, bishop of Troyes; Claudianus Mamertus, the philosophically minded brother of the bishop of Vienne (who argued against Faustus's view that the soul was corporeal); and Ruricius, a fellow aristocrat and bishop of Limoges. Sidonius's letters show that although circumstances were difficult and clergy were often under suspicion for their political affiliations, it was possible for the life, rituals, and theological debates of the churches to go on, and even for new church buildings to be constructed in the midst of the uncertainty and changes. Even the worst consequences of military strife—famine, disease, suffering, and death—gave the churches an important role in the administering of charity and relief to the needy.

Besides the Visigoths, the other major Gothic group to emerge in this period were the Ostrogoths. They were made up of eastern Goths who had settled in Pannonia and Thrace during the supremacy of the Huns and after much rivalry and conflict had united behind Theoderic the Great (ca. 453–526). Under Theoderic's leadership the Ostrogoths went from being an unstable assortment of barbarians in the Balkans to being part of a kingdom situated at the traditional heart of the Roman Empire, in Italy itself.

Theoderic

The background to the Ostrogoths' arrival in Italy lay in the autumn of 476, when the last of the puppet-emperors in the West, Romulus Augustulus, was removed from office by the barbarian general Odoacer, commander of the Germanic forces in Italy, who determined to make himself "king" of Italy in his stead.[5] Odoacer sent the imperial insignia of Romulus to the Eastern emperor Zeno in Constantinople on the grounds that they were no longer required, and Zeno in turn granted him the rank of "patrician" and de facto recognition, though theoretically he himself was now the sole emperor.

Because of this coup by Odoacer, it has long been conventional to see the year 476 as marking the end of the Roman Empire in the West, but in reality the transition was of little significance in its own time. The real blow had been struck two generations earlier, and all that had followed thereafter in the West was but a facade of Roman imperialism. Odoacer brought Italy a few years of peace, going out of his way to promote good relations with his public, but his own position was insecure, and by the late 480s Zeno's officials were encouraging Theoderic, with whom Constantinople had volatile and uneasy relations (sometimes they were in alliance; increasingly they were at war), to take his people and seek his own place in Italy.

In 493, after a lengthy siege of Ravenna, Theoderic defeated and executed Odoacer and established himself as king of Italy in his place. Like Odoacer, he remained nominally subject to the authority of the emperor (now Anastasius) in Constantinople, and it took several years of negotiations with the East before his position was clarified, for he had almost certainly gone beyond the expectations of the Eastern court in what he had secured. In the end, it was agreed in the late 490s that he would be guaranteed regal independence in his own sphere, but he was certainly not intended by Constantinople to present himself as comparable in status to the emperor; formally he was a representative, not an equal. That was the theory, at least; the authorities in the East were in no position to see that it was adhered to in practice.

Theoderic had been brought up in Constantinople, and he had an instinctive respect for Rome's traditions and culture. As far as he was concerned, although he was formally king and not emperor, his kingdom was to be identified in the West with the Roman Empire continuing, and his Italy was by far the most conspicuously Roman of all the barbarian successor states in Europe. Theoderic and his people may have held the power, but the great majority of his subjects were of course Romans, and he was eager that there should be cultural integration and social harmony. Theoderic continued Odoacer's policy of conciliating as far as possible, and he retained the imperial senatorial and administrative order and kept a large proportion of Odoacer's officials. His capital at Ravenna contained splendid buildings after the fashion of those in Constantinople, his court favored Roman literature and art, and under his reign many literate Goths began to take Roman names and learned to speak Latin.[6]

Religious Policies

Theoderic was himself an Arian, but he was keen that doctrinal differences should not impede his political aspirations. Catholics were in a clear majority among his Christian subjects, and he favored a policy of toleration towards them.[7] For the most part he endeavored not to interfere in ecclesiastical affairs, expressing a willingness to let the clergy operate in their sphere while he kept to his. Some bishops were, of course, subject to political manipulation, but they were usually treated with great respect, and many were very willing to recognize Theoderic as a sincere believer and a champion of Christ's cause.

On his sole recorded visit to Rome in 500, Theoderic is said to have greeted Pope Symmachus as if he were the apostle Peter himself, and in the following years he was invited to settle a schism in the Roman church caused by supporters of a rival pope, Lawrence. Whatever the nature of his personal feelings (and his own inclinations in the case of the schism are difficult to gauge), Theoderic could act in ways that earned him praise from believers of quite different opinions, and his virtues were celebrated by many churchmen, such as the former rhetorician Ennodius, who as a deacon of the church of Milan[8] delivered a public panegyric before the king in 507.

Theoderic devoted significant sums of money to the building and decoration of remarkable Arian churches and baptisteries in Ravenna,[9] symbolizing the wealth and status with which his capital was endowed. Such activities naturally provoked rival expressions of enterprise from the local catholics, who were also very prosperous compared with many of their fellow Christians elsewhere in the West. No repressive measures were taken, and for the largest part of his reign Theoderic enjoyed positive relations with the catholic hierarchy. A number of talented catholic Christians were able to attain to high office in his government, and as time went on there were in fact significant numbers of conversions of Arian Ostrogoths to the Nicene faith.

Theoderic's appeal to "Romanness" was in part designed to legitimize an expansionist foreign policy, and over the years he extended his dominions considerably, over the Vandals, the Burgundians, and, most significantly, the Visigoths. The stability of his regime also depended heavily on the maintenance of a coolness or hostility towards Constantinople on the part of the Western senatorial aristocracy, and Theoderic recognized that if this mood were to change he would face a potential political crisis. When the schism that had seriously divided the churches of Rome and Constantinople since 482 came to an end in 518–519 (see pp. 220–22, 224–25), Theoderic was alarmed that Constantinople might seek to use the rapprochement in the interests of reasserting its political authority over the West. Already there were signs that this was likely, and Theoderic was also experiencing mounting problems in the West, with difficulties in both Gaul and Spain. In the midst of it all, his nominated heir died, and there were many complications surrounding the choice of an alternative successor.

Boethius

In Theoderic's bid to impose control, Christians were among the victims. His chief civil administrator or "Master of Offices" was the gifted aristocrat, Anicius Manlius Torquatus Severinus Boethius (ca. 480–524). A wealthy senator, educated in Athens and Alexandria, Boethius was a philosopher with a first-rate knowledge of the works of Plato and Aristotle who wrote translations of and commentaries on Greek thinkers and a series of tractates in defense of orthodox Christian theology. In 523 he was accused of treason when he played down the significance of disloyalty—or correspondence with Constantinople—on the part of another eminent senator, Albinus, and he was condemned to death. His father-in-law, Symmachus, incurred a similar fate.

While awaiting his execution under house arrest on a country estate, Boethius wrote the work for which he would become most famous, the *Consolation of Philosophy*. A dialogue in prose and verse between the author and a personified "Philosophy," it draws heavily on classical sources. It offers a vision of the acceptance of undeserved suffering and contentment with one's own reason and virtue, and the tone is Stoic at least as much as it is Christian. Boethius's work became greatly influential in later thought, and in many ways he belongs at the beginning of the intellectual traditions of the Middle Ages as a figure for whom theology and philosophy were intimately intertwined. In his literary project more widely, he anticipated the scholastic theologians of the twelfth century and beyond with his synthesis of Christian doctrine and Aristotelian logic.

Boethius's fate at the hands of Theoderic was a tragic waste of talent, but Boethius cannot be seen as a religious martyr. He had clearly made a number of notable enemies at court, and his advice on various policy issues was at odds with the interests of other parties. In particular, he had close links to one of the candidates to succeed Theoderic, the king's nephew Theodahad, whom Theoderic himself did not favor. His fall was a sign that his master was quite prepared to assert his authority by making an example of prominent individuals, Christian or not, who were suspected of having dubious connections or treasonable leanings towards Constantinople's political agendas.

The Downfall of Theoderic

It required more than gestures like these, however, to save Theoderic. His empire was breaking apart, and although he had some successes in taking action against insurgents, notably the Burgundians, and he nursed ambitious plans to pursue the Vandals, he was losing his grip on power. Constantinople willingly used these problems to further its objectives of crushing the Ostrogothic dream, and the emperor Justin set about persecuting his Arian subjects, including large numbers of Goths. Forced conversions to catholicism took place, and it is possible that Arian churches were sequestered for catholic use.

Theoderic's protests through the agencies of Pope John I (523–526) proved mostly ineffective, for although Justin gave way on several requests he would not accede to the restoration of converts. To make matters worse, on his embassy of mediation, the pope, who had been lavishly welcomed in Constantinople, chose to give Justin his blessing as emperor, and he had received in turn a generous gift to the churches in Rome. If, as may have been the case, the embassy was also intended to win recognition of Theoderic's young grandson, Athalaric, as his successor, it also evidently failed. Theoderic was furious, and on their return to Ravenna, John and his fellow legates were imprisoned; John himself, already advanced in years and infirm, died shortly afterwards.

Theoderic is said by various Christian sources to have hatched plans to oppress catholics more widely in his last months, but there is little evidence that this actually happened, though there were obvious tensions surrounding the replacement of Pope John in Rome. Theoderic died in 526, and within a matter of a few years his kingdom collapsed, as fierce struggles went on regarding the political guardianship of his young successor and opinions were sharply divided over what line to take with regard to the authorities in the East. At the same time, all around other barbarian peoples were on the ascendant. All of these changes would in turn have consequences for the churches. But so too did other developments that had already taken place elsewhere in the West, while Theoderic was still on his throne in Ravenna.

12

A New West: Gaul, Italy, Spain

▼

The Franks

The chief rivals of the Visigoths in northern Gaul were the Franks, made up of a disparate group of warrior tribes who had proved fierce harriers of Roman forces on the Rhine frontier over many generations. Over the course of the late third and fourth centuries, numbers of Franks had succeeded in pressing across into northern Gaul and settling as allies of the Romans in what is now Belgium and the Rhineland. Significant contingents had come to serve as auxiliaries in the Roman armies, and several of the most prominent military officers of the fourth century were Franks. Such individuals were typically highly Romanized, and many of them proved capable and loyal officials who fought on Rome's behalf against other barbarian peoples.

There were large groups of other Franks, however, dominated by the so-called "Salians" from farther north, who were far less enthusiastic about Rome, even though they remained subject to its influences. Under their bellicose leader Childeric in the 470s, these tribes caused considerable trouble for the Romans in northern Gaul. Childeric was a "Merovingian," a scion of the great fighter Merovech, the "sea-warrior" who was believed to have been conceived by a union of a Frankish queen and a sea-god.[1] In the 480s Childeric's son and successor, Clovis (or more accurately Chlodovech, "pillaging warrior"), inherited his father's authority and interests and determinedly expanded his dominions, first westwards into the Loire Valley and then beyond, both up the Rhine against the Alamanni and south of the Loire into Visigothic territory.

Childeric and Clovis were pagans, though Childeric's final burial place lay close to a Christian church and Clovis received good wishes from Remigius, the catholic bishop of Reims, when he took over the leadership of his people. In the early 490s Clovis married a Burgundian princess named Clotilde, who was a catholic believer. Significant numbers of other Burgundians were converted around this time, including Sigismund, son of King Gundobad, who was influenced by the impressive Bishop Avitus of Vienne. Under Clotilde's influence, and with additional encouragement from Remigius, who was a zealous missionary, Clovis was nudged towards a profession of Christian faith.

The Conversion of Clovis

The traditional story goes that Clovis, like Constantine, accepted the Christian faith in the context of battle. It is said that he vowed to become a Christian if he succeeded in defeating the Alamanni, and kept his word when he did so. Perhaps around 499, he was baptized along with a significant number of his soldiers, possibly as many as three thousand in all. The event is said to have been the first mass conversion of a Germanic group to the catholic faith.

It is hard to be sure about almost any of the details of this conventional account, and there is much scholarly dispute over the dating of Clovis's first expressions of interest in Christianity, the circumstances of his conversion, and the context of his final reception of baptism. There is no doubt that he had already made some military progress southward before he acknowledged the name of Christ, and it is likely that his acceptance of Christianity was significantly connected with his calculations as to how his expansionist strategy might be advanced. In that sense, Clovis's profession of belief almost certainly had as much to do with politics as with personal faith.

By no means did all of the Franks come over to the Christian faith; the first conversions, nominal or otherwise, were among leaders rather than common people, and it is plainly wrong to think of the Franks in general as pagans one day and Christians the next. Certainly the character of Clovis's regime was not much changed in moral terms: it continued to be characterized by violence, intrigue, and brutality. While his reign witnessed a skillful revolution of the structures of Frankish political governance—a loosely confederate system of tribal chieftains was replaced by an overarching kingship held only by Clovis's own Merovingian dynasty—his own plans were shot through with the designs of naked power. Pagan beliefs and practices continued to be widespread among his ordinary subjects, and the laws and customs of the enlarged Frankish kingdom continued to embrace many aspects of traditional religion such as animal sacrifices.

By espousing the catholic Christian position, Clovis may have hoped to win valuable support from many of the bishops and landowners of Gaul, to whom he might portray his military campaign as a holy war against pagans and heretics. He had already defeated the Alammani, brought the Burgundians over to his side, and taken a variety of lands along the Upper Danube; now he was gambling on taking on the might of the Visigoths. By aligning himself doctrinally with the enemies of Visigothic Arianism, he may well have speculated that he could further his chances of success in confronting the powerful domain in the south.

In practice, however, plenty of the catholics of southern Gaul were not at all enthusiastic about Clovis's advance. They preferred control by the Visigoths—doctrinal deviants or not—to conquest by the warriors from the north. To many it was apparent that Clovis was a ruthless imperialist; the claims that he was fighting a crusade on behalf of orthodoxy probably only came together later on, once Clovis's military prowess had achieved a number of its objectives. When the Visigoths and their king Alaric II were decisively crushed at the battle of Vouillé near Poitiers in the summer of 507, among the vanquished were both Arians and catholics. Bordeaux and Toulouse were taken; Clovis himself returned to Paris, but the Burgundians and a contingent of Franks continued south and besieged Arles (latterly the most important city of the old Roman Gaul) in 507–508, which was tenaciously defended by both Goths and Gallo-Romans. In the end the attackers were defeated by forces sent by Theoderic, and the Ostrogoths went on to establish control over the southeast.

The Merovingian Church

By the time Clovis died in 511 he had doubled the size of his empire, and the vast bulk of Gaul had officially been restored to catholicism. The Visigoths held on to just a small strip of land in the south, around

Narbonne. Theoderic had recovered the southeast, but over the course
of the following generations Clovis's sons and grandsons succeeded in
exploiting the decline of Ostrogothic power and expanded the Frankish
domain still further to cover most of the territory that would become the
basis of modern France. Bishop Gregory of Tours (ca. 539–594), writing
his highly influential history of the Franks more than half a century later,
could picture the reign of Clovis as attended by many miraculous signs
of divine approval and his victories as a providential defeat of evil and
error. The new Constantine had triumphed, and his empire of truth had
arrived. The subsequent enlargement of the Frankish territories seemed
only to confirm the divine blessing that shone upon the regime in its
commitment to the true faith.

In reality, as Gregory's own evidence of the generations after Clovis
makes abundantly clear, Merovingian Gaul was a society presided over
by autocratic rulers whose hold on power was continually under threat
in internecine strife, where corruption and immorality were rife, and
where the leaders of the churches were much under the sway of their
political masters. There was an attending decline in spiritual standards,
and it is doubtful if the church in Gaul was much better off under the
catholicism of the Merovingians than it was under the Arian Visigoths.
Even the catholic creed itself was by no means secure: as Gregory also
testifies, Arianism was in no wise a spent force, and it continued to be
influential in many quarters. In a period in which the cult of the saints
expanded considerably in its popular appeal, there was also a good
deal of syncretism—both deliberate and unthinking—between old-style
Frankish rituals and the symbols, shrines, and relics of Christian piety.
Those endeavoring to spread an unambiguously Christian message did
not find their lot easy.

Many of the bishops were themselves the natural elite of their society—old-fashioned Gallo-Roman gentlemen who were concerned to
negotiate the best possible terms for themselves as the figureheads of
a new kind of social establishment. The old Roman order was no more,
and indeed numbers of churchmen were beginning to filter through
from expressly Frankish backgrounds, but it was possible for the heirs
of the traditional system to build up a new position as the powerful regional representatives of a faith that enjoyed royal sanction. When the
Merovingian rulers summoned councils to meet, as they did on many
occasions, the preoccupations of the assembled churchmen tended to be
conventional, in so far as a good deal of the legislation was concerned
with the enshrining of ecclesiastical prerogatives; but the attitudes adopted by the bishops were often politically compliant, for those who

framed the canons looked to their king as their overall protector and patron.

Nevertheless, it would be wrong to imagine that all was confusion, or that all churchmen were self-serving or merely the puppets of their royal masters. There were also some genuine evidences of spiritual vitality and some notable signs of Christian cultural consolidation. Gregory of Tours may have lamented the state of decline that marked the Gallic church in his time, but he could also document the lives of numerous saints of the recent as well as the distant past—bishops, aristocrats, hermits, and ascetics—whose character displayed special spiritual qualities. Over against the allurements of episcopal self-indulgence through political cooperation lay other convictions, most notably the enduring strength of Gallic asceticism, which continued to play a positive part in the shaping of spirituality, especially in the areas most affected by earlier monastic influences. There were also some impressive cultural achievements. One of Gregory's contemporaries and friends was the gifted poet Venantius Fortunatus, whose compositions, as we noted in chapter 9, evinced a rich quality of spiritual insight and anticipated the textures of medieval work in various respects (see p. 266).

Caesarius of Arles

Around the time when Clovis was proclaiming his Christian faith, the church in the south of Gaul, in what was still at that time Visigothic territory, was dominated by a particularly impressive figure, who combined a natural gift for leadership with a strong spiritual zeal. Caesarius (ca. 470–542), bishop of Arles from 502 to 542, came from an aristocratic Gallo-Roman family, but his formation included a period as a monk at Lérins, and he was convinced that the leaders of the church were called to reflect exemplary lives of spiritual devotion. He criticized his fellow bishops who showed signs of being more attached to their own interests than to their vocation to look after their flocks. He organized part of his own clerical community on ascetic lines, according to the precedent made most famous by Augustine, founded an additional monastery for women, and sought to spread the influences of monastic spirituality to his church as a whole.

Caesarius called upon his congregation to pursue not only the traditional virtues of a respectable community—justice, honesty, and the avoidance of gross evil—but qualities of Christian self-denial and charity that transcended conventional decency. He challenged the endurance of "uncouth" practices in Christian circles, which to him meant moral behavior that was no better than the lifestyle of coarse pagan peasants. As he reminded his people, such "rusticity" was found not just among those still enmeshed in the magic and superstition to be found out in the countryside, but also in the lives of supposedly cultivated city-dwellers when they engaged in the social and sexual activities of a world that had supposedly accepted the gospel.

Caesarius was a gifted preacher who communicated in a deliberately direct style; he was also well-read in Christian literature and capable of adapting ideas and themes from Augustine and other authorities. He could edit and recycle Augustine's homilies for Provence as distinct from North Africa. As his many surviving sermons show, his counsel was often ignored or rejected as impractical even while his rhetorical gifts were admired, but his ideals were clear. An indefatigable moral teacher, he persisted in his efforts to raise the tone of his church despite opposition and indifference to his plain speaking; on one occasion he is reported to have closed the doors of his church to prevent people from leaving before the sermon. In his wholehearted effort to stand at the heart of his city's life, he labored to build up his Christian community as an example to its wider society. The pursuit of holiness was not at odds with the duty to promote social order in difficult times.

Not that this image was always easily sustained. Arles was a diverse society, and its religious spectrum embraced not only Christians but devotees of older cultic practices, and a sizable number of Jews. Caesarius expressed admiration for Jewish piety and strongly discouraged ill-treatment of Jews in society, but he was careful to differentiate between Jewish and Christian beliefs, and the presence of such religious others inevitably challenged his vision of a community in which Christianity and civil society merged. There were also palpable signs that a bishop himself could still be vulnerable. When Arles was under pressure from the Burgundians and Franks in 507–508,[2] Caesarius was suspected by the defending Goths of having sympathies with the enemy, and he was arrested and charged with treason. After a brief period in exile in Bordeaux, he succeeded in clearing himself and returning to his see, but the suspicions concerning his loyalties did not entirely disappear.

After the Burgundians and Franks were repulsed by the Ostrogoths, Caesarius further antagonized some of the inhabitants of the city by selling off church silver in order to pay for the redemption of prisoners of war, most of them from the enemy side. Such actions, he pointed out, had been undertaken by bishops before, but they were naturally controversial in that they involved the disposal of church assets in which Christian donors had often invested great spiritual significance. Nevertheless, Caesarius's charitable works both to locals and to their enemies said a good deal for his commitment to compassionate leadership in a time of crisis, and many of his congregation were prepared to contribute alms to his causes. By reaching out to those who had caused the troubles in the first place, Caesarius made plain his belief that his gospel was also for those on the other side.

Caesarius impressed Theoderic with his abilities, and he also won the favor of Pope Symmachus in Rome. Symmachus restored to Arles the authority of being the primary see in Gaul, a status that had been removed in the late 440s by Pope Leo when one of Caesarius's predecessors, Hilary, had caused offense at Rome. Caesarius was granted the right to wear the papal *pallium* (see p. 282) throughout Gaul and to act as the pope's vicar in all of its regions. Such a position elicited some controversy elsewhere in Gaul, not least in nearby Aix, where the bishop was deeply resistant to the elevation of Arles, but it gave Caesarius a powerful responsibility for ecclesiastical discipline and liturgical practices over a very large area, which, with the Ostrogothic expansion, extended farther and farther into Gaul and also into Spain. As well as bolstering his own authority, it furthered the territorial diffusion of Roman practices in the West.

Caesarius presided over a number of church councils, most famously at Orange in 529, which reaffirmed the Augustinian teaching on grace against its lingering critics in Gaul (see pp. 187–88). Orange condemned the kind of views that had been advanced in the not-too-distant past by churchmen such as the late Faustus of Riez, who had contended that Augustine's doctrine of predestination left no place for human free will. While the council declared that there is no predestination to evil, it strongly asserted the priority of grace over faith and the utter necessity of divine enabling if human beings are to perform good works.

Alongside Caesarius's activities as a leader and confessional champion, his episcopate may have one other claim to fame. One of his sermons contains a version of a creed dubbed the *Quicunque vult* (from its opening words, "Whosoever wishes to be saved . . ."), which also came to be better known as the "Athanasian Creed." The work has in fact nothing to do with Athanasius himself; it was first written in Latin, and in both its origins and its usage it is a Western confession of faith. It asserts a firmly anti-Arian position, and its other theological emphases are identifiably Augustinian and anti-Nestorian. There is no evidence to suggest that Caesarius himself was its author, but there is good reason to believe that the so-called Athanasian Creed did originate in the context of southern Gaul around the turn of the fifth and sixth centuries, and it is quite possible that it owed something of its subsequent popularity to Caesarius's influence.

Caesarius's latter years were spent amid much political upheaval, as the Franks finally succeeded in annexing Provence and taking over Arles. These changes brought new challenges to his ability to exercise his ecclesiastical power, and in the aftermath of his death these difficulties intensified, as his successors in Arles became susceptible to greater degrees of influence from their new masters and more limited in their authority over their fellow bishops. Some of these other churchmen, it seems, discerned little need to adopt the comprehensive ideals of pastoral reform and spiritual commitment Caesarius had championed when they could instead pass comfortable lives running their regional fiefdoms and reaping the rewards of assured social status, wealth, and power.

Benedict of Nursia

If Caesarius's work in Gaul went on within the regular structures of the church's life, some other energetic Christians in the West were concerned to address the moral character of their times by a somewhat more independent approach. In Italy, Benedict (ca. 480–547), a native of Nursia in Umbria, was distressed by the corruption he witnessed in society while

pursuing his education in Rome, and he withdrew to live the life of a hermit in a cave near Subiaco, east of the city. He attracted a number of admirers and imitators, but, like many ascetics before him, he disturbed some official clergy by his behavior. Around 529 he founded a monastery at Monte Cassino, midway between Rome and Naples, and there he lived for the rest of his life.

The pattern of Benedict's monastic regime was based upon a

Icon of St. Benedict. Illustration from Holy Transfiguration Monastery, Boston, MA. Used by permission.

combination of spiritual and practical activities. His monks were primarily laymen, and their lives were made up of a carefully regulated daily round of prayer and work. The primary emphasis was on worship, structured around seven canonical hours, a system that had already been adopted by other Christian monastics who took their cue from the psalmist's confession, "Seven times a day I praise you" (Ps. 119:164). Benedict's system also repudiated leisure as a spiritual enemy, and the bulk of each day was spent in work. This might consist of labor in the fields or other forms of manual activity such as the writing out of a biblical or Christian manuscript. Benedict himself had received a good secular education, but he held a low opinion of classical texts and did not believe that these should be studied by his monks. Sacred, not secular, literature was the worthy object of attention.

Benedict set out his directives for both spiritual and practical behavior in his *Rule* (ca. 540), a charter that drew upon a variety of monastic authorities,[3] especially an anonymous document from approximately the same period in Italy known as the *Rule of the Master*. From the details of his prescriptions, it is clear that his monks were offered a way of life that was strict but by no means unusually harsh. Like John Cassian, whose work he commended to his followers, Benedict held to the principles of moderation, prudence, and humanity rather than extreme self-denial. His monks were forbidden to move to another monastery, and lived their entire lives in the same house where they took their vows. They were committed to chastity, common ownership of goods, and obedience to the discipline of their abbot. But they were also allowed benefits that by no means all ascetics enjoyed, such as wine in moderation. Some other ostensibly limiting requirements brought benefits of their own: the obligation to belong to one house over an entire lifetime, for example, might seem restrictive, but for many of Benedict's monks it afforded a measure of security and quasi-familial intimacy they would not have known otherwise.

In Benedict's mind, his teaching was "a little rule for beginners," and he was not establishing an order as such. After his death his style of monasticism continued as only a local phenomenon in Italy. Only gradually did the Benedictines become an outward-looking movement with principles that caught on over a much larger area. From the seventh century onward, the Benedictine pattern started to make significant inroads in Gaul, gradually eclipsing other monastic rules, and from the time of the Synod of Autun in 670 Benedict's *Rule* was declared binding on all Merovingian monasteries; it also came to be very widely followed in Britain and Germany.

By then the scholarly work in which Benedictine monks were engaged had come to include much more than the copying of Scripture or the works of only Christian authors, and the Benedictines became vital custodians of many of the great texts of classical antiquity. They emerged as a large and multifaceted order, with a crucial place at the heart of the religious culture of the Middle Ages. A version of Benedict's *Rule* continues to be the basis for the Benedictines to this day, though various adaptations were introduced over the centuries according to changes in circumstances.

Cassiodorus

Benedict himself may not have advocated the interest that his followers came to show in secular learning, but the same was not true of other Christian reforming figures in the sixth-century West. Cassiodorus (ca. 485–580), a Roman aristocrat and catholic Christian who attained high office in Ravenna under Theoderic and his successors, was a dedicated scholar and an enthusiast for education. Influential in Theoderic's promotion of the cultural legacy of the Roman imperial past, he planned a Christian academy of higher learning, after the fashion of the great schools of the East in Alexandria and Nisibis, to be established in Rome, and he was keen to further the civilization of the Goths in the humane traditions of classical liberal studies.

Although a library was collected in Rome in collaboration with Pope Agapetus in 535–536, the collapse of the Ostrogothic kingdom and the military campaigns in Italy by imperial forces in the mid-530s brought an end to Cassiodorus's initial plans. After spending a number of years in Constantinople, away from the turmoil in his own country, he returned to his country estate at Squillace near Naples, called Vivarium ("fish-pond," due to its landscaped gardens), where around 554 he set up his own monastic community. Here, unlike at Monte Cassino, there was an explicit attention to intellectual activity that went beyond the fulfillment of just religious aims. Cassiodorus seems not to have imposed a formal rule, but his monks were expected to pursue a course of secular studies. His monastery was equipped with a library and writing room in which the works of Christian and classical authors alike were studied, copied, and translated.

Cassiodorus was a talented biblical commentator; he was also a man with a deep interest in philosophy, history, literature, and language. In his *Institutes of Divine and Secular Studies* he proposed a strong synthesis of biblical scholarship with the liberal arts. In the first part he offered instruction on such matters as biblical manuscripts and versions, textual criticism, and commentaries; in the second he set out the importance of the standard educational subjects of his time, including grammar, literature, rhetoric, and philosophy. Like Augustine before him, he believed that secular studies would further the ability of Christians to understand and expound the Scriptures. Unlike Augustine, however, he was not dealing with what were still in some sense competing cultures. For Cassiodorus, pagan learning was no longer to be viewed as a discrete entity; it had long ago been definitively assimilated into Christian thinking.

Cassiodorus was critical of those who considered it frivolous or unnecessary to study the literary bequests of great classical authors. At the same time, he urged familiarity with earlier Western theology, especially Augustine's, oversaw the translation of important works by Greek churchmen such as Clement and Didymus of Alexandria, and wrote his own biblical commentaries, most notably on the Psalms. His aim was to equip an intellectual and spiritual elite for a changed world in which secular learning and Christian wisdom could form a single, coherent package, and his desire was to give such leaders the tools to function in an environment where "education" might mean one thing in all contexts. Cassiodorus was perhaps the first writer to think of himself and his readers as living in a "modern" age, and there is no doubt that he stands as one of the founding figures of the medieval period, when his *Institutes* would be widely studied as an educational guide. As it happens, the Benedictine tradition in particular was almost certainly encouraged to take up the concern for learning for which it became famous thanks in part to the influence of Cassiodorus's ideals.

Justinian and the Recovery of the West

All of the work of Benedict at Monte Cassino and the formative years of Cassiodorus's community at Vivarium took place during the reign of the emperor Justinian (527–565). As we saw in chapter 8, Justinian presented himself as a ruler with a mission to restore the Roman world to its former greatness, and he labored to effect a reunification of East and West in political, cultural, and religious terms. In a series of ambitious military campaigns stretching from the 530s to the 550s, Justinian succeeded in recapturing a great deal of the West. His able general Belisarius regained North Africa from the control of the Vandals in

533–534, a major achievement in both strategic and economic terms. This success was followed by a number of sustained assaults on Italy, first by Belisarius, then by an Armenian commander called Narses. The war in Italy was neither swift nor straightforward, and Justinian's plans suffered numerous setbacks, but at length the peninsula was successfully recovered from Ostrogothic control.

The costs, however, were considerable: cities had been devastated, the countryside had been ravaged, and the agricultural economy had been left in ruins. Landowners who had done very well under the Ostrogoths confronted the ruin of their estates, and there were large numbers of displaced, hungry, and indigent people. The country had also been severely affected by the plague that devastated so many other parts of the Mediterranean world in the 540s. Italy had officially been restored to the empire, but imperial bureaucracy in the West was greatly scaled down, and important administrative offices that had been retained by the Ostrogoths fell into abeyance. After a few years power came to be vested in individuals imported from the East who reported directly to Eastern superiors. The emperor's sovereignty was represented at Ravenna by a viceroy known, from the 580s onward, as his "exarch"; there was little meaningful Western government as such.

Much disaffection and festering disloyalty ensued in Italy, both among the military and governing classes and in the country at large. Intellectual life also suffered. Men such as Cassiodorus had withdrawn from public life at the height of the troubles, and in the aftermath of war Cassiodorus's scholarly community at Vivarium was a refuge rather than a reflection of any kind of cultural mood in society more widely. The fact that this community, for all its importance, was a monastic fellowship based on a private estate rather than the kind of grand school of learning originally envisioned for Rome itself testifies to the major decline in the cultural atmosphere as a result of the upheavals between the 530s and the 550s.

Ironically, there was a much more flourishing interest in Greek literature in Italy before the Byzantine conquest than there was afterwards. Rich culture there was in Justinian's world, in art, architecture, and legal studies, but its finest expressions were overwhelmingly to be found in the East, not the West, and even there it is highly questionable if the range of intellectual life was nearly so broad by the later period of Justinian's rule as it had been at the beginning of it. In Italy, certainly, there were many who looked back wistfully on the days of the Ostrogoths as a preferable regime in this as in other respects. To them, the reinstatement of their land into the empire was an idea that had sounded a lot better in principle than it proved to be in practice.

The seeming ambivalence of Justinian's achievement in the West extended into the effects of his religious policies. As we have seen, he was firmly committed to the promotion of a single catholic faith throughout his empire, and he played a direct role in the doctrinal debates of his time. To many Western Christians, this was all very well so long as his efforts were unambiguously aimed at the suppression of Arianism and the promotion of Chalcedon. However, when he took it upon himself to issue his edict on the Three Chapters, his interference was seen as being at odds with Chalcedon's teaching, and his treatment of the (admittedly very indecisive) Pope Vigilius did little to assist the imperial image in the West (see pp. 229–31). Vigilius's successor, Pelagius I (556–561), was regarded by many as the emperor's pawn, who had betrayed the West by yielding to Justinian's wishes on the question of the Three Chapters. Justinian had issued a so-called "Pragmatic Sanction" decree guaranteeing important rights and privileges to Italian bishops, and Pelagius worked hard to implement its details. But despite some local success in Rome, there was much ongoing resentment elsewhere over what the new imperial order appeared to mean for the leadership of the Western church, and the major northern sees of Aquileia and Milan renounced communion with Rome.

Justinian's armies had retaken the major islands of the Western Mediterranean and gained a foothold in southeastern Spain, but most of Spain, together with southern Gaul, remained in the hands of the Visigoths. Roman arms could not automatically prevail against Arian enemies. In all of the reclaimed regions of the West, not least in Africa, there was enduring opposition in many Christian circles to the emperor's complicated agendas for theological unity, and a sense that he had gone much too far in trying to appease the "Monophysites" in the East. Firm measures taken by the authorities against some of his most vocal critics did not help. For many, Justinian's regime was far too centralized and his efforts at personal control far too ambitious.

Justinian saw himself as the chief legislator, charged with upholding the common good of all the peoples of the Roman world, and he oversaw the systematic codification of Roman laws and the production of influential legal textbooks; but to many his attempt to administer a large imperial system without ever venturing much beyond Constantinople was both naïve and clumsy. His efforts to enforce Christian confession by taking legal sanctions against practitioners of other faiths were highly problematic morally, and both pagans and Jews suffered badly under his prescriptions. The social prestige of Christianity was beyond doubt, as was evidenced powerfully by the many magnificent churches that Justinian built, restored, and adorned, especially in and around his capital,[4] but his rhetorical evocation of a unified Christian realm as the bastion of righteousness and good order was betrayed by all-too-obvious realities on the ground.

Not only were believers divided among themselves and Christian officials capable of some very questionable behavior; not all barbarians could automatically be regarded as bad rulers or even as heretics. The Franks, notably, had aligned themselves with catholic orthodoxy. They had behaved deviously with the Ostrogoths, alternately attacking and allying themselves with them according to their calculations of their own advantages, and in the aftermath of the Ostrogoths' fall they were a serious menace to Justinian's plans as they plundered and appropriated large parts of northern Italy. Dislodging them from the country proved difficult enough; extending operations deeper into the Franks' established territories to the north was simply impracticable. This was not only for military reasons. To engage with the Franks seriously was not to confront a religious foe but to attack those who were supposedly fellow believers in the true God. Ostensibly the Franks were just as much an occupying barbarian power as the Vandals or the Goths, and their conduct was sometimes far worse than the Goths' in Italy had ever been, but whatever was said of them, they could not plausibly be depicted as enemies of truth.

Viewed in retrospect, Justinian's regime can be said to have succeeded to an impressive degree in recapturing the spirit of Roman imperial glory, but it can equally be said to have represented this spirit in that way for the last time in history. Justinian achieved a very great deal in political and cultural terms, and some of the finer accomplishments of his reign in areas such as art and architecture anticipated the more splendid aspects of the later Byzantine world. However, it was clear that his vision of an integrated political and ecclesiastical order in the context of the sixth century did not and could not succeed. He was no more able to win the general favor of Christians in the West than he was to unite their divided brothers and sisters in the East.

In any event, while the West mattered enormously to him, it was in the East that he concentrated almost all his symbolic and practical apparatus of power. Justinian may have been the last Roman emperor who could with any legitimacy claim that his dominion embraced large parts of the Western as well as the Eastern Mediterranean world, but he also ensured that the center of gravity in that world was located as

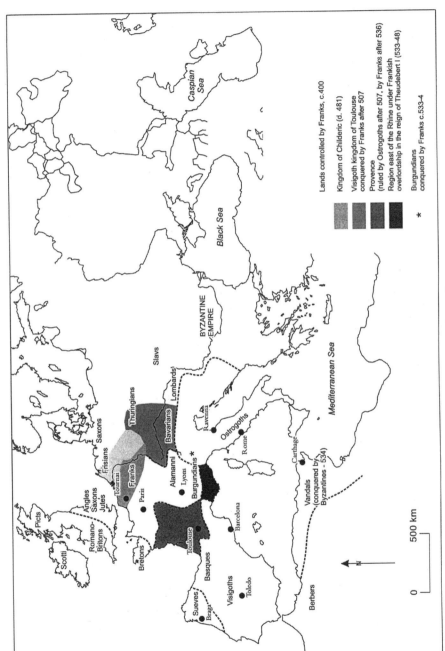

Lands controlled by Franks, c.400

Kingdom of Childeric (d. 481)

Visigoth kingdom of Toulouse
conquered by Franks after 507

Provence
(ruled by Ostrogoths after 507, by Franks after 536)

Region east of the Rhine under Frankish
overlordship in the reign of Theudebert I (533-48)

Burgundians
conquered by Franks c.533-4

*

Western Europe by the sixth century.

never before in Constantinople, and as such he was one of the primary architects of what would be a distinctively Byzantine as opposed to a Roman Empire.

Justinian's later years were marked by mounting problems on various fronts as fresh challenges presented themselves socially, economically, and militarily, and he had to contend with much personal unpopularity, political infighting, and civil unrest. New threats emerged that his order was incapable of meeting, from the Berbers in Africa, from the Slavs and the Avars in the Balkans, and from the mighty reemergence of the Persian challenge in the East. In Italy the problem came from another source, but it proved equally irresistible. In theory, the emperor's authority held sway; in reality, there was little to impede a new influx of invaders ready to make the most of a highly unstable situation.

In 568–569, just three years or so after Justinian's death, yet another Germanic people entered Italy from the northeast and soon succeeded in placing the imperial control of the country under intolerable strain. Once again there would be major implications for the churches.

The Lombards

The Lombards, or Longobards, whose first attested homeland lay around the river Elbe close to modern Denmark, had in the mid-520s crossed the Danube and occupied part of Pannonia, and over the ensuing generation they had expanded their power base considerably and established positive relations with Constantinople. They were recognized as confederates with territory of their own, and they had fought on the side of the Romans in several contexts, including the final stages of Justinian's reconquest of northern Italy.

The Lombards' diplomatic and military contacts with other Germanic peoples had brought them an awareness of Christianity, primarily of an Arian creed, though some Lombard nobles may have converted to catholicism in order to win favor at Constantinople. Their king, Alboin (560–572), was reportedly a convinced Arian, despite his marriage to a catholic Frankish princess. Most Lombards, however, still remained pagan, and those among their leaders who espoused Christian faith probably did so as much for political as for spiritual reasons. The influences of Christianity would certainly expand among them in the years ahead, but the evidence suggests that pagan religion continued to be very much a part of many Lombards' lives for several generations.

When the Lombards first invaded Italy in 568, they met with weak resistance, and within a few years they succeeded in capturing most of the north of the country. "Dukes" were given charge of conquered cities and regions, and similar arrangements were made in other annexed territories farther to the south at Spoleto and Benevento. Various attempts were made by Constantinople to play upon internecine feuding among the Lombards (who were led by these dukes rather than by a king from 574 to 584) and to undermine their power by bribery and by utilizing the Franks against them, but by the early 590s most of these efforts had come to nothing, mainly due to the unreliability of the Franks. The imperial governor in Ravenna had managed to hold on to some territories, notably the coastal areas, the islands, parts of southern and central Italy, the hinterland of Ravenna, southern Tuscany, and a bitterly contested corridor of land between Rome and Ravenna. The imperial control of Italy had, however, been destroyed once and for all. In the years ahead, a Lombard kingdom would be consolidated that would last for two centuries.

In a country already on its knees, the Lombard invasions in Italy brought further upheaval for Christians. As had been the case in other contexts of large-scale barbarian immigration, the newcomers were naturally suspicious of bishops as collaborators with the imperial authorities, and many church leaders fled, especially in the early years of the conquests, taking what they could of their churches' material resources with them. In some northern areas the disturbances were less severe, perhaps in part because the churches of Aquileia and Milan had recently broken off communion with Rome over the Three Chapters affair (see p. 327), and thus in the Lombards' eyes their hierarchies were already usefully estranged from the imperial regime. In far more cases, however, the patterns of the churches' lives were severely disrupted. The Lombard conquests brought plenty of suffering to Christians, with much bloodshed, looting, and devastation of property. Churches and monasteries were destroyed (Monte Cassino was among the casualties), ecclesiastical treasuries were plundered, and many ordinary believers were forced to flee.

When Christianity spread among the Lombard nobility, most professed Arian belief over against the official faith of the empire, but there also came to be growing catholic influences among Lombard leaders, especially following the marriage of a catholic princess from Bavaria, Theodelinda, first to the Lombard King Authari (584–590) and then to his successor Agilulf (590–616). Authari allegedly forbade catholic baptism among his people, but Agilulf consented to allow his son and

heir, Adaloald, to be baptized as a catholic, and there were signs of a
reasonable catholic presence at the Lombard court in the 590s. A number
of Lombard dukes also had catholic wives. No matter what professions
of faith existed formally among their leaders, though, the Lombards
seemed to many Christians to be sacrilegious, murdering criminals,
intent only on pursuing their own selfish ends regardless of the cost to
their innocent victims.

However natural the judgment, a somewhat more nuanced view was
required of one who had to deal with the Lombard hierarchies at close
quarters and was obliged to negotiate a relationship with the new regime
that would allow him to function as a Christian leader in these vastly
challenging times.

Gregory the Great

Gregory, traditionally known as "Gregory the Great," was born into
a distinguished and wealthy Roman family around 540. His family was
noted for its piety: his great-great-grandfather was Pope Felix III (483–
492), another pope, Agapetus (535–536), was also a relative, and three
of Gregory's aunts had taken vows of chastity and devoted themselves
to a life of domestic consecration.[5] After a good education, Gregory had
pursued a career in public service, and in 573 he had become prefect of
the city of Rome. Shortly afterwards he resigned his office to become
a monk, determined to detach himself from the cares of the world and
pursue a full-time vocation to the spiritual life. He disposed of his inherited wealth and turned his father's home on the Caelian hill in Rome
into an ascetic house; he also founded a number of other monastic
communities on family estates in Sicily.

After a period spent in ascetic retreat, Gregory was called in 579 to
serve the Roman church in a more prominent capacity. He was ordained
as a deacon by Pope Pelagius II and was sent as special representative
or *apocrisiarius* to the imperial court in Constantinople. Although this
role obviously placed him much more in the public domain once again
and brought him into contact with many prominent individuals in both
the political and ecclesiastical spheres, he continued to nurse his ascetic
ideals, and when he returned to Rome in 585 he reverted to a monastic
existence, pursuing the study of the Scriptures and spiritual matters,
albeit with some additional work in the service of his bishop. In 590,
however, Pelagius II died, and Gregory was chosen as his successor.

It was a dreadful time to assume office. Not only was there war with the Lombards; disease and famine were also rife (Pelagius had died of the plague), and heavy rains had caused the river Tiber to flood, causing considerable devastation. Civil government was in ruins, and the task of becoming bishop was a calling to far more than the leadership of a church, even of a church at the heart of its society; it was an obligation to take on the job of holding together a disintegrating social and economic world. Gregory, whose deepest affinities lay with the quest for contemplation and monastic seclusion, was inevitably reluctant to be thrust into such a task, and only agreed once it was clear that the emperor Maurice in Constantinople endorsed his appointment. While he awaited confirmation of the imperial sanction, however, he had already begun to tackle the urgent humanitarian needs of his city. Whether he liked it or not, there was to be no ambiguity about his new calling, back into the stormy seas of the temporal affairs from which his monastic life had been a cherished retreat.

Gregory's Pastoral Vision

The fourteen years of Gregory's pontificate until his death in 604 proved to be a period of remarkable achievement. Gregory showed himself to be a gifted and imaginative administrator, a dedicated pastor, and a committed evangelist and moral reformer. He set out his clerical vision in his *Pastoral Rule*, written during the first year of his office, a brief work that would be very widely read and admired in subsequent centuries. Many of its ideas were also anticipated in earlier work, especially in a set of moralizing expositions of the book of Job, based upon talks he had given while in Constantinople, and in a number of his letters.

Very much as a result of his own wrestlings with his calling, Gregory appreciated that the pastoral vocation was a commission to both an active and a contemplative life. Both of these dimensions he traced in the life of Christ, who combined an immense dedication to prayer and meditation with a great commitment to the practical needs of those around him. They were also witnessed eloquently in the apostle Paul, who could range in a single epistle from sublime heights of spiritual insight to the mundane realities of the daily conduct of his addressees.

Gregory recognized that the need to attend to everyday demands could seem like a distraction from a higher life of contemplation, but he saw it as the task of the faithful minister to serve the church as a body and not just to cultivate a personal or private spirituality. At the same time, the whole range of practical obligations—whether in preaching, teaching, or showing material care—was for him vitally nourished and given proper shape by the pursuit of inner holiness. "The art to end all arts," he wrote, "is the governing of souls."[6] For Gregory, this supreme task called for a dynamic fusion of the public and the private, the outward and the inward aspects of spiritual devotion.

Administrator and Politician

Gregory's own immediate duties were certainly practical as well as spiritual: he had to feed and care for a needy populace in a time of social turmoil and military danger. His church was a place where the hungry were fed, the sick received treatment, the victims of war were given charity, and the destitute were shown hospitality—though dishonest suppliants were resisted with a firm hand. He also had to act as a defender against the Lombards' assaults. His natural instinct was to evangelize the invaders, in the conviction that conversion would dissuade them from their destructive ways, but it was also necessary to stand against them where the military peril was immediate.

Between 592 and 594, first under Duke Ariulf of Spoleto and then under King Agilulf, the Lombards brought the combat virtually to the gates of Rome. When it became clear that little or no help was forthcoming from Ravenna, Gregory resorted to his own means of dealing with the crisis, organizing his own defenses and engaging in negotiations with the enemy. He successfully concluded a truce with Ariulf, but when this was subsequently broken by the exarch in Ravenna and Agilulf descended on Rome and besieged it, Gregory reached his own terms with the king, at the price of a large quantity of gold.

Gregory's arrangements were highly controversial with the emperor, who thought he had acted like a fool in negotiating with the barbarians. But faced with the official government's indifference to the plight of innocent people, Gregory had been left to assume the responsibilities of a civil protector, and it is clear that significant hardship and suffering were alleviated by his actions. The lifting of the siege of Rome did not in itself produce lasting peace with the Lombards, as Gregory hoped it might, and he was soon embroiled in further negotiations, this time as an intermediary between the imperial authorities and the Lombard court. These negotiations were long and uneasy, and Gregory's behavior attracted much ill-will in Ravenna, but he was able to build up a positive relationship with Queen Theodelinda and use other contacts to further his aims.

Over the years Gregory acted as a de facto protagonist in the maelstrom of Italian political life. A natural patriot, he discharged these responsibilities with considerable aplomb, issuing orders with the expectation that they would be fulfilled and using his skills of organization, diplomacy, and patronage to secure the best terms he could for his church and his country. The more the old West had fragmented and the more it had become clear that the representatives of the East in Ravenna were either culturally ill-equipped or politically impotent to deal with the new order, the more it fell to the papacy to assume the role of social linchpin and guarantor of at least some kind of continuity. If church and state were, as Gregory believed, interdependent for their well-being, the assumption of such a role by the bishop of Rome could be seen as simply another expression of the convergence of public and private spheres; such were, he might reason, the responsibilities to be shouldered by the representative of the church's leading see.

The church of Rome was by this time easily the largest landowner in Italy and Sicily, and it possessed extensive holdings elsewhere too, in North Africa, Gaul, Corsica and Sardinia, and Dalmatia. The church's estates were its investment portfolio, and it was very important to maximize their revenue in order to fund the structural and charitable requirements of the ecclesiastical machine. Gregory overhauled the vast structures for administering the system and took a very close personal interest in its efficiency and accountability. He spent little money on building new churches in Rome but gave very large sums to welfare programs. As well as sustaining its own significant bodies of clergy, monks, and nuns, his church paid for grain for general distribution among the populace in times of serious shortage, fed and looked after the vulnerable, ransomed prisoners, and sent impromptu donations to a range of causes. In an age when public finances were regularly crippled, Gregory also often advanced subsidies and loans to the authorities for needs such as soldiers' pay, and as his actions with the Lombards showed, he was not above using the church's funds to bribe enemies in the interests of peace.

Church Business

Over 850 of Gregory's letters are extant, collected in his *Register* of correspondence. This must be only a small part of his overall output, and it is quite possible that he and his immediate staff issued as many as twenty thousand epistles over the course of his pontificate. Gregory corresponded with rulers, civil officials, and ecclesiastical leaders all over the West. A large proportion of his extant letters is made up of "rescripts," or rulings in response to requests from officials, and a significant number relate to administrative matters. The main objects of his attention were naturally the churches within his own metropolitan province in Italy, but through his wide-ranging contacts with other churchmen and the extensive network of "rectors" who oversaw his papal estates, Gregory stayed well-informed on the affairs of churches much farther afield.

Gregory expected these "rectors" to act as his regional representatives as well as his fiscal managers, and although their responsibilities varied widely according to circumstances they were often granted significant powers to ensure that local clergy carried out their duties and the will of Rome in matters of procedure was not thwarted. Through their agencies and through direct injunctions to bishops and metropolitans Gregory made sure that preferred candidates were appointed to clerical and monastic positions and discipline was carried out in accordance with his wishes. Such extensive impositions of Rome's authority sometimes proved controversial among regional officials who felt that their own prerogatives were being undermined. This was especially true where Gregory's ideas about clerical standards were stricter than those favored in the local situations, as they not infrequently were.

Gregory particularly denounced the evil of simony, or the practice of ordaining those who offered gifts or favors in return for their elevation (see p. 156). This behavior had been forbidden by various church councils, but it remained a widespread problem, especially in an age of royal patronage. Gregory had no objections to kings such as the Merovingian rulers showing favor to bishops, but he was sharply critical of any suspicion of open corruption in such relationships, or of laymen being elevated to clerical posts because of their political affiliations, and he had some blunt things to say to the Gallic churches in particular in this connection. He strongly encouraged reforming measures to root out such habits.

Relations with the East

Gregory's relations with Constantinople were decidedly delicate. He of course knew the workings of the system in the capital from his previous years there as an ambassador of his church, but he was never at ease with the culture of the East. He professed to have known no Greek, and although his claims occur in a context where he is denying responsibility for works circulating in Greek under his name and may not be entirely reliable, it does seem that he had never been comfortable with the fashions of Constantinople. For much of his time in the East he had been attached to a small circle of Latin-speaking associates.

As pope, Gregory expressed loyal and courteous deference to the emperor, despite Constantinople's failure to do much to help in Italy's military crisis. With his ecclesiastical counterpart in the Eastern capital, however, his dealings were marked by thinly disguised suspicion. The familiar tensions between the old Rome and the new were by now of very long standing and had been made considerably worse by the schism of a century earlier (see pp. 220–22, 224–25). They were still all too apparent in reactions to ostensibly quite small matters. The title "ecumenical patriarch" had been used in Constantinople since at least the time of Patriarch John II (518–520), and it had evidently become customary among his successors. It became a bone of contention for Rome in the late 580s, and a few years later Gregory protested furiously that its continuing use was an unacceptable sign of pride on the part of his episcopal brother. Implicitly, he saw it as an attempt to usurp the status of the bishop of Rome. Despite an attempt to whip up wider ecclesiastical opposition to the title, Gregory's campaign was largely a failure, and the appellation continued to be used and accepted in the East.

Gregory resented any gesture that he saw as an encroachment on the effective jurisdiction of Rome over the church universal. By insisting on the supreme authority of the Roman pontiff, Gregory was reinforcing the kinds of papal claims that had been proffered by the bishops of Rome from at least Damasus onward and intensified under Leo I (440–461) and Gelasius I (492–496) in the fifth century.[7] Gregory's vision of his own office marked the decisive turn toward the comprehensive claims of the medieval papacy, and the ways in which he viewed Constantinople reflect the degree to which the churches of the West and the East had moved farther and farther apart under the differing cultural influences of Rome and Byzantium. At the same time, Gregory's sense of the unity of the catholic church, and of Rome's centrality within that tradition, was sufficiently pragmatic to grant that there could be quite widespread diversity of liturgical practice and procedural process. The oneness of the church was to be located in its shared commitment to the authentic Christ whom it served and presented to the world, not in a forced pattern of uniformity on every matter of behavior.

Influences of Asceticism

As the first bishop of Rome to have been a monk, all of Gregory's activity was shaped in one way or another by his ideals of the church as a community led by those with an obligation to practice holiness. He damaged his health through his personal austerities, and he took extremely seriously the need for servants of Christ to renounce the flesh. He pressed the requirement of celibacy on junior deacons as well as on men in senior orders and in various ways linked the ascetic duties of clergy with those of monks, partly under the influence of the writings of John Cassian and Augustine, to both of whom he remained much indebted. Gregory was also very strongly influenced by Benedict in particular, and although his own prescriptions on the monastic life were not a straightforward repetition of Benedict's he contributed to the later popularity of the Benedictine pattern by his rich praise of Benedict's example and his achievements as a holy man.

Yet alongside this prizing of the achievements of a spiritual elite, Gregory evinced a deep concern to affirm and represent the piety of ordinary believers both in his preaching and in his advocacy of popular expressions of devotion. He was well aware of the evocative power of the cult of the martyrs and of the veneration of sacred relics among Christians of widely differing social classes, and in a society where so many remained illiterate and unable to read the Scriptures for themselves, he vigorously defended the use of visual aids and images in worship. He was also keen to identify recent and contemporary evidences of spiritual power and to trace meaningful emblems of sanctity amid the secular insecurity and pressures of his own time.

His *Dialogues*, written in the early 590s, contain a collection of miracles and prodigies associated with Italian holy men and women, presented as signs of the times.[8] Gregory recognized that a society radically changed by the influx of new peoples needed to be reached in ways that were accessible to everyday imagination, and though many of his stories of spiritual wonder-working sound outlandish and incredible to modern ears they reflect his concern to interpret the circumstances in which he ministered. Although Gregory was tempted to think that the age of miracles was past, he was encouraged to believe that the richness of saintly wonders still to be found even in the Italy of the Lombards was evidence that God had not abandoned his people.

Other Horizons: Spain and Beyond

One of the most far-reaching of Gregory's influences was his concern for mission. It was a natural compulsion. As Gregory looked out from Rome, he could see striking developments and significant opportunities. The Franks, whose kingdom extended over most of Gaul, were already converts to catholicism, and whatever real problems existed in the fulfillment of the church's responsibilities in their society it seemed clear that the orthodox faith there was not in danger of being eclipsed. Reforms were certainly necessary, and Gregory engaged in much correspondence from the late 590s onward with both bishops and royalty to urge that these were carried through, but in his mind Gaul had already been won over to the true faith.

Farther West, quite remarkable things had happened in Spain. Under the Visigothic King Leovigild (569–586), the country had been almost entirely united into a single kingdom, bringing together the divided territories of the north and the south and at last incorporating the realm of the Sueves. In 587, Leovigild's son and successor, Reccared (586–601) had been converted to catholicism, and in 589 a great council of Spanish bishops, nobles, and royalty had gathered at Toledo to affirm the official renunciation of Arianism in the kingdom.

The new creed appears to have been accepted in Spain with very little resistance, and Gregory rejoiced to hear of its progress from his friend Leander, bishop of Seville, whose acquaintance he had made in Constantinople. Christianity in Visigothic Spain in the seventh century would become a remarkably unified and vibrant force, thanks not least to the efforts of its greatest representative, Leander's brother and successor in Seville, Isidore (ca. 560–636), who proved to be the outstanding scholar, educator, and ecclesiastical organizer of his age in the West, with an immense influence upon the later medieval world. Isidore did not become bishop of Seville until about 600, and thus his achievements mostly postdate Gregory's time, but the situation of the churches in Spain was already starting to look a good deal different by the 590s.

Thus, although Gregory recognized various problems in the Western churches—including what he took to be a revival of Donatism in North Africa—and while many of the Lombards in Italy proved painfully resistant to change (in some Lombard cities such as Pavia, there were two bishops, one catholic and one Arian), he could also see many signs of encouragement in the strengthening of the catholic faith in the West. Despite all that had happened in the centuries of revolution wrought by the barbarian invaders, the gospel had advanced, and peoples who had previously been outside the Roman Empire or converts to a false version of the truth had—at least nominally—been brought within the realm of orthodox Christianity.

But there was also another context to which Gregory looked, simultaneously with his interest in Europe and North Africa. That context was a place that has not yet received much attention in this book—Britain, and in particular the part of it that we call England. It is to the intriguing story of early Christianity not just in England but in the disparate environments of the British Isles as a whole that we turn in our remaining chapters.

13

BRITAIN AND IRELAND: THE FIRST PHASE

Roman Britain

Britain as we think of it today did not exist as a geopolitical entity in the early Christian period. *Britannia* was a Roman province from around A.D. 43 to 410, but to a Roman of the late first century or beyond this province consisted roughly of the equivalent of modern-day England and Wales plus a shifting fringe in southern Scotland. None of these modern names—England, Wales, or Scotland—existed as the designation of a national territory in the manner that it does today. What we think of as England and Wales had from the last quarter of the first century onward been a single imperial region, and the names "England" and "Wales" had yet to be conceived. The *Scotti* or "Scots" lived in Ireland, and much of the later kingdom of Scotland from the Forth-Clyde line northward was inhabited by the tribes of the Caledonians and other Highland peoples, known from the late third century as the "Picts."

In the later first century the Romans penetrated quite far into the northeast of what we call Scotland, and in the 140s they built a turf wall (the Antonine Wall) across the Forth-Clyde isthmus to mark the northern frontier of their domain, but from the later second century onward the intended boundary of the empire lay along Hadrian's Wall, the great stone wall erected in the 120s from the Tyne to the Solway Firth.[1] Some further campaigning took place in Scotland in the early third century, and Roman armies again reached the northeast, but Roman Britain never did include the Highlands and Islands, and Lowland Scotland also received no long-term Roman settlement.

Britain was an asset-rich island and a major supplier of grain and mineral resources to the Romans, but the degree to which its disparate regions were affected by Roman civilization varied significantly. The greatest concentrations of Roman influence lay in the south, especially the southeast. There the greatest natural prizes had been identified, and the forces of conquest had been least impeded in their business. Prosperous Roman towns grew up with all the usual evidences of Roman culture, art, and architecture—temples, baths, aqueducts, shops, schools, spacious houses, and amphitheaters. The countryside in these regions was also dotted with Roman villas, some of which were very elaborate farm complexes with magnificent properties; by the early fourth century, when the villa-economy was at its height, there were many hundreds of these estates all over the most fertile southern parts of the country.

In other areas, in the rougher and poorer regions of the Welsh mountains, the Pennines, and the moorlands of Devon and Cornwall, the nature of the Roman presence was dominated by military necessities, and the systems of roads, garrison towns, forts, and camps reflected the demands of keeping the peace. These regions lacked the more prosperous and politically advanced nobility of the lowlands, and for many of their peoples warmongering was a way of life. Their tribes caused plenty of trouble for the Romans with their sporadic uprisings and outbreaks of guerilla warfare.

To people in the Mediterranean Roman world, Britain lay at the ends of the earth, and to be stationed in its dreary upland regions in particular, charged with keeping control of the unruly natives and warding off the attacks of the barbarians from the north and from Ireland, was a thoroughly unpopular posting. The degree to which the Romans considered it worthwhile to devote resources to preserving their hold on areas such as southern Scotland depended very much on military, political, and economic exigencies elsewhere, and it was a combination of such pressures in other areas of the empire as well as local problems that eventually led to the decline in Roman commitment to Britain as a whole in the early fifth century.

Christian Origins and Development

Compared with the situation in many other parts of the Roman world, the story of early Christianity in Britain remains remarkably obscure. Most of our primary sources for the history of the churches in the East, Europe, and Africa show no knowledge of the situation this far north, and even archaeology, which so often yields crucial information not available in literary resources, in this case gives us little further access to the picture. Overall, we have very little knowledge of the impact of the Christian faith in Britain prior to the fourth century.

Various later legends make connections between early Christian figures and Britain, most famously an association of Joseph of Arimathea with the church of Glastonbury in Somerset, but these are all pious fictions. Tertullian, writing around 200, and Origen, about forty years later,[2] both speak of the faith as extending as far as the barbarians of Britain in their times. We have no means of knowing whether these were well-founded claims or just exaggerated rumors, intended to illustrate how true the gospel was and how far-reaching its impact—it had brought peace even to the savage tribes of these far-flung islands. Perhaps the gospel did reach British shores quite early on; perhaps it came unusually late. We cannot say one way or the other—though it is not clear that Tertullian's testimony that Christianity was already present in Britain by the late early third century should necessarily be discounted.

Whenever the story of Christ arrived, it was most likely through the agencies of merchants, soldiers, or travelers, or it may have been carried by Britons themselves who came in contact with the new faith while overseas. The Celtic-speaking peoples of Britain had their own roots somewhere in Continental Europe; Celtic cultures of one kind or another occupied very significant swaths of European territory, and there had been centuries of contacts between Britain and the wider world before the Romans first arrived in force in the middle of the first century B.C. The links of trade and travel naturally intensified under the imperial system, and there was plenty of traffic by the British as well as by their conquerors. As was so often the case in the spread of Christianity, the most important dissemination of the faith is likely to have come not from the work of just one or two primary figures but from the witness of ordinary individuals talking about their experience of conversion and testifying to its attractions by the quality of their lives.

The earliest British martyr for whom we have any solid attestation is a soldier named Albanus (Alban), who was put to death at Verulamium (later known as St. Albans), most probably in the early third century, around 208–209, during the reign of Septimius Severus. Alban is said to have been converted while offering shelter to a Christian presbyter who was in flight from an outbreak of persecution. Amid the elaborate legends surrounding his suffering the actual circumstances are impossible to determine, but if it was the case that he was put to death during a time of particular harassment of Christians in Britain then the persecution was short-lived, for there is little evidence of such oppression in the third century.[3]

We know of just two other martyrs by name, Julius and Aaron, who were reportedly executed at Caerleon in Gwent (the site of a major Roman military presence since the 70s). These victims may have suffered in the same period as Alban or perhaps later, in the persecutions of Decius or Valerian, but we are aware of no other martyrs in Britain in the pre-Constantinian age. As was the case in Gaul, the Great Persecution appears to have had little or no serious effect in Britain, thanks to Constantius's lukewarm application of Diocletian's policy;[4] there may well have been some destruction of places of worship, but it is difficult to be sure.

Archaeological evidence for British Christianity prior to the fourth century is, on the whole, very slender. There are some possible indications of a Christian presence, but the data are ambiguous. The following inscription was discovered scratched on wall-plaster in a Roman house at Cirencester:

R O T A S
O P E R A
T E N E T
A R E P O
S A T O R

This seemingly nonsensical sequence of letters can just about be read as a Latin sentence, albeit an odd one ("Arepo the sower holds the wheels with care"). It is possible that it ought to be understood a different way, as a Christian cryptogram, drawn by a believer when his faith was illegal and perhaps under attack. The square possibly contains the opening words of the Lord's Prayer in Matthew's Gospel, *Pater noster*, "Our Father" (Matt. 6:9), surrounded by the letters A and O to represent the Greek *alpha* and *omega*, a biblical designation of the exalted Christ (Rev. 1:8; 21:6; 22:13). If this is so, the double use of the letter N implies that the words are to be arranged in the shape of a cross. Thus the stanza is perhaps to be read as follows:

```
                              A

                              P
                              A
                              T
                              E
                              R
          A  PATERNOSTER  O
                              O
                              S
                              T
                              E
                              R

                              O
```

Archaeologists have found "magic squares" of similar or identical types in a wide variety of places in the Roman Empire; the interpretation of them is much contested, and many scholars do not believe that they were necessarily Christian in origin. Complete skepticism about Christian associations is probably unwarranted, but even if such a symbol was adopted by Christians in some places, it is very difficult to establish that a given example has a definite Christian connection.[5] This is no less true of the Cirencester square. Its date is uncertain and may in fact lie as late as the fourth century. As a straightforward indication of an early Christian presence in Britain, it is therefore highly questionable. We cannot say categorically that the Cirencester square is *not* Christian, but nor can we say for certain that it *is*.

Even where we do have evidence of undoubtedly Christian activity, scholars are increasingly wary of drawing hasty conclusions about its chronological setting. A hoard of silver plate containing vessels used in Christian ritual was discovered at Water Newton in Cambridgeshire in 1975.[6] Some of the items have similarities with other plate from non-Christian contexts in the third century, but it is likelier overall that most if not all of the pieces originate in the fourth century. The vessels clearly come from a Christian shrine, and perhaps from a shrine located not far from where they were buried. It is possible that they point to the existence of a Christian community in or near Water Newton's ancestral settlement, the Roman town of Chesterton, in the later third century, but the artifacts themselves cannot be used to establish this beyond dispute, and it is in fact much more probable that they date from the fourth century.

The Fourth Century

The evidence for Christian belief and practice begins to become more extensive from the time of Constantine onward, though even then we know a lot less in the case of Britain than we do for many other regions. It was in Britain that Constantine was first acclaimed as Augustus, by his troops at York in July 306, and it was from Britain that he set off on the lengthy campaign that would ultimately see him enthroned as the first Christian emperor. Whether or not Constantine had any kind of association with Christian influences in Britain is a matter on which we have no information; the obvious signs of his journey towards Christian profession certainly all stem from later on. Nevertheless, the beginnings of the peace of the church that ensued under his leadership rendered the situation of believers in Britain no less than elsewhere quite different from any that had prevailed before.

From almost the earliest point at which Christianity became legal, we hear of church leaders from Britain, but very little is known about either the government or the liturgy of such British churches at this time. It is even possible that it is only from around Constantine's era that an organized system of episcopal oversight was formed in Britain, though the lack of evidence for such structures prior to this clearly cannot be assumed to indicate that they did not exist. Three British bishops together with a priest and a deacon attended the Synod of Arles in 314, summoned to deal with the first of the protests of the Donatists against the condemnation of their eponymous leader in Carthage. They came from London, York, and perhaps Lincoln (though Colchester remains an alternative possibility)—sees based in three of the four major provincial regions that the Romans had recently set up in Britain.

British bishops were probably also present among the ranks of the Western representatives at a number of the councils held amid the controversies over Arianism over the ensuing two generations. There was certainly a British presence at the Council of Ariminum in 359. We do not know how many British clergy came to the council, but we do know that three British bishops were unable to meet their traveling expenses and had to rely upon imperial funding in order to attend. This may perhaps suggest that at least some of the British churches were still relatively poor, though it is again dangerous to draw general inferences from an isolated piece of evidence.

The middle decades of the fourth century saw serious structural problems in Roman Britain, and there was much economic and social upheaval. Political turmoil erupted in the revolt of Magnus Magnentius (see p. 54), followed by vicious reprisals on those who were held (correctly or otherwise) to have supported him. There were also extremely serious barbarian attacks from the Picts and the Scots, who in the later 360s managed to penetrate well into the south of the country. Simultaneous raids took place on the east by Saxon pirates from across the North Sea, and the Romans faced further pressures from the Saxons and the Franks on the Continent. These concerted challenges overwhelmed Roman defensive resources. The commander of the northern frontier forces in Britain was overpowered, and one of his key generals was killed. Stability was restored under Count Theodosius, father of the future emperor Theodosius I, who took decisive action to clear the raiders out of Roman territory, repaired defensive installations and towns, and brought back some security and order to British life. But the prosperity and organization that had characterized much of Romano-British society over earlier generations had been irreparably damaged by the incursions, and the recovery that did take place was only partial and temporary.

As the towns and cities suffered amid the ravages of the raiders and the ensuing disruption of administration, trade, and agriculture, effective power, both politically and economically, shifted away from the traditional population centers toward the villa-estates of the countryside. It is likely that Christianity in Britain was already stronger among the most Romanized elements of society than it was in the populace as a whole, and there seems to have been a significant connection between the profession of Christian faith and the identification with Latin as opposed to indigenous British culture. There is some reason to believe that as the villas became increasingly important, so Christian practice also came to be located more and more on these estates as well as in the main centers. Some of the Christian proprietors of the villas may have been members of an established Romano-British gentry; others were perhaps wealthy immigrants from the Continent, especially from Gaul. Whatever their background, if it is right to suppose that the numbers of such people increased, then we may perhaps speculate that this had some positive effects upon the overall economic status of the church in Britain, but again it is hard to establish this directly.

We do still have many indications of fourth-century Christian ritual in town contexts through the archaeological evidence of church plate, baptismal fonts, and especially cemeteries, such as the very large number of Christian burials uncovered at Poundbury in Dorset. It is also clear that Christian practice was by no means confined to the rich or the representatives of obvious cultural sophistication. Overall, however, the

archaeological picture of British Christianity in this period does reveal
a relative absence of freestanding church buildings in towns and cities.[7] What we find, for the most part, are strong evidences of Christian
worship going on in other contexts, both in the large country houses
and in other, more humble settings in urban areas.

The owner of a villa at Lullingstone in Kent had rooms in his house
decorated with Christian murals, which included the common *Chi-Rho*
motif[8] and praying figures, and it is clear that these rooms were set
apart for Christian worship. Christian mosaics also survive from the
public rooms of other fine villas at Hinton St. Mary and at Frampton in
Dorset. It is plausible to suppose that the patrons of such treasures did
not simply practice their faith in private but also strongly encouraged or
enforced Christian observance among those who worked on their lands
and in their local areas more generally. Some probably had their own
clergy present on their estates. The importance of the villa-economy
declined in Britain in the later fourth century, but it is possible that for
the generation or so in which the system was at its height it did a little
to further the expansion of Christianity in the countryside.

The Endurance of Paganism

Alongside the signs of Christian practice, however, it is very clear
that paganism endured with remarkable tenacity in Britain, and as
always its influences remained strongest in rural areas, though they
were certainly not confined there. While some pagan shrines fell into
disuse in the first half of the fourth century and others were destroyed
either by Christians or in barbarian raids, a large number of temples
remained in use, despite imperial orders to close all shrines in the
340s and 350s, and many centers of pagan cults continued to flourish.
Even as traditional temples were being abandoned or put to different
purposes in some places, in others new ones were being built well into
the 360s and beyond.

Even where the archaeological data concerning Christian observance
are clear, there are also indications of competing religious influences
and lingering pagan symbolism. At Lullingstone villa, the same rich
Christian with his private household chapel had other murals that min-
gled Christian images with scenes from pagan mythology: the triumph
of Christ over the forces of evil was equated with the classical myth of
Bellerophon slaying the Chimera. Similar syntheses occur in other villa
mosaics. Explanations and assessments of their historical evolutions

vary, but it is at least noteworthy that the juxtaposition of Christian and pagan motifs can be found in a number of instances.

One particular rival to the spread of Christian faith was the powerful Eastern mystery cult of Mithras. Restricted to men only, this religious system had long attracted a strong following among military officers, merchants, and other similarly consequential members of society. Despite the imperial patronage of Christianity and official orders that all troops had to recite a prayer to "the supreme God," Mithraism remained the most popular religion among army officers. We have far stronger evidence of Mithraic worship among soldiers, particularly in the frontier regions of the north of England, than we do of Christian practice. While Mithraic shrines and images were sometimes subject to Christian vandalism, some of the destruction came from competitor cults or barbarian assaults, and pagans as well as Christians sometimes had to bury their treasures to prevent them being plundered by their enemies.

Even in the last quarter of the fourth century, paganism remained well entrenched. For almost half of the reign of the emperor Theodosius, when pagan religion was definitively proscribed (see pp. 112–14), Britain was outside of Theodosius's direct control, first under the usurper Maximus (383–388) and then during the revolt of Eugenius (392–394). Maximus, first acclaimed by his troops in Britain, was a strong sponsor of the Nicene cause who took action both against alleged heretics such as the Priscillianists (see pp. 116–18) and against temple sites, yet pagan practices continued during his regime. Eugenius was prepared to show open favor to religious traditionalists in Rome, and under the government that he administered with Arbogast paganism was again tolerated in the West. Even after Theodosius regained control of his empire, pagan beliefs continued to be widespread in Britain despite the legislation outlawing cultic practices, and a number of temples still received patronage and funding well into the fifth century. The persistence of paganism in military circles was fostered by Rome's increasing reliance on barbarian soldiers as confederate forces. Many of these troops continued to observe their own religious conventions even where they were supposedly fighting on behalf of an empire officially committed to a unitary Christian faith.

Although the example of Martin of Tours was admired in Britain, the country appears to have had no direct parallel to him. We know of no single leader making organized missionary efforts to evangelize the countryside directly and suppress its traditional religious practices. One of Martin's disciples, Victricius, bishop of Rouen (c. 330–407), undertook mission work along the Channel coast on the Gallic side and visited

Britain around the turn of the fourth and fifth centuries in order to deal with some kind of ecclesiastical dispute, but there is no evidence that the kind of general outreach work that went on in northern Gaul crossed over into Britain.

The Demise of Roman Britain

The early fifth century saw the winding down of Roman power in Britain. As Rome's political difficulties escalated elsewhere, there were moves to withdraw troops from Britain for much-needed service on the Continent, and by 409–410 direct Roman rule in the country had come to an end, as the Western empire started to disintegrate, Britain revolted from Roman authority, and Rome itself fell to the Goths. In 410 the emperor Honorius told the cities of Britain to look to their own defense. The move was a procedural expedient at a time of crisis, and its significance has often been exaggerated. It was not intended to signal a permanent severance of Britain from Roman power: the expectation was that Rome would resume control in due course, once the storm had passed.

In the event this did not happen, but there was no abrupt transition to a different order. Despite the disturbances caused by raids in both the south and the north, and some disruption to mercantile exchanges because of events in Europe and increased piracy around the coasts, there was no great destabilizing of overall economic prosperity, and for the most part life in Britain went on in a reasonably orderly fashion. The regional British leaders had to look after themselves against their invaders, and there was no longer any possibility of a centralized system of administration, but the influences of Roman culture remained strong for many years to come.

Some historians have attempted to argue that the putative spread of Christianity among an elite in Roman Britain may in the end have encouraged an attitude of political detachment among the most powerful classes and an indifference regarding the value of restoring Roman authority, but it is much too simple to suppose that the final demise of Roman power can be attributed in any primary sense to religious factors. Even so, the suspension of Britain's status as an imperial territory naturally served to heighten the significance of any doctrinal differences that existed between believers in Britain and their brothers and sisters who continued to live within the Roman system, however friable that system was itself becoming. One illustration of this can perhaps be found in the apparent effects of Pelagianism in Britain in the early fifth century.

Pelagianism in Britain

There appears to have been some significant sympathy in some quarters of the British church for the ideas of Pelagius, which caused such a storm in the Mediterranean world in the early fifth century (see pp. 179–90). Pelagius was probably British himself, and although he and his followers became controversial far from his native shores and there is no reason to suppose that his ideas were necessarily first generated in his homeland, his teaching found its way back to Britain quite early on. We do not know where or among what sorts of believers it gained a following, but if there were any similarities with other contexts it is likely to have found particular support among members of a prosperous class, who were attracted by its emphasis on serious moral effort as a hallmark of spiritual grace.

The evidence is frustratingly slight and a good deal less decisive than it has sometimes been claimed to be, so it is necessary to be cautious in speculating. We have tantalizing glimpses of the activities of a Pelagian bishop in Britain named Severianus, whose son Agricola was a leading figure in the late 420s, and of one Fastidius, also apparently a bishop around the 430s, who seems to have been won over to Pelagian views while visiting the Continent, but it is not known exactly where these figures were operating or what the real impact of their teaching was. Nevertheless, from the few clues we do possess a tentative picture can be constructed to suggest that Pelagianism came to be regarded by some on the Continent as a problem in Britain.

By the 420s Pelagianism had been expressly condemned by imperial decree, but such decrees no longer had any automatic validity in Britain, and there may well have been people in leadership roles in Britain who saw no reason to pay any attention to the denunciation of Pelagian theology one way or another. Some may have been sympathizers with Pelagian ideas themselves; others may have been non-Christians and simply indifferent to all such matters. At the same time, there were clearly others in Britain who favored something like an Augustinian catholicism and who saw it as important to remain in identifiable continuity with the Roman tradition as officially endorsed by a majority in the Western churches at large. Though again it must be stressed that we are obliged to speculate on the basis of slender and partly conflicting historical clues, it is possible that a group of Christians in southern Britain, perhaps a group based in an important center such as London, appealed for help from Europe in combating the influences of Pelagianism, either within their own church or over a wider area.

In 429, perhaps in response to such a request, Pope Celestine I sent a delegation to Britain led by the strongly Augustinian Germanus, bishop of Auxerre, and including at least one other churchman from Gaul, Lupus, bishop of Troyes. Germanus made commendable endeavors in preaching, teaching, and administering discipline, and his visit seems to have had some impact. He and his companions are said to have visited the shrine of Alban, where the martyr's cult was by this time well established. Pelagians tended to disapprove of the veneration of such shrines, and it is quite likely that the visitors intended to encourage the practice in order to score a point against their opponents. Nevertheless, it is clear that Germanus's mission encountered stiff opposition. Despite achievements that are reported to have included baptizing and leading a Romano-British army to victory in battle against Saxon and Pict invaders (triumph was allegedly won under the cry of "Alleluia"),[9] he remained unsuccessful in his primary objective of dispelling Pelagian sympathies.

We are heavily reliant for our information upon a hagiographical *Life* of Germanus, written in the second half of the fifth century, which in fact offers us relatively little hard detail on its hero's activities in Britain and must be used with some care as a witness. Nevertheless, it is safe to infer from what we are told that things certainly did not all go Germanus's way. According to the *Life*, Germanus was recalled for a second mission to Britain some years later, perhaps not long before his death in about 448. It is unclear if this was indeed the case, but even if the story of a second expedition is simply a hagiographical fiction, its inclusion may suggest an awareness on the part of the author[10] that Pelagianism was still an issue in the British church a good many years after the expedition of 429.

The suppression of Pelagianism may also have been on the mind of Celestine when he sent another bishop to the British Isles in 431. This time, however, the destination was not Britain, but Ireland.

The Gospel in Ireland

Ireland never had been part of the Roman Empire. Some plans had been entertained by the great Roman governor Agricola (77–83) for an invasion of the island in the early 80s, but these had yielded only a brief exploratory assault before resources had to be diverted elsewhere, and to the Romans *Hibernia* had remained in principle just another barbarian realm beyond the boundaries of the civilized world, its otherness

Significant sites in the history of early Christianity in Britain and Ireland.

reinforced by its physical separation from the officially pacified territory of *Britannia*.

It would be quite wrong, however, to think of Ireland as a place cut off or unaffected by much wider influences. The early Irish were extensive traders, raiders, and plunderers over a very large area, and they had many contacts, peaceful and otherwise, with Continental Europe and beyond. There is plenty of evidence of widespread commerce between Ireland and the Roman world, and Roman customs had an impact upon

Irish burial customs and other aspects of social and religious culture. Ireland received visitors from the Roman Empire, and some Irish fighters probably served as mercenaries or auxiliary troops on behalf of Rome. From the end of the third century onward there were also established colonies of *Scotti* along the western seaboard of Britain, in what became Cornwall and Wales and farther to the north, in the future Scotland. Ireland may have remained a prehistoric iron age society for far longer than anywhere else in western Europe, but it was by no means a country untouched by other cultural forces.

Though the origins of the gospel in Ireland are as obscure as they are in Britain, and for all we know the name of Christ may even have been heard there earlier than it was in Britain, it is once again probable that the faith first arrived through trading contacts. Britain, Gaul, and Spain were the likeliest sources. Some of the people captured in Irish raids in Britain and Western Europe and transported to Ireland as slaves were almost certainly Christians. Others were uprooted in the opposite direction by British warlords, and perhaps there were among them some who were converted and who at some stage took their new faith back to Ireland. The cultural exchanges in areas surrounding Irish settlements on the British mainland must equally have included religious as well as other influences. In addition, there were probably also groups of Roman Britons living in Ireland, engaged in commercial activities and the business of providing sailing links between the two countries, and they too are likely to have included Christians.

Certainly there were already Christian believers in Ireland by the late fourth and early fifth centuries, and their numbers may have been increased by refugees from the barbarian invasions in Gaul. It is clear that the object of the mission initiated by Celestine in 431 was not so much the conversion of pagans as the consolidation of an existing work. Although we continue to rely on only a possible as opposed to a confident appraisal of the extent of Pelagian influence in Britain, if it is right to suppose that Pelagianism was indeed an issue in at least parts of the British church, then it is conceivable that some of its effects may have traveled across the sea to Ireland. A key part of Celestine's purpose may have been to root them out and to bring the Irish Christians into line with the orthodox Roman position.

Palladius, a deacon who seems to have been influential in arranging the sending of Germanus to Britain, was commissioned to be a leader to an existing constituency of Irish believers. Palladius is said to have established churches in Leinster, but if the challenging of Pelagianism was part of his orders we do not know how successful he was in this task. In any event, his episcopal ministry was short, for he died not long into his work. His activities were continued by a number of others from Britain, but whatever achievements were associated with their efforts they were soon to be totally eclipsed by the work of another Christian worker in Ireland—Patricius, better known as St. Patrick, the so-called "apostle of the Irish."

Patrick

Just about everything to do with Patrick is disputed in historical terms, and the various accounts of his life and ministry are highly contested and overlaid with many legendary accretions. Even the dates of his birth and death are uncertain. Most of what we do know about him must be pieced together from his few extant authentic writings, and even then there are numerous difficult questions.

We know that Patrick was born in Britain, probably in the northwest, the son of a Romano-British decurion (a minor local government official) and landowner. His father was a deacon of the church and his grandfather a priest. In his midteens Patrick was captured in a raid by Irish invaders and taken to Ireland, where he worked in captivity for a period of around six years as a herdsman, perhaps on the Atlantic coast of County Mayo. It is not entirely clear whether he was yet a Christian at the time of his abduction, or whether he had professed faith but had still not been baptized (he himself speaks of having been as yet "ignorant of the true God"), but certainly during his time as a captive he developed deep Christian convictions. At length he escaped from his captors and returned to Britain, where some time later he experienced a vision in which he felt called to go back to Ireland as a preacher of the gospel. After some kind of training and ordination, he progressed to the rank of bishop and returned to Ireland. The conventional year for his arrival in the island is 432, but this date is almost certainly just a calculated guess made by medieval writers, not a definite point of reference.

Most of Patrick's ministry, which seems to have extended over almost a thirty-year period, took place in the northern part of Ireland, in Ulster and north Connaught, and he traveled extensively in regions that were, to the Roman mind, on the outer edges of the known world. If Palladius had a responsibility for the correction of Pelagianism, this was not Patrick's preoccupation. His priorities lay in primary evangelism—in preaching, baptizing, and nurturing new converts to Christ. He made efforts to spread the gospel through the tribal kings and their families in particular, and as his message met with success he received from them in turn significant tokens of their wealth in the interests of his cause. He is said to have baptized thousands of converts and by his displays of spiritual power to have significantly dented the authority of the druids and their magical powers in the popular consciousness of the Irish.

As we can see from his *Confession*, the meditative account of his spiritual pilgrimage that he wrote in his later years, Patrick was himself conscious of being an alien and a stranger among the Irish, taking his gospel, at some personal cost, to those who dwelt at the ends of the earth, and thus fulfilling the commission of the risen Christ that his followers must be witnesses to all nations. Like many of his fellow evangelists in rural Gaul and elsewhere, Patrick almost certainly saw his mission as spreading not only the truth of the Christian faith but also the civilizing influences of Roman culture to barbarian people. Yet his written Latin—one of the vital elements of that culture—was in fact quite crude and colloquial, and he was criticized for his meager education and his rustic style. Patrick was censured by clergy in Britain as a maverick and an extremist who profited personally from his success in persuading the highborn of Ireland to part with their money and jewels. To some of his contemporaries he seemed like a rough-and-ready upstart who had taken it upon himself to exploit the Irish for his own ends, and he had brought the British church into disrepute by his conduct. He also had his inevitable critics within Ireland. His *Confession* was designed in part to refute the charges of both kinds of detractors.

Modern evaluations of Patrick's intellectual gifts, at least, tend to be somewhat more positive than the judgments of these contemporaries. Patrick clearly possessed a deep knowledge of Scripture and a capacity for communicating successfully not only in Latin but also in the differing Celtic languages of Ireland and Britain. Though his written Latin is certainly far from classical, it perhaps evinces a greater degree of stylistic sophistication than was once supposed. Some recent work has suggested that Patrick's writing displays a subtle ability to organize words in suggestive patterns, and even if this evidence cannot be pressed too far it is true that his prose was not necessarily as rustic as has often been claimed. At the very least, if Patrick's written Latin is to be criticized in the light of classical paradigms, it is also worth remembering that his extant writings are the first significant pieces of Latin to survive from beyond the frontiers of the Roman world.

For all the Britishness of his background and the degree to which he is likely to have associated the expansion of his faith with the spread of Roman conceptions of civilization, it is apparent that Patrick did make some real efforts to enculturate his gospel in the patterns, practices, and values of ancient Irish life. Though he was sharply critical of many aspects of ancient Celtic religion, he also had an understanding of the spiritual traditions of those to whom he preached, and he was prepared to appeal to elements of their pagan past in order to earth his evangel in symbols and ideals with which his hearers could identify. Whether or not he ever actually referred to the shamrock as an emblem of the Trinity, as he is famously supposed to have done, his version of the catholic trinitarian faith was deliberately communicated in simple language.

Just as his doctrine may have represented something of a fusion of the international and the local, so too did his methods. His theology of grace stressed the incorporation of all believers into a universal ecclesial body and made reference to Christian practices elsewhere such as in Gaul, but Patrick did not shun local social structures as media for the transmission of his gospel. He was undoubtedly hard on those who carried over too much of their pre-Christian past, but his style of evangelism was manifestly not confrontational by some standards. It is striking that there are no recorded martyrdoms at all in the early expansion of Christianity in Ireland.[11]

Whatever his perceived shortcomings in some circles, Patrick made a significant impact in Ireland as a charismatic leader and spiritual exemplar. He was very willing to admit his personal unworthiness and his shortcomings, and he understood full well the dangers of making mistakes and being misunderstood in his efforts to spread his message. That message was also more than spiritual in its impact; Patrick was a dedicated promoter of peace in an age of piracy, devastation, and (as he knew from firsthand experience) a savage slave trade. When Coroticus, a western British warlord, raided Ulster and carried off prisoners who included Christians, Patrick wrote to his soldiers protesting against their cruelty, warning them of God's judgment upon evil and setting out the moral obligations incumbent upon those who professed Christian faith. His letter conveyed a sense of moral outrage at the ill-treatment of believers, but it also achieved other purposes as well, notably the instruction of new converts, who were given clear teaching on how they were to behave, and further self-defense on Patrick's part against those who objected to the legitimacy of his methods as a leader.

Tradition has it that Patrick established the episcopal see of Armagh, which he deliberately took as his base because of its proximity to the royal seat of the kings of Ulster. After the defeat of the Ulaid, the dominant dynasty in the north of Ireland, by the northern Uí Néill and their allies in the middle of the fifth century, Patrick is said to have transferred his headquarters to the new Ulaid capital east of the Bann, at what became Downpatrick, where he was eventually buried. These contentions are explicit in a *Life* of Patrick written by Muirchú, a priest of the church of Armagh in the later seventh century. The historical realities underlying them are, however, extremely difficult to determine, and we cannot say for certain whether the medieval association of the church of Armagh in particular with Patrick's name is an authentic claim or simply part of a later effort to establish Armagh as the premier see of the Irish church. Patrick undoubtedly saw himself as a bishop, but this does not necessarily mean that he set up a permanent center for his church or that he followed exactly the kind of diocesan system that applied in Britain or Gaul. He may have done this, but we cannot be sure.

Though later legends connecting Patrick with a monastic formation in Gaul are probably unreliable (they stem from confusions with Palladius), Patrick was certainly a great admirer of asceticism, and he exhorted his converts to pursue serious devotion to Christ. He took special pride in the fact that sons and daughters of pagan rulers were won over to a life of spiritual consecration, even though such commitment was often opposed by their families. It was in the generations after Patrick, though, that monasticism really took off in Ireland, as we shall see in due course.

The Political Landscape of Britain

We shall return to the story of Irish monasticism and its contribution to the history of Christianity both in the British Isles and farther afield in the next chapter. First, however, it is important to notice what was happening to the political landscape of Britain in the middle and later decades of the fifth century, in order to understand the church's position in this and subsequent generations. Around the approximate period of Patrick's established ministry in Ireland, and over the next generation or so, southern Britain was beginning to evolve into a much more obviously post-Roman society. Our knowledge of the process by which the changes took place is a lot less complete than we should like, but it is clear that the impetus came from the combined effects of invasions and the ways in which these were handled by the British leaders.

As we have seen, Roman Britain had been subject to repeated and sometimes serious pressure from barbarian incursions for generations, and in the late fourth and early fifth centuries there were ongoing problems on various fronts from the Picts, the Scots, and the Saxons. Traditionally these pressures had consisted of sporadic raids and opportunistic adventures, but from around the late 430s onward the invaders began to arrive in larger numbers, and there was an influx of Germanic forces in particular in the southeast. It is not entirely certain why this was so, but conventional wisdom has it that the Saxons were invited to Britain in greater numbers in order to assist the new leaders of Britain to deal with the difficulties of other attackers, especially the Picts and the Scots. A prominent southern British overlord called Vortigern is said to have invited two Saxon brothers, Hengest and Horsa, to the southeast to help with the defense of the country, but after a short while these Saxon leaders reneged on the alliance and staked a territorial claim of their own, resulting in the establishment of the kingdom of Kent.

This account is heavily invested in legend, and it is far from clear what the real historical circumstances were or what the actual status was of the figure known as Vortigern. We have no confident knowledge of how many invaders arrived from the Continent or of what their forms of organization were. Nonetheless, it is true that there had been a long-standing tradition in Roman times of using Germanic mercenaries against other peoples, and some of these allied soldiers and their relations had already come to be settled in areas of the southeast, so it is not implausible to assume that the Roman successor states might have continued with such a policy, resulting at some stage in a migration of those who preferred to pursue the possibilities of force rather than the more limited rewards of confederate status. Whatever the circumstances and scale of their arrival, though, it is clear that the newcomers soon made significant advances, and news of the rich pickings to be had in Britain must have traveled fast to the Continent, enticing other adventurers to follow where the first warriors had led.

However many they may have been, the invaders were no homogeneous group but an eclectic mixture of various Germanic and southern Scandinavian peoples, including not only Saxons but Jutes, Frisians, and especially Angles, whose roots lay in and around the equivalent of today's Schleswig-Holstein area of northern Germany. Before long these disparate groups had established themselves in the south and east and were placing the existing British population and its leadership in serious difficulties.

Many of the realities of these years lie buried beneath a mass of traditions and uncertain historical claims, and it is very hard to be sure about the details. However, we know enough from a combination of archaeological and limited literary evidence to say that the invaders began to establish a patchwork of territories characterized by their own distinctive traditions of language, kinship, governance, agriculture, essentially nonurban life, and pagan religion. Though there were some instances of peaceful integration with existing British peoples, much of the time the new settlers showed little concern to spare those whose land they were appropriating. The invasions were frequently violent and brutal, and there was much destruction of life and property and an enforced depopulation of conquered areas. If appeals were made by the British for further defensive assistance from the Continent, they went unheeded amid the chaos of other developments across the water.

There was some successful British resistance spearheaded by a number of native leaders, some of whom became famous military heroes. The most conspicuous success achieved by the British is said to have been won at a battle that took place at a place called *Mons Badonicus* or Mount Badon, which seems to have occurred around the year 500 in the area that would later be known as Wiltshire. The invaders were apparently quite heavily defeated, and their recovery and further advance was checked in a series of subsequent campaigns. It is approximately in these years that the fabled exploits of the British war-leader Arthur are to be placed. We know virtually nothing about the historical Arthur, but it seems likely that he was some kind of senior tribal chieftain or overlord who managed to galvanize some of the former provincial forces for the last time into challenging successfully the onslaught of the invaders.

In the end, however, the Germanic progress proved unstoppable. The Angles, Saxons, Jutes, and Frisians occupied not only the hinterland of the southeastern seaboard but areas well into the heart of central-southern Britain and right up the east of the country beyond the Humber. As time went on, some of the occupiers of these regions began to coalesce, either as a result of internecine struggles or through the formation of strategic federations, and a diverse series of Anglo-Saxon kingdoms evolved—the network of states with enduring names like Sussex, Wessex, East Anglia, Mercia, and Northumbria.[12] The early foundations of all of these territories are again mixed up in all kinds of folklore and traditional legends, and most of the story of the kingdoms' development lies outside the time-frame of this book, but already by the later sixth century the Anglo-Saxons had come to acquire permanent control of virtually half of Britain.

Their success drove the native British farther and farther to the west. The primary enclave was Wales, which developed kingdoms of its own such as Gwynedd, Dyfed, Powys, and Gwent. As far as the invaders were concerned, the inhabitants of these regions were *wealh*, "foreigners" (the origin of the name "Welsh"), who lived like peasants in wild, mountainous places—though ironically many of their forms of social organization were probably not so different from those of the Anglo-Saxons themselves. Another British zone lay in the kingdom of

Dumnonia, covering the later Cornwall, Devon, and Somerset. In the north there were British domains in Elmet, centered in the southwest of Yorkshire, Rheged, on the Solway Firth, and Strathclyde, with its capital at Dumbarton.[13]

British Christians in a Changed World

By the sixth century, the great majority of Christians in Britain were confined to these western and northern areas, while some others fled overseas to Brittany or Ireland. Some did remain in the Anglo-Saxon territories, but it is unlikely that their numbers were significant. Christians were perhaps not specially singled out for violent treatment by the invaders, but many inevitably experienced abuse, loss of property, and privation, and some were killed. Large numbers of churches lay in ruins, their assets plundered, their buildings left to decay. In the midst of the upheaval, there is little to suggest that the British clergy performed the kinds of roles that their peers fulfilled in the invasions in Gaul, acting as leaders of their communities in times of crisis. Flight and survival were valued over defiance and the risk of losing all.

Around the late 540s, in south Wales or southwestern England,[14] a learned Christian author named Gildas wrote a famous tract *On the Ruin and Conquest of Britain*. Gildas's purpose in writing, as his title suggests, is to denounce the evils of his times in no uncertain terms. He looks back on the era of Roman rule in Britain as a golden age of sound government and good order, blames the demise of this system on the moral delinquency and treachery of the British, and sees the coming of the Saxons as an indication of the folly of the British leaders and a judgment upon their wicked behavior. He bemoans the havoc caused by the marauding pagans who, invited to become confederates of the British, turned on their allies, laying waste to towns and killing without scruple. A period of peace had eventually ensued, but this, Gildas's own age, is marked by the disgraceful slavery of the British to their evil conquerors.

Gildas upbraids the lamentable condition of his society and the corruption of those in authority, both civil and religious. Church leaders are guilty of supporting the tyrants who administer the political regimes of post-Roman Britain. Gildas traces a simultaneous decline in the spiritual and moral qualities of the time and the demise of the civilizing influences of the study of Latin language and literature. The barbarians are God's scourge on an errant people, and only when the British repent of their transgressions and turn in obedience to God will there be any prospect of deliverance in the form of righteous leadership and a renewal of cultural as well as religious life.

Gildas's lament cannot be taken at face value; cleverly constructed though his work is and important though it remains as a historical asset from an age for which we have very limited textual resources, it contains too many inaccuracies, gaps, and mistaken judgments to be treated as a straightforward witness to the condition of Britain in the sixth century. The author's idealized view of the Roman past is naïve, and his moralizing explanation of the ruin of his country is obviously overdrawn and subjective; he offers his readers a sermon rather than a piece of history.

Even so, it can hardly be unreasonable to suppose that the changes wrought by the coming of the Saxons brought many new challenges for Christians in Britain. Even if a period of relative political stability had been realized after three generations or so of turmoil and Britain had begun to take on something of the new shape in which it would exist in an Anglo-Saxon as opposed to a Roman world, all can hardly have been well in the organizational, cultural, and spiritual life of the churches. Though we can only conjecture, it is indeed quite conceivable that the leadership of the churches was less than efficient and that standards of commitment were mixed. There is every likelihood that there was much uncertainty about how best to adapt the structures and the witness of the churches to this post-Roman scene, when the obvious landscape of Christianity in Britain had shrunk so considerably.

To what extent were Christians to continue to identify with Roman culture, and to what extent were they to cherish and expand upon their own regional traditions? What was to be the relationship between the churches of western and northern Britain and their counterparts on the Continent, where—despite all the multitude of profound changes that had affected European societies as well—there were still very obvious ties to Rome? What would it mean to spread the truth of the gospel and testify to the name of Christ in an environment in which powerful pagan kingdoms were all around, and where there were new temptations to compromise the moral integrity of Christian witness? In what ways was the faith to be lived, taught, and broadcast in this kind of world?

In the working out of answers to these and similar questions, many different forces contributed. However, one Christian tradition in particular, monasticism, would play an especially outstanding role, nourishing the spiritual life of the churches, fueling their missionary zeal, and rendering some of the Christians of Britain and Ireland among the most remarkable people of their times.

14

FROM CELTIC MONASTICISM TO THE EVANGELIZING OF THE ENGLISH

▼

Celtic Society

In the main centers of Christian concentration in Britain and Ireland in the late fifth and sixth centuries, the structures of society were different from those that had traditionally existed in the wider Roman world. In Ireland, in Wales, in the southwest, and in the north the political map consisted of independent tribal kingdoms, and power was organized primarily around local dynasties and family hierarchies. The landscape was overwhelmingly rural, and there was for the most part an absence of the kinds of administrative and economic centers that had been found over the centuries in imperial territories. While there were lingering evidences of the effects of Roman culture and other signs of contact with Roman influences, on the whole the Celtic heartlands of the West were distinctive in their social and political makeup.[1]

At the same time, Christianity in all of these areas was of course an imported phenomenon, which inevitably reflected in various ways the patterns and forms of larger Western traditions. The foundations of the

363

Irish church lay in a message that had traveled from the Roman world, and the Christians of Ireland had been subject to significant Roman influences over many years. An evangelist such as Patrick may have gone some way towards enculturating his teaching in the existing social conventions and religious ideas of the people he evangelized, but Patrick also regarded himself as the emissary of a gospel that was proclaimed in identifiably similar terms all over the world, and he was a representative of Roman culture to the Irish.

Christianity in Ireland, as we saw in the last chapter, did not develop in independence from beliefs, values, and practices also espoused by believers in other places. The same holds true for the nature of the faith in other Celtic areas such as Wales, Devon, and Cornwall. Indeed, since these latter regions had officially been part of the Roman Empire, there is every likelihood that the effects of Roman influences there were stronger still. Even if these territories had remained a lot less Romanized overall than more central parts of *Britannia*, they had been technically subsumed under the authority of the *pax Romana* and had thus been exposed in some measure to the forces of what we think of as mainstream Western Christianity.

Both of these realities—the sociocultural differentness of Celtic societies and the strong links between the faith professed by Christians in these contexts and their peers elsewhere—were significant for the shaping of spiritual ideals in Britain and Ireland in the sixth century. If the coming of the Saxons and the gradual emergence of their successor states obliged the believers in their western British enclaves to confront the demands of their times and to think about their spiritual obligations in an altered world, the ways in which some of these believers responded to the challenge naturally reflected the joint influences of their own social circumstances and of traditions overseas.

The most important product of this process—the evolution of Celtic monasticism—bore the imprint of both legacies. The monastic traditions that developed in the British Isles displayed the characteristics of their particular contexts, and the effects of these traditions were in turn naturally connected with regional conditions. At the same time, such monasticism certainly did not arise in a vacuum but was much affected by ideals and patterns from abroad.

The Growth of Monasticism in Ireland

The ways in which the gospel spread in Ireland bound the church there closely to existing social structures. Christianity had made significant inroads among the elite of Irish society, eliciting powerful (and, in the case of Patrick's mission, controversial) patronage of the church from tribal chieftains and their families. There were also strong encouragements to take spiritual discipline seriously, and one of the fruits of the work of evangelists such as Patrick lay in the adoption of ascetic ideals by members of these ruling classes.

As gifts of money, lands, and resources came to be handed over to the church for the cause of Christ's work, traditional patterns of kin and kingship favored the development of monastic foundations as significant institutions. Ireland's most prestigious monastic houses were based close to the traditional centers of tribal power, and the largest ones were settlements of some size. In a country where there were few major towns, monasteries formed a nucleus for significant communities of people and often owned large areas of land, some of which might be looked after by client-workers. Abbots came to function as territorial overlords, with guaranteed rights and responsibilities.

But while the growth of Irish monasticism was furthered by indigenous social patterns, the system also combined many elements from both eremitic and coenobitic traditions overseas, and its representatives were practitioners of an ascetic faith that had existed over several centuries in other contexts. The life of monks in many Irish monasteries was not very different from that of many zealous spiritual devotees elsewhere, and the faithful saw themselves as believers in essentially similar doctrines and ideals. The daily pattern typically consisted of a combination of prayer, manual work, and study, especially of the Scriptures and the church fathers. Monastic influences from Gaul in particular were strong, with writers such as John Cassian widely read, and ideas derived from these sources were deeply absorbed into Irish conceptions of the spiritual life. The details of the monks' existence varied, but regimes were deliberately austere: food was modest, fasting frequent, and poverty and simplicity of life mandatory. As elsewhere, the duties of giving hospitality to travelers and caring for the sick were taken seriously.

Many monasteries were of simple design—collections of small huts clustered around a central church. Buildings were usually constructed of wood or of wattle and daub; stone was for the most part used only where timber was unavailable. Stone of course is more durable, and it is the vestiges of the stone edifices that have survived into modern times. Beehive cells were a standard type of stone building. They were erected by a process of "corbelling," or projecting each layer of stones over the one below in an inward sequence, so that the edifice grew narrower as it rose. Communal monasteries often had their internal space symbolically divided into zones of varying degrees of sacredness, ranging from the sanctuary of the church through to areas in which manual work might go on or visitors might be housed; inmates would perform ritual gestures such as the sign of the cross as they passed from one area to another.

A good number of monasteries were established on island sites, such as Inishmore in the Aran Islands, and a number were in particularly isolated places, such as Skellig Michael off the coast of County Kerry, where detachment from worldly distractions and proximity to nature might facilitate spiritual devotion. Similar ideals often influenced the choice of locations in Britain and elsewhere in Europe, where islands both offshore and in lakes and rivers were regularly favored. Contemplation was seen as a very important aspect of the monastic life, and even communal foundations in less remote places typically contained hermitages or chapels to which monks could retreat for periods of solitary meditation.

Abbots and abbesses acted as overall spiritual directors of their houses, and they possessed absolute disciplinary authority. In Ireland clerical celibacy tended to be the exception rather than the rule, and it was not unusual for monastic leaders to be married. In accordance with Irish inheritance laws, it became routine for such leaders to bequeath their entitlements to their offspring, and thus important ecclesiastical offices and their entitlements were passed on from father to son. Monasteries with a common founder were often linked together in "families," bound by a common rule; individual houses tended to follow their own rules, though these often included some fairly generic features. The most famous founders attracted many disciples, and after their deaths their bases frequently became great centers of pilgrimage, with flourishing cults in their honor.

It would be quite wrong to suppose that the Irish church was ever primarily a monastic entity or to imagine that the prominence of the abbots meant that bishops and dioceses had little or no role. In some cases an abbot and a bishop would coexist in a monastery, each with different responsibilities; in others, the bishop's duties would be assumed by the abbot, but even in these instances episcopal obligations were not dismissed as irrelevant—they were explicitly absorbed into the monastic office. Disciplines such as penance, which was taken very seriously in Ireland, were commonly administered by both bishops and monastic leaders. The exercise of episcopal authority such as existed in Gaul or Italy was a lot less prominent in Ireland in the sixth century, but this does not mean that regular clerical structures were somehow displaced altogether. For all the importance of abbots and abbesses, the pastoral needs of the Irish church were served primarily by conventional means.

Ninian

Such a coexistence of a strong monastic tradition and an active episcopal authority was not confined to Ireland. At a date that is very difficult to pin down and that could lie either in the early fifth century or in the early sixth, among the Christians in Galloway was a leader called Nynia or Ninian.[2] Ninian is an elusive figure, and much about his life and work remains unclear. The great Anglo-Saxon scholar Bede (c. 673–735), whose *Ecclesiastical History* is the most important source for our knowledge of early medieval England, describes Ninian as a British bishop who had been trained in Rome. He is said to have built a stone church (as yet an unusual phenomenon in Britain) dedicated to Martin of Tours at a place called *Ad Candidam Casam*, "At the White House," where he was eventually buried.[3] Ninian's church and grave were at Whithorn, south of Wigtown, where modern archaeological excavations have yielded some impressive evidence of early Christian activity in Scotland.

Ninian became famous for an extensive mission that he is said to have undertaken to the north, among the Picts. The details of this work and its impact are very difficult to ascertain, and it is in fact likely that most of Ninian's work was confined to what we consider southern Scotland. If he did venture farther north, it was probably only to the most southerly representatives of the Picts, who lived south of the Forth, and it is possible that his work also got him embroiled in political troubles. Some traditional depictions of Ninian's achievements are undoubtedly overstated. In the twelfth century it was claimed by Ailred, abbot of the Cistercian monastic house at Rievaulx in Yorkshire, that Ninian organized an entire national church in Scotland, with a structure of bishops, presbyters, dioceses, and parishes. That claim is definitely false.

Another of Ailred's contentions is that Ninian was directly associated with Martin of Tours, and that he even visited Martin on his way back to Britain from Rome. There is no reason to doubt the possibility that Ninian went to Rome—such journeys came to be quite common for British churchmen—but the truth or falsehood of the story that he met with Martin depends on where he is to be located chronologically. If a later rather than an earlier setting is to be preferred for his episcopate, then the reported meeting with Martin is of course impossible.

Archaeological evidence suggests the presence of an organized church in Galloway in the later fifth century, and a church and monastery did exist at Whithorn from around that period. We cannot be sure, however, whether the foundations at Whithorn were first established by Ninian himself or whether they predate him. None of our literary sources actually claims that he was their founder, and the original power base of the church in Galloway may in fact have lain somewhere else, perhaps as far to the east as Carlisle. Those who favor a later date for Ninian argue that Whithorn was already an established monastic center prior to his time and that he himself may actually have trained there. If this is correct, his primary work later on as a bishop lay in consolidating the center's influence and building it up as a hub of pastoral oversight for an existing Christian community in Galloway.

We do not know whether Ninian himself dedicated his church to Martin or whether the association had only come to exist by Bede's time. By then a cult had already started to gather around the resting place of Ninian and the "many other saints" (as Bede describes them) who had come to lie beside him. In Bede's day, Whithorn was an important part of the English church, and it is quite possible that he was concerned to identify reasons for the antiquity of Ninian's foundation over against other strands of Christianity farther north. Martin was nevertheless the example *par excellence* of an ascetic missionary, and there is every reason to envisage an early idealization of him at Whithorn. It is quite possible that Ninian himself dedicated a new church building to Martin, even if the monastic community at Whithorn was not begun at Ninian's own initiative.

Whatever the ambiguities surrounding Ninian's work and the origins of the church at Whithorn, it is clear that the community there, as in other places, could embrace both a lively monastic tradition and an organized ecclesiastical authority. It is equally clear that regardless of precisely how this church evolved, it came to exercise a significant influence over monasticism farther afield. Whithorn was closer to Ireland than it was to most of Scotland, and a number of Irish monks in the sixth century were either trained there or visited its community, particularly those who operated in the northern half of Ireland. Celtic monasticism was no isolated force, but a network of closely related centers and figures. Not only did monks study or work for periods in different places; many also traveled extensively, preaching, teaching, organizing, and inspiring. The influences of spiritual traditions in one region spread to others, and ideas and practices were shared in widely diverse places.

Monasticism in Wales

In southern Wales, a region that, to judge from the recorded martyrdoms of Julius and Aaron (see p. 344), had been subject to Christian influences from a reasonably early date in the history of the British church, there were also several prominent exemplars of monasticism from the later fifth century onward. The most renowned was Illtyd or Illtud, who established a large monastery at Llantwit Major in the Vale of Glamorgan toward the end of the fifth century. According to later tradition, he was a native of Brittany who was converted to Christianity in Britain, but the details of his life are elusive. Other ascetics known to us from around the sixth century include Cadoc, founder of a monastery at Llancarfan; Dyfrig (Dubricius), whose name is associated with various locations, especially the see of Llandaff; Samson, who was ordained by Dyfrig and became abbot of an existing monastery on Caldey Island, off the coast near Tenby, before becoming bishop of Dol in Brittany; Padarn, who is associated especially with the founding of a monastery at Llanbadarn Fawr near Aberystwyth; and Teilo, who is said to have succeeded Dyfrig as bishop of Llandaff (though the origins of that see are more complex).

The most famous of the Welsh monastic leaders is of course David (Dewi), who became celebrated as the patron saint of Wales. His dates are unclear, but he is undoubtedly to be placed in the second half of the sixth century. According to tradition, David was a member of a leading noble family who abandoned his privileged life to devote himself to a spiritual calling, first as a priest and then as a monk. His name is attached to numerous monastic sites, and above all to the origins of the church in Mynyw (Menevia), subsequently St. Davids, where he is said to have established a monastery with a strict ascetic regime and served as the first bishop of this see. David was plainly a remarkable figure, a gifted organizer, and an impressive man of faith, but amid the many legends about his life very little can be established with any certainty, and some of the feats attributed to him, such as the story that he made a pilgrimage to Jerusalem and was consecrated as archbishop of Wales by the patriarch of the holy city, are undoubtedly false.

Other monastic pioneers were active farther north in Wales, such as Deiniol, who is honored as the founder of the large monastery of Bangor-is-coed near Wrexham and the first bishop of Bangor; Cybi, who is commemorated at Caergybi (Holyhead) and at other sites on or near the coast; and Seiriol, who is connected with other foundations on the island of Anglesey. Whether we are looking at the south or the north, our knowledge of the careers of all of these saints depends upon later medieval *Lives*, which must be read with a good deal of caution as historical witnesses. It is likely that the degrees of asceticism that such monastic leaders practiced and the ways in which they operated as evangelists and organizers varied considerably, and things were certainly not always as they are presented in the hagiographies.

Many of the most renowned figures were not settled ascetics, living a life of quiet detachment from the world, but busy evangelists, teachers, and spiritual directors who traveled widely in pursuit of their cause, not just within Wales but much farther afield. Leaders such as Samson were active not only in their own country but also in Ireland, Cornwall, and Brittany. They symbolized a monasticism that was both outward-looking and influential, and monastic expansion and the strengthening of diocesan territories often went hand in hand. Not surprisingly, there were well-established links with Ireland in particular, fostered by the settlements of Irish in southern Wales and the regular exchanges of trade and travel between the two regions, and many Irish monks in areas such as Leinster and Munster were trained in Welsh monasteries.

In Cornwall, the most famous saint, Petroc, who set up a monastic foundation at Padstow and lived for a time on Bodmin Moor, had Welsh connections, and he too studied for a period in Ireland. Other saints commemorated in Devon and Cornwall also had Welsh, Breton, and Irish associations, such as Paul Aurelian, a disciple of Illtyd who worked both in Cornwall and in Brittany, and Budoc, whose heroic exploits are also remembered on both sides of the English Channel.

Monks as Scholars

One of the most important functions of the larger monasteries, in Ireland especially, consisted in the furthering of education. Literacy lay at the heart of the ideal of religious devotion, and the learning of Latin was prized as a vital tool in the study of the Scriptures, for the Latin Bible was the primary subject of instruction. The Psalter in particular and portions of the Gospels were committed to heart. It became common for the royal households of Ireland to send their sons to monasteries for schooling, and a number of the major monastic houses, such as those at Clonard, Clonmacnois, and Clonfert, became notable centers of learning. There was a significant exchange of ideas and scholarly knowledge between Ireland, Gaul, and Spain in particular. Similar patterns evolved in a number of places in Wales and elsewhere, but monasticism in Ireland far outstripped its peers in Britain in the levels of resources and sophistication it enjoyed as a result of its political privileges.

As well as providing vital teaching in language and literature, the monks spent a good deal of their time making copies of the texts that they studied, and these came to include not only sacred and theological works but also classical authors. In later times the Irish monks in particular would become additionally famous for their lavish illustration of the books that they produced. In all of these ways, Christian scholars situated on the fringes of the officially civilized world performed a remarkable role in the preservation of a rich literary and artistic culture in Western Europe in the period between the demise of Rome and the High Middle Ages.

The Lives of the Saints

Gaining access to the real lives of the leading figures of Celtic monasticism is nevertheless extremely difficult. Much of what we have inherited about them is a dense mixture of hagiographical elaboration and local legend, and there are often substantial quantities of pagan as well as Christian tradition mixed in with the stories of their achievements. The protagonists are regularly said to have been of royal lineage, to have been set apart from their childhood, to have enjoyed uncanny degrees of attunement to the natural world, and to have possessed various miraculous powers. Certain aspects of some of these claims may perhaps have been true in individual cases, but the genre of saintly characterization tends so to apportion standard qualities and so to blend ideas from varying religious contexts that it is very hard to determine the boundaries of fact and fiction.

One of the most celebrated of Irish saints, Brigit, who generally ranks after Patrick as the most venerated of fifth- and sixth-century spiritual exemplars, may well have been genuinely associated with the founding of a monastery for men and women at Cill Dara (Kildare) in Leinster,[4] as tradition insists, but she is also conflated in various ways with the Celtic goddess of fertility and healing, Brig, and her fame is further blended with elements of the burgeoning medieval cult of the Virgin Mary. Some scholars have even questioned whether she existed at all.

St. Kevin, who set up a monastery in the valley of Glendalough in what is now County Wicklow, is much connected with Celtic ideals of the veneration of nature; one of the most common images depicts him tenderly holding a blackbird's nest while waiting for its eggs to hatch.

Similar stories about saintly affinities for birds, plants, and animals abound in the traditions of other leaders.

Brendan, abbot of Clonfert in County Galway, is said to have gone with a group of companions on an epic sea voyage lasting seven years, searching for the mythical Isles of the Blest. The story of his odyssey became very popular in later medieval times and was translated into many languages. The tale is a mishmash of many fantasies, though it is quite possible that it has some basis in a real journey. In the 1970s an expedition in a replica sixth-century Irish boat succeeded in crossing the Atlantic and reaching Newfoundland via the Hebrides, the Faeroe Islands, Iceland, and Greenland. Perhaps Brendan the Navigator did go on a missionary journey along the northwest of Scotland, and perhaps he made it as far as Iceland or even beyond. We are unlikely ever to know, however, for his exploits are obscured by the complexities of many mythical accretions.

With many of the heroes and heroines of monasticism, it is not even easy to identify firm connections with particular sites, for the fame of individual saints, coupled with the tendency of some abbots and abbesses to travel quite widely, meant that their names came to be linked with several different places. Finnian of Clonard, one of the giants of the scholarly monasticism that flourished in the Irish midlands in the 540s and whose example attracted numerous disciples, is to be distinguished from Finnian of Moville in County Down, who was probably educated at Whithorn, and both are to be differentiated from a later individual with a similar name, Findbarr, who came to be venerated in Cork. In later medieval practice it was very common to commemorate the honor of saints in place-names and church dedications, and some of the great names of the Celtic saints are attached to dozens of locations in widely divergent regions.

Columbanus and His Associates

At the monastery in Bangor in County Down, founded by the revered abbot Comgall in the 550s, there was a typically impressive fusion of learning and austerity. The most famous product of this house was Columbanus. A great scholar, steeped in the Scriptures and the church fathers and also well-read in classical authors, Columbanus was passionate about the importance of learning as a vital element in Christian devotion. After spending many years as a teacher at Bangor, in midlife he led a party of companions from Ireland to Gaul, which by this time was under

Merovingian control. He set up a monastery at Annegray in the Vosges mountains, on a former Roman site, converting a pagan temple into his church, and rapidly attracted a large number of local followers.

So powerful was the growth of this community that further monasteries were soon established in the region, at Luxeuil and then at Fontaines. These houses were governed by very strict rules, and the efforts of Columbanus and his associates to reinstate serious standards of discipline did much to revitalize the wider church in Burgundy in an age that had seen a good deal of spiritual decline. However, Columbanus also made himself deeply unpopular with both religious and secular authorities for his belligerent adherence to his own Irish traditions and for his condemnations of royal behavior, and around 610 he and his associates were forced to leave Gaul.

After managing to escape their decreed fate of being deported back to Ireland, they traveled for several years through the kingdom of Austrasia and worked their way southward through the part of Swabia that became modern Switzerland, before finally crossing the Alps into Italy. On the way they undertook missionary work and established a number of other monastic houses, but political events as well as a sense of pilgrimage drove them on. The most renowned of the monasteries that they set up was that of St. Gall in Swabia, which was overseen by one of Columbanus's disciples. Columbanus himself finally settled at Bobbio, a small town in the Apennines, where he established another monastery that soon became renowned as a center of piety and learning. It was there that he died in 615.

Columbanus's principles were shared by many other Irish monks who also traveled and worked overseas around the same time and over subsequent centuries. The ideal of *peregrinatio*, "pilgrimage," was a fundamental element in their faith. It was connected with conceptions of penitential self-discipline. To travel was not to go off on an interesting sightseeing tour or even to seek out particular holy places; it was to set out on a deliberate exile from the comforts and temptations of the familiar. The aim was not to see the world, but to renounce it morally. Such expeditions might take various forms, but pilgrimage abroad was regarded as a sign of special dedication, more eminent in spiritual terms than pilgrimage within Ireland itself.

By the later Middle Ages the influences of Celtic monastic culture would be felt in places as far away from Ireland as Eastern Europe and the South of Italy. Although our information about the activities of its representatives is invariably much more restricted than we should wish, there is no doubt that many of these figures performed a striking service

The Abbey of Iona as it exists today—a much more substantial building than the basic monastery (of timber, wattle and daub) first erected on the site in Columba's time. Illustration from author.

in diffusing the aims and aspirations of their style of monasticism over a very wide area of Europe and in combining precious elements of spirituality and scholarship from which later generations would greatly benefit. If the Irish monks themselves had inherited rich legacies of Christianity from Continental Europe, so they in turn came to share with Europe their own distinctive contributions to the Christian life.

Columba

The most famous of Irish missionary saints, however, took his pattern of monasticism not to Gaul and Italy but to somewhere much closer to home, and in circumstances that were much more directly connected with political developments. In 563, an Irish monk and a small group of followers (traditionally said to have been twelve in number) sailed from Ulster to the west coast of Scotland. We are not sure exactly where they first made landfall, but at length—perhaps in the same year, though perhaps some time later—they reached the shores of the tiny island off the coast of Mull that would later come to be known as Iona.[5] There they built a monastery and launched a work that was to have a profound impact on the subsequent history of Christianity both in Scotland and farther afield. Yet the circumstances in which they came to be on Iona and their leader's place in the wider story of the church in Scotland have been much misunderstood and unhelpfully romanticized over the centuries.

The monk who led the group was Columba (ca. 521–597). Possibly a native of Donegal,[6] he came from an important family that was a member of the northern branch of the Uí Néill ("descendants of Niall") dynasty, one of the chief lineages of Ireland. Columba's name, according to medieval tradition, was originally Criomhthann, and it was as a monastic that he acquired the Latin name *Columba*, "Dove." In Irish he became Colum Cille, "Dove of the Church," the name by which he is still more commonly known in Ireland. It seems that he was educated under Finnian of Clonard, the most prominent teacher of his day, and perhaps in a number of other monastic schools as well, and he was ordained as a presbyter. We know nothing for certain about his life between the completion of his training and his departure from Ireland in 563.

According to a famous *Life* of Columba by Adomnán, a distant kinsman of his who became abbot of Iona in the late seventh century, Columba left Ireland "choosing to be a pilgrim for Christ," according to standard ideals of monastic endeavor. However, Adomnán also hints that Columba had made some enemies among the leaders of the Irish church and had even been temporarily excommunicated for certain (allegedly minor) offenses. In addition, Adomnán's account mentions that Columba's departure took place about two years after a battle fought at a place called Cúl Dreimne, north of Sligo. This battle saw victory go to Columba's kinsmen, the northern Uí Néill, against the forces of the southern Uí Néill overlord and high king of Ireland, Diarmait mac Cerbaill, and the victory was later attributed to the prayers of Columba; others speculated that Columba had deliberately engineered the battle on account of differences with the household of Diarmait. Although Adomnán himself does not say so, legends later grew up that Columba's departure from Ireland was connected with the battle and that he went into exile either as a punishment or as a chosen penance for having caused the deaths of many warriors.

The historical realities are impenetrable, but it is certainly plausible that Columba would have supported his own side against the high king and that this entanglement in dynastic politics, perhaps together with some already strained relations with other churchmen, had compromised his reputation. Maybe he left Ireland partly in a bid to remove himself from these difficulties and to find a place where he might pursue a spiritual life in a more conducive environment. Whatever his motives, he arrived in Scotland as no minor itinerant but as a well-connected leader with strong political associations. In any event, he did not leave politics behind when he left Ireland, and it is in fact altogether probable that he ended up on Iona for strategic reasons.

At this time much of the area of what became Argyll was controlled not by the Picts but by Irish settlers (*Scotti*) from the area of the northeast of Ireland known as Dál Riata, and there were quite close connections between this Scottish Dál Riata and its related domain in Ireland. Scottish Dál Riata had steadily encroached on the territory of the Picts, but in the period prior to Columba's arrival the northern Picts had fought back significantly and reduced the Scottish power. In Ireland, meanwhile, the ascendancy of the Uí Néill was also challenging the Irish Dál Riata. To at least some in the Scottish Dál Riata, already suffering from the Pictish recovery, Columba's arrival in Scotland may not have been at all welcome, for it may well have seemed as if the Uí Néill were trying to establish a base of their own in or close to Dál Riata territory.

Columba undoubtedly played a prominent political role in Scotland. He carved out an influential place for himself within the Scottish Dál Riata and is reported to have been "given" the island of Iona by King Conall mac Comgaill. In 574 Columba consecrated Aedán mac Gabráin as Conall's successor and the following year accompanied him to a conference in Ireland, held at Druim Cett near Limavady, where negotiations took place concerning the responsibilities of the king of Dál Riata toward the high king of Ireland. One of the probable outcomes of the conference was that Aedán came to side more closely with the king of the northern Uí Néill. Columba exercised some influence over other political situations as well. He had a number of contacts with the Picts and paid one particularly important visit to Bruide, the powerful king of the northern Picts, in his fortress near Inverness, when he apparently persuaded Bruide sufficiently of his spiritual powers to obtain some kind of understanding on behalf of his kinsmen. Contrary to what was reported by Bede and others, there is no solid evidence that Columba converted either Bruide or his men. But by impressing the northern Picts with his personal authority, Columba furthered the position of Dál Riata, and his skills thus helped to secure the status of the Scottish kingdom on both sides of the water.

But Columba was not just a politician. He was also a monk, a preacher, a pastor, a healer, a teacher, and a poet, and his life and ministry clearly made a charismatic impact in spiritual terms. His monastery rapidly became a place of powerful influence as a religious foundation and drew monks from many parts of Ireland and Britain. Iona came to be at the heart of a whole network of churches and to be the mother-house of an extensive family of cognate monasteries in Ireland, the Hebrides, and the western Scottish mainland. Travel to and from these various centers was frequent, and there was much exchange of news, ideas, and learning between the monks in the various locations. Columba himself traveled extensively throughout Dál Riata, and aside from his visits to the territory of the Picts seems to have concentrated most of his energies on this territory.

Columba's disciples, however, engaged in evangelistic efforts over a much wider area, among both the northern and the southern Picts and the northern Britons. The legacy of their work can be traced in place-names, church dedications, and religious traditions across a significant stretch of modern Britain, from the northeast of Scotland to northern England. Not all of the impact of this activity, by any means, was achieved while Columba was still alive, but his example does seem to have proved a lasting inspiration.

For all that, it would be quite wrong to imagine that Columba and his followers were by any means the first to take the gospel to peoples such as the Picts of central and northern Scotland or to other parts of northern Britain. There is good evidence that there had already been significant numbers of Irish and British evangelists at work in these regions before Columba's time, and there were certainly many other active missionaries in the north during and after his day, both monastics and others, who probably had little or no connection with him. Saints such as Kessog, Serf, Blane, and Ternan all played important parts in the story of the Christian advance in the territory of the Picts, even if the identification of their historical details amid a welter of traditions is a nearly impossible task.

One of the best known of Columba's contemporaries was Kentigern (also known as Mungo), an energetic bishop who reevangelized the British kingdom of Strathclyde, centered on Dumbarton. Strathclyde had already been affected by earlier missionary endeavors, but Kentigern consolidated this work and extended the outreach both to the south and the north, in the latter case apparently reaching into Aberdeenshire and beyond. He is also said to have carried out work at various times in Cumbria and in north Wales, where he is credited with the foundation of the church of St. Asaph in Clwyd, though there is much uncertainty about some of these claims, not least as to whether or not he ever did go to Wales. Kentigern is acclaimed in particular as the founder of the church of Glasgow, where his tomb lies in the cathedral later built in his honor.[7] Some traditions depict Columba and Kentigern meeting, but it is at least as likely that Kentigern represented an entirely independent British missionary endeavor. Columba came to eclipse all the other ambassadors of Christ in later Scottish tradition, but the reality is that this had as much to do with his social status, his political significance, and the influence of Adomnán's portrayal of him as it had with his personal impact as a missionary.

Adomnán's narrative of Columba's achievements is, as we might expect, a hagiographical account, aimed at persuading readers a century later that Columba was every bit the equal of the Continental saints whose lives were greatly admired at that time. Even so, amid its celebratory anecdotes of Columba's prophecies, visions, and miraculous feats we encounter a man who obviously possessed genuine piety and zeal as well as political and organizational talents. Much of the devotional verse that has been attributed to Columba is of dubious authenticity, but from the poetry that may more securely be attached to his name we glimpse a person with a deep reverence for the Scriptures, a genuine love of creation, and a strong sense of the majesty and the providence of God.[8] At the same time, Columba was evidently an individual with a very strong personality, who brooked little dissent and believed in strict discipline and few compromises with the flesh. Columba was a figure of passion and intensity, and he was not given to indulging delicate inclinations when it came to the practical realities of acting upon his convictions.

Later traditions concerning Columba have yielded a variety of images, ranging from the sentimental to the superstitious; on the whole, the tone is more positive in the Hebrides than it is in Donegal. Columba's spiritual aura and his powers became an essential element in much popular Celtic folklore, in prayers, and in rituals. Many of the pictures ignore the degree to which Columba was more than an idealized holy man and forget that his journey to Iona and his work there were almost certainly about more than the realization of a purely spiritual vision. It is also a pity that the prestige attached to Columba has overshadowed the importance of other contributors to the expansion of the gospel in Scotland. Nevertheless, whatever amalgam of truth and superstition exists within the popular assessments, and whatever firm qualifications need to be presented to any assumptions that he stood alone as an evangelist of the north, Columba's status as one of the great pioneers of Christianity in the British Isles seems assured.

Interpreting "Celtic Christianity"

Amid the apparent secularism of modern Western society, it has become common to view the legacy of saints like Ninian, David, Columbanus, and Columba as part of a distinctive "Celtic Christianity" that deserves to be appropriated as a cure for the materialism, externalism, and spiritual sterility of much Western Christian life in the twentieth and twenty-first centuries. Highly lucrative industries have grown up around the promotion of all things "Celtic," and "Celtic spirituality" in particular is hailed by many believers all over the Western world as a holistic, creation-centered, and "alternative" type of Christian faith from which a great deal can be learned. The wisdom of the Celtic saints, expressed not only in their teaching but also in the artistic and musical traditions with which their ideals have come to be associated, is held to present a much-needed corrective to the formalism and authoritarianism of dominant Western Christian traditions.

"Celtic" liturgies, prayers, retreats, and pilgrimages abound as ways of getting in touch with and appropriating spiritual insights and qualities that mainstream "Romanized" Christianity is said to have either neglected or suppressed, such as the importance of the feminine in spirituality, the mysticism of the natural world, or the value of indigenous traditions of art and culture in the telling of the Christian story. The mysterious "Celtic knot," depicted on the crosses, monuments, and manuscripts bequeathed by these saintly forebears, is often taken as a symbol of the endlessly intertwining and dynamic pattern of the Celts' conceptions of nature and faith, over against the allegedly formal and static understandings adopted by the official voices of the Latin church. The Celtic saints are said to have been far more liberated in their views of God, the world, and themselves than were the churchmen under whose authority the bulk of the Western church took its shape, and they are sometimes even held not to have shared such pessimistic ideas as doctrines of original sin or divine judgment.

A great deal of the modern revival of "Celtic Christianity" and fascination with "the Celtic church" deserves to be handled with considerable caution. Modern images of "Celtic Christianity" as a magical spiritual environment of practical good sense, mystical attunement to nature, and indifference to the legal and political preoccupations of organized church life are often wide of the mark in historical terms. The ideals of Celtic monasticism in both Ireland and Britain, as we have seen, certainly did not grow up independently of outside forces but were deeply shaped by a variety of external influences, and ascetics avidly studied the writings of eminent spiritual authorities from many different parts of the Christian world. Romantic notions of the Celtic monks as representatives of an aboriginal form of Christianity untainted by Roman traditions are in reality quite mistaken.

Many of the theological views of the famous figures of Irish and British monasticism were essentially similar to those of most Western churchmen who thought of themselves as orthodox on matters such as the centrality of Scripture, the trinitarian nature of God, and the close relationship between creation and redemption. The monks may have been world-affirming in one sense, in that they did very often relish the beauty, order, and power of God's creation and stressed a combination of physical as well as spiritual activity as part of the regular monastic routine. But they also believed very strongly in what they held to be the dangers of the secular world, and in general they were anything but enthusiasts for notions of intrinsic human goodness or potential. If in the seventh century some of the Irish monks were accused of Pelagian tendencies, this probably had as much to do with their enthusiasm for the works of John Cassian as it had with the gist of their views on natural human capacity.

Nor did they endorse a straightforward appeal to personal instinct or intuition in expressing the content of faith. Monastic patterns of spiritual life may have placed great importance on meditation and on the joyful celebration of the all-encompassing presence of God, but the saints' vigorous devotion to Scripture and to the study of traditional authorities meant that their reflection was not a free-ranging exercise of the religious imagination. Their faith may have had deep—and, for many of us from traditions in which such dimensions have been rather neglected, genuinely instructive—investments in the value of poetry and symbol, but it was typically a cerebral as well as an aesthetic affair, and its doctrinal substance was intentionally consonant with Christian belief elsewhere.

So far from being easygoing nature lovers who went through life unburdened by concepts such as guilt or unconcerned about the dangers of the world, Celtic monks frequently held very serious opinions concerning the realities of indwelling sin, divine omniscience of human failure, and the importance of personal discipline. So far from shunning the kinds of ecclesiastical authority adopted by the Western churches more widely, they tended to believe in forms of self-denial, submission, and penance that were at least as rigorous as any practiced in most other contexts.[9] For the monks, "pilgrimage" was not what it might sometimes be for those who experience it today—a period of withdrawal from the pressures of a frenetic urban life in order to visit some tranquil place in which to meditate or find spiritual refreshment. Rather, it was a deliberate "martyrdom" of the flesh through exile from the regularities of an already austere life.

Nor can we assume that those who engaged in such disciplines were necessarily antagonistic to many of the normal patterns of church authority. Even if structures of ecclesiastical organization were originally somewhat more fluid in places such as Ireland than they were elsewhere, that certainly does not mean they were nonexistent. The sporadic merging of the power of abbots with that of the episcopate there and in other Celtic territories had more to do with political factors and the particular ways in which Christianity had spread in these regions than it had with any purposeful rejection of hierarchy or clerical jurisdiction. As we have observed, bishops and dioceses were still of primary significance in the great majority of contexts. Sometimes it was the very monks who set off on pilgrimage to other regions who became the bishops of the areas in which they worked, such as was the case with Samson in Brittany.

It is true that in the seventh and eighth centuries there would be significant tensions between the convictions and practices of some Christians in the British Isles and the agendas of other ecclesiastical strategists, as certain established patterns came into conflict with other increasingly powerful forms imported from Europe. We shall briefly consider some examples of these problems in due course. For now, though, it is sufficient to stress that such differences cannot be characterized entirely as a clash between an indigenous "Celtic" church and a repressive "Roman" force determined to stamp an alien type of uniformity upon the churches in Britain and Ireland. As we shall see, the dynamics were much more complex than that.

Those who regard the trajectory of faith to which figures like Columba belonged as representing an authentic form of non-Roman or even proto-Protestant Western Christianity tend to underestimate the degree to which that same line contained some strongly "Roman" emphases, such as belief in the veneration of Mary and the intercessory powers of the saints, as well as ideas of sacramentality and of tariffed penance that would undoubtedly be problematic for many modern Protestant sensibilities. Certainly some of the accounts of miracles, visions, prophecies, and angelic interventions that suffuse the stories of the monastic saints were not very different from those that might be found in obviously Roman traditions. It is simply incorrect to view the Celtic leaders as untainted by mainstream Western notions of spirituality, however awkward the implications of this fact for some of the would-be champions of the Celtic saints today.

Celtic monasticism performed an outstanding role in maintaining the vitality and energy of the churches in Britain and Ireland in the early medieval period, and its story is deservedly inspiring for many Christians in the modern world.[10] At the same time, it is necessary to take a much more critical line with regard to the historical evidence than some popular versions of this legacy have done. However well-intentioned some of the most enthusiastic advocates of Celtic Christianity may be, a good deal of what is claimed concerning the Celtic past reflects a mixture of cultural romanticism, hagiography, and religious idealism built up out of various influences over the past two hundred years. The great names of the early centuries were figures from whom we may undoubtedly learn a great deal, but we do them no favors at all when we confuse their contributions with notions that owe more to "New Age" spiritualities or neopagan conceptions of the natural world than they do to the faith to which these believers so zealously sought to bear witness.

The Launch of Another Monastic Mission

Columba died on Iona on 9 June 597, his last days marked, according to Adomnán, by many wonders and angelic visitations. Only a matter of weeks before, a new missionary work had been launched hundreds of miles to the south, in the southeastern corner of England. It too was led by a monk and a group of his colleagues. In this case, however, the ecclesiastical background of the individual in question lay not in the British Isles but in Rome, and he came not with the authority of a Celtic abbot (even one with political connections) but in the name of the bishop of Rome himself.

Pope Gregory probably conceived the idea of a mission to England around 595. He may have seen an opening in the fact that the ruler of the kingdom of Kent, Aethelberht, who was now recognized as the overlord of all the Germanic settlers south of the Humber, had married a Frankish catholic princess named Bertha. Aethelberht was somewhat suspicious of Christianity, but he tolerated it in his queen, and there were probably some other Christians in or not far from his court. Bertha had a Frankish bishop as her personal chaplain, and she was given the use of a partly ruined church originally built in honor of St. Martin, which Aethelberht probably restored for her.

We cannot be sure how much knowledge Gregory had regarding the political climate in Britain, and it is likely that he was not especially well-informed as to the details of Aethelberht's position. Nevertheless, it is conceivable that with his extensive range of contacts he knew enough to calculate that the time was right to embark on some kind of work among the Anglo-Saxons. According to his own later claims, his vision of the spread of the gospel to all nations meant that he was naturally anxious to see its extension to the idolatrous pagans of this benighted land, set in its remote corner of the world. As far as he was concerned, Britain had once been a place where the praise of God had resounded, but now its organized church structures were in serious disarray and much of the country was controlled by heathen rulers. Gregory himself would insist that his desire to evangelize the English went back a long way, and in the legends of subsequent generations his plans were said to have been laid as far back as in the days before he became bishop.

One particularly famous tale to this effect is mentioned by the historian Bede.[11] The story goes that one day Gregory saw some attractive, fair-skinned boys for sale in the slave market in Rome, and on enquiring who they were he was told that they were *Angli*, "Angles" from England, and pagans. To this he is said to have replied that they were not *Angli* but *angeli*, not "Angles," but "angels," and they deserved to be fellow heirs with the angels of heaven: they and their people ought to be converted to Christianity. The story is clearly apocryphal. It is likely to have arisen from pious elaboration of an actual incident that took place in 595, when Gregory ordered his representative-designate in Gaul to organize the purchase of clothes for some poor English slave boys who were apparently to be sent to Rome to be trained in monasteries with a view to serving the church. Perhaps Gregory did have it in mind that one day these young men might be sent back to their own country, for it was not long after this that he dispatched his mission to England. It is extremely unlikely, however, that he had hatched plans to evangelize the English as early as the 570s or 580s.

In 596, though, the situation was different. Gregory commissioned Augustine, the prior in charge of his papal monastery in Rome, to set out for England, accompanied by a party of forty other monks. Their journey was protracted, as they stayed en route at various church centers in Gaul, including Lérins, Aix, Arles, Autun, and Tours, in accordance with orders to make contacts with the Frankish churches as they ventured toward their destination. The group was apprehensive about their mission, and at one stage Augustine went back to Rome to convey their feelings. He returned with a message of encouragement from Gregory and confirmation of his status as their authoritative leader. At length they arrived on the Isle of Thanet just before Easter 597, and proceeded to Canterbury, Aethelberht's seat.

Augustine's Work at Canterbury

The visitors were given a polite though very cautious reception by Aethelberht, who insisted upon meeting them in the open air, fearing that they possessed magical powers. Despite the king's initial suspicions, however, there is no evidence that there was significant opposition to their activities. Aethelberht was sufficiently impressed by the monks' sincerity to offer them provisions, permission to preach, and the freedom to use old Roman churches in and around Canterbury.

Before long the king himself was won over to the Christian faith, and he may at length have consented to be baptized, though the details here are very unclear. By the following year it was reported that significant numbers of his subjects had been baptized—Gregory heard stories of more than ten thousand individuals thus professing faith. This figure was certainly an exaggeration, but it is clear that Aethelberht's espousal of Christianity brought some kind of tribal change of allegiance, akin to that reported of the Franks in the context of the conversion of Clovis (see pp. 316–17). By this time Augustine had been consecrated as a bishop,[12] and he had established his church and started a monastery dedicated to Peter and Paul, just to the east of the city of Canterbury.

In 601 Augustine sent a party of his followers back to Rome with the news of the progress of their mission and requests for further helpers and supplies of books and items such as sacred vessels, relics, and vestments. A second wave of monastic missionaries arrived from Rome in 601, led by an abbot named Mellitus. The work was now well established, and Augustine was given authority to install a number of other bishops as the churches grew. It seems that Gregory planned that a restored catholic Christianity in Britain should be organized around the old structures of the Roman provincial system, in which London and York were the chief cities. The idea was that Augustine, as the senior leader, would become archbishop of London, and as the gospel spread there would also in time be an archbishopric at York, the incumbent of which would in turn be authorized to consecrate a further number of bishops in the north of England. In practice, however, Augustine opted to remain in Canterbury, and thus Canterbury came to be the primary see of England, the status it retains to this day.

Gregory's expectations were that the conversion of the Anglo-Saxons would proceed rapidly. The shrines and idols of pagan religion would be speedily destroyed, the social prestige of pagan practices would be unreservedly undermined, and people would soon be induced to abandon the old ways. As in earlier generations in the Britain of the Romans, however, so too in the England of the Germanic peoples: the hold of paganism proved tenacious. Despite the presence of an officially Christian ruler, the process of Christianization did not advance anywhere near as smoothly as the pope anticipated. Gregory exhorted Aethelberht to play his part in promoting the faith, but the strength of opposition from committed pagan subjects limited the king's ability to fulfill this role, especially amid the delicate political relations between Kent and the regimes in other areas.

Augustine had many good qualities, but he was an unimaginative leader, and he wrote to consult Gregory on all kinds of details. These included issues of discipline, morality, and observance among converts as well as ecclesiastical procedures such as the proper practices for episcopal consecrations and the appropriate ways of organizing financial affairs. He was even unsure whether he ought to follow the liturgical conventions of Rome or those of Gaul (which varied in a number of respects), despite the fact that some flexibility was already tolerated by Rome.

As Gregory's knowledge of the actual conditions in England grew through these enquiries and other reports, so he came to concede that the program of evangelism in the country would have to advance more gradually than had at first been intended. By the time Mellitus was on his way to join the work, Gregory had realized that there could be no coercion, only persuasion, and he sent instructions to say that, contrary to previous advice to Aethelberht, there was, after all, little point in destroying pagan religious buildings; pagan sanctuaries were certainly to be stripped of their idols, but it was acceptable for them then to be reconsecrated as places of Christian worship.

Tensions with Other Christians

Gregory's emissaries had, in effect, been charged with reclaiming British Christianity for Rome and with restoring the fortunes of churches that had been pushed to the margins by the forces of invasion. But although Gregory would gradually acquire a clearer picture of the challenges of the real conditions on the ground in England, he had at no stage been well-informed about the situation of the Christians who lived in other areas of the British Isles, who had already been busy for generations keeping the faith alive and spreading it in adjacent regions. Many of these believers may have been pleased to hear of the spread of the gospel among the English, but they were unimpressed by what looked like the papal patronage of an Anglo-Saxon regime and resentful of the ascendancy of a new episcopal structure with claims to large-scale jurisdiction.

It must be stressed once again that a majority of these Christians in the west, the north, Wales, Ireland, and Scotland cannot be assumed to have been instinctively antagonistic toward wider European traditions. As the influence of Gallic monasticism in the Celtic churches showed, there was much willing assimilation of Continental ideas and practices and a concern to cherish the same broad doctrinal principles as were espoused by the Western churches more widely. As we have indicated already, it is quite wrong to suppose that these believers were naturally hostile toward Rome in particular, for much of their theology was either implicitly or self-consciously faithful to the principles of the same essential orthodoxy over which Rome professed to be the preeminent guardian. Contrary to widespread modern impressions, the problems that arose in the early seventh century between the leaders of the Anglo-Saxon mission and these Celtic Christians cannot be depicted straightforwardly as a collision of "Roman" and "non-Roman" forms of Christianity.

Nevertheless, the tensions between the assumptions of Gregory's ambassadors and the representatives of other churches in the British Isles were not trivial. In a number of areas the Celtic Christians had distinct practices of their own. Many of them operated with an old eighty-four-year cycle for calculating the date of Easter,[13] based on Jewish ways of reckoning the date of the Passover. Such a system seems to have gone back to the origins of Christianity in Britain, and versions of the same principle had been widely followed elsewhere in the West, including Rome itself, well into the fifth century. However, after a series of protracted disputes on the matter, most of the Western churches had by this time come to use the nineteen-year cycle, a variant of which had been favored by the Alexandrian church since the late third century, and this had been formally adopted by Rome in 525 (see p. 271). The Celtic believers also differed on the limits within which Easter Sunday could fall in relation to the spring equinox.

In addition, there were some differences on matters such as baptismal practices, the procedures for episcopal ordinations, and the shape of the tonsure given to monks and priests. The convention of cutting the hair in a particular fashion had been a part of religious dedication in many Eastern contexts in antiquity, and from the fourth century onward it had started to be applied in Christian circles as a sign of spiritual devotion, first for monks and then to distinguish those in clerical orders. The Celts seem to have favored the cutting of a broader vertical band at the front of the head as a mark of consecration, while the Roman preference was for a round tonsure on the crown.

When Augustine met with churchmen from the southwest and Wales in 603, he insisted that they should adopt the nineteen-year method of calculating the date of Easter and abandon their independent practices on this and other matters. The Celtic leaders were unwilling to change their customs, despite much argument. The compiling of ecclesiastical calendars was a highly valued activity in monastic circles, and they were convinced that their way of reckoning was older and superior. The same was true of their other traditions. Their attachments were deep-seated and widely shared; on the Continent, Columbanus was incurring similar opposition for his insistence upon similar views, though he made bold to defend his teachings to the highest ecclesiastical authorities.

In Britain, however, the feelings were becoming increasingly bitter. At a second conference, attended by seven British bishops and a number of scholars led by Dinoth, abbot of the monastery of Bangor-is-coed, the Welsh delegates were deeply insulted when Augustine allegedly failed to rise to greet them. The divisions remained unhealed. In the opinion of Bede, the intransigent Welsh were judged for their obstinacy when around 613 a large group of churchmen were killed in a battle near Chester with the pagan king Aethelfryth of Northumbria; their fate was allegedly a result of their refusal to comply with Augustine's requests.[14]

The "Synod" of Whitby

It is conventional to assume that the dispute over the dating of Easter and the other issues was at length more or less resolved in 664, when a meeting of churchmen was convened at Whitby by King Osuiu of Northumbria. By this time many in the west of Britain and in the south of Ireland had already decided to adopt the nineteen-year cycle for reckoning Easter, and this had now been standard in their circles for a generation, but the older Celtic pattern was still insisted upon by a significant constituency in the north of Ireland, on Iona, and in Northumbria, which was heavily influenced by northern Irish traditions.

In Bede's famous account of the gathering at Whitby,[15] the protagonists on each side were as follows: for the "Celts," Colman, an Irishman and former monk of Iona who was then bishop of Lindisfarne, the tiny island off the Northumbrian coast that had been established in the 630s as the chief monastic and missionary center in the kingdom by Aidan, another monk of Iona; for the "Romans," Wilfrid, bishop of York, who had become disillusioned with Celtic traditions and was now an enthusiast for the Roman positions. Colman refused to accept the Roman argument and left, to spend the rest of his days in Ireland, but Osuiu was persuaded to adopt the Roman line.

In Bede's eyes, Whitby marked the beginnings of a definitive shift toward uniformity in the English church, in accordance with the over-arching authority of Peter's see in Rome. His perspective has powerfully influenced traditional accounts of British ecclesiastical history, and the so-called "Synod of Whitby" has been seen as a major event in the story of the relations between "Roman" and "Celtic" Christian traditions. In reality, Osuiu's reasons for accepting the "Roman" arguments were probably political as much as anything, and had to do with domestic maneuverings and his own ambitions to win papal acknowledgment of his supremacy in England. More significantly still, the meeting had fairly limited impact beyond Northumbria, except perhaps among the East Saxons, whose bishop, Cedd, a former monk of Lindisfarne, was persuaded to take the Roman position back to his people in Essex.

In the long run of history, Whitby does represent a somewhat defin-ing moment in the gradual movement toward a certain standardizing of church practices, but it was not the kind of landmark synod that it has classically been taken to be, and its effects should not be overstated. There was only slow acquiescence in the different dating of Easter in many areas, including the north of Ireland and Iona, and the Welsh churches did not finally yield until 768, more than a century later.

Whitby certainly cannot be reduced, as it often has been, to a stand-off between a powerful Roman Christian bureaucracy and a brave and outnumbered "Celtic church," nor to a collision between two entirely disparate cultures. Diverse factors were at work on both sides of the debate: by no means all among those whom modern-day parlance might deem the "Celtic" constituency were by the mid-seventh century opposed to the Roman practices, and the "Roman" system had for its part come to be symbolic of an already mature Saxon tradition.

Assessing the English Mission

By the 660s, two generations had passed since Augustine and his monks had landed on the south coast of England. Augustine himself had died some time between 604 and 609, after consecrating one of his Roman colleagues, Lawrence, as his successor. He had also established sees at Rochester and among the East Saxons of London. Augustine's mission had accomplished some quite impressive things. He and his associates had preached the gospel, made converts, and established or reestablished churches in the midst of a pagan culture. He had also introduced Latin learning and classical art to England's Germanic society and assisted Aethelberht in the framing of the first written legal code in the country, produced not in Latin but in Anglo-Saxon. The Christian church had come to be an integral part of the social fabric of the kingdom. Despite strong opposition from paganism, some significant work had been done in the planting of the Christian message in the changed soil of southeastern Britain.

In the end, however, the continuation of all these achievements was closely dependent upon the acquiescence or support of Aethelberht. After the king's death in 616 the preeminence of the kingdom of Kent was weakened, and there was also a strong revival of paganism, which once again presented many challenges to the churches. Though advances were achieved by Lawrence and his successors, there were also many setbacks. Paulinus, one of the group of workers who arrived from Rome to reinforce Augustine's mission in 601, became chaplain to the Kentish princess Aethelburg and went north with her when she married King Edwin of Northumbria. His work led to the conversion of Edwin and his chiefs in the 620s, and Paulinus became for a time bishop of York, but he eventually had to retreat south to Rochester on the defeat and death of Edwin in 633.

Overall, the evangelization of England advanced far more through the energies of missionaries from Ireland and from the north than it did through the work in the south, and Christianity was primarily consolidated in Northumbria through the efforts of dedicated monks from Iona, who in turn carried their gospel southward to the Humber and beyond. In the west, there were also significant labors by Welsh, Irish, and Cornish missionaries, and by others who came across from Gaul. Nor did these Celtic workers cease to operate after the Synod of Whitby: Irish and other monks continued to be very active in England long after 664.

The task upon which Pope Gregory had sent his representatives in the 590s thus proved to be, in itself, only a small part of the process by which England would at length be more generally converted to Christianity.[16] Despite the achievements that had been made, as far as Gregory's own plans were concerned the mission was, in the short term, a failure, for it did not yield a transformation of English society, nor, despite the pretensions, did it succeed in establishing a network of churches with a uniform degree of attachment to the opinions of Rome. In several respects, in fact, it could be argued that Gregory's outreach to the English did almost as much for the Frankish churches as it did for England, for the contacts of his emissaries with the bishops of Gaul greatly strengthened the network of papal relations with both ecclesiastical and political leaders in Continental Europe and consolidated Gregory's influence over their affairs.

Gregory's vision was one of Frankish and English churches working together in a harmonious partnership to extend the impact of the gospel, all in conformity with the purposes of Rome. That dream was not fulfilled, but it proved a powerful image for later generations to evoke—the ideal of a single orthodox church unifying the disparate peoples of the Western world. The quest for such uniformity would always prove more elusive than Gregory or any later visionary could conceive, but the lingering potency of the notion testified to its beguiling possibilities. In Britain, at least, things would always be far more complex, but there did slowly emerge some evidences of the kind of consensus that Gregory had in mind.

It is perhaps fitting that one of the first attempts to write a *Life* of Gregory should have been made early in the eighth century by a resident of the monastery at Whitby founded in 657 by the abbess Hild, a former pupil of Aidan's. It was certainly not through the efforts of Gregory's own time that the English had been won over to Christ, nor would Gregory's notion of an undivided catholic witness in England ever be realized. But the work that was begun under his inspiration, however limited and complex its consequences, deserves to be remembered for its contribution to the longer-term story of Christianity in Britain as a whole.

EPILOGUE

A Public Faith

With the evolution of seventh-century Christianity, our journey in this book comes to an end. As we survey the position of the Christian faith at this point in history it is worth casting our minds back over the course of our narrative and reminding ourselves of the route we have taken.

Our title speaks of "A Public Faith," and that indeed is what our story has been about. In the first three centuries, Christianity had traveled a very considerable distance from its beginnings in Galilee and Judea, but for all its statistical growth and evolution in form it remained a faith without any official status in its primary political world. By the later third century there were far too many Christians in the Roman Empire for their presence to be ignored, but believers could never be entirely sure of what might happen to them if the manifestations of their faith rubbed against the sensibilities of the power-brokers of their day, or if those authorities found reasons of their own to take measures against them. If Christians were for the most part allowed to get on with living their lives in peace, and if their gospel continued to spread to larger ethnic and social constituencies, they were also subject to a great deal of suspicion, popular hostility, and intellectual critique, and intermittently they became the victims of the worst kinds of physical persecution and suffering. As the trials of the early fourth century proved, the expansion of the church's presence in imperial society brought no guarantees of security, and commitment to Christ in the Roman world could still cost everything.

The profession of Christian belief never would cease to be potentially offensive, and at an individual level no one could ever be sure that spiritual enthusiasm would not bring considerable difficulties or dangers. In the end, however, Christians were far too deeply embedded in the structures of Roman society to be dealt with by political decree, and the early fourth century signaled the recognition of this fact at the height of the imperial machine. The years that followed witnessed the emergence of a new kind of climate, in which Christian faith could be expressed in public in ways that had never previously been possible. The changes that ensued did not come all at once, and their overall cultural effects can readily be exaggerated, but over the course of the next few generations the conditions of Christians and their communities had nevertheless altered dramatically.

The descendants of once persecuted believers had become representatives of a favored social system, their leaders honored with status, prestige, and degrees of power that far exceeded anything afforded to clergy in earlier times. The overseers of once impoverished Christian communities had become the custodians of significant economic resources, dispensers of charity not only to their own but benefactors of their local societies and even lenders to civil authorities. A once clandestine movement celebrated its beliefs and rituals in some of the most splendid public buildings to be found in the towns and cities of the ancient world and expressed its ideas in rich traditions of art, music, and literature. Those who had been scorned as fools had come to have among their number some of the greatest thinkers and scholars of their times, whose books and ideas would dominate intellectual culture in Europe and elsewhere for centuries to come.

Revolution in Retrospect

As we saw, the conversion of Constantine and his lavish generosity to the churches and their leaders had certainly not turned the Roman Empire into a Christian realm. There was still a very great deal of pagan religion about, and there would still be many different kinds of significant intellectual and social opposition to the Christian faith over the following generations. But the Christians' social success seemed to confirm a growing sense that there had to be a single transcendent divinity behind all the diverse religious traditions of humanity, and that the traditional cults were no longer quite as important as they had been in cultural terms. For most of the inhabitants of the Roman world, it was true, life went on much as before, but for both town-and even country-dwellers there were signs of change. Those who lived in the larger cities in particular could hardly miss the new churches that were being built and dedicated all over the empire, the increasing style of their officials, the confidence of their rituals, and the displays of popular devotion that attended their major festivals and martyr cults.

If a majority of the residents of the empire as a whole remained indifferent toward the Christians' outreach or resentful of the growing political significance of their bishops, others must have been curious enough to go to hear the churches' preachers for themselves or to experience other aspects of the Christians' communal devotion firsthand. As the prestige of Christianity grew, the profession of Christian faith could also carry social, economic, or professional advantages, and this too led to unprecedented interest in the Christians' way of life. While some were won over by genuine intellectual and spiritual conviction, others had more pragmatic reasons for aligning themselves to the Christian cause. The task of sorting out true commitment from false became more complex than it had ever been, and the moral demands of faith needed to be spelled out with renewed vigor. For the most part, the gospel must still have had its greatest impact at the level of personal witness and in the practical evidences of good works expressed within the immediate social networks of families, friends, and neighborhoods.

The really big change wrought in cultural terms in the fourth century lay within the thinking of Christians themselves, who for the first time could view their faith as that of the emperor himself, and could present it as such. Even so, they certainly could not assume that the state was automatically on the side of particular Christian causes. When Christians quarreled among themselves—as they continued to do with as much if not more passion than ever, given that imperial favors were now at stake—the emperor and his representatives had to take one position or another. Within the churches as a whole there were inevitably losers as well as winners in that process. The Donatists would discover this repeatedly, and parties on all sides in the Arian disputes also found it out to their cost. Sometimes the losers in controversial cases ended up the tragic victims of injustice, like Priscillian of Avila and his devout followers who were executed in the 380s. Others suffered lesser fates, but they suffered all the same. Much depended upon the shifting calculations of those in power and upon the ability of differing ecclesiastical factions to elicit official sanction for their particular positions. Non-Christians could also influence events, playing one Christian cause off against another in the interests of their own independent objectives.

The enormous doctrinal divisions that occurred in the fourth century over the various theologies described as "Arian" testify to the deep politicization of Christian discourse in this changed social context. Christian exchanges always had been political in one way or another, but in the post-Constantinian era they were political as never before. If the authorities sponsored a specific theological position, that position possessed an official status that could be acquired no other way. Only in this environment could there be councils after the fashion of those held in Nicaea, Constantinople, Ephesus, and Chalcedon, at which doctrinal formulae were hammered out with the aid of—or threats from—civil authorities, and enshrined as official teaching to be followed by believers everywhere. Only in this world could there be recourse to harassment, exile, imprisonment, or even execution for those who refused to comply with the prevailing political will about which theological stance was to be preferred.

Christians will always debate whether the conversion of Constantine and the social privileging of Christianity that followed were in the end a good or a bad thing for their faith. Broadly similar questions might be asked of the conversion of other rulers such as Clovis, or indeed at any point where a political overlord became a sponsor of a particular conception of the church's interests, whether in Armenia, Ethiopia, Spain, or England. In Constantine's case, however, the issue assumes unparalleled importance—not because he was the first ruler to be converted, for he was not, but because the consequences of his turn to Christianity proved of such momentous weight for the future of the faith.

As we suggested, simplistic answers to this question can never be adequate, for it is clear that the Constantinian revolution produced a complicated mixture of blessings and banes for the churches. Those who have followed Eusebius in viewing the emergence of Constantinian Christianity as a joyous vindication of the truth of the gospel and a marvelous opening up of new opportunities and advantages tend to see only one side of the picture. On the other hand, those who regard the process as a fateful co-opting of the church by political interests and a tragic dissolution of the vital distinction between the imperatives of the gospel and all natural frameworks of human culture may equally be identifying only a part of the truth.

The Positive and the Negative

In reality, the changes that took place in the fortunes of the churches were both positive and negative. Without the empire of Constantine and his Christian heirs, there might never have been the expansion of the faith into large areas of the ancient world at the pace and in the fashion that occurred from the fourth century onward, and the churches might never have attained the kind of economic or cultural position to enable them to be what they became socially, politically, and intellectually in subsequent history.

There might never have been, for example, the great age of theological energy and spiritual leadership characterized by such remarkable Christian scholars, preachers, and organizers as Athanasius, the Cappadocian Fathers, Ambrose, John Chrysostom, Augustine, Cyril of Alexandria, and Gregory the Great. Certainly the tenor of some of these individuals' work, and its implications for the future of the church, would have been very different. The designation of such figures as "the Fathers of the Church" indicates the reverence that came to be attached to their teaching, their sanctity, and their enduring influence on Christian thought.[1] While we may regret the limitation of primary status to just a few, and in particular lament the absence of any comparable recognition for the many women who also played vital roles as spiritual exemplars and channels of the gospel (there are no official "Mothers" of the church), the achievements of all of the giants, both greater and lesser known, only had the impact they did because of the world in which they existed.

At the same time, such a world certainly contained dangers for Christianity. For rather a long time it was all too easy for Christian belief to be equated, in the minds of some, with "Romanness," and for the drive for consensus around an official doctrinal orthodoxy to be motivated by visions of political and cultural unity as much as by spiritual considerations. Social and economic privileges also brought considerable risks of moral corruption, materialism, and complacency. Thankfully, there were always believers who recognized that Christianity was not just for the Roman world but for everyone, and generations before Constantine had ever set about implementing his pro-Christian policies the faith had already been carried to other constituencies far outside the empire, in the East, in Africa, and in northern Europe. The differing varieties of belief espoused by some of these groups would invite their own problems, of course, but it was impossible to deny that there were countless spiritually active Christians and highly developed traditions of theology and worship far beyond the boundaries of the Roman world. Major churches had existed in Asia and non-Roman Africa long before the fourth century. The considerable expansions that would take place among non-Roman peoples in the fifth and sixth centuries made the reality of a faith that far transcended Roman dominions all the more obvious. As we have seen, Christianity evolved in a rich variety of forms outside of imperial territory, and the early church's story cannot be confined—as it too often has been—to the context of the Mediterranean world, far less to "the West." Christianity was flourishing in many parts of the Middle East, Asia, and Africa when it was still struggling to become established in large areas of northern Europe. The Christian faith had been practiced with lavish devotion in Ethiopia for centuries when the Anglo-Saxons were only beginning to be converted. At every stage in our story in this book—and indeed for long centuries beyond our period—the overwhelming majority of believers were not to be found in Europe, and the typical Christian face was certainly not pale-skinned.

As for the perils of moral decadence for an institutionalized Christianity, the vitality of the ascetic movement in all its forms served as a potent reminder of the obligations of holiness, and one of monasticism's complex influences upon the churches lay in its capacity to confront regular ecclesiastical structures with the challenges of more comprehensive—and often more independent—species of sanctity. The relationship between organized church authority and asceticism was often uneasy, but in many places, such as in Basil's Cappadocia or Augustine's Hippo, it became possible to subsume monasticism under the bishop's control while also absorbing its key emphases. As ascetic forces came to shape more and more members of the clergy, so the churches assimilated patterns of moral conviction and practical devotion that served to check some of the temptations to spiritual inertia that lurked in the shadows of social respectability and structural prestige.

It is certainly likely that if things had taken a different course in the fourth century the perils of "Caesaropapism," the domination of church affairs by secular powers, and the deficiencies of a religion marked by convention and expediency rather than conviction and commitment might never in the longer term have become so powerful in the later regimes of Europe and their daughter states. That said, the fact that Christianity obtained a privileged public profile from the fourth century onward does not mean that it was seriously corrupted in all respects by the experience, or that the churches were rendered incapable of bearing a faithful moral and intellectual testimony to Christ amid the enormous challenges of their world. If we would do justice to the complexities of late antiquity and beyond we must acknowledge both the dangers and the possibilities that were presented by the cultural affirmation of the Christian faith, and avoid the temptation to oversimplify the consequences by presenting them in black-and-white terms. A nuanced assessment of what was implied by the social changes of the fourth century may well be all the more necessary as we view history from the perspective of an increasingly post-Christian Western world.

Politics, Beliefs, Images

As the brief renaissance of pagan religion under Julian in the 360s showed, Christianity was not automatically secure in the Roman Empire even after Constantine, and there were many ongoing intellectual and social challenges for believers. Julian's efforts to revive the traditional religions of the classical past were, however, short-lived, and in the aftermath of his fall those who shared his personal ideals lacked the power and the opportunity to carry them any further, as an emperor of Christian profession was very soon on the throne once again. Despite what had happened in the early 360s, Christianity was too deeply embedded to be easily uprooted.

For Christian leaders, especially in the East, the middle decades of the fourth century were dominated not by political circumstances but by the highly divisive disputes generated by the Arian crisis. The Arian controversies were both complex and tragic for the churches, and many of the protagonists on all sides behaved in ways that seem plainly disreputable to Christians today. In the end, though, whatever we say of the tactics deployed by individuals and parties, the issues were of profound importance to the logic of the gospel, and the thinking that went on yielded some of the most important doctrinal reflection ever undertaken in Christian history on the status of Jesus and his relationship to God, on the nature and role of the Holy Spirit, and thus—putting both of these areas together—on the triune character of the God revealed in Christ. However fraught their circumstances and however divisive their prescriptions, occasions such as the Councils of Nicaea in 325 and Constantinople in 381 were of very great significance in the doctrinal story of Christianity, and some of the theological work done in the course of the fourth century by figures such as Athanasius and the Cappadocians was of a quality equal to anything in later centuries.

As far as many average believers were concerned, it was true, the debates went on over their heads a good deal of the time, and there was often only limited understanding of the issues, even if popular ferment could be whipped up by zealous partisans. The same could also be said of quite a lot of clergy, whose levels of engagement with the details variously depended upon the degree to which they were educated or upon the availability of guidance from other churchmen in their areas.

Nonetheless, the best-informed leaders labored to inculcate more ac-
curate understandings among their people through their catechetical
instruction, their sermons and letters, and not least through the powerful
medium of hymns. Misapprehensions and honest dissent doubtless
remained widespread, and there certainly never was anything like a
wholesale renunciation of Arian ideas anywhere in the churches. If
Arianism suffered defeat at the level of official orthodoxy, it never died,
and its influence continued to be obvious beyond the boundaries of the
empire, where peoples such as the Goths were evangelized by expressly
Arian missionaries. The doctrinal tensions caused by such differences
would be considerable in later generations.

In terms of Roman society more generally, Christianization of a
more pervasive kind only took place in the reign of Theodosius, whose
edicts against paganism gradually ensured the official demise of other
expressions of belief and gave impetus to forms of religious coercion
that would prove far more effective than the anti-Christian measures
of earlier Roman authorities had ever been. Even then, there was no
mass conversion to Christianity, nor was there any serious effort to root
out private belief in other ideas, and paganism never did die, despite
widespread destruction of its public symbols. Nevertheless, there was
no doubt that the fourth century had seen a significant elevation in the
status of the churches. There had been much consolidation of the rights,
privileges, and responsibilities of clergy, and especially of bishops, who
came to be seen as a new class of political managers. The leaders of the
largest metropolitan churches emerged as very important public figures,
with obligations and entitlements that marked them out as belonging
among the elite of their time. Some were better prepared to play this
role than others.

The most conspicuous ecclesiastical example of splendor, wealth,
and authority lay in the church of Rome, and it was from the later
fourth century onward that the papacy began to function as a powerful
political force in its own right. It claimed natural overall jurisdiction
and leadership over all the other churches of the West and proffered
practical guidance in disciplinary matters to other Western bishops,
who were increasingly expected to fall into line with Rome's wishes. In
reality, a great deal of regional variety continued, especially in regard
to liturgical practice, though influences spread with mounting speed.
Rome's claims extended eastwards as well, but here there were much
greater difficulties still because of the powerful profile of other ancient
sees, especially Antioch and Alexandria. Long-lasting problems began

to arise over the status of Constantinople vis-à-vis not only Rome but other churches as well.

Morality and Doctrine

The liturgical developments of the fourth century and beyond typified the advances wrought by increased cultural and theological sophistication; they also reflected the challenges posed by social expansion. Patterns of worship, feasts, and ceremonies testified to new advantages; the elaboration of catechesis, the mysticizing of the sacraments, the efforts of bishops to educate their staff, and the endeavors made by preachers and writers in Christian moralizing pointed to the concern to deal with unprecedented needs. Would-be reformers of the church frequently found their lot none too easy. Some, like Jerome, were simply too acerbic in their denunciations of other churchmen, or, like John Chrysostom, far too outspoken in their allegations about prominent individuals and far too interfering toward other churches. Others ran into problems on account of their theological ideas. In the last years of the fourth century and the first decades of the fifth, Pelagius and his supporters attracted many followers for their impassioned advocacy of moral effort in the Christian life, but they increasingly found themselves in trouble for the ways in which they came to undergird this ideal doctrinally.

To Augustine in particular, the assumptions of Pelagius and his followers, especially the redoubtable Julian of Eclanum, struck at the heart of the gospel of free grace and the fundamental Christian conviction that salvation is a divine gift, bestowed upon those who by nature are incapable of redeeming themselves. The dispute between these two different approaches was exacerbated by various misunderstandings. The Pelagians for their part did not wish to deny the necessity of grace for salvation, only to qualify some prevalent ideas as to how grace operated and what this implied for Christian behavior. In the end, however, Augustine's reasoning exposed the reality that it was not possible to ground conceptions of Christian ethical endeavor in optimistic views of human capacity.

If the fourth century produced a widespread consensus that Christ could not be less than God, though only with much difficulty a consensus as to how best to state this fact, the late fourth and early fifth centuries saw further protracted efforts to pin down an appropriate way of speaking of the relationship between Christ's divinity and his humanity. In the debates between the Greek theologians of the Alexandrian and

Antiochene traditions, differing emphases were examined and contested. Although there was some broad agreement against the extremes on both sides, there were also strong feelings about the legitimacy or otherwise of certain ways of speaking about "persons" and "natures."

As in previous generations, there was a good deal of unseemly behavior by church politicians, and in the midst of the battles there were innocent casualties, such as Nestorius, who almost certainly never held what his enemy Cyril accused him of believing. Nevertheless, the underlying issues were, as before, of great importance. Just as it mattered crucially to the logic of Christian salvation that Christ was fully equal to God, it was also of comparable moment that he was absolutely human, and it was necessary to find a way to affirm both of these realities without compromising the integrity of either.

The Council of Chalcedon in 451 attempted to find a settlement that would do justice to the enduring concerns on both sides, and although surrounded by controversy and heavily influenced by particular agendas it yielded a carefully balanced formula. The incarnate Lord was confessed to be fully consubstantial with God in relation to his divinity and fully consubstantial with us in relation to his humanity, yet also one reality: he was, and is, one person made known in two natures. This confession won widespread approval in the West and among a large number in the East, but there were also a great many Eastern dissenters who felt that for one reason or another it did not represent a true exposition of their faith.

The disputes that ensued between Chalcedonians and "Monophysites" in particular involved significant political as well as theological divisions, and the doctrinal differences that emerged in this period contributed in their own ways to the fragmentation of Christianity in the Eastern and the Western worlds. The arguments over doctrine dominated the East for centuries and indeed have never really been overcome to this day, as new churches evolved out of the divisions and consolidated their own distinctive traditions of faith and practice. Despite all the problems, however, there was continued expansion of the Christian message, as non-Chalcedonian missionaries of both "Monophysite" and Antiochene varieties carried the gospel to new contexts in Asia, Africa, India, and beyond, and strong independent traditions of spirituality continued to develop in all of these contexts even in the midst of changing political circumstances. The churches of the non-Roman East, of Asia, Africa, India, and China must never be overlooked in the narrative of Christian endeavor.

Challenges and Opportunities

As the regime of every Christian ruler showed, political favor certainly did not mean an end to problems for the churches, or even an end to physical dangers. From the time of Constantine to the age of Justinian and far beyond, sincere Christians continued to know very well what it was to suffer when their personal beliefs on salvation or the nature of the church or the person of Christ did not coincide with those of their political masters. Nor did government by officially Christian rulers remotely mean that righteousness and justice automatically prevailed in social terms. Sometimes pagan authorities were much better behaved than were those who professed Christianity, and sometimes the heretics revealed much better manners than the catholics. As the fifth and sixth centuries showed abundantly, there was plenty of wanton violence and destruction wrought by the armies of those who called themselves Christian, and innocent believers were not spared their share of the costs. The upheavals raised many questions about God's purposes in allowing such trials. For some, the suffering was an urgent call to awake from moral and spiritual lethargy; for others, it could only presage the end of the world and the return of their Lord to judge the earth for its wickedness.

In the midst of it all, however, the churches went on, and the boundaries of the faith were enlarged. There were conversions among the Franks, and the consolidation of a catholic Merovingian church. There were successes in bringing some of the Goths over to the catholic faith, most notably the Visigoths in Spain, and there were some inroads made among the Lombards in Italy. In Britain and Ireland, after an apparently slow start, evangelism had also advanced among the Britons, the Scots, the Picts, and most recently the Anglo-Saxons, and there were particularly lively traditions of monasticism, scholarship, and missionary commitment in the Celtic territories, which in turn had a significant impact upon the churches on the Continent.

Paganism was an enduring force, and the Christianizing of society in any meaningful sense in every one of these contexts proved an infinitely more difficult challenge than has often been supposed. There never would be wholesale conversion anywhere, and in northern Europe the social effects of Christian expansion were frequently much more limited than pious narratives of later times would claim. Political, economic, and social problems over the generations brought countless setbacks and ups and downs, and there were many questions about the ways in which the gospel was enculturated, about the independence of church leaders from the civil authorities, and (as always) about relationships between local churches and those elsewhere. Yet in each case there were new opportunities alongside the new challenges, and in many situations the churches assumed a vital role as agents of social stability, welfare, and cultural stewardship in the complex world of the early medieval West.

If the fourth century had marked the beginning of one new age, the dawn of the seventh century brought another. At just the time Gregory the Great and his heirs in Rome were appreciating the opportunities in the West, ominous changes were afoot in the East, in comparison with which all that had happened politically in Europe would prove of limited consequence. The protracted struggle between the Byzantine Empire and Persia increased the gulf that had opened up between the Christians of the Byzantine realm and their counterparts outside it, and exacerbated the theological differences between them. In Arabia, Islam appeared at first to be just a local tribal movement, but the influence of the new faith would grow with astonishing rapidity, and in the long run it would prove the greatest challenge ever posed to the prosperity of Christianity in very large parts of the Mediterranean world and beyond. The real impact of all these developments was as yet still far in the future, but the first seeds of the process toward it had been sown. In the medieval era, the map of the Christian world would be radically redrawn.

Time Line

The dating of many events, personalities, and texts is controversial. The following time line assumes approximations in several instances; specialist discussions of chronological questions can be found in some of the literature cited in the Suggestions for Further Reading.

Date	Major Developments
303–304	"The Great Persecution" begins
304–313	Lactantius works on the *Divine Institutes*
305	Diocletian and Maximian abdicate
306	Constantine proclaimed Augustus by his troops at York
306–312	Easing of persecution in West
	Continuing oppression in East
	Beginnings of Melitian schism in Egypt
ca. 310	Armenia becomes first officially Christian state
311	Galerius issues edict of toleration
	After Galerius's death, continued persecution under Maximin, especially in Egypt
	Beginnings of Donatist schism in North Africa
312	Constantine defeats Maxentius at Milvian Bridge
313	"Edict of Milan" issued by Constantine and Licinius: universal toleration
313–315	Lactantius's *On the Deaths of the Persecutors*
	War begins between Constantine and Licinius
318	Beginnings of controversy around Arius in Alexandria
321	Constantine promotes Sunday as special day

Date	Major Developments
321–324	Christians persecuted in Licinius's territories
324	Constantine defeats Licinius and becomes sole emperor
325	Completion of Eusebius of Caesarea's *Ecclesiastical History*
	First "ecumenical" Council of Nicaea: Christ confessed to be *homoousios* with God the Father
late 320s –330s	Growth of ascetic *lavrae* in Palestine
328	Athanasius becomes bishop of Alexandria
330	Dedication of Constantinople
335	Council of Tyre: Athanasius condemned and sent into exile
336	Marcellus of Ancyra exiled
	Death of Arius in Constantinople
337	Baptism and death of Constantine
	Division of empire between Constantine II, Constantius, and Constans
	Amnesty for exiled bishops
ca. 338	Eusebius's *Life of Constantine*
339	Athanasius and Marcellus in exile once again, in Rome
	Christians persecuted in Persia during war with Rome
340	Civil war between Constantine II and Constans
	Death of Constantine II
340s	Mission of Ulfila to Goths and translation of Scriptures into Gothic language
	(?) Evangelism in northern Ethiopia/Aksum
ca. 343	Council of Sardica
346	Athanasius returns to Alexandria
	Death of monastic leader Pachomius
ca. 349	Cyril becomes bishop of Jerusalem
350	Hilary becomes bishop of Poitiers
	Constans killed by usurper Magnentius
	Reputed conversion of Georgian royal household
350s	Western bishops exiled for opposition to Constantius's Arianizing strategies for doctrinal unity
late 350s	Intensification of "Arian" and "Nicene" parties
356	Athanasius exiled once more
	Death of celebrated Egyptian ascetic, Antony
357	"Blasphemy" of Sirmium

Date	Major Developments
late 350s –360s	Further debates emerge about status of Christ and Holy Spirit
	Flourishing of monastic movement
359–360	Twin councils of unity (Seleucia and Ariminum) and gathering at Constantinople confirm political victory of *homoian* Arian theology
361–363	Reign of Julian "the Apostate": concerted effort to restore paganism; intellectual attacks on Christianity; restrictions on Christians as teachers; toleration of rival doctrinal positions within churches (return of exiled bishops)
362	Council of Alexandria
late 362–363	Athanasius in exile again
mid-late 360s	Major writings of Ephrem the Syrian produced at Edessa
	Martin (later of Tours) builds up ascetic community at Ligugé
364–375	Valentinian I emperor in West
364–368	Valens emperor in East
364	Athanasius returns to Alexandria
365–366	Fifth and final exile of Athanasius
366	Damasus becomes bishop of Rome
later 360s – 370s	Significant expansion of the Messalians in the East
367–383	Gratian joint emperor in the West
370s	Controversies over Apollinaris's Christology
	Cappadocian Fathers, especially Basil of Caesarea, active
	Further significant expansions of ascetic movements under way
ca. 371	Martin becomes bishop of Tours
373	Death of Athanasius
374	Ambrose becomes bishop of Milan
mid-370s	Fierce attack on Origen's teaching by Epiphanius of Salamis
	Intensifying disputes over "Origenism" for many years
late 370s	Priscillianism emerges in Spain
378	Roman defeat and death of Valens at Adrianople
	Antiochene scholar Diodore becomes bishop of Tarsus
379	Theodosius becomes emperor in East
380	Heresies including Arianism condemned by Theodosius
381	Second "ecumenical" Council at Constantinople: curtailing of "Arianism"; ecclesiastical status of Constantinople affirmed as second only to Rome
early 380s	Further writings by Gregory of Nazianzus and Gregory of Nyssa

Date	Major Developments
	Missionary work of Martin of Tours
	Beginnings of Jerome's translations of Scriptures
	Egeria writes of her travels in the East
	Tyconius's *Book of Rules*
	Pelagius arrives in Rome
382	Evagrius of Pontus moves to Egyptian desert
384	Siricius becomes bishop of Rome
385	Jerome leaves Rome for East
	Execution of Priscillian and some of his followers at Trier
385–386	Height of Ambrose's trials with his Arian opponents and court of Valentinian II in Milan
386	Conversion of Augustine at Milan
	Jerome settles at Bethlehem
	John Chrysostom ordained as priest in Antioch
387–388	Invasion of Italy and defeat of Maximus
390	Massacre at Thessalonica; subsequent penance of Theodosius
	Birth of Simeon "the Stylite"
391	Ban on pagan sacrifices and closure of temples; popular destruction or Christian appropriation of pagan shrines
early 390s	Further legislation against paganism and movements such as Manichaeism
	Paulinus arrives at Nola
392	Theodore becomes bishop of Mopsuestia
392–394	Revolt and defeat of Eugenius
395	Death of Theodosius
	Augustine becomes coadjutor bishop of Hippo and sole bishop the following year
397	John Chrysostom becomes bishop of Constantinople
	Death of Ambrose
397–401	Origenist controversy very intense
	Didymus the Blind active in Alexandria
	Augustine writes *Confessions*
	Victricius of Rouen visits southern Britain
ca. 399–412	Augustine active against Donatists
ca. 399–419	Augustine writes *On the Trinity*
ca. 402–407	Prudentius's hymns written

Date	Major Developments
406–407	Vandals, Sueves, and Alans cross Rhine into Roman territory and begin to advance southward across Gaul and Spain
407	Death of John Chrysostom in exile
409–410	Romans withdraw from Britain
410	Paulinus becomes bishop of Nola
	Fall of Rome to Goths under Alaric
	Pelagius and many of his followers leave Italy
411	Conference at Carthage condemns Donatists
	Pelagian teacher Celestius condemned in Carthage
412	Donatist church declared illegal
	Beginnings of Augustine's polemic against Pelagianism
	Cyril becomes bishop of Alexandria
413–426	Augustine writes *The City of God*
415	Murder of Neoplatonist teacher Hypatia in Alexandria
415–430	John Cassian's work as monastic leader in Gaul
	Controversy emerges in Gaul over Augustine's theology of grace
417–432	Pelagianism condemned in Rome
420	Death of Jerome
420s	Julian of Eclanum active as Pelagian controversialist
423	Theodoret becomes bishop of Cyrrhus
428–431	Fierce disputes over teaching of Nestorius, bishop of Constantinople; strong opposition from Cyril of Alexandria
	Support for Pelagian theology in Britain
429	Vandals invade North Africa
	Mission of Germanus of Auxerre to Britain
430	Death of Augustine
early 430s	Defenses of Augustine's teaching by Prosper of Aquitaine
431	Third "ecumenical" Council at Ephesus: Nestorius and Pelagian Celestius condemned
	Palladius undertakes Christian work in Ireland
ca. 432	Conventional date of arrival of Patrick in Ireland
433	Formulary of Reunion attempts to relieve tensions between Antiochene and Alexandrian theologians on person of Christ
437	Nestorius exiled to Egypt
439	Carthage falls to Vandals; Vandal kingdom in North Africa will favor Arianism and harass catholic believers for generations
440	Leo becomes bishop of Rome

Date	Major Developments
440s	Aggressive expansion of Huns under Attila
	Tracts and letters by Nestorius
444	Death of Cyril of Alexandria
446	Flavian becomes bishop of Constantinople
448	Eutyches condemned in Constantinople for allegedly undermining the humanity of Christ
449	"Robber council" at Ephesus
	Leo's *Tome*
	Death of Vincent of Lérins (?)
late 440s	Salvian writes in Marseilles
450	Death of Theodosius II; Marcian and Pulcheria take over
451	Fourth "ecumenical" Council at Chalcedon: Christ declared to be "one person acknowledged in two natures"
450s–470s	Extensive disputes over Chalcedon in the East; hardening of "Monophysite traditions" in Egypt, Palestine, Syria
453	Death of Attila
470	Sidonius Apollinaris becomes bishop of Clermont
476	Last Western emperor Romulus Augustulus removed from power by Odoacer
482	Zeno's *Henotikon*
484	Acacius of Constantinople excommunicated in Rome; schism opens up between the two churches
490s	Expansion of Antiochene Christianity in Syria and Persia
492–493	Marriage of Frankish King Clovis to Burgundian Christian princess Clotilde
493	Theoderic becomes king of Italy
ca. 499	Conversion of Clovis and ensuing expansion of Christianity among Franks
502	Caesarius becomes bishop of Arles
512	Severus becomes bishop of Antioch
	Public riot in Constantinople over use of *Trisagion* in worship
519	End of "Acacian" schism
520s	Persecution of "Monophysite" believers in much of East
523–524	Boethius writes the *Consolation of Philosophy* while awaiting execution for treason against Theoderic
527–565	Reign of emperor Justinian
late 520s	Consolidation of distinct "Monophysite" church in East
529	Council of Orange upholds Augustine's doctrine of grace (but condemns predestination to evil)

Date	Major Developments
	Benedict of Nursia founds monastery at Monte Cassino
530s–540s	Extensive disputes between pro- and anti-Chalcedonian polemicists in East
	Diverse attempts at reconciliation by Justinian
	Military campaigns to recover large areas of Western empire from barbarian control
	Possible date of Ninian's ministry in southern Scotland (though traditional date is from ca. 397–398)
533–534	Belisarius regains North Africa from Vandals
ca. 540	Benedict's *Rule*
541–543	Empire ravaged by plague
	Origenist controversy reignited in Palestine
ca. 542	Jacob Baradaeus secretly consecrated as "Monophysite" bishop of Edessa; itinerant ministry to "Monophysite" churches over subsequent years
543–544	Justinian's edict on the "Three Chapters" attempts to condemn extreme versions of Antiochene theology
mid-540s	"Monophysite" expansion in Nubia and Aksum
late 540s	Gildas writes on British church
550s–560s	Monasticism expands in Ireland and Wales
553	Fifth "ecumenical" Council in Constantinople condemns the "Three Chapters" and endorses pro-Cyrilline interpretation of Chalcedon
554	Cassiodorus establishes a scholarly monastic community on his estate near Naples
555	Armenian church aligns itself with non-Chalcedonian Syrian believers
563	Columba leaves Ireland for Scotland; he and his companions settle on Iona, either the same year or later
568	Lombards invade Italy
570	Birth of Mohammad
570s–590s	Hymns of Venantius Fortunatus
ca. 576	Gregory of Tours begins his *History of the Franks*
587	Conversion of Visigothic Spanish King Reccared to catholicism
589	Council of Toledo renounces Arianism in Spain
590	Gregory the Great becomes pope
590s	Columbanus travels from Ireland to Gaul and sets up monasteries
597	Arrival of Augustine's mission to Anglo-Saxons in Kent
	Death of Columba
ca. 600	Isidore becomes bishop of Seville

Date	Major Developments
604	Death of Gregory the Great
622	Migration of Mohammad and his followers to Medina
630	Establishment of Mecca as Islam's spiritual center
630s	Beginnings of Monothelite/Dyothelite controversies
662	Death of Maximus the Confessor
664	"Synod" of Whitby
680–681	Sixth "ecumenical" Council in Constantinople affirms Dyothelite theology

SUGGESTIONS FOR FURTHER READING

There is a vast literature on almost everything to do with early Christianity, and numerous catalogs and indexes record a flood of annual additions to this bibliography. Material of many kinds influenced the writing of this book; the following suggestions are only a small selection of pointers for readers who would like to pursue particular topics in more depth. The list is restricted to literature available in English, though very extensive resources are to be found in other languages, especially in French, German, and Italian. The selection is also confined to book-length studies, though an enormous amount of journal literature exists on all topics, and vital discussions often take place in this context. The list reflects a wide range of historical and theological perspectives and is not necessarily representative of the interpretations offered in this book.

Sources

1. Ancient Christian Authors

Various English-translation series exist for ancient Christian authors. Among the most important are:

Ancient Christian Writers. Edited by J. Quasten and J. C. Plumpe. Westminster, MD, and New York: Newman Press, 1946–.
Classics of Western Spirituality. Edited by R. J. Payne. Ramsey, NJ: Paulist Press; London: SPCK, 1978–.
The Fathers of the Church. Washington, DC: Catholic University of America Press, 1946–.

411

Library of Christian Classics. Edited by J. Baillie, J. T. McNeill, and H. P. van Dusen. Philadelphia: Westminster; London: SCM Press, 1953–69.

The Library of Early Christianity. Washington, DC: Catholic University of America Press, 2002–.

Loeb Classical Library. Cambridge, MA: Harvard University Press; London: Heinemann, 1912–.

Oxford Early Christian Texts. Edited by H. Chadwick. Oxford: Oxford University Press, 1970–.

The Oxford Library of the Fathers. Edited by M. Dods. Edinburgh: T. & T. Clark; New York: Eerdmans, 1838–81.

Popular Patristics. Crestwood, NY: St. Vladimir's Seminary Press, 2001–.

A Select Library of Nicene and Post-Nicene Fathers of the Christian Church. Edited by P. Schaff and H. Wace. Reprint. Grand Rapids: Eerdmans, 1975–.

Translated Texts for Historians. Liverpool: Liverpool University Press, 1985–.

Other significant translations have been issued in series such as the Penguin Classics (Harmondsworth, England: Penguin) and by publishers such as Cistercian Publications (Kalamazoo, MI) and Liturgical Press (Collegeville, MN).

2. Useful Anthologies

Bettenson, H., ed. *The Later Christian Fathers*. Oxford: Oxford University Press, 1970.

Stevenson, J., ed. *A New Eusebius: Documents Illustrating the History of the Church to* A.D. *337*. Rev. ed. by W. H. C. Frend. London: SPCK, 1987.

———. *Creeds, Councils and Controversies: Documents Illustrative of the History of the Church* A.D. *337–461*. Rev. ed. by W. H. C. Frend. London: SPCK, 1989.

Wiles, M. and M. Santer, eds. *Documents in Early Christian Thought*. Cambridge: Cambridge University Press, 1975.

Valuable collections of texts on a variety of doctrinal, social, and moral themes, accompanied by introductory essays, can be found in the series *Message of the Fathers of the Church* (Wilmington, DE: Michael Glazier; Collegeville, MN: Liturgical Press, 1983–).

Early Christian exposition and application of biblical texts can be sampled in the excellent series *Ancient Christian Commentary on Scripture* (Downers Grove, IL: InterVarsity, 1998–).

3. On the Role of Archaeological Resources

Frend, W. H. C. *The Archaeology of Early Christianity: A History*. London: Geoffrey Chapman; Minneapolis, MN: Fortress Press, 1996.

4. On Legal Texts

Coleman-Norton, P. R., *Roman State and Christian Church: A Collection of Legal Documents to A.D. 535*. 3 vols. London: SPCK, 1966.

5. On Councils

Davis, L. D. *The First Seven Ecumenical Councils: Their History and Theology (325–787)*. Collegeville, MN: Liturgical Press, 1990.

Tanner, N. P., ed. *Decrees of the Ecumenical Councils*. Vol. 1, *From Nicaea I to Lateran V*. Washington, DC: Georgetown University Press; London: Sheed and Ward, 1990.

Reference Works

Ackroyd, P. R. and C. F. Evans, eds. *The Cambridge History of the Bible*. Vol. 1, *From the Beginnings to Jerome*. Cambridge: Cambridge University Press, 1970.

Altaner, B. *Patrology*. 6th ed. Translated by H. C. Graef. Freiburg, Germany: Herder; Edinburgh and London: Nelson, 1960.

Apostolos-Cappadona, D. *Dictionary of Christian Art*. New York: Continuum, 1994.

Armstrong, A. H., ed. *The Cambridge History of Later Greek and Early Medieval Philosophy*. Cambridge: Cambridge University Press, 1967.

Atiya, A. S., ed. *The Coptic Encyclopedia*. 8 vols. New York and Toronto: Macmillan, 1991.

di Berardino, A., ed., with bibliographies by W. H. C. Frend. *Encyclopaedia of the Early Church*. 2 vols. Cambridge, England: James Clarke, 1992.

Bowersock, G. W., P. Brown, and O. Grabar, eds. *Late Antiquity: A Guide to the Postclassical World*. Cambridge, MA: Harvard University Press, 1999.

Bradshaw, P., ed. *The New SCM Dictionary of Liturgy and Worship*. London: SCM Press, 2002. U.S. edition: *The New Westminster Dictionary of Liturgy and Worship*. Louisville: Westminster John Knox Press, 2002.

Chadwick, H. and G. R. Evans, eds. *Atlas of the Christian Church*. London: Guild Publishing, 1987.

Cross, F. L., ed. *The Oxford Dictionary of the Christian Church*. 3rd rev. ed. Edited by E. A. Livingstone. Oxford: Oxford University Press, 1997.

Farmer, D. H. *The Oxford Dictionary of Saints*. 2nd ed. Oxford: Oxford University Press, 1987.

Ferguson, E. *Backgrounds of Early Christianity*. 3rd ed. Grand Rapids: Eerdmans, 2003.

———, ed. *Encyclopaedia of Early Christianity*. Rev. ed. 2 vols. New York: Garland, 1997.

Fitzgerald, A. D., ed. *Augustine through the Ages: An Encyclopedia*. Grand Rapids and Cambridge, England: Eerdmans, 1999.

Hornblower, S. and A. Spawforth, eds. *The Oxford Classical Dictionary*. 3rd ed. Oxford: Oxford University Press, 1996.

Johnston, W. M., ed. *Encyclopedia of Monasticism*. 2 vols. Chicago and London: Fitzroy Dearborn Publishers, 2000.

Kelly, J. F., ed. *The Concise Dictionary of Early Christianity*. Collegeville, MN: Liturgical Press/Michael Glazier, 1992.

Kelly, J. N. D. *The Oxford Dictionary of Popes*. Oxford: Oxford University Press, 1986.

McGuckin, J. A. *The Westminster Handbook of Patristic Theology*. Louisville: Westminster John Knox Press, 2004.

van der Meer, F. N. S. and C. Mohrmann, eds. *The Atlas of the Early Christian World*. Translated by M. Hedlund and H. H. Rowley. London: Nelson, 1958.

Parry, K., D. J. Melling, D. Brady, S. H. Griffith, and J. F. Healey, eds. *The Blackwell Dictionary of Eastern Christianity*. Oxford and Malden, MA: Blackwell, 1999.

Quasten, J. *Patrology*. 3 vols. Utrecht, Netherlands, and Antwerp, Belgium: Spectrum; Westminster, MD: Newman Press, 1962–64. Supplemented by 3 further vols. by A. di Berardino, 1978–2001.

Young, F., L. Ayres, and A. Louth, eds. *The Cambridge History of Early Christian Literature*. Cambridge: Cambridge University Press, 2004.

Other Historical Guides

On the period from Jesus to Constantine:

Davidson, I. J. *The Birth of the Church: From Jesus to Constantine*, A.D. *30–312*. The Baker History of the Church/Monarch History of the Church. Vol. 1. Grand Rapids: Baker, 2004; London: Monarch Books, 2005.

Other, more general guides on the era covered in the present book include the following:

Introductory

Brown, P. R. L. *The World of Late Antiquity: From Marcus Aurelius to Muhammad*. London: Thames and Hudson, 1971.

———. *The Rise of Western Christendom: Triumph and Diversity*, A.D. *200–1000*. 2nd ed. Oxford and Malden, MA: Blackwell, 2003.

Brox, N. *A History of the Early Church*. Translated by J. Bowden. London: SCM Press, 1994.

Chadwick, H. *The Early Church*. Harmondsworth, England: Penguin, 1967.

Frend, W. H. C. *The Early Church*. Reprint. London: SCM Press, 1982.

Hazlett, I., ed. *Early Christianity: Origins and Evolution to A.D. 600*. London: SPCK, 1991.

Herrin, J. *The Formation of Christendom*. Oxford: Blackwell, 1987.

Lietzmann, H. *A History of the Early Church*. Vol. 2, parts 3–4. Translated by B. L. Woolf. Foreword and bibliography by W. H. C. Frend. Cambridge, England: James Clarke, 1993.

Markschies, C. *Between Two Worlds: Structures of Earliest Christianity*. Translated by J. Bowden. London: SCM Press, 1999.

Rousseau, P. *The Early Christian Centuries*. London: Darton, Longman and Todd, 2002.

More Advanced

Chadwick, H. *The Church in Ancient Society: From Galilee to Gregory the Great*. Oxford History of the Christian Church. Oxford: Oxford University Press, 2001.

————. *East and West: The Making of a Rift in the Church, from Apostolic Times until the Council of Florence*. Oxford: Oxford University Press, 2003.

Esler, P. F., ed. *The Early Christian World*. 2 vols. London and New York: Routledge, 2000.

Frend, W. H. C. *The Rise of Christianity*. London: Darton, Longman and Todd; Philadelphia: Fortress Press, 1984.

General History of the Period

Invaluable discussions of late antiquity and the early medieval world can be found in relevant volumes of the *Cambridge Ancient History* and *The New Cambridge Medieval History* (Cambridge: Cambridge University Press). Other very useful sources include:

Cameron, A. *The Later Roman Empire*, A.D. *284–430*. London: Fontana; Cambridge, MA: Harvard University Press, 1993.

————. *The Mediterranean World in Late Antiquity*, A.D. *395–600*. London and New York: Routledge, 1993.

Garnsey, P. and R. Saller. *The Roman Empire: Economy, Society and Culture*. London: Duckworth, 1987.

Jones, A. H. M. *The Later Roman Empire, 284–602: A Social, Economic, and Administrative Survey*. 3 vols. + maps. Oxford: Oxford University Press, 1964.

Lançon, B. *Rome in Late Antiquity*: A.D. *313–604*. Translated by A. Nevill. London and New York: Routledge, 2001.

MacMullen, R. *Christianizing the Roman Empire (*A.D. *100–400)*. New Haven and London: Yale University Press, 1984.

————. *Christianity and Paganism in the Fourth to Eighth Centuries*. New Haven and London: Yale University Press, 1997.

On Ideas, Doctrine, and Practice

Ayres, L. *Nicaea and Its Legacy: An Approach to Fourth-Century Trinitarian Theology*. Oxford: Oxford University Press, 2004.

Behr, J. *The Way to Nicaea: Formation of Christian Theology*. Vol. 1. Crestwood, NY: St. Vladimir's Seminary Press, 2001.

————. *The Nicene Faith: Formation of Christian Theology*. Vol. 2. Crestwood, NY: St. Vladimir's Seminary Press, 2004.

di Berardino, A. and B. Studer, eds. *History of Theology*. Vol. 1, *The Patristic Period*. Translated by M. J. O'Connell. Collegeville, MN: Michael Glazier/Liturgical Press, 1997.

Daley, B. E. *The Hope of the Early Church: A Handbook of Patristic Eschatology*. Cambridge: Cambridge University Press, 1991.

Evans, G. R. *A Brief History of Heresy*. Oxford and Malden, MA: Blackwell, 2003.

————, ed. *The First Christian Theologians: An Introduction to Theology in the Early Church*. Oxford and Malden, MA: Blackwell, 2004.

Greer, R. A. *Broken Lights and Mended Lives: Theology and Common Life in the Early Church*. Reprint. Philadelphia: Pennsylvania State University Press, 2001.

Grillmeier, A. *Christ in Christian Tradition*. Vol. 1, *From the Apostolic Age to Chalcedon (A.D. 451)*. Rev. ed. Translated by J. Bowden. London and Oxford: Mowbray, 1975. Vol. 2, *From the Council of Chalcedon (451) to Gregory the Great (590–604)*. Part 1, *Reception and Contradiction: The Development of the Discussion about Chalcedon from 451 to the Beginning of the Reign of Justinian*. Translated by P. Allen and J. Cawte. London and Oxford: Mowbray; Atlanta: John Knox Press, 1987, 1995. Part 2 (with T. Hainthaler), *The Church of Constantinople in the Sixth Century*. Translated by P. Allen and J. Cawte. London: Mowbray; Louisville: Westminster John Knox Press, 1995. Part 4 (with T. Hainthaler), *The Church of Alexandria with Nubia and Ethiopia after 451*. Translated by O. C. Dean, Jr. London: Mowbray; Atlanta: Westminster John Knox Press, 1996.

Hall, C. A. *Reading Scripture with the Church Fathers*. Downers Grove, IL: InterVarsity Press, 1998.

———. *Learning Theology with the Church Fathers*. Downers Grove, IL: InterVarsity Press, 2002.

Hall, S. G. *Doctrine and Practice in the Early Church*. London: SPCK, 1991.

Hanson, R. P. C. *The Search for the Christian Doctrine of God: The Arian Controversy 318–381*. Edinburgh: T. & T. Clark, 1988.

Kelly, J. N. D. *Early Christian Creeds*. 3rd ed. London: Longman, 1972.

———. *Early Christian Doctrines*. 5th ed. London: A. & C. Black, 1977.

Pelikan, J. *The Christian Tradition: A History of the Development of Doctrine*. Vol. 1, *The Emergence of the Catholic Tradition (100–600)*. Chicago and London: Chicago University Press, 1971.

Prestige, G. L. *God in Patristic Thought*. 2nd ed. London: SPCK, 1952.

Ramsey, B. *Beginning to Read the Fathers*. London: SCM Press, 1993.

Studer, B. *Trinity and Incarnation: The Faith of the Early Church*. Translated by M. Westerhoff. Edited by A. Louth. Edinburgh: T. & T. Clark, 1993.

Tanner, N. P. *The Councils of the Church: A Short History*. New York: Herder and Herder/Crossroad, 2001.

Torrance, T. F. *The Trinitarian Faith: The Evangelical Theology of the Ancient Catholic Church*. Edinburgh: T. & T. Clark, 1988.

Turner, H. E. W. *The Patristic Doctrine of Redemption: A Study of the Development of Doctrine during the First Five Centuries*. London: Mowbray, 1952.

Wilken, R. *The Spirit of Early Christian Thought: Seeking the Face of God*. New Haven and London: Yale University Press, 2003.

Young, F. *From Nicaea to Chalcedon: A Guide to the Literature and Its Background*. London: SCM Press, 1983.

———. *The Making of the Creeds*. London: SCM Press, 1991.

The Dawn of a New Age

Barnes, T. D. *Constantine and Eusebius*. Cambridge, MA, and London: Harvard University Press, 1981.

Baynes, N. H. *Constantine the Great and the Christian Church*. 2nd ed. Oxford: Oxford University Press, 1972.

Bowder, D. *The Age of Constantine and Julian*. London: Paul Elek, 1978.

Cameron, A. and S. G. Hall, ed. and trans. *Eusebius: Life of Constantine*. Oxford: Oxford University Press, 1999.

Drake, H. A. *Constantine and the Bishops: The Politics of Intolerance*. Baltimore: Johns Hopkins University Press, 2000.

Frend, W. H. C. *Martyrdom and Persecution in the Early Church*. Oxford: Blackwell, 1965.

Jones, A. H. M. *Constantine and the Conversion of Europe*. London: Macmillan, 1962.

Kee, A. *Constantine versus Christ*. London: SCM Press, 1982.

Lieu, S. N. C. and D. Montserrat, eds. *Constantine: History, Historiography and Legend*. London and New York: Routledge, 1998.

Pohlsander, H. A. *The Emperor Constantine*. London and New York: Routledge, 1996.

Chapter 1

In addition to the above literature on Constantine:

Cameron, A. *Christianity and the Rhetoric of Empire: The Development of Christian Discourse*. Berkeley and Los Angeles: University of California Press, 1991.

Digeser, E. D. *The Making of a Christian Empire: Lactantius and Rome*. Ithaca, NY: Cornell University Press, 1999.

Frend, W. H. C. *The Donatist Church: A Movement of Protest in Roman North Africa*. 3rd ed. Oxford: Oxford University Press, 1985.

Grant, R. M. *Eusebius as Church Historian*. Oxford: Oxford University Press, 1980.

Greenslade, S. L. *Church and State from Constantine to Theodosius*. London: SCM Press, 1954.

Gregg, R. C. and D. E. Groh. *Early Arianism: A View of Salvation*. Philadelphia: Fortress Press, 1981.

Hanson, R. P. C. *The Search for the Christian Doctrine of God: The Arian Controversy 318–381*. Edinburgh: T. & T. Clark, 1988.

Hunt, E. D. *Holy Land Pilgrimage in the Later Roman Empire, A.D. 312–460*. Oxford: Oxford University Press, 1982.

Mendels, D. *The Media Revolution of Early Christianity: An Essay on Eusebius's Ecclesiastical History*. Grand Rapids: Eerdmans, 1999.

Walker, P. W. L. *Holy City, Holy Places: Christian Attitudes to Jerusalem and the Holy Land in the Fourth Century*. Oxford: Oxford University Press, 1993.

Wilkens, R. L. *The Land Called Holy: Palestine in Christian History and Thought*. New Haven and London: Yale University Press, 1992.

Williams, R. *Arius: Heresy and Tradition*. London: Darton, Longman and Todd, 1987.

Chapter 2

Anatolios, K. *Athanasius: The Coherence of His Thought*. London and New York: Routledge, 1998.

———. *Athanasius*. London and New York: Routledge, 2004.

Ayres, L. *Nicaea and Its Legacy: An Approach to Fourth-Century Trinitarian Theology*. Oxford: Oxford University Press, 2004.

Barnes, M. R. and D. H. Williams, eds. *Arianism after Arius: Essays on the History of the Fourth Century Trinitarian Conflicts*. Edinburgh: T. & T. Clark, 1993.

Barnes, T. D. *Athanasius and Constantius: Theology and Politics in the Constantinian Empire*. Cambridge, MA, and London: Harvard University Press, 1993.

Borschardt, C. F. A. *Hilary of Poitiers' Role in the Arian Struggle*. The Hague: Nijhoff, 1966.

Brakke, D. *Athanasius and the Politics of Asceticism*. Oxford: Oxford University Press, 1995.

Gregg, R. C., ed. *Arianism: Historical and Theological Reassessments*. Cambridge, MA, and Philadelphia: Philadelphia Patristic Foundation, 1985.

Hanson, R. P. C. *The Search for the Christian Doctrine of God: The Arian Controversy 318–381*. Edinburgh: T. & T. Clark, 1988.

Kopecek, T. A. *A History of Neo-Arianism*. 2 vols. Cambridge, MA: Philadelphia Patristic Foundation, 1979.

Newlands, G. M. *Hilary of Poitiers: A Study in Theological Method*. Berne, Switzerland: Peter Lang, 1978.

Pettersen, A. *Athanasius*. London: Geoffrey Chapman, 1995.

Thomson, R. W., ed. and trans. *Athanasius,* Contra Gentes *and* De Incarnatione. Oxford: Oxford University Press, 1971.

Vaggione, R. P. *Eunomius of Cyzicus and the Nicene Revolution*. Oxford: Oxford University Press, 2000.

Widdicombe, P. *The Fatherhood of God from Origen to Athanasius*. Oxford: Oxford University Press, 1994.

Wiles, M. *Archetypal Heresy: Arianism through the Centuries*. Oxford: Oxford University Press, 1996.

Chapter 3

Athanassiadi, P. *Julian: An Intellectual Biography*. London and New York: Routledge, 1992.

Bowder, D. *The Age of Constantine and Julian*. London: Paul Elek, 1978.

Bowersock, G. W. *Julian the Apostate*. Cambridge, MA: Harvard University Press, 1978.

Browning, R. *The Emperor Julian*. Berkeley and Los Angeles: University of California Press, 1976.

Coakley, S., ed. *Rethinking Gregory of Nyssa*. Oxford and Malden, MA: Blackwell, 2003.

Fedwick, P. J., ed. *Basil of Caesarea: Christian, Humanist, Ascetic*. 2 vols. Toronto: Pontifical Institute of Medieval Studies, 1981.

Haykin, M. A. G. *The Spirit of God: The Exegesis of 1 and 2 Corinthians in the Pneumatomachian Controversy of the Fourth Century*. Leiden, Netherlands: E. J. Brill, 1994.

McGuckin, J. A. *Saint Gregory of Nazianzus: An Intellectual Biography*. Crestwood, NY: St. Vladimir's Seminary Press, 2001.

Meredith, A. *The Cappadocians*. London: Geoffrey Chapman, 1995.

———. *Gregory of Nyssa*. London and New York: Routledge, 1999.

Momigliano, A., ed. *The Conflict between Paganism and Christianity in the Fourth Century*. Oxford: Oxford University Press, 1963.

Pelikan, J. *Christianity and Classical Culture: The Metamorphosis of Natural Theology in the Christian Encounter with Hellenism*. New Haven and London: Yale University Press, 1993.

Raven, C. E. *Apollinarianism: An Essay on the Christology of the Early Church*. Cambridge: Cambridge University Press, 1923.

Rousseau, P. *Basil of Caesarea*. Berkeley and Los Angeles: University of California Press, 1994.

Seitz, C. R., ed. *Nicene Christianity: The Future for a New Ecumenism*. Grand Rapids: Brazos Press; Carlisle, England: Paternoster Press, 2001.

Shapland, C. A. B., ed. and trans. *The Letters of Saint Athanasius Concerning the Holy Spirit*. London: Epworth Press, 1951.

Smith, R. *Julian's Gods: Religion and Philosophy in the Thought and Action of Julian the Apostate*. London and New York: Routledge, 1995.

Stewart, C. *"Working the Earth of the Heart": The Messalian Controversy in History, Texts, and Language to* A.D. *431*. Oxford: Oxford University Press, 1991.

Torrance, T. F., ed. *The Incarnation: Ecumenical Studies in the Nicene-Constantinopolitan Creed,* A.D. *381*. Edinburgh: Handsel Press, 1981.

Chapter 4

Brown, D. Vir Trilinguis: *A Study in the Biblical Exegesis of Saint Jerome*. Kampen, Netherlands: Kok Pharos, 1992.

Brown, P. R. L. *Authority and the Sacred: Aspects of the Christianisation of the Roman World*. Cambridge: Cambridge University Press, 1995.

———. *Power and Persuasion in Late Antiquity: Towards a Christian Empire*. Madison: University of Wisconsin Press, 1992.

Burrus, V. *The Making of a Heretic: Gender, Authority and the Priscillianist Controversy*. Berkeley and Los Angeles: University of California Press, 1995.

Cameron, A. *Christianity and the Rhetoric of Empire: The Development of Christian Discourse*. Berkeley and Los Angeles: University of California Press, 1991.

Chadwick, H. *Priscillian of Avila: The Occult and the Charismatic in the Early Church*. Oxford: Oxford University Press, 1976.

Curran, J. *Pagan City and Christian Capital: Rome in the Fourth Century*. Oxford: Oxford University Press, 2000.

Davidson, I. J. *Ambrose,* De Officiis: *Edited with an Introduction, Translation, and Commentary*. 2 vols. Oxford: Oxford University Press, 2002.

Hagendahl, H. *Latin Fathers and the Classics: A Study on the Apologists, Jerome, and other Christian Writers*. Gothenburg, Sweden: Gothenburg University Press, 1958.

Hayward, C. T. R. *Saint Jerome's Hebrew Questions on Genesis, Translated with an Introduction and Commentary*. Oxford: Oxford University Press, 1995.

Homes Dudden, F. *The Life and Times of Saint Ambrose*. 2 vols. Oxford: Oxford University Press, 1935.

Humphries, M. *Communities of the Blessed: Social Environment and Religious Change in Northern Italy,* A.D. *20–400*. Oxford: Oxford University Press, 1999.

Kamesar, A. *Jerome, Greek Scholarship, and the Hebrew Bible: A Study of the* Quaestiones Hebraicae in Genesim. Oxford: Oxford University Press, 1993.

Kelly, J. N. D. *Jerome, His Life, Writings, and Controversies*. London: Duckworth, 1975.

King, N. Q. *The Emperor Theodosius and the Establishment of Christianity*. London, SCM Press, 1961.

Lieu, S. N. C. *Manichaeism in the Later Roman Empire and Medieval China*. 2nd ed. Tübingen, Germany: Mohr Siebeck, 1992.

Matthews, J. *Western Aristocracies and Imperial Court*, A.D. *364–425*. Oxford: Oxford University Press, 1975.

McLynn, N. B. *Ambrose of Milan: Church and Court in a Christian Capital*. Berkeley and Los Angeles: University of California Press, 1994.

Moorhead, J. *Ambrose: Church and Society in the Late Roman World*. London and New York: Longman, 1999.

Ramsey, B. *Ambrose*. London and New York: Routledge, 1997.

Rebenich, S. *Jerome*. London and New York: Routledge, 2002.

Wiesen, D. S. *St. Jerome as a Satirist: A Study in Christian Latin Thought and Letters*. Ithaca, NY: Cornell University Press, 1964.

Williams, D. H. *Ambrose of Milan and the End of the Nicene-Arian Conflicts*. Oxford: Oxford University Press, 1995.

Williams, S. and G. Friell. *Theodosius: The Empire at Bay*. London: Batsford, 1994.

Chapter 5

Binns, J. *Ascetics and Ambassadors of Christ: The Monasteries of Palestine, 314–631*. Oxford: Oxford University Press, 1994.

Brock, S. *The Luminous Eye: The Spiritual World Vision of St. Ephrem*. Rev. ed. Kalamazoo, MI: Cistercian Publications, 1992.

———, ed. and trans. *St. Ephrem the Syrian: Hymns on Paradise*. Crestwood, NY: St. Vladimir's Seminary Press, 1990.

Brown, P. *The Body and Society: Men, Women and Sexual Renunciation in Early Christianity*. New York: Columbia University Press, 1988.

Burton-Christie, D. *The Word in the Desert: Scripture and the Quest for Holiness in Early Christian Monasticism*. New York: Oxford University Press, 1993.

Caner, D. *Wandering, Begging Monks: Spiritual Authority and the Promotion of Monasticism in Late Antiquity*. Berkeley and Los Angeles: University of California Press, 2002.

Chadwick, O. *John Cassian*. 2nd ed. Oxford: Oxford University Press, 1968.

Chitty, D. J. *The Desert a City*. Oxford: Blackwell, 1966.

Chryssavgnis, J. *In the Heart of the Desert: The Spirituality of the Desert Fathers and Mothers*. Bloomington, IN: World Wisdom, 2003.

Clark, E. A. *The Life of Melania the Younger: Introduction, Translation, and Commentary*. New York: Edwin Mellen Press, 1984.

———. *The Origenist Controversy: The Cultural Construction of an Early Christian Debate*. Princeton, NJ: Princeton University Press, 1992.

Conybeare, C. *Paulinus Noster: Self and Symbols in the Letters of Paulinus of Nola*. Oxford: Oxford University Press, 2000.

Cunningham, M. and P. Allen, eds. *Preacher and Audience: Studies in Early Christian and Byzantine Homiletics*. Leiden, Netherlands: E. J. Brill, 1998.

Dunn, M. *The Emergence of Monasticism: From the Desert Fathers to the Early Middle Ages*. Oxford and Malden, MA: Blackwell, 2000.

Dysinger, L. *Psalmody and Prayer in the Writings of Evagrius Ponticus*. Oxford: Oxford University Press, 2004.

Elm, S. *"Virgins of God": The Making of Asceticism in Late Antiquity.* Oxford: Oxford University Press, 1994.

Gould, G. *The Desert Fathers on Monastic Community.* Oxford: Oxford University Press, 1993.

Griffith, S. H. *Faith Adoring the Mystery: Reading the Bible with St. Ephrem the Syrian.* Milwaukee: Marquette University Press, 1997.

Harmless, W. *Desert Christians: An Introduction to the Literature of Early Monasticism.* New York: Oxford University Press, 2004.

Kelly, J. N. D. *Golden Mouth: The Story of John Chrysostom—Ascetic, Preacher, Bishop.* London: Duckworth, 1995.

Liebeschuetz, J. H. W. G. *Barbarians and Bishops: Army, Church, and State in the Age of Arcadius and Chrysostom.* Oxford: Oxford University Press, 1990.

Lienhard, J. *Paulinus of Nola and Early Western Monasticism.* Cologne and Bonn, Germany: P. Hanstein, 1977.

Mayer, W. and P. Allen. *John Chrysostom.* London and New York: Routledge, 2000.

McVey, K. E., trans. *Ephrem the Syrian: Hymns on the Nativity, Hymns against Julian, Hymns of Virginity and on the Symbols of the Lord.* New York: Paulist Press, 1989.

Murray, R. *Symbols of Church and Kingdom: A Study in Early Syriac Tradition.* Cambridge: Cambridge University Press, 1975.

Rousseau, P. *Ascetics, Authority and the Church in the Age of Jerome and Cassian.* Oxford: Oxford University Press, 1978.

———. *Pachomius: The Making of a Community in Fourth-Century Egypt.* Berkeley and Los Angeles: University of California Press, 1985.

Rubenson, S. *The Letters of St. Anthony: Monasticism and the Making of a Saint.* Minneapolis: Fortress Press, 1995.

Stancliffe, C. *St. Martin and His Hagiographer: History and Miracle in Sulpicius Severus.* Oxford: Oxford University Press, 1983.

Stewart, C. *Cassian the Monk.* New York: Oxford University Press, 1998.

Trout, D. *Paulinus of Nola: Life, Letters and Poems.* Berkeley and Los Angeles: University of California Press, 1999.

Ward, B. *The Sayings of the Desert Fathers: The Alphabetical Collection.* London: Mowbray; Kalamazoo, MI: Cistercian Publications, 1975.

Wilken, R. L. *John Chrysostom and the Jews: Rhetoric and Reality in the Late Fourth Century.* Berkeley and Los Angeles: University of California Press, 1983.

Wilkinson, J. *Egeria's Travels.* London: SPCK, 1971.

Wimbush, V. L. and R. Valantasis, eds. *Asceticism.* New York: Oxford University Press, 1995.

Chapter 6

Babcock, W. S., ed. and trans. *Tyconius: The Book of Rules.* Atlanta: Scholars Press, 1989.

Bonner, G. *Augustine and Modern Research on Pelagianism.* Villanova, PA: Villanova University Press, 1972.

———. *God's Decree and Man's Destiny: Studies on the Thought of Augustine of Hippo.* London: Variorum Reprints, 1987.

————. *St. Augustine of Hippo: Life and Controversies*. Rev. ed. Norwich, England: Canterbury Press, 1986.

Brown, P. R. L. *Augustine of Hippo: A Biography*. London: Faber & Faber, 1967.

————. *Religion and Society in the Age of Saint Augustine*. London: Faber & Faber, 1972.

de Bruyn, T. S., ed. and trans. *Pelagius's Commentary on St. Paul's Epistle to the Romans*. Oxford: Oxford University Press, 1993.

Burnaby, J. *Amor Dei: A Study of the Religion of Saint Augustine*. London: Hodder and Stoughton, 1938.

Burt, D. X. *Friendship and Society: An Introduction to Augustine's Practical Philosophy*. Grand Rapids: Eerdmans, 1999.

Burton, P., ed. and trans., with introduction by R. Lane Fox. *Augustine: The Confessions*. London: Everyman, 2001.

Chadwick, H. *Augustine*. Oxford: Oxford University Press, 1986.

————. ed. and trans. *Saint Augustine: Confessions*. Oxford: Oxford University Press, 1991.

Clark, M. T. *Augustine*. London: Geoffrey Chapman, 1994.

Dodaro, R. and G. Lawless, eds. *Augustine and His Critics: Essays in Honour of Gerald Bonner*. London and New York: Routledge, 2002.

Evans, G. R. *Augustine on Evil*. Cambridge: Cambridge University Press, 1982.

Evans, R. F. *Pelagius: Inquiries and Reappraisals*. London: A. & C. Black, 1968.

Ferguson, J. *Pelagius: A Historical and Theological Study*. Cambridge: Cambridge University Press, 1956.

Frend, W. H. C. *The Donatist Church: A Movement of Protest in Roman North Africa*. 3rd ed. Oxford: Oxford University Press, 1985.

Gilson, E. *The Christian Philosophy of Saint Augustine*. Translated by L. E. M. Lynch. London: Victor Gollancz, 1961.

Harrison, C. *Augustine: Christian Truth and Fractured Humanity*. Oxford: Oxford University Press, 2000.

Kirwan, C. *Augustine*. London and New York: Routledge, 1989.

Lancel, S. *St. Augustine*. Translated by A. M. Nevill. London: SCM Press, 2002.

Lawless, G. *Augustine of Hippo and His Monastic Rule*. Oxford: Oxford University Press, 1987.

Markus, R. A. *Saeculum: History and Society in the Theology of St. Augustine*. Cambridge: Cambridge University Press, 1970.

Merdinger, J. *Rome and the African Church in the Time of Augustine*. New Haven and London: Yale University Press, 1997.

O'Daly, G. J. P. *Augustine's Philosophy of Mind*. London: Duckworth, 1987.

O'Donnell, J. J. *Augustine, Confessions*. 3 vols. Oxford: Oxford University Press, 1992.

Rees, B. R. *The Letters of Pelagius and His Followers*. Woodbridge, Suffolk, England: Boydell Press, 1991.

————. *Pelagius: A Reluctant Heretic*. Woodbridge, Suffolk, England: Boydell Press, 1988.

Rist, J. *Augustine: Ancient Thought Baptized*. Cambridge: Cambridge University Press, 1994.

Scott, T. K. *Augustine: His Thought in Context*. Mahwah, NJ: Paulist Press, 1995.

Stump, E. and N. Kretzmann, eds. *The Cambridge Companion to Augustine*. Cambridge: Cambridge University Press, 2001.

TeSelle, E. *Augustine the Theologian*. New York: Herder & Herder, 1970.

Wetzel, J. *Augustine and the Limits of Virtue*. Cambridge: Cambridge University Press, 1992.

Willis, G. G. *Saint Augustine and the Donatist Controversy*. London: SPCK, 1950.

Chapter 7

Bagnall, R. S. *Egypt in Late Antiquity*. Princeton, NJ: Princeton University Press, 1993.

Bethune-Baker, J. F. *Nestorius and His Teaching*. Cambridge: Cambridge University Press, 1908.

Greer, R. A. *Theodore of Mopsuestia: Exegete and Theologian*. London: Faith Press, 1961.

Keating, D. A. *The Appreciation of Divine Life in Cyril of Alexandria*. Oxford: Oxford University Press, 2004.

McGuckin, J. A. *Cyril of Alexandria: The Christological Controversy*. Leiden, Netherlands: E. J. Brill, 1994.

Norris, R. A. *Manhood and Christ: A Study in the Christology of Theodore of Mopsuestia*. Oxford: Oxford University Press, 1963.

Russell, N. *Cyril of Alexandria*. London and New York: Routledge, 2000.

Sellers, R. V. *The Council of Chalcedon: A Historical and Doctrinal Survey*. London: SPCK, 1953.

———. *Two Ancient Christologies: A Study in the Christological Thought of the Schools of Alexandria and Antioch in the Early History of Christian Doctrine*. London: SPCK, 1940.

Torrance, T. F. *Divine Meaning: Studies in Patristic Hermeneutics*. Edinburgh: T. & T. Clark, 1995.

Wallace-Hadrill, J. S. *Christian Antioch: A Study of Early Christian Thought in the East*. Cambridge: Cambridge University Press, 1982.

Weinandy, T. G. and D. A. Keating, eds. *The Theology of St. Cyril of Alexandria: A Critical Appreciation*. Edinburgh: T. & T. Clark, 2003.

Wessel, S. *Cyril of Alexandria and the Nestorian Controversy: The Making of a Saint and of a Heretic*. Oxford: Oxford University Press, 2004.

Wickham, L. R., ed. and trans. *Cyril of Alexandria: Select Letters*. Oxford: Oxford University Press, 1983.

Young, F. *Biblical Exegesis and the Formation of Christian Culture*. Cambridge: Cambridge University Press, 1997.

Chapter 8

Atiya, A. S. *A History of Eastern Christianity*. London: Methuen, 1968.

Attwater, D. *The Christian Churches of the East*. 2 vols. Milwaukee: Bruce Publishing Company, 1947–48.

Berkey, J. P. *The Foundation of Islam: Religion and Society in the Near East, 600–1800*. Cambridge: Cambridge University Press, 2003.

Brown, D. W. *A New Introduction to Islam*. Oxford and Malden, MA: Blackwell, 2004.

Chesnut, R. C. *Three Monophysite Christologies*. Oxford: Oxford University Press, 1976.

Frend, W. H. C. *The Rise of the Monophysite Movement: Chapters in the History of the Church in the Fifth and Sixth Centuries*. Cambridge: Cambridge University Press, 1972.

Gray, P. T. R. *The Defense of Chalcedon in the East (451–553)*. Leiden, Netherlands: E. J. Brill, 1979.

Gregorios, P., W. H. Lazareth, and N. A. Nissiotis, eds. *Does Chalcedon Divide or Unite? Towards Convergence in Orthodox Christology*. Geneva: WCC Publications, 1981.

Hussey, J. M. *The Orthodox Church in the Byzantine Empire*. Oxford: Oxford University Press, 1986.

Kamil, J. *Christianity in the Land of the Pharaohs: The Coptic Orthodox Church*. London and New York: Routledge, 2002.

Louth, A. *Denys the Areopagite*. London: Geoffrey Chapman, 1989.

———. *Maximus the Confessor*. London and New York: Routledge, 1996.

Mango, C., ed. *The Oxford History of Byzantium*. Oxford: Oxford University Press, 2002.

McCullough, W. S. *A Short History of Syriac Christianity to the Rise of Islam*. Chico, CA: Scholars Press, 1982.

Meyendorff, J. *Byzantine Theology: Historical Trends and Doctrinal Themes*. Rev. ed. Crestwood, NY: St. Vladimir's Seminary Press, 1978.

———. *Christ in Eastern Christian Thought*. Rev. ed. Crestwood, NY: St. Vladimir's Seminary Press, 1975.

———. *Imperial Unity and Christian Divisions: The Church 450–680 A.D.* Crestwood, NY: St. Vladimir's Seminary Press, 1989.

Norwich, J. J. *Byzantium: The Early Centuries*. London: Macmillan, 1991.

Pelikan, J. *The Christian Tradition: A History of the Development of Doctrine*. Vol. 2, *The Spirit of Eastern Christendom (600–1700)*. Chicago and London: University of Chicago Press, 1974.

Sarkissian, K. *The Council of Chalcedon and the Armenian Church*. 2nd ed. New York: Armenian Prelacy, 1975.

Torrance, I. R. *Christology after Chalcedon: Severus of Antioch and Sergius the Grammarian*. Norwich, England: Canterbury Press, 1988.

Trimingham, J. S. *Christianity among the Arabs in Pre-Islamic Times*. London and New York: Longman, 1979.

Watson, J. H. *Among the Copts*. Brighton, England: Sussex Academic Press, 2000.

Chapter 9

Aland, K. *Did the Early Church Baptize Infants?* Translated and edited by G. R. Beasley-Murray. London: SCM Press, 1963.

Bradshaw, P. F. *Early Christian Worship: A Basic Introduction to Ideas and Practice*. London: SPCK, 1996.

———. *The Search for the Origins of Christian Worship: Sources and Methods for the Study of Early Liturgy*. 2nd ed. Oxford: Oxford University Press, 2002.

Jeremias, J. *Infant Baptism in the First Four Centuries*. Translated by D. Cairns. London: SCM Press, 1960.

Johnson, M. E. *The Rites of Christian Initiation: Their Evolution and Interpretation*. Collegeville, MN: Liturgical Press, 1999.

Jungmann, J. A. *The Early Liturgy to the Time of Gregory the Great.* Translated by F. A. Brunner. Notre Dame, IN: University of Notre Dame Press, 1959.

McGuckin, J. A. *At the Lighting of the Lamps: Hymns of the Ancient Church.* Harrisburg, PA: Morehouse Publishing, 1997.

McKinnon, J. W. *Music in Early Christian Literature.* Cambridge: Cambridge University Press, 1987.

Palmer, A.-M. *Prudentius on the Martyrs.* Oxford: Oxford University Press, 1989.

Riley, H. M. *Christian Initiation: A Comparative Study of the Interpretation of the Baptismal Liturgy in the Mystagogical Writings of Cyril of Jerusalem, John Chrysostom, Theodore of Mopsuestia, and Ambrose of Milan.* Washington, DC: Catholic University of America Press, 1974.

Taft, R. *The Liturgy of the Hours in East and West: The Origins of the Divine Office and Its Meaning for Today.* Collegeville, MN: Liturgical Press, 1986.

Westermeyer, P. *Te Deum: The Church and Music.* Minneapolis, MN: Fortress Press, 1998.

Whitaker, E. C. *The Baptismal Liturgy.* 2nd ed. London: SPCK, 1981.

White, C. *Early Christian Latin Poets.* London and New York: Routledge, 2000.

Yarnold, E. J. *The Awe-Inspiring Rites of Initiation: The Origins of the R.C.I.A.* 2nd ed. Collegeville, MN: Liturgical Press, 1994.

———. *Cyril of Jerusalem.* London and New York: Routledge, 2000.

Chapter 10

Bacchiocchi, S. *From Sabbath to Sunday: A Historical Investigation of the Rise of Sunday Observance in Early Christianity.* Rome: Pontifical Gregorian University Press, 1977.

Brown, P. R. L. *The Cult of the Saints: Its Rise and Function in Latin Christianity.* Chicago: University of Chicago Press, 1981.

Cantalamessa, R. *Easter in the Early Church: An Anthology of Jewish and Early Christian Texts.* Translated by J. M. Quigley and J. T. Lienhard. Collegeville, MN: Liturgical Press, 1993.

Carson, D. A., ed. *From Sabbath to Lord's Day.* Grand Rapids: Zondervan, 1982.

Clark, E. A. *Ascetic Piety and Women's Faith: Essays on Late Ancient Christianity.* Lewiston, NY: Edwin Mellen Press, 1986.

Clark, G. *Women in Late Antiquity: Pagan and Christian Lifestyles.* Oxford: Oxford University Press, 1993.

Cloke, G. *This Female Man of God: Women and Spiritual Power in the Patristic Age,* A.D. *350–450.* London and New York: Routledge, 1995.

Eisen, U. E. *Women Officeholders in Early Christianity.* Translated by L. M. Mahoney. Collegeville, MN: Liturgical Press, 2000.

Finney, P. C. *The Invisible God: The Early Christians on Art.* Oxford: Oxford University Press, 1994.

Gambero, L. *Mary and the Fathers of the Church: The Blessed Virgin Mary in Patristic Thought.* Translated by T. Buffer. New York: Ignatius Press, 1999.

Hobbs, H. C. and W. C. Wuellner, eds. *The Role of the Christian Bishop in Ancient Society.* Berkeley and Los Angeles: University of California Press, 1980.

Janes, D. *God and Gold in Late Antiquity.* Cambridge: Cambridge University Press, 1998.

Jensen, A. *God's Self-Confident Daughters: Early Christianity and the Liberation of Women*. Louisville: Westminster/John Knox Press, 1996.

Jensen, R. M. *Understanding Early Christian Art*. London and New York: Routledge, 2000.

Kaufman, P. I. *Church, Book, and Bishop: Conflict and Authority in Early Latin Christianity*. Boulder, CO, and Oxford: Westview Press, 1996.

Limberis, V. *Divine Heiress: The Virgin Mary and the Creation of Christian Constantinople*. London and New York: Routledge, 1994.

Milburn, R. L. *Early Christian Art and Architecture*. Berkeley and Los Angeles: University of California Press, 1988.

Pelikan, J. *Mary through the Centuries: Her Place in the History of Culture*. New Haven and London: Yale University Press, 1998.

Salisbury, J. *Church Fathers, Independent Virgins*. London and New York: Verso, 1991.

Talley, T. J. *The Origins of the Liturgical Year*. New York: Pueblo Publishing Company, 1986.

Telfer, W. *The Office of a Bishop*. Reprint. London: Darton, Longman and Todd, 1962.

White, L. M. *The Social Origins of Christian Architecture*. 2 vols. Valley Forge, PA: Trinity Press International, 1996–97.

Chapter 11

Chadwick, H. *Boethius: The Consolations of Music, Logic, Theology, and Philosophy*. Oxford: Oxford University Press, 1981.

Drinkwater, J. F. and H. Elton, eds. *Fifth-Century Gaul: A Crisis of Identity?* Cambridge: Cambridge University Press, 1992.

Fletcher, R. *The Barbarian Conversion: From Paganism to Christianity*. Berkeley and Los Angeles: University of California Press, 1999.

Harries, J. *Sidonius Apollinaris and the Fall of Rome, A.D. 407–485*. Oxford: Oxford University Press, 1994.

Heather, P. J. *The Goths*. Oxford and Malden, MA: Blackwell, 1996.

———. *Goths and Romans, 332–489*. Oxford: Oxford University Press, 1991.

Marenbon, J. *Boethius*. Oxford: Oxford University Press, 2003.

Mathisen, R. W. *Ecclesiastical Factionalism and Religious Controversy in Fifth-Century Gaul*. Washington, DC: Catholic University of America Press, 1989.

Moorhead, J. *Theoderic in Italy*. Oxford: Oxford University Press, 1992.

Thompson, E. A. *A History of Attila and the Huns*. London: Oxford University Press, 1948.

———. *The Huns*. Rev. ed. Oxford and Malden, MA: Blackwell, 1996.

———. *Romans and Barbarians: The Decline of the Western Empire*. Madison: University of Wisconsin Press, 1982.

Wolfram, H. *History of the Goths*. Translated by T. J. Dunlap. Berkeley and Los Angeles: University of California Press, 1988.

———. *The Roman Empire and Its Germanic Peoples*. Berkeley and Los Angeles: University of California Press, 1997.

Chapter 12

Christie, N. *The Lombards: The Ancient Longobards*. Oxford and Malden, MA: Blackwell, 1995.

Evans, G. R. *The Thought of Gregory the Great*. Cambridge: Cambridge University Press, 1986.

Fry, T., ed. *The Rule of St. Benedict*. Collegeville, MN: Order of St. Benedict, Vintage Spiritual Classics/Random House, 1998.

Homes Dudden, F. *Gregory the Great: His Place in History and Thought*. 2 vols. London: Longmans Green and Co., 1905.

James, E. *The Franks*. Oxford and Malden, MA: Blackwell, 1988.

Kelly, J. N. D. *The Athanasian Creed*. London: A. & C. Black, 1964.

Klingshirn, W. E. *Caesarius of Arles: The Making of a Christian Community in Late Antique Gaul*. Cambridge: Cambridge University Press, 1994.

Markus, R. A. *The End of Ancient Christianity*. Cambridge: Cambridge University Press, 1990.

———. *Gregory the Great and His World*. Cambridge: Cambridge University Press, 1997.

Moorhead, J. *Justinian*. London and New York: Longman, 1994.

O'Donnell, J. J. *Cassiodorus*. Berkeley and Los Angeles: University of California Press, 1979.

O'Donovan, P. *Benedict of Nursia*. London: Collins, 1980.

Richards, J. *Consul of God: The Life and Times of Gregory the Great*. London and Boston: Routledge and Kegan Paul, 1980.

———. *The Popes and the Papacy in the Early Middle Ages, 476–752*. London and Boston: Routledge and Kegan Paul, 1979.

Straw, C. *Gregory the Great: Perfection in Imperfection*. Berkeley and Los Angeles: University of California Press, 1988.

Van Dam, R. *Leadership and Community in Late Antique Gaul*. Berkeley and Los Angeles: University of California Press, 1985.

———. *Saints and Their Miracles in Late Antique Gaul*. Princeton, NJ: Princeton University Press, 1993.

Wallace-Hadrill, J. M. *The Barbarian West, 400–1000*. 3rd ed. London: Hutchinson, 1967.

———. *The Frankish Church*. Oxford: Oxford University Press, 1983.

Wood, I. N. *The Merovingian Kingdoms, 450–751*. London and New York: Longman, 1994.

———. *The Missionary Life: Saints and the Evangelization of Europe, 400–1050*. London and New York: Longman, 2001.

——— and K. Mitchell. *The World of Gregory of Tours*. Leiden, Netherlands: E. J. Brill, 2002.

Chapter 13

Barley, M. W. and R. P. C. Hanson, eds. *Christianity in Britain, 300–700*. Leicester, England: Leicester University Press, 1968.

Carver, M., ed. *The Cross Goes North: Processes of Conversion in Northern Europe,* A.D. *300–1300.* York, England: York Medieval Press, 2003.

Dumville, D. N., et al. *St. Patrick,* A.D. *493–1993.* Woodbridge, Suffolk, England: Boydell Press, 1993.

O'Loughlin, T. *St. Patrick: The Man and His Works.* London: SPCK, 1999.

de Paor, L. *Saint Patrick's World: The Christian Culture of Ireland's Apostolic Age.* Dublin: Four Courts Press, 1993.

Petts, D. *Christianity in Roman Britain.* Stroud, Gloucestershire, England: Tempus, 2003.

Thomas, C. *Christianity in Roman Britain to* A.D. *500.* London: Batsford, 1981.

Thompson, E. A. *Who Was Saint Patrick?* Woodbridge, Suffolk, England: Boydell Press, 1985.

Watts, D. *Christians and Pagans in Roman Britain.* London and New York: Routledge, 1991.

Winterbottom, M., ed. and trans. *Gildas: The Ruin of Britain and Other Works.* London: Phillimore; Totowa, NJ: Rowman and Littlefield, 1978.

Chapter 14

Atherton, M., ed. *Celts and Christians: New Approaches to the Religious Traditions of Britain and Ireland.* Cardiff: University of Wales Press, 2002.

Bradley, I. *Celtic Christianity: Making Myths and Chasing Dreams.* New York: St. Martin's Press, 1999.

Chadwick, N. K. *The Age of the Saints in the Early Celtic Church.* London: Oxford University Press, 1961.

Charles-Edwards, T. M. *Early Christian Ireland.* Cambridge: Cambridge University Press, 2000.

Clarke, H. B. and M. Brennan, eds. *Columbanus and Merovingian Monasticism.* Oxford: BAR, 1981.

Dales, D. *Light to the Isles: Missionary Theology in Celtic and Anglo-Saxon Britain.* Cambridge, England: Lutterworth Press, 1997.

Davies, O. *Celtic Christianity in Early Medieval Wales: The Origins of the Welsh Spiritual Tradition.* Cardiff: University of Wales Press, 1996.

Herren, M. W. and S. A. Brown. *Christ in Celtic Christianity: Britain and Ireland from the Fifth to the Tenth Century.* Woodbridge, Suffolk, England: Boydell Press, 2002.

Hughes, K. *The Church in Early Irish Society.* London: Methuen, 1966.

Lacey, B. *Colum Cille and the Columban Tradition.* Dublin: Four Courts Press, 1997.

Macquarrie, A. *The Saints of Scotland: Essays in Scottish Church History,* A.D. *450–1093.* Edinburgh: John Donald, 1997.

MacQueen, J. *St. Nynia.* Edinburgh: Polygon, 1990.

McNeill, J. T. *The Celtic Churches: A History,* A.D. *200 to 1200.* Chicago: University of Chicago Press, 1974.

Meek, D. E. *The Quest for Celtic Christianity.* Edinburgh: Handsel Press, 2000.

O'Loughlin, T. *Celtic Theology: Humanity, World and God in Early Irish Writings.* London and New York: Continuum, 2000.

Sharpe, R., ed. and trans. *Adomnán of Iona: Life of St. Columba*. Harmondsworth, England: Penguin, 1995.

Sheldrake, P. *Living between Worlds: Place and Journey in Celtic Spirituality*. London: Darton, Longman and Todd, 1995.

Victory, S. *The Celtic Church in Wales*. London: SPCK, 1977.

Walsh, J. R. and T. Bradley. *A History of the Irish Church, 400–700 A.D.* Dublin, Ireland: Columba Press, 1991.

NOTES

The Dawn of a New Age

1. Fuller details on the political context sketched in the following paragraphs can be found in *The Birth of the Church*, pp. 334–42.

2. Lactantius, *On the Deaths of the Persecutors* 44.5–6.

3. Eusebius, *Life of Constantine* 1.28, written after Constantine's death, allegedly recalling Constantine's own account of the matter toward the end of his life.

Chapter 1: Constantine and the Churches

1. Lactantius also wrote interesting works on the divine creation of the human body (*On the Workmanship of God*, ca. 303) and on the wrath of God as expressed in the punishment of human sin (*On the Anger of God*, produced some time in the period 313–324, during which years he also produced an *Epitome of Divine Institutes*).

2. On the persecutions of Valerian, see *The Birth of the Church*, pp. 331–32.

3. The principle that sites did not possess supernatural qualities in themselves but were rendered holy by holy individuals applied in Christian thinking about pilgrimages in general; it was not confined to the status of the Holy Land.

4. As West and East became increasingly fragmented and the Western empire collapsed in the fifth century (see pp. 295–306), Constantinople would be the capital of the "East Roman" or Byzantine realm, which survived for another thousand years.

5. Later legend claimed that the episcopal privileges included much more, stretching to sovereignty over all Italy and the West, but this was a pious fiction.

6. For all its extensive eulogizing, the *Life of Constantine* contains some important historical material. Eusebius also composed a rhetorical tribute in commemoration of the thirtieth anniversary of Constantine's accession to power in 336. His other writings ranged across history, apologetics, biblical interpretation, and theology.

7. On the context, see *The Birth of the Church*, pp. 325–31.

8. On Tertullian, see *The Birth of the Church*, pp. 239–47; on Cyprian, pp. 325–32.

9. On Novatian and his followers, see *The Birth of the Church*, pp. 328–30.

10. On the status of such "confessors," see *The Birth of the Church*, p. 324.

11. On the problems identified with "modalist" thinking in earlier theology, see *The Birth of the Church*, pp. 237–38, 244–46.

12. On Origen, see *The Birth of the Church*, pp. 256–69.

13. See *The Birth of the Church*, pp. 233, 262–69.

14. Eusebius, *Epistle to the Church of Caesarea* 4.

15. See *The Birth of the Church*, pp. 268–69.

16. On Manichaeism, see further pp. 114–16.

17. Cf. note 11 on "modalism."

18. The rights of metropolitan churchmen were in fact quite variable in many places for generations to come after Nicaea, and some bishops came to hold very significant positions of regional influence without being recognized officially as metropolitans.

19. See *The Birth of the Church*, pp. 230–32.

20. On the earlier history of penitential discipline, see *The Birth of the Church*, pp. 309–11.

21. It was subsequently rumored in some quarters that one of those thus ordained was Arius himself, but this was almost certainly untrue.

22. The origins of the usage may lie in the third century, and in a secular context, to describe a "worldwide" guild of professional actors and athletes who gained exemptions from taxes.

23. See *The Birth of the Church*, pp. 237–38.

Chapter 2: The Politics of Arianism

1. For some reflections on the social complexion of the Christian communities and on the processes of conversion and belonging in earlier times, see *The Birth of the Church*, pp. 101–30. On patterns of initiation, organization, and practice from the fourth century onward, see chapters 9 and 10 of this volume.

2. This was probably the first time this phrase was used in a credal context.

3. Liberius subsequently reneged on his Nicene loyalties in order to return to his see, before finally reverting to his true position after the death of Constantius in 361.

4. Several of which provide valuable evidence on the history of ideas at this time.

5. Nor, however, would all of them have owned the unqualified assertion that the Son is always to be thought of as "unlike" the Father.

6. This Basil is not to be confused with his much more famous namesake, Basil of Caesarea (see pp. 84–93, 145–47).

7. The *homoiousians* have often been identified with a kind of "semi-Arianism," but this designation is misleading, for, whatever problems may have attached to their position, their intentions were to steer away from Arianism proper.

8. Hilary of Poitiers, *On the Synods* 10.

9. The church of Rome was not represented.

10. Jerome, *Dialogue Against the Luciferians* 19. See the further discussion of Jerome that follows, pp. 122–32.

11. The text as we have it belongs to a two-part treatise, *Against the Pagans—On the Incarnation*. The first part is a conventional apologia for Christianity against Greek culture, while the second is a more directly theological engagement on the logic of the overall relationship between God and creation. The dating of the work is much disputed. Conventionally, it was dated very early, prior to Nicaea and perhaps as early as 318, due to its lack of explicit reference to Arianism. It is more likely, however, that it should be located some time in Athanasius's early years as a bishop, prior to his exile to Trier in 336.

12. Athanasius, *On the Incarnation* 54.

13. E. Gibbon, *The History of the Decline and Fall of the Roman Empire*, vol. 2, edited by D. Womersley (London: Allen Lane/Penguin Press, 1994), ch. XXI.III.3.

14. For further information on Irenaeus, see *The Birth of the Church*, pp. 225–28.

Chapter 3: The Churches in the Greek East, 361–381

1. In theurgy, the worshiper might typically seek to animate a statue of a god, causing the image to reveal some visual response to an entreaty and thus manifest divine presence.

2. As we have seen, however, this title had also been retained by Christian emperors, including Constantine (see p. 19).

3. The last of the great Roman historians, Ammianus (ca. 330–395) was an army officer of Greek origin who was born in Antioch. He wrote an extensive history of the Roman Empire from the late first century down to his own day. The first thirteen of the thirty-one books of his account are lost, but the remainder, covering the period 354–378, are a vital historical resource, not least on Julian, whose reign is presented as a pivotal phase in the imperial story. For all his esteem for Julian, Ammianus strongly criticized the religious excesses of his revival of paganism, and he had a positive view of various aspects of Christianity. It has been suggested by one or two scholars that Ammianus may even have been a Christian himself, but this is unlikely.

4. On the earlier traditions of Christian apologetics, see *The Birth of the Church*, pp. 212–20.

5. On Cyril, see further pp. 200–208.

6. See *The Birth of the Church*, p. 321.

7. Philostorgius, *Ecclesiastical History* 7.15.

8. Theodoret, *Ecclesiastical History* 3.25.7.

9. On Sabellianism, see *The Birth of the Church*, pp. 237–38.

10. Ammianus, *History* 30.9.5.

11. On the earlier history of the New Testament canon, see *The Birth of the Church*, pp. 172–78.

12. Contrary to some interpretations of his language, there is much in Athanasius's logic that is consistent with the affirmation of a human soul in Christ, though it can certainly be argued that he did not give due weight to the theme.

13. Athanasius, *Tome to the Antiochenes* 7.

14. See *The Birth of the Church*, pp. 268–69.

15. Gregory of Nyssa produced remarkable mystical expositions of such scriptural themes as the life of Moses, the Song of Songs, the Lord's Prayer, and the Beatitudes, as well as other biblical and ascetic subjects. All of the Cappadocians were influenced in a range of ways by Origen; for one example of the debt, cf. p. 435n23.

16. Gregory of Nazianzus, *Epistle* 101.32. In Greek, the phrase "the unassumed is the unhealed" is just three words.

17. Athanasius, *Tome to the Antiochenes* 3.

18. Not to be confused with Eustathius of Antioch, whom we encountered earlier (see pp. 31, 78).

19. It was attached to a set of texts attributed to an ascetic teacher called Macarius of Egypt. These so-called "Macarian homilies," not all of which are in fact homilies, cannot in reality be by this Macarius (ca. 300–390) but are of a Syrian origin. They survive from a variety of collections in several languages including Greek, Syriac, and Arabic. Their relationship to Messalianism is disputed, since there are differences as well as parallels with Messalian teaching, but some of the early-fifth-century Messalians' claims do appear to be taken from these works.

20. This phrase was once fashionable in scholarly depictions of the history of trinitarian theology in this period.

21. Again, this is contrary to some widespread modern assumptions that the analogy of three human beings was basic to his thinking.

22. It is worth noting that the significance of *To Ablabius* as a window upon Gregory's thought has often been overstated, and recent scholars have been concerned to broaden

the study of his trinitarian logic to include a range of his other exegetical and spiritual writings. The summary of his reasoning here mentions themes that are further developed and clarified by Gregory elsewhere.

23. The term *perichoresis* is not, however, used this way by the Cappadocians, and later trinitarian construals of the concept cannot always be reliably read back into their language.

24. The number of such nominal Christians in high places by this stage of the fourth century was not inconsiderable and shows how much social change had occurred from Constantine's time—a profession of faith could be an aid rather than an impediment to professional advancement.

25. Gregory of Nyssa, *On the Deity of the Son and the Holy Spirit*, PG 46.557 B–C.

26. The fourfold designation is often referred to in later theology (especially from the period of the Reformation onward) as the four "Nicene notes" of the church, the marks that characterize the nature of what the church is at its deepest level of being.

27. Gregory of Nyssa's *To Ablabius: On Why There are Not Three Gods*, for example, may have been written later in his career, in the 380s (though some scholars place it earlier).

Chapter 4: Consolidation in the West

1. For one famous example of the effect, see pp. 162–63.

2. Mary's womb is thus seen as a place of paradox: it is at one and the same time a "royal hall of chastity" and a spiritual "bridal chamber" where divinity and humanity are mysteriously joined together at God's initiative.

3. Books 1 and 2 of the work were probably published in the autumn of 378 (though some scholars date them to the spring of 380); books 3–5 were written in late 380–early 381.

4. Ambrose, *Epistle* 76 [20].2.

5. Soon to be known as the Basilica Ambrosiana, it was where the bishop himself was later laid to rest.

6. Ambrose, *Epistle* 74 [40].

7. The young Augustine attached himself to the Manichees as such a "Hearer" for almost a decade prior to his conversion to Christianity: see p. 161.

8. Ursinus himself survived well into the 380s, and though banished from Rome he never gave up hope of attaining to its papal throne; he and his followers continued to be accused of stirring up trouble in various parts of the West.

9. The factions had both been determined to lay claim to Rome's holy places.

10. Jerome, *Against John of Jerusalem* 8.

11. All the same, if social respectability brought such an inroad into the Roman aristocracy, so too there were increasing tensions when some upper-class believers, especially women, began to adopt wide-ranging forms of asceticism, which threatened to destabilize cherished social and economic patterns. A Christianity that led the rich to abandon marriage and disburse long-accumulated wealth was, not surprisingly, far more divisive than a faith that might be confined to respectable piety. See further pp. 144, 148, 285–86.

12. Augustine, *On Christian Doctrine* 2.16.36.

13. See *The Birth of the Church*, p. 258.

14. See *The Birth of the Church*, p. 173.

15. Eastern Christians have generally followed the view of Epiphanius (see pp. 152–53) that the relatives of Jesus were sons of Joseph by an earlier marriage. A further suggestion made in modern times has been that these persons were indeed cousins of Jesus, and their parents were indeed Mary and Clopas, but that this Mary was not the sister of Jesus's mother; rather, Clopas was Joseph's brother. A straightforward reading of the

New Testament references, as proposed by Helvidius, nevertheless remains the most coherent option.

16. Jerome, *Epistle* 22.30.

Chapter 5: Christians as Ascetics

1. See *The Birth of the Church*, pp. 311–16.

2. See *The Birth of the Church*, pp. 31–32, 34.

3. Another classic was the *Life* of the famous first-century Neopythagorean itinerant teacher and wonder-worker, Apollonius of Tyana (d. ca. 98), written in the 220s by Flavius Philostratus (ca. 170–249).

4. See *The Birth of the Church*, p. 175.

5. See *The Birth of the Church*, pp. 285–86.

6. The column is said to have increased in height over the years.

7. A monastery and church were built around his pillar, the remains of which can be seen to this day; see the illustration on p. 137.

8. They continued to exist into the seventh century.

9. On Origen's asceticism, see *The Birth of the Church*, p. 315.

10. The traditional site of the Inner Mountain became a Coptic monastery that can still be visited today.

11. Palladius (ca. 364–420s) served as a bishop in Bithynia and in his native Galatia. He suffered for his friendship with John Chrysostom (see pp. 153–57). In his youth he spent a number of years among the monks in Egypt and was a great admirer of their devotion. His account of the character of these "friends of God" is known as the *Lausiac History* because it is dedicated to Lausus, an official of the emperor Theodosius II (ca. 419).

12. Palladius, for example, was one of his pupils.

13. In the late fourth and early fifth centuries, the Pachomian model also had its stringent disciplinarians, notably the formidable Shenoute, abbot of Athribis (d. ca. 466), who exercised a very strict system, with a written code of obedience and sanctions that included floggings and imprisonment for those who broke the rules. Shenoute was a prominent ally of the great Cyril, bishop of Alexandria (see pp. 200–208).

14. The text of Egeria's *Travels* was lost for seven hundred years, until a manuscript copy from the Middle Ages was discovered in the late nineteenth century in Italy.

15. Melania the Younger's virtues are celebrated in a hagiographical *Life*, which exists in different versions in Greek and Latin. As well as containing standard evocation of ascetic ideals, the work provides important evidence of the social and economic conditions affecting Rome's senatorial aristocracy at the time.

16. Cyril also wrote popular biographical sketches of five other leaders of Palestinian monasticism: John, Cyriacus, Theodosius, Theognius, and Abraham.

17. Eustathius's name was associated with Messalianism after his death, but this was an unwarranted slur.

18. Often popularly designated his *Rule*.

19. From the later second century, veils had symbolized the solemn status of consecrated women as spiritually "married" to Christ, in imitation of the veiling associated with the Roman marriage ceremony. Practices varied considerably as to when the veil was taken. Sometimes it was adopted by young women on their entrance upon the ascetic life; in other cases this final public expression of devotion was postponed until later years.

20. A wealthy lawyer from Aquitania, Sulpicius was converted to asceticism after the death of his wife in the early 390s. Influenced both by his friend Paulinus and by Martin, he set up a religious community on his estate. In addition to his very popular *Life* of Martin, he wrote *Dialogues*, in which Martin's wonder-working powers are compared to

those of the saints of Egypt, and a work called *Chronicles*, which attempts to narrate the history of the Old Testament and the Christian church up to the year 400. The latter is an invaluable source on the course of the Priscillianist movement (see pp. 116–18).

21. In addition to his writings on monasticism, Cassian also produced in 430 a work entitled *On the Incarnation of the Lord*, framed in opposition to the views of the controversial churchman of Constantinople, Nestorius (on whom see pp. 199–208).

22. See *The Birth of the Church*, pp. 265–67.

23. One notable example of their enduring popularity can be seen in an anthology of passages from Origen compiled by Basil and Gregory of Nazianzus in the late 350s or early 360s known as the *Philokalia* ("Love of Beautiful Things"). This work contains a great many excerpts from texts that have otherwise been lost from our corpus of Origen's original Greek writings.

24. Epiphanius's earlier work, *Panarion*, or "A Medicine Chest for the Cure of All Heresies," attacked every example of false teaching known to him since the beginning of the church. A staunch defender of Nicene orthodoxy and critic of those he considered to have a weak grasp of its importance, he was also involved in opposition to other controversial ideas, including the views of Apollinaris (see pp. 82–87) and of the Melitians (see pp. 37–38).

25. Jerome, *Epistle* 95.

26. John also attacked Judaism, which seems to have been exercising a certain attraction for some Christians in his context, much to his fury.

Chapter 6: Augustine of Hippo

1. The work consists of thirteen books. After the personal narrative of books 1–9, Augustine engages in reflection on his current condition in a fallen world as only the beginning of his search for God (especially in book 10), and books 11–13 take the form of an imaginative commentary on the opening of the book of Genesis, with consideration of the nature of time and God's relationship to it.

2. Augustine, *Confessions* 7.9.13.

3. On Plotinus and Porphyry, see *The Birth of the Church*, pp. 320–21.

4. And others, including the Stoics.

5. Marius Victorinus resigned his position after Julian's edict of 362 barring Christians from holding teaching posts. A thinker of considerable depth if difficult style, his Christian writings included an important series of commentaries on some of Paul's Epistles and a number of works against Arianism, which offered a sophisticated Neoplatonist doctrine of the Trinity that in certain respects anticipated Augustine's later thinking on the subject. Three hymns by Victorinus on the Trinity also survive.

6. Augustine, *Confessions* 8.12.28–30.

7. Ibid., 1.1.1.

8. Though he did know Punic, the dominant language of rural North Africa, which was also a Semitic tongue.

9. Augustine, *On the Trinity* 5.9.10.

10. Tyconius's Revelation commentary survives in fragments, pieced together by later scholars.

11. The death penalty for the recalcitrant, however, was not an option.

12. See *The Birth of the Church*, pp. 325–32.

13. See ibid., pp. 330–31.

14. Augustine, *Confessions* 10.29.40, 31.45, 37.60.

15. On infant baptism generally, see further pp. 253–54.

16. Ambrosiaster was one notable exception.

17. This idea, however, was not in fact expressly to be found in Augustine in any case. A doctrine of "double predestination"—the election of some to life and others to death—was argued in some quarters in the ninth century, notably by Godescalc of Orbais (ca. 804–869), whose views were condemned. It was reawakened at the Reformation.

18. One was by Orosius, whom Augustine sent to Palestine to enlist supporters such as Jerome in the fight against Pelagianism. At Augustine's request, Orosius completed in 417–418 a chronicle of world history in seven books, from Adam to his own day, designed to refute the pagan complaint that Christianity had been fatal for Rome's prosperity. His work was fairly crudely executed.

19. Somewhat similar claims would also be made by Salvian, a priest in Marseilles in the middle of the fifth century, who equally contrasted the decadence of Roman society with the virtues of its conquerors (see p. 307).

Chapter 7: Further Reflection on Christ

1. See *The Birth of the Church*, pp. 260–61. Among the most impressive of fourth-century Alexandrian exegetes was the immensely learned ascetic scholar Didymus (c. 313–398), who despite being blind from infancy produced a very large body of commentaries and other theological works. He taught figures such as Jerome and Rufinus, and his readers included Ambrose of Milan. Much of his work was strongly influenced by Origen, an association that rendered him suspect in the fifth and sixth centuries, and a large proportion of his writings was lost after he was retrospectively condemned as an Origenist in 553.

2. He would succeed Nestorius in 434.

3. Alexandrian Jewry was, of course, extremely large; see *The Birth of the Church*, p. 45.

4. John and his party had also been late in setting out from Antioch, owing to public disturbances in Antioch caused by famine.

5. It was widely assumed in the East that Rome was in a position to speak for a majority in the West.

6. Interestingly, the analogy of the unity of body and soul had also been cited by some who espoused an essentially Antiochene approach. One such was Nemesius, the scholarly bishop of Emesa in Syria in the late fourth century. In a treatise called *On Human Nature*, Nemesius argued that human beings are a psychosomatic unity; however complex in structure, the nature of the relationship between the body and the soul is so intimate that it constitutes something of a parallel to the union of divinity and humanity in Christ. For Nemesius, however, the incarnational union was cast in "Word-man" not "Word-flesh" terms.

7. Though Ibas's predecessor in Edessa, Rabbula, was a passionate convert to Cyril's ideas and a fierce critic of Theodore's writings. Rabbula had been vigorously opposed by Ibas.

8. The title "archimandrite," literally "ruler of the fold," emerged in the East from the fourth century.

9. The term for such a representative was *apocrisarius*, a name that is still used of an ecclesiastical envoy in a number of contexts.

10. The numbers in attendance varied from session to session; the statement of faith issued by the Council carried 452 signatures.

11. Juvenal temporarily lost control of his see as a result of a revolt organized by Palestinian monks, though he recovered his position late in 453 thanks to the aid of his allies.

Chapter 8: Arguing over Chalcedon: Division and Expansion

1. Though the designations "Monophysite" and "Monophysitism" have unfortunately become familiar over centuries of such usage, they continue to be regarded as offensive by those who hold similar views today, and there is an enduring danger that the terms may mislead, precisely because of such long-standing deployment by their critics. However varied the ideas of the so-called "Monophysites," they all sought to distance themselves from the position associated with the name of Eutyches. The need to treat the terminology with caution is signaled by the use of quotation marks around it at each appearance in this book.

2. The designation "Aelurus," from the Greek for *cat*, is said to have been due to his small, weaselly appearance.

3. Timothy "Wobblecap."

4. Peter "the hoarse one."

5. In addition to works of commentary on the Old Testament (all of which have been lost), Narsai produced attractive hymns and verse-homilies, a large number of which survive. Metrical homilies were a rich feature of both Persian and Syriac Christianity. Another significant poet-expositor was the Syriac author, Jacob, bishop of Serugh in Osrhoene (ca. 451–521), who supported the opposite christological tradition to Narsai (but adopted an irenic stance on doctrinal controversy—so much so that he has been revered by both pro- and anti-Chalcedonian Christians). Jacob wrote some remarkable poetic celebrations of the spiritual senses of Scripture.

6. Bishop of Hierapolis (Mabbug) from 485, Philoxenus was a theologian of originality whose extensive writings on theological, biblical, and moral themes combined a knowledge of Greek thinking with the distinctive emphases of his own Syriac tradition. A "Philoxenian" version of the New Testament in Syriac was produced for him in 508.

7. In fact it was also backed by some pro-Chalcedonian monks.

8. The dating of Leontius is uncertain. Traditional estimates place him somewhere in the middle of the sixth century, but it has recently been suggested that he may belong as late as the early seventh century.

9. Leontius of Byzantium and Leontius of Jerusalem have often been confused in the history of scholarship, but it is important to differentiate them.

10. Several further outbreaks of a similar pestilence, a version of the bubonic plague, would occur over generations to come.

11. Greek *Indikopleustes*.

12. Jacob may have been known as "Baradaeus" because of his habit of traveling around in disguise, dressed in a horse cloak (Syriac *burd' ana*).

13. All of the Syrian Christians of Malabar trace the origins of their church to the evangelism of the apostle Thomas, thus styling themselves the "Thomas Christians" (see *The Birth of the Church*, p. 154). There are a number of different traditions among these Syrian communities; a good many were originally of Nestorian sympathies and ended up in alliance with pro-Chalcedonian Western churches over the centuries as a result of historical developments, especially the arrival of the Portuguese in the fifteenth century. Others, however, rejected communion with Rome, and joined themselves to the Syrian Orthodox Church. While further divisions ensued in later centuries, a sizable segment of the Thomas Christians today belongs to one or the other of two branches of this tradition.

14. However, there were probably some believers in the region from the fourth century.

15. On the initial spread of Christianity in Ethiopia, see p. 57. Further impetus had also come from the influences of a group of monks, probably from Syria, in the fifth century, who promoted asceticism in the region.

16. Another notably learned Armenian churchman was a disciple of Mesrob's named Eznik, who in the 440s wrote a significant treatise *Against the Sects*, refuting, in four books, pagan beliefs, Persian religion, Greek philosophy, and Marcionite theology.

17. Honorius was dead by the time the document was issued.

18. Strictly speaking, the correct spelling of the words is "Monothelete" and "Dyothelete" (hence also "Monotheletism," "Dyotheletism"), but it is more common to use the forms adopted here.

19. Recognition of the 553 council in particular by some in the West proved slow and complex, however, and some others remained fairly lukewarm about the significance of the Dyothelite victory.

20. It should however be noted that the Armenian church has never been in full communion with the other Oriental Orthodox traditions.

21. The Ethiopian church in particular had cultural and linguistic links to the ancient Israelites and was strongly affected by Jewish influences; its biblical canon included a range of Jewish pseudepigrapha such as *1 Enoch* and the *Book of Jubilees*.

Chapter 9: Christian Worship

1. The designation originates in the seventeenth century.

2. See *The Birth of the Church*, p. 276.

3. In the fifth century, the Nicene Creed began to be recited in the service of the Eucharist in parts of the East. This tradition would eventually become customary, but it did not gather general momentum until the Middle Ages.

4. See *The Birth of the Church*, pp. 278–79.

5. Cyprian, *Epistle* 64.5.2 and Origen, e.g., *Commentary on Romans* 5.9.

6. Gregory of Nazianzus, *Oration* 40.28.

7. See further *The Birth of the Church*, pp. 279–84, esp. p. 283.

8. Cyril of Jerusalem, *Mystagogical Catecheses* 5.21–22.

9. Ambrose, *On the Sacraments* 4.14.

10. Sometimes "Lift up your hearts" was replaced with the simple "Hearts up." In North Africa, the singular "Heart up" was standard.

11. On the second- and third-century roots of such a pattern, see *The Birth of the Church*, pp. 281–82.

12. This is, however, missing from our major source for the Syriac rite, a liturgy which was traditionally attributed to Addai and Mari, the believed pioneers of Christianity in Mesopotamia in the first century, but which has perhaps third-century roots instead.

13. Greek *kathedra* means "throne"; a "cathedral" was the place where the bishop's official seat was located, and thus it was the symbolic center of the whole church in a particular area.

14. See *The Birth of the Church*, p. 286.

15. Both Prime and Compline are in Benedict's *Rule*, though they had earlier roots.

16. A collection of liturgical material drawn from a variety of sources, including the *Didascalia* and the *Didache* (see *The Birth of the Church*, p. 277 and p. 180), it was almost certainly drawn up in Syria by an author of Arian sympathies. Its final chapter consists of a series of eighty-five so-called *Apostolic Canons*, mostly on the ordination and moral responsibilities of clergy.

17. The collection also includes hymns for the festivals of Christmas and Epiphany (see pp. 272–74) and one for the burial of the dead.

18. Sedulius perhaps wrote in Italy some time around the year 430. His *Carmen Paschale* ("Easter Song") was informed not only by Scripture but also by Virgil, whose influence upon Christian authors in the fourth- and fifth-century West was considerable. A number

of examples could be cited; two must suffice. Around 330 a Spanish presbyter, Juvencus, issued a hexameter poem on the life of Christ that was heavily evocative of Virgil as well as the Gospels. A generation later, an aristocratic Roman lady called Proba produced a *Cento* or "patchwork" poem on the course of biblical history, composed entirely of lines and half-lines from Virgil. Her understanding of Christian teaching was decidedly confused, but it and other such patchwork poetry based upon classical sources would be much read in later centuries. In Christian verse more generally, not only Virgil but a wide range of other classical authors—including Horace, Ovid, Lucretius, Statius, Juvenal, and others—were exploited.

19. The name *kontakia* for these sermons was first used in the ninth century; it derives from the Greek word *kontos*, for the "rod" or "pole" around which the vellum text of the hymn was wound.

20. Augustine, *Confessions* 9.6.14; 10.33.49–50.

Chapter 10: Organization, Ministry, and Symbolism

1. The Anatolian system would also come to be known as the Dionysian cycle, after the Scythian monk Dionysius Exiguus who compiled the model adopted in Rome in the sixth century. (It is also to Dionysius that the system of dating events from the birth of Christ—the B.C./A.D. convention—is to be attributed, though Dionysius's scheme was based on miscalculations.)

2. The sixth century also saw the reconciliation of the Alexandrian and Constantinopolitan versions of the scheme.

3. Note also the examples of Moses (Exod. 34:28) and Elijah (1 Kings 19:8).

4. The English name "Maundy" Thursday derives from the Latin *mandatum novum*, describing the "new commandment" of Jesus to his disciples to love one another (John 13:34), a verse that was recalled in the liturgy of the ceremony of foot-washing.

5. See *The Birth of the Church*, pp. 205, 292.

6. Two of Paulinus's poems are on the life of Felix, his patron saint at Nola (see p. 148), and fourteen of them are *Natalicia* or "birthday poems" dedicated to Felix on his annual feast day of 14 January.

7. So called because the names were inscribed on a hinged, two-leaved tablet, often made of ivory (in Greek, a *diptuchon*). Such folding tablets were first used by Roman gentlemen as invitation cards for special occasions, such as the taking up of public office.

8. In the East the preferred name for the Feast of the Assumption is the *Koimesis*, or the feast of the "falling asleep" of the Virgin.

9. See *The Birth of the Church*, pp. 297–309.

10. The date is uncertain; the conventional guess is that the gathering took place ca. 306, but it may have been as late as 310.

11. The practice of living with such *subintroductae*, as they were often called in Latin, had existed in some places from the second century.

12. One interesting instance of this was Synesius (ca. 370–413), a native of Cyrene who was nominated bishop of Ptolemais around 410–411, largely on account of popular admiration for the part he had played in his community in Cyrenaica (which had included going on a mission to the imperial court in Constantinople to negotiate tax-relief for the province). Synesius was an educated Neoplatonist (a former student of the ill-fated Hypatia in Alexandria, pp. 113, 200), and was married to a Christian wife. He was anxious that he might have to give up either his philosophical beliefs (in such matters as the preexistence of the soul or the nature of resurrection) or his wife (or both) if he became bishop, and he only accepted the role once he had been assured by the patriarch

Theophilus of Alexandria that neither sacrifice was necessary. Synesius's writings reveal a deeply Platonized construal of the Christian faith.

13. In addition to such obvious giants as Ambrose, Gregory of Nazianzus, John Chrysostom, and Augustine, we have many other examples of less well-known figures who also evinced both passion and gift in communicating with their people. Peter, bishop of Ravenna in the first half of the fifth century (d. ca. 450), left an extensive collection of sermons; he came to be known as Peter Chrysologus (Greek *Chrysologos*, "golden-worded"), apparently to imply that he was the Western counterpart of John Chrysostom. Another north Italian churchman two or three decades earlier, Maximus, bishop of Turin (d. perhaps ca. 420), bequeathed several dozen homilies, most of them quite short, which combine rhetorical flair with a popular vigor and offer an interesting window on Christian life in his region at this time. The study of the dynamics of early Christian preaching and the rhetorical strategies that underpinned the work of the greatest pulpit performers is an area of growing fascination for scholars today.

14. The wearing of a tonsure, or the cutting of the hair in a particular fashion as a symbol of religious vows, spread from monastic practice to the clergy in the sixth century; see pp. 386–87.

15. See *The Birth of the Church*, pp. 168–70.

16. Vincent of Lérins, *Commonitorium* 2.3.

17. On the background, see *The Birth of the Church*, pp. 116, 127–30, 301–9.

18. As a number of scholars have argued, the choice of continence in itself represented a challenge to traditional ideas of the role of women as primarily sexual partners and mothers.

19. On the background, see *The Birth of the Church*, pp. 287–89.

20. See *The Birth of the Church*, pp. 292–96.

21. Eusebius of Caesarea, *Ecclesiastical History* 7.18.1–4.

22. Not to be confused with Rabbula, bishop of Edessa in the fifth century (see p. 436n7).

Chapter 11: Christians and Barbarians: The Churches in a Changing World

1. Jerome, *Epistle* 127.12.

2. See also p. 436n18 on Orosius.

3. Orientius, *Commonitorium* 2.184. Orientius was perhaps bishop of Auch, west of Toulouse. He was a poet, and his *Commonitorium* is an elegiac exhortation to pursue Christian holiness and avoid moral vices.

4. Under Gunthamund, a lawyer from Carthage named Dracontius was imprisoned for writing a poem addressed to the Byzantine emperor Zeno. While in prison he wrote further poetry, including his major work, *On the Praises of God*, which extols the greatness of God as creator, sustainer, and savior of humanity.

5. The title of "king" had been traditionally detested by the Romans ever since the overthrow of their early kings and the establishment of the Roman Republic in ca. 509 B.C.

6. Some Romans also learned Gothic.

7. As he also did, notably, towards the Jews, whose interests he sought to safeguard in a number of instances.

8. He later became bishop of Pavia, ca. 513.

9. A number of these buildings and their magnificent mosaics can still be seen today; the most celebrated are those of the court church, S. Apollinare Nuovo. Another of the great treasures of Ravenna's art is the so-called *Codex Argenteus*, now held in the University

Library in Uppsala in Sweden—an exquisite book of the Gospels in Gothic, of which 188 folios remain, written in gold and silver letters on very fine purple parchment.

Chapter 12: A New West: Gaul, Italy, Spain

1. Childeric's burial chamber at Tournai was discovered in 1653 and further excavated in modern times. It revealed a splendid hoard of ornaments, weaponry, and coins testifying both to Childeric's wealth and to the Franks' contacts with a network of other peoples.

2. Caesarius's monastery for women was largely destroyed during the final siege in 507–508 and was subsequently rebuilt on a safer site within the city walls. It was presided over in the first instance by Caesarius's sister and subject to a rule that the bishop himself composed, arguably the first such rule written specifically for a female ascetic community. A later version of the rule was produced towards the end of Caesarius's life.

3. Including, interestingly, Caesarius of Arles.

4. Justinian is reported to have erected or restored as many as thirty-three churches in Constantinople and its suburbs, and numerous others in other imperial cities. The most famous is the magnificent Basilica of Sancta (or in Greek, *Hagia*) Sophia (Church of the Holy Wisdom), consecrated in 537, which was constructed after its predecessor, dedicated in 360, was destroyed in a serious popular riot early in 532. It remains as one of the primary landmarks in Istanbul to this day, variously affected by its colorful history as church, mosque, and museum. See p. 289.

5. One had abandoned the calling in order to marry one of her staff. The marriage is said by Gregory to have been unhappy.

6. Gregory the Great, *Pastoral Rule* 1.1.

7. In the fourth century, Damasus and Siricius had made much of the primacy of Rome as the see of Peter, the "rock" upon which the church was built (see Matt. 16:18); the association was emphasized very strongly by Leo, and its jurisdictional implications were further invoked by Gelasius in the context of the protracted schism between Rome and the East (see pp. 220–22, 224–25).

8. The authenticity of the *Dialogues* has been challenged in recent years, but a majority of scholars continue to defend Gregory's authorship of the work. The whole of the second book of the *Dialogues* is devoted to Benedict.

Chapter 13: Britain and Ireland: The First Phase

1. The western two-fifths of Hadrian's Wall were originally built of turf but were then rebuilt in stone to match the remainder of the wall, which had been constructed in stone from the first. The wall was garrisoned by thousands of auxiliary troops. Contrary to popular misconception, it was not intended to prevent all movement across the frontier, and there was plenty of traffic in both directions. Nevertheless, the wall was certainly designed to present a psychological barrier to would-be military invaders. For all its remarkable symbolism and its immense impact on local economic and social conditions, ultimately it proved no obstacle to the Picts and the Scots in their determination to raid imperial territory.

2. Tertullian, *Against the Jews* 7; Origen, *Homilies on Ezekiel* 4.

3. Some scholars place his death later than the early third century, opting instead for the context of the persecutions under the emperor Decius in 250 (see *The Birth of the Church*, pp. 322–23). The great historian of the early British church, Bede (ca. 673–735), locates the incident as late as the Great Persecution of the early fourth century (*Ecclesiastical History* 1.7), but this is unlikely on a variety of counts.

4. See *The Birth of the Church*, pp. 334–38.

5. The most famous examples are to be found among graffiti discovered in the ruins of the ancient cities of Pompeii and Herculaneum in Italy. Scholars debate whether or not these examples are Christian; a reasonable prima facie case can be made for the claim that they are. If this is so, the squares suggest the presence of at least one believer in each of these places prior to the destruction of both cities by the eruption of Mount Vesuvius in 79.

6. The hoard included twenty-seven silver objects, the most remarkable of which is a striking two-handled chalice. There is also a single gold piece.

7. Some independent churches have been found in urban contexts, such as one at Silchester in Hampshire, though the dating of them, together with other details surrounding their original settings, remains open to dispute.

8. See *The Birth of the Church*, pp. 343–45.

9. It is impossible to tell what element of truth lies in these reports. If a mass baptism of any kind did take place, it is a further hint of the extent to which paganism was still a serious force among the Britons at this time.

10. Constantius, a presbyter of Lyons.

11. Some later Irish writers were in fact troubled by this fact, seeing it as a sign that the church had been too lax and accommodating in its style. Some later forms of extreme asceticism were driven by a need to remedy this perceived weakness. Ireland's day for martyrdoms of a more literal kind, however, would yet come.

12. The last was made up of two kingdoms with designations that proved somewhat less durable: Deira in the south (from the Humber to the Tees) and Bernicia in the north (which eventually reached as far as the Forth).

13. Of these, only Strathclyde would survive beyond the seventh century; the others were swallowed up by Northumbria.

14. Both the date and the geographical origin of the work are disputed.

Chapter 14: From Celtic Monasticism to the Evangelizing of the English

1. The terms *Celtic* and *Celts* are highly complicated and controversial in their application. Those whom Greco-Roman writers called *Celts* had at one time inhabited a large amount of Europe north of the Alps, and a good deal of what we think of as Western Roman culture in fact represented (not least in the area of religion, as it happens) a complex fusion of Roman and Celtic cultures. Though Roman influences may have dominated from around the end of the first century B.C., identifiably Celtic languages, social customs, and material culture continued to be widespread in Roman territory, especially in rural areas. However, after the disintegration of Roman power in Europe under the weight of Germanic cultures in the fifth century A.D., distinctively Celtic traditions were crushed in much of Europe and Britain, and those who spoke one or another version of an identifiably related group of Celtic languages came to be concentrated in a small collection of western areas: Ireland, Scotland, Wales, Cornwall, the Isle of Man, and Brittany. In what follows, the designations "Celtic" and "the Celts" appear not as descriptors of ethnicity but as broad ways of referring to the linguistic and cultural representatives of non-Germanic traditions in these parts of the British Isles and northern Europe.

2. The most favored date for Ninian traditionally has been the early fifth century, with the establishment of his see around 397–398, but there have been suggestions more recently that he ought to be located as late as the second quarter of the sixth century. The evidence is fairly inconclusive, though the case for the later context may have a slight edge over the conventional dating.

3. Bede, *Ecclesiastical History* 3.4.

4. Brigit is also said to have exercised some influence in Scotland. A monastery was established in her honor at Abernethy around 600, and her name is commemorated widely in place-names stretching from Aberdeenshire to Galloway.

5. Its Gaelic name was simply "I" (pronounced *ee* as in "see," and meaning literally "island"). The later name derives from a misreading of a seventh-century adjectival coinage, *Ioua insula* ("Island of I").

6. The village of Gartan is celebrated as his birthplace, though the tradition on which this association rests is quite late and is open to some objections.

7. He perhaps died around 612, a few years after Columba. The modern Glasgow cathedral dates from the late thirteenth and early fourteenth centuries, though the first stone church on the site was dedicated in 1136. There are large gaps in our knowledge of the see of Glasgow in the centuries immediately after Kentigern.

8. The best known of the Latin poems attributed to Columba is a piece known as the *Altus prosator*, the "High Creator" (from its opening words), a celebration of the majesty of God as creator, redeemer, and judge. The poem is structured in an "abecedarian" fashion, with the first letter of each verse beginning with a successive letter of the alphabet, from A to Z but excluding J, U, and W.

9. The Celtic churches evolved a distinctive system of penitential discipline in which lists ("penitential books") were written out prescribing the appropriate grades of discipline for particular sins. The tariffs stipulated different periods of fasting or varying degrees of almsgiving according to the gravity of a specific offense. Such practices were controversial, not least because they appeared to reduce penance to a mechanical process and because there were considerable inconsistencies in the demands placed upon the sinner by different registers. In later times it also became possible to commute penances by handing over money. Despite the abuses that developed, the practice of using penitential books spread very widely in the West in the medieval period; in its Celtic origins it often called for arduous expressions of remorse for even quite minor sins.

10. One of the most notable instances of a consciously Celtic tradition in modern church life has been the work of the Iona Community, founded in 1938 by George MacLeod (later Lord MacLeod of Fuinary). This movement advocates the incarnation of the gospel in practical ways through economic witness, political activity, and the promotion of justice and peace. Its members were originally drawn primarily from the Church of Scotland but are now representative of a wider range of churches. The activities of the Iona Community include encouraging the rediscovery of Celtic spirituality in various forms, though in principle the movement is opposed to romanticized versions of Iona's past.

11. Bede, *Ecclesiastical History* 2.1.

12. It is likely that he was consecrated in Gaul, but the location and the date are uncertain, and it is not clear whether Augustine returned to the Continent for this ceremony or whether he had already been created a bishop on the way to England.

13. On the origins of the name "Easter" itself in English around this time, see *The Birth of the Church*, p. 384n9.

14. Bede, *Ecclesiastical History* 2.2.

15. Ibid., 3.25.

16. Even then, of course, we can only speak of a general as opposed to a wholesale adoption of the Christian faith in sociopolitical terms, as there never was a conversion of all the various peoples of England en bloc. Paganism remained a force that never would be extinguished.

Epilogue

1. The title "father" had been given to bishops from an early date; from the later fourth century it came to be used particularly of certain specific churchmen whose status was regarded as special and whose authority could be invoked in the cause of doctrinal claims. Classifications varied, and there never would be any single agreed list of Church Fathers, but the significance of those who were regarded this way was great. In the Middle Ages, Ambrose, Jerome, Augustine, and Gregory the Great would also come to be known as the primary "doctors" or teachers of the church. The study of the Fathers and their writings is known as "Patristics" (from the Latin *Patres*, "fathers"), and manuals on their work are traditionally called "Patrologies." The early Christian centuries are commonly designated "the patristic age."

INDEX

Page number in italics refer to maps and illustrations.

445